Handling the Big Jets

D. P. Davies

Handling the Big Jets

An explanation of the significant differences in flying qualities between jet transport aeroplanes and piston-engined transport aeroplanes together with some other aspects of jet transport handling.

Civil Aviation Authority
CAA House, 45-59 Kingsway, London WC2B 6TE

First published in April, 1967
Second edition May, 1968
Reprinted January, 1969
Reprinted April, 1970
Third edition December, 1971
Reprinted April, 1973
Reprinted December, 1975
Reprinted December, 1977
Reprinted November, 1979
Reprinted April, 1985
Reprinted February, 1988
Reprinted April, 1990
Reprinted January, 1994
Reprinted July, 1995
Reprinted June, 1996

ISBN 0 903083 01 9

NOTE: Since this edition was published, the Air Registration Board has become part of the Civil Aviation Authority and now operates as the Airworthiness Division of the Authority. Any references to 'Air Registration Board', 'ARB', 'Board' should be understood to mean CAA.

Illustrations by Phoenix Artwork, Gloucester.
Printed in England by Borough Press, Swindon.

THE AUTHOR

David Davies was born in 1920 at Neath in South Wales: he was married with two sons; now lives at Wickwar in South Gloucestershire. He joined the Royal Navy in 1940, served for two years on the lower deck as a torpedo-man and was a survivor of H.M.S. *Patia*. He then trained as a pilot and was commissioned in the Fleet Air Arm, later serving in 818 Swordfish Squadron in H.M.S. *Unicorn* off Norway, Biscay and in the Salerno landings. This was followed by service in 854 Avenger Squadron over the Channel during the D Day landings and in H.M.S. *Illustrious* in the Far East off Sumatra and Japan. He attended the Naval Maintenance Test Pilots' Course at the end of the war and No. 4 Empire Test Pilots' Course at Cranfield in 1946. He then served for three years in the Handling Squadron E.C.F.S. Hullavington during which he carried out handling trials on new types of military aircraft.

Davies joined the Air Registration Board in August, 1949, as Chief Test Pilot and carried out the certification testing of the world's first jet transport aircraft in 1950. He has since been responsible for the certification flight trials of most British civil prototypes and a number of the larger validated aeroplanes. His experience ranges from ultra-light powered aircraft to current jet transports, including Concorde, and covers gliders and helicopters. He has flown jet aircraft since early 1946 and civil jet transports from 1950 onwards. His experience totals over 5,000 hours on 175 different types and significant variations of aircraft both military and civil and mostly on test flying duties.

He was awarded the Distinguished Service Cross in 1945 and was made an Officer of the Order of the British Empire in 1957. He has been the recipient of the R.P. Alston Memorial prize awarded by the Royal Aeronautical Society, the Cumberbatch Trophy by the Guild of Air Pilots and Air Navigators, the Dorothy Spicer Memorial Award by the Society of Licensed Aircraft Engineers and Technologists, the Technical Publications Award by the Flight Safety Foundation, the Douglas Weightman Safety Award, the Founders Medal of the Air League and the Britannia Trophy of the United Service and Royal Aero Club. He is a Master Air Pilot of the Guild and a Fellow of the Royal Aeronautical Society.

Davies is well known in many parts of the world and has been much in demand in recent years to talk on the subject which he has now committed to paper. His specialised experience, coupled with the fact that he has flown significant flight trials on more individual types of jet transport aeroplane than anyone else in the world, enables him to write with authority on the subject of handling the big jets.

Preface to the third edition

There are five reasons for this Third Edition at this time. I want to give some, more or less, advance information on the flying qualities of Very Big Jets; I am pleased to take the opportunity of speaking well of an aeroplane, for a change; I wanted to make good my promise to write about engine out ferrying and to take the opportunity of having my say on asymmetric flight training; to up-date the present text; finally to acknowledge the help of the people concerned with the mechanics of making this book available.

It is difficult to hit exactly the right time to publish anything on a new type of aeroplane. It is no good doing it too early because there is no indication of the problems which might be generated in the first few years of operation—equally it is a pity if the information is late. With the first of the jumbo jets about eighteen months into service, now seems to be a good time to start talking about it. Figure 0.1 shows just where this Third Edition fits—the comparatively small but interesting jump from big jets to jumbos. Complexity of design and increasing weight or speed is plotted against time. The change from piston-propellered to turbine-propellered aircraft was small and rather lost by the dominating influence of the propeller. The change to straight jet aircraft was rather a big one—see Edition One and Two! The change to Very Big Jets is another comparatively small jump and it is this change which this Third Edition attempts to explain. To look further ahead yet is tempting. Clearly the SST is on its way; that will be the next major progression and will call up the need for a lot more knowledge. If I'm still around, qualified and have any steam left I might just tackle it. I could write a decent sized book already as a result of eight hours flying on the Concorde prototype.

In the first two editions all the aeroplanes were anonymous. It wasn't necessary to identify them because there were so many around with common design features and failings. Now that I wish to discuss a very big aeroplane I have to name it because its identity is obvious. This is a relief to me in many ways and with the release that it offers I feel freer already to make comparisons with preceding types by name. Coincidentally, the B747 is a hell of a good aeroplane anyway; after so much writing about the poorer qualities of aeroplanes it's a pleasant change to be able to talk about the better qualities. I feel it balances this Third Edition somewhat. Certification pilots do not waste time on the good points of aeroplanes but concentrate on the bad points; naturally, this is where the difficulties are and where everyone has to co-operate and work hard to get an aeroplane through. This leads to a bit of a gloomy flavour to one's existence, not unexpectedly if one chooses to live one's life as a professional critic. Occasionally, however, something pleasant happens and life becomes much more cheerful. The certification of the 747 turned out to be one of these pleasant occasions. When I first started work on the aeroplane several years ago, while I was impressed by the line Boeing were taking in many areas I had my doubts about the level of response of the aeroplane in terms of short period changes to the flight path. I couldn't quite get rid of the momentum effect of 710,000 lb., 322,000 kg., of aeroplane. In the event the Boeing predictions were correct and my doubts groundless. But more of this later.

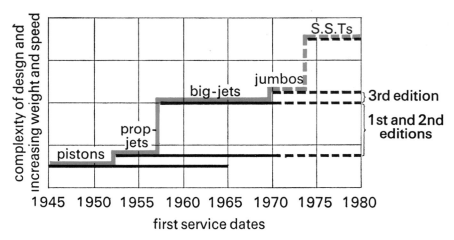

Figure 0.1

While Chapter 10 is headed Asymmetric Flight it is not a full treatment of the subject: just as Edition 1 assumed that a pilot could fly a piston-engined aeroplane before progressing to a jet aeroplane so the assumption continues that any transport pilot reader will of course be familiar with the basic principles of asymmetric flight. This chapter deals only with two specific items; training, particularly with two engines out and engine out ferrying. The first subject is very controversial. My write up is equally controversial but I was not able to express my feelings any other way. Two engines out flying on a four-engined aeroplane is neither difficult nor dangerous. It cannot be properly simulated—its practice is essential. To improve the training accident record the proper course of action is to improve the training organisations. If this means money—pay it. The saving in hull losses alone would justify it.

The text has been improved in lots of areas, too many to identify here. Apart from a re-write of some of the stalling there is a discourse on the use of reduced thrust for take-off.

Finally, the pleasant part of any preface—thanking the people who helped out. Firstly, Paul Soderlind of North West Airlines, apart from a couple of days flying his 720B and chewing the fat generally, which was most useful, he was kind enough to allow me to use his superb diagram of the 747 flight controls and hydraulic system. Secondly, ARB staff. I have a bunch of pilots, flight test engineers and aerodynamics people who are, in their lines, without peers. In the middle of their busy professional lives no problem however small in relation to the exact wording of a particularly difficult passage has been beyond their patience, understanding and willingness. The girls too; apart from my three secretaries over eight years who have typed literally tens of thousands of words with accuracy and cheerfulness there are the many production experts in our publications office who have pitched in with all the co-operation in the world. I am grateful to them all—but particularly Harry Hartland, the ARB Managing Editor. It was he who, many years ago, first read the initial draft of Edition One and saw its value and possibilities. As the author and in essence a modest person, I had little confidence in it. I am still astonished by its success. If indeed it has done some good the credit is due as much to Harry Hartland as to myself. Without his foresight and native publications ability it would never have achieved the success it now enjoys.

D. P. Davies,
Air Registration Board,
Redhill, Surrey.
5th August, 1971.

Preface to the second edition

Just as I found it necessary in the Preface to the First Edition to explain why I wrote this book I now feel the same need to say something about this Second Edition.

Obviously I was pleased with the book's general reception and the breadth of the readership which it obtained; but at the same time I became aware of improvements which could be made to a future edition. The necessary work has now been completed and this new edition is improved in several respects as well as being brought up to date in the light of my most recent experiences. The photographs which have been introduced should highlight many of the points in the text, certain errors have been corrected and various expansions of the text have been made to explain some of the more intricate points more simply and clearly. An index has also been added.

Of the many people who read and reviewed the first edition, I am grateful to three in particular: Mr. Jack Karran, formerly of the Ministry of Aviation, Captain Frank Brown of Qantas and Mr. Oscar Ingham of BOAC. They took the trouble to make detailed, critical and honest analyses which were of great help to me in the preparation of the revised text. I would also like to mention Captain 'Jacko' Jackson, Executive Secretary of the International Federation of Air Line Pilots Associations, who lent his support to the project from the first day of publication and who negotiated an arrangement with the ARB for the supply of the book to Pilot Associations throughout the world.

To the many people who have already asked for a much expanded version to cover the more 'interesting' problems (engine-out ferrying is a good example) I can only say '*Perhaps, under another cover*'. There is nothing in, say, engine-out ferrying peculiar to jet transports and to expand in directions such as this would be to move away from the accuracy of the balance of the book. The sub-title makes a complete statement of my present aims.

The most significant feature of this edition, and one which I must point out, is the change in flavour of part of my Conclusions addressed to Training Captains. I suggested that the too-rigid writing and imposition of flying techniques was a bad thing in that it reduced initiative, reduced command responsibility and prevented pilots from thinking for themselves. I have been universally condemned for taking this line. Having had time to think it over I must admit my error and do a *volte face*. I now accept that in a modern airline employing thousands of pilots it is quite impossible for all the pilots to be top grade and for the chief pilot to be personally acquainted with each one. The only system which can survive, therefore, is one which spells out in detail all operating procedures and insists on their application through a very high level of personal and crew discipline.

I am still surprised, when I meet an airline crew for a supernumerary ride, if, for example, the flight engineer introduces the first officer to the captain— all three perhaps having served the same airline for some years. This, I think, high-lights the problem and makes it clear that strict adherence to a well-written Operations Manual is one of the key-stones to a good safety record.

D. P. Davies,
Air Registration Board,
Redhill, Surrey.
21st February, 1968.

Preface to the first edition

I feel that some explanation for this book is necessary or, if it is not actually necessary, then I would at least like to put the following point across. It was never my intention to become an author — I was perfectly happy sculling along as a certification pilot just flying aeroplanes. But as the years went by I realised that a lot of basic flying experience on a wide variety of types was bound to accumulate in the flight test department of any certification authority and that it was wrong, in a broad sociological sense, that this experience should remain in such a tight circle. I felt it ought to be shared and that the information should be made available to airline pilots. It was partly because of this that I started to give a series of talks to various interested organisations and was pleased to find that these went down well. After one such talk in October, 1963, to the Society of Licensed Aircraft Engineers and Technologists, it was suggested that I should put pen to paper and deal with the subject of the significant differences in flight handling qualities between the 'big jets' and the traditional piston-engined transport aircraft; this I agreed to do. It was some task and one which I am not anxious to repeat. I had great difficulty in finalising parts of the book for, while I am happy to admit to being an expert on handling qualities, I make no such claim for performance, structures, engines and aerodynamics — or meteorology for that matter. I had to work long and hard to get quite complicated matters down in a reasonably simple form without losing too much of the truth. Thus a simple idea grew into a major task.

The information which follows is intended primarily for the use of those pilots who are about to make their first conversion to jet equipment. At the same time it is hoped that pilots who are already so qualified will find it useful. In any case it is assumed that the reader is a fairly senior transport pilot with a good background of basic airmanship and considerable experience of 'traditional' aeroplanes.

I recognise that it is impossible when writing for a large number of pilots, whose ability and experience vary over fairly large ranges, to pitch the level of discussion to suit them all. Thus I am bound to talk down to some and up to others but, in order to encompass the majority range, each subject has been given a simple introduction and then developed sufficiently for a fairly full understanding to be achieved.

Some of the subject material has been elaborated in detail quite recently, but it is nevertheless included because it is necessary to complete the picture and because it bears repeating. Those readers sufficiently interested to probe further into specific areas will find plenty of reading material in airline, official and professional publications.

I am anxious that this book should be received in the way in which it is offered, that is, purely as an expression of my personal opinions. It is not an official ruling on the subject, but is based on my experience of a wide variety of jet transports and includes the advice of many pilots specially qualified in specific subjects and the advice of engineering specialists. I am the first to admit that there are probably errors of fact in the book. I can only ask those who identify them to forgive me and let me know the truth as they see it. In some of the more contentious areas one of my biggest difficulties was to get two experts to agree on a particular point and it was amusing to find myself acting as an umpire in a field in which I was completely unqualified. Perhaps the best excuse for any errors which exist is that if the book had been delayed for a sufficient length of time to allow every section to be debated at length then it would never have appeared at all.

I am grateful for the assistance of my colleagues and of a number of distinguished pilots and engineers in the Industry and Airlines. My thanks are also due to my employers, the Air Registration Board, who have allowed considerable freedom in the expression of personal opinions, in the belief that to be unduly restrictive would not be in the best interests of the many pilots who have to be ready to adjust themselves to rapidly changing techniques.

Originally commissioned by the Ministry of Aviation, this book is published by the Air Registration Board and has the full support of the Civil Aviation Department of the Board of Trade.

Circumscription

Two years ago, when work on this book was started, the title 'Handling the Big Jets' was chosen because development was in a particular weight range and the title was descriptive of this range. Since that time little jet transports (down to, say, 20,000 lb.) have been developed and soon even bigger jet transports will come into service. It is already clear that the information as written is equally applicable to the little jet and it is probable that it will also apply to the even bigger jet.

In spite of these developments I decided to retain the original title if only because I had become accustomed to its sound! This decision made it possible to leave the text substantially as written so as to give a broad picture of the handling of jet transport aeroplanes in general and to attempt an explanation in this circumscription of why little jets fly like big jets in spite of the fact that they are not heavy aircraft.

It is certainly true that all jet aircraft have substantially similar flying qualities. This is so, as will be explained, because of their aerodynamic and engine qualities and because they all operate at higher speeds and higher altitudes. These environments encourage the same qualities in all aircraft regardless of size and type of propulsion unit. It is only in the mass part of the momentum formula (where momentum is the product of mass and velocity) that some further explanation becomes necessary. It is simply that the aerodynamic, engine and environmental qualities of the little jet impose on it a general level of behaviour which gives it the feel of flying just like its bigger brother and completely suppresses the fact that the small aeroplane weighs comparatively little.

With this qualification and accepting that the speed term in the momentum formula for a small jet aeroplane is much more dominant than the weight term, all the material which follows is generally applicable to jet transports of all weight ranges.

WARNING

> Throughout this book there appear certain suggestions and recommended flying techniques and drills for a number of both normal and abnormal flight conditions.
>
> These suggestions are made in good faith but without, however, naming the particular aeroplane types involved. There is, therefore, the possibility that a generic suggestion, while being compatible with the design philosophy of most jet transport aircraft, might be incompatible with a particular aeroplane or design philosophy.
>
> It is left to the good sense of the reader to be alive to this possibility and then to translate the suggestion in a fashion which keeps it compatible with his particular aeroplane.

D.P.D.,
Air Registration Board,
Redhill, Surrey.
13th January, 1967.

Contents

1. Introduction

2. First order differences

3. The consequences of increased size and weight

4. The flight handling significance of turbine engines

5. Flying faster

6. Flying higher

7. Take-off and landing

List of plates

Language comparison

A mixture of English and American terms is used throughout this book. The following is a table of broad equivalents.

ENGLISH	AMERICAN
accelerate-stop	— RTO (rejected take-off)
airworthiness requirements B.C.A.R.	— CAR4b + SR 422b or FAR part 25
allowable deficiency	— no-go item, despatch deviation or minimum equipment item
boost pressure	— manifold pressure
coaming	— glareshield
compressor	— spool
clamshells	— buckets
EAS	— CAS (at sea level only)
engine acceleration	— spool-up
inter-com.	— inter-phone
Mach trimmer	— pitch trim compensator
maximum continuous	— METO (maximum except take-off; piston engines only)
relight	— flight start
spectacles	— yoke
tailplane	— stabiliser
throttle	— thrust lever
undercarriage	— gear
unstick	— lift-off
V_{AT}	— Vref

1 Introduction

The table of differences

The heart of this book is the Table of Differences which follows. Although the colour presentation should make the main arteries immediately clear, some explanation and qualification of the table are felt to be necessary.

It was constructed quite simply by first identifying in isolation all areas of significance in the flying qualities of jet transports, then attempting to arrange them in a logical overall pattern. It was soon found that certain qualities stemmed immediately from other more fundamental qualities, and the broad framework of first, second, third and fourth order differences became apparent.

Many of the derivation paths are correct, easy to follow and beyond dispute. The derivation paths of some others are more obscure and the author's justification of these will be found in the text. Certain derivations are wide open to debate and the layout eventually chosen in these instances should be regarded as one of convenience. Nevertheless there is sufficient technical accuracy to serve the purposes of this book, which is intended for the use of pilots rather than aerodynamicists who might be expected to dispute some of the derivations.

A similar defence can be made of the four first order differences chosen. They are the most elementary qualities in which a jet transport differs from a piston-engined transport and they lead conveniently to an expansion which eventually covers all the defined areas of flying qualities.

The remainder of the book is essentially an elaboration of the Table of Differences and the chapters are planned accordingly. The four first order differences are discussed in Chapter Two and the reasons for the existence of these differences are given. It should be noted that in this chapter there is an explanation of why the difference exists but nothing relating to the consequences of the difference; the immediate consequences of the first order differences are of course the second order differences.

Each first order difference is given a chapter to itself for further elaboration of its consequences and to suggest, in each case, at least one acceptable method of dealing with the resulting flying qualities.

There are three phases of flight in which all the differences in flying qualities discussed in this book combine to make the jet transport an aeroplane of entirely different character from any other. It is in these phases — take-off, landing and flight through severe weather — that the pilot's knowledge of the basic differences must be applied, and they can therefore be regarded as first order differences   second order differences

1 **BIGGER AND HEAVIER**
1.1. momentum (1. & 3.)
1.2. powered controls (1. & 3.)
1.3. large weight range (1.)
1.4. large C.G. range (1.)
1.5. long wheelbase (1.)

2 **TURBINE ENGINES**
2.1. thrust to thrust lever relationship (2.)
2.2. acceleration times (2.)
2.3. absence of propeller slipstream (2.)
2.4. absence of propeller drag (2.)
2.5. high consumption at low altitude (2.)
2.6. noise abatement techniques (2.)
2.7. engine locations (2.)
2.8. general operation (2.)

3 **FASTER**
3.1. low drag (3.)
3.2. poor lift at low speeds (3.)
3.3. sweep (3.)
3.4. spoilers (3.)
3.5. high ground speeds (3. & 1.)
3.6. flight through severe weather (1.2.3. & 4.)

4 **HIGHER**
4.1. high Mach number (4. & 3.)
4.2. emergency descent (4.)
4.3. high altitude characteristics (4.)

third order differences   fourth order differences

1.2.1. artificial feel (1.2.)
1.3.1. large changes in reference speeds (1.3.)
1.4.1. variable incidence tailplanes (1.4. & 3.)

2.7.1. auto-ignition and fuel dippers (2.7.)

3.1.1. speed margins (3.1. & 2.)
3.2.1. high lift devices (3.2.)
3.3.1 dutch roll (3.3.)   3.3.1.1. yaw and roll dampers (3.3.1.)
3.3.2. spiral stability (3.3.)   3.3.2.1. directional and lateral trim (3.3.2.)
3.3.3. stalling (3.3. & 3.1.)   3.3.3.1. stick shakers & pushers (3.3.3.)
3.3.4. speed stability (3.3.)
3.3.5. high sink rates
on the approach (3.3. & 3.2.)
3.3.6. reduced roll freedom
on the ground (3.3.)

3.5.1. tyre and brake temperatures (3.5. & 1.)
3.5.2. mishandled rotations (3.5. & 2,3.)
3.5.3. reverse thrust (3.5. & 2.4.)
3.5.4. aquaplaning (3.5.)
3.5.5. slush (3.5.)
3.5.6. take-off techniques (3.5. & 2.3.)
3.5.7. landing techniques (3.5. & 2.3.)
3.5.8. overshoot techniques (3.5. & 2.3.)
3.5.9. operation on contaminated
runways (3.5.)
3.6.1. recovery from upsets (3.6.)

4.1.1. Mach trimmers (4.1.)
4.2.1. high drag devices (4.2. & 3.1.

Figure 1.1   The table of differences.

The diagram shows the derivation paths of the significant differences in flying qualities between jet transport aeroplanes and piston-engined transport aeroplanes. The difficulties in making this diagram entirely self-explanatory are referred to in the Introduction. For example, Flight Through Severe Weather is considered to be a direct result of all four first order differences, but, for convenience, it has been related to FASTER. This is because, as the diagram clearly illustrates, FASTER is the most critical of the first order differences.

The figures in brackets after each item refer to the root of that item.

3

the most important parts of any discussion of the significant differences in handling qualities between a jet transport and a piston-engined aeroplane. The two chapters in which these subjects are discussed form an essential part of the book.

Certain subjects have been included in the book despite the fact that they are not unique to jet transports and have been with us for years; some examples are aquaplaning, slush and spiral stability. The reason for this is that their significance has increased enormously in their application to jet transports.

Glossary of terms

Most of these will be well remembered but some need elaboration in order to support the text material and to avoid repetition. This list is not a complete glossary of terms — only those used in this book appear here. The definitions do not, in most cases, use the 'official' words; the intention has been merely to make the point as simply and as briefly as possible.

Aerodynamics

Buffet threshold For a given set of conditions, the point at which buffet (either low or high speed) is first felt.

Buffet boundary For a given set of conditions, the line of speed and altitude combinations at which buffet will be experienced.

Buffet margin For a given set of conditions, the amount of 'g' which can be imposed for a given level of buffet.

Compressibility effect The effect of shock waves on the aeroplane at the critical Mach number.

Free stream The air conditions close to but uninfluenced by the aeroplane.

Friction range of trim The range of speeds that the aeroplane will maintain, stick free, for a given longitudinal trim setting, due to control circuit friction.

Hinge moment The twisting effect exerted at the hinge line of a control surface due to its deflection.

Incidence The angle between the wing chord line and the free air stream. (Also referred to as 'angle of attack').

Lift The force supporting the aeroplane; $=\frac{1}{2}\rho V^2 SC_L$.

Stagnation point That point on the leading edge of an aerofoil surface where the upper and lower air streams last separate and where the airstream is locally brought to rest.

Engines

B.H.P. Brake horsepower.

S.H.P. Shaft horsepower. B.H.P. and S.H.P. are generally synonymous. B.H.P. is usually employed when it is desired to emphasise the method of determining the power, e.g. by dynamometer; S.H.P. is used to emphasise the value of the power at the output shaft, which is available to drive a propeller for example.

T.H.P. Thrust horsepower; the power equivalent of the thrust exerted on the aircraft by the propulsive device. In the case of a propeller system it may be expressed as the product of the S.H.P. and the propeller efficiency.

Bleed air Air which has been compressed in the main engine compressor and utilised for cabin pressurisation and the driving of various services.

B.T.U. British Thermal Unit; a unit of energy defined as the quantity of heat required to increase the temperature of 1 lb. of water by 1°F.

By-pass ratio The ratio of the total air mass flow through the fan stage of a by-pass engine to the air mass flow which passes through the turbine section.

E.P.R. Engine pressure ratio; a ratio of pressures, usually the maximum cycle pressure (compressor delivery pressure) to air intake pressure or ambient pressure (depending on specific applications) which is an important turbine engine parameter and can be displayed to the pilot.

H.P. (and L.P.) High (and low) pressure rotating systems.

J.P.1 Petroleum distillate fuel blended from Kerosene fractions.

J.P.4 Wide boiling range petroleum distillate fuel blended from Naphtha and Kerosene fractions.

Mechanical efficiency The power output of a mechanical system expressed as a fraction of the power input. A reduction gear, for example, has power losses due to friction at the gear tooth profiles and in the bearings.

N_1 (and N_2) The rotational speed of the low (and high) pressure compressor of a two-spool engine expressed either as r.p.m. or a percentage of the maximum value.

Propeller efficiency The thrust horsepower expressed as a fraction of the shaft horsepower at any flight condition.

S.F.C. Specific fuel consumption; the quantity of fuel consumed in pounds per hour divided by the thrust of the engine in pounds.

Surge   A condition of aerodynamic instability in the compressor which can cause cyclic reversal of the airflow.   It may be caused by disturbance of the air intake flow or by a fault condition and may lead to overheating and serious mechanical damage.

T.G.T.   Turbine gas temperature; a temperature which may be used for engine control purposes, measured between the turbine stages of a multistage turbine engine: sometimes loosely employed for E.G.T.

E.G.T.   Exhaust gas temperature; also known as J.P.T. (jet pipe temperature).   The temperature used for control purposes in many engines but less satisfactory than T.G.T. in certain applications.

Thermal efficiency   The energy which can be converted to useful work expressed as a fraction of the total energy available in the fuel.

Thrust line   The line along which the thrust acts.   Where a propeller is employed this will coincide with the centreline of the propeller shaft. In a turbine engine the thrust line will be the centreline of the total exhaust flow, including the exhaust from the fan stage where applicable.   The thrust line may not always coincide with the engine centreline since the exhaust ducts may be angled.

Performance

Compressibility error   The error in flight instrument readings due to Mach number effect.

Position error   The error in flight instrument readings due to the position and system limitations of the static and dynamic pressure sensing sources.

Gross performance   The measured performance of a test aeroplane adjusted so as to be representative of the type and reflecting either a fleet mean or minimum guaranteed engine power.

Net performance   The gross performance adjusted downwards to account for reasonable errors in operational variables and flying techniques.

Net flight path   The engine out climb after take-off providing adequate obstacle clearance under adverse circumstances.   It covers the segment from screen height at V_2 to the beginning of the en route climb and specifies powers, airspeeds and flap retraction details.

I.S.A. — sea level   The international standard atmosphere; at sea level the following conditions are assumed:—

> temperature — 15°C
> pressure   — 29.92"Hg or 1013.2 mb.
> density   — 0.002378 slugs/cu.ft.

W.A.T. (limiting conditions) Conditions of aeroplane weight which, when combined with the aerodrome altitude and temperature, reduce the performance level to the airworthiness minima.

Rate of climb Climb performance expressed in rate = feet per minute.

Gradient of climb Climb performance expressed as a gradient = the vertical height gained expressed as a percentage of the horizontal distance travelled.

Speeds

ASIR Airspeed indicator reading; the uncorrected reading on an airspeed indicator.

IAS Indicated airspeed; ASIR corrected only for instrument error.

EAS Equivalent airspeed; IAS corrected for position error and compressibility error.

TAS True airspeed; the true speed of the aeroplane relative to undisturbed air: $EAS/\sqrt{\sigma} = TAS$.

Mach number The ratio of TAS to the speed of sound for the ambient conditions.

MMR Mach meter reading; the uncorrected reading on a Mach meter.

IMN Indicated Mach number; MMR corrected only for instrument error.

TMN True Mach number; IMN corrected for position error.

V_S Stall speed; the speed at which the aeroplane exhibits those qualities accepted as defining the stall.

V_{MS} The minimum speed in the stall; the minimum speed achieved in the stall manoeuvre.

V_{S_1} The (not more than) zero thrust stall speed at a specified flap setting.

V_{S_0} The (not more than) zero thrust stall speed at the most extended landing flap setting.

V_1 Decision speed in the event of an engine failure on take-off; at which the take-off may be either abandoned or continued.

V_R Rotation speed; the speed at which the pilot starts to rotate the aeroplane for take-off.

V_2 Take-off safety speed; the lowest speed at which the aeroplane complies with those handling criteria associated with the climb after take-off following an engine failure.

V_3 The all engines screen speed; the speed at which the aeroplane is assumed to pass through the screen height with all engines operating on take-off.

V_4 The all engines steady initial climb speed; the speed assumed for the first segment noise abatement take-off procedure.

V_{AT} The target threshold speed for a specified flap setting; for landing in relatively favourable conditions.

V_{AT0} As for V_{AT} except that the final suffix denotes the most extended landing flap setting only.

V_{AT1} The target threshold speed for an engine out landing.

V_{AT2} The target threshold speed for a two engines out landing.

V_{Tmax} The maximum threshold speed; the speed above which there is an unacceptable risk of overrunning: normally assumed to be V_{AT} + 15 knots.

V_{MU} The minimum demonstrated unstick speed; the minimum speed at which it is possible to leave the ground, all engines, and climb out without undue hazard.

V_{MCG} The minimum control speed on the ground; the minimum speed at which it is possible to suffer an engine failure on take-off and maintain control of the aeroplane within defined limits.

V_{MCA} The minimum control speed in the air in a take-off configuration; the minimum speed at which it is possible to suffer an engine failure and maintain control of the aeroplane within defined limits.

V_{MCL} The minimum control speed in the air in an approach or landing configuration; the minimum speed at which it is possible, with an engine inoperative to maintain control of the aeroplane within defined limits while applying maximum variations of power.

V_{NO}/M_{NO} Normal operating speed; the maximum permitted speed for normal operations.

V_{NE}/M_{NE} Never-exceed speed; a higher maximum permitted speed when operationally desirable.

V_{MO}/M_{MO} Maximum operating speed; the maximum permitted speed for all operations.

V_{DF}/M_{DF} The maximum demonstrated flight diving speed; the highest speed demonstrated during certification.

V_{RA}/M_{RA} The rough-air speed; the recommended speed for flight in turbulence.

V_B Design speed for maximum gust intensity; one of the parameters used in establishing V_{RA}.

V_C Design cruising speed; one of the speeds used in establishing the strength of the aeroplane.

V_D Design diving speed; another of the speeds used in establishing the strength of the aeroplane.

V_F Flap limiting speed; maximum speed for flight with the flaps extended.

V_{IMD} Speed for minimum drag.

V_{IMP} Speed for minimum power.

Screen speed (and screen height)   The speeds assumed at 35 feet above the runway after take-off and at 30 feet above the runway on approaching to land used in establishing the field performance of the aeroplane.

Zero rate of climb speed   The speed at which, for a given thrust from the operating engines, the drag of the aeroplane reduces the climb gradient to zero.

Stability

Static stability   The tendency of an aircraft following a disturbance from a trimmed condition to return to or diverge from the initial trimmed condition.

Stick fixed static stability   The stability as measured with the control surface remaining fixed in the initial trimmed condition throughout the manoeuvre.

Neutral point   The C.G. position at which the stick fixed static stability is zero.

Static margin   The distance of the C.G. forward of the neutral point expressed as a percentage of the wing chord.

Stick free static stability   The stability as measured with the control surface free throughout the manoeuvre: the neutral point, stick free, may be forward or aft of the stick fixed neutral point depending on the aerodynamic balance of the control surface.   The stick free static stability is measured by the way in which stick force varies with speed from a trimmed condition.

Manoeuvre point   The C.G. position, usually aft of the neutral point, at which the stick force per g becomes zero.

Manoeuvre margin   The distance of the C.G. forward of the manoeuvre point expressed as a percentage of the wing chord.

Structures

Proof strength   The strength required to sustain the product of the maximum load anticipated in normal operation and the proof factor of safety; this usually results in load factors of $+2\frac{1}{2}$g and -1g flaps up and $+2$g flaps extended.

Ultimate strength The strength required to sustain the product of the maximum load anticipated in normal operation and the ultimate factor of safety; this results in load factors of 1.5 times the proof values.

> Notes (1) The gust strength requirements can separately require additional strength.
>
> (2) In simple terms, up to proof, while the structure might bend, it should not remain bent; beyond proof it might remain bent; at and above ultimate it might break.

V_{gh} The old, post-war type of flight recorder which continuously recorded V (speed), g (normal acceleration) and h (height), on a metal foil or wire. (There was a pre-war Vg recorder which scratched speed and g only on a smoked glass screen.)

Wing bending relief The relief of wing bending by the spreading of the total weight across the span: this is most advantageous when, for example, the engines are mounted on the wing and the wings are full of fuel.

Symbols

α	alpha	—	incidence
η	eta	—	efficiency
ε	epsilon	—	downwash angle
γ	gamma	—	flight path angle to horizontal
ρ	rho	—	density
ρ_0	rho nought	—	density at sea level
σ	sigma	—	relative density (ρ/ρ_0)
θ	theta	—	pitch attitude
C_L		—	coefficient of lift
C_D		—	coefficient of drag
C_m		—	coefficient of pitching moment
C_{mo}		—	coefficient of pitching moment at zero lift
'g'		—	normal acceleration
'q'		—	dynamic pressure ($\frac{1}{2}\rho V^2$)
S		—	total wing planform area.

10

Weights

APS weight   Aircraft prepared for service weight: a fully equipped operational aeroplane — but empty; i.e. without crew, fuel or payload.

Maximum zero fuel weight   This is the weight of the aeroplane above which all weight must consist of fuel.   This is a simplified definition which is satisfactory for current transport aeroplanes in which most of the fuel is contained in tanks in the wing.   This limitation is always determined by the structural loading airworthiness requirements; unlike the other weight limitations, it is not associated with any handling or performance qualities. Its effect is to impose a limit on the amount of load which may be carried in the fuselage.   The designer is able to achieve a higher maximum take-off weight by being able to take into account the relieving effect of the weight of fuel in the wing tanks on the loads imposed on the wing structure.   Similarly he is able to achieve higher operating speeds by reducing the maximum zero fuel weight.

Miscellaneous

ADC   Air data computer; a device for correcting the information from the usual pressure and static sources and supplying it to servo driven flight instruments, the autopilot and flight director.

Autopilot manometric locks   Height, airspeed, Mach and rate of descent holding facilities and height acquire capture facility.

Autopilot auto-trim   An autopilot facility for maintaining the aeroplane substantially in trim longitudinally; on a variable incidence tailplane aeroplane it is usual for the autopilot to fly through the elevator and the auto-trim through the stabiliser.

Clean   The aeroplane configuration with all extensible devices (gear, flaps, etc.) retracted; also referred to as 'en-route'.

Droop   On a fixed wing leading edge this refers to a drooped nose profile to improve lift at high incidence: some aeroplanes have an extensible droop leading edge to the wing.

Green band   The range of stabiliser trim settings for take-off against weight and C.G. marked as a green segment (exceptionally — white (!)) on the longitudinal trim scale.

INS Inertial Navigation System   The fundamental element of this complex system is ISS, Inertial Sensor System.   This comprises a stable platform of high quality gyros and accelerometers and a computer.   The computer integrates the accelerometer outputs with time to give velocity and integrates velocity to give distance travelled.   From this is available pitch and roll

11

attitude and true heading and a whole range of navigational knowledge (true track and heading, drift, and, in numerical read out form, present position in Lat. & Long., ground speed and wind). A further computer section turns ISS into INS by providing ability to inject and store waypoints and then compute track angle error, distance and time to go to reach them. This information can be used for autopilot, flight director or manual flying. The latest equipment can be continuously updated by reference to available radio navigation information.

LCN Load classification number. A numerical method for matching the footprint pressures of an aeroplane to the strength of rigid and 'flexible' pavements.

PCU Power control unit (refers to powered flying controls).

Pickle switches The thumb-operated electrical longitudinal trim switches mounted on the control column.

Slat A wing leading edge flap which extends to increase lift.

Slot Either the space between the wing and an extended slat or flap, or a gap, either permanently open or openable, aft of the fixed wing leading edge.

VASI Visual approach slope indicator; a system of coloured light beams defining a safe approach angle to a runway.

VSI Vertical speed indicator.

IVSI Instantaneous vertical speed indicator.

ILVSI Instant lead vertical speed indicator.

VSI's in which a vertically sensing accelerometer gives an advance signal by blowing or sucking air into or out of the capsule.

2 First order differences

Bigger and heavier

In the science of air transport, and probably in all methods of transportation, there must be an optimum unit size from an overall economic point of view. This will vary from route to route and will depend on a great number of inter-relating factors, such as demand, seat-mile cost, desirable frequency and speed. An independent factor is the state of the art at the time.

In operating an aeroplane, some of the costs are fixed, regardless of its size, and many others increase very slowly with increased size. The result is that seat-mile costs generally decrease with increasing aeroplane capacity. For any given route therefore, there is a need to use the largest aeroplane that traffic can justify without decreasing the frequency to an unacceptable level. At the same time there has been a demand for increased fuel capacity due, in part, to the increased fuel consumption of jet engines; for short-haul aeroplanes this gives the advantage of several short sectors without the need to refuel, and for long-haul aeroplanes it gives the direct connections on long routes which traffic now justifies. Where London – New York seemed adequate some years ago, London – Los Angeles is now required.

These two requirements of increased seating capacity and increased range have resulted in much larger aeroplanes; and larger aeroplanes are of course heavier aeroplanes.

The development of large piston-engined aeroplanes ceased with the advent of the jet engine, and the jet engine has undoubtedly permitted a more rapid increase in size and weight than a piston engine would have done. The result is that present jet transports are very much bigger and heavier than the largest piston-engined transports.

Turbine engines

The reason for aircraft having jet engines is simply that only the jet engine can produce the qualities required to satisfy the demands made by the modern transport aeroplane.

It is worth examining briefly the requirements of the modern transport aeroplane in relation to speed and size. The economic benefits of speed are twofold; utilisation and passenger appeal. If the flight speed is doubled, in theory only half the number of aeroplanes are required to perform a given task, with a consequent saving in capital expenditure and total running costs, even though the running cost of each aeroplane may be higher. Short

3

journey times will attract passengers, thus giving higher load factors to the faster aeroplane. This effect is especially pronounced in a fare structure that contains no speed differential.

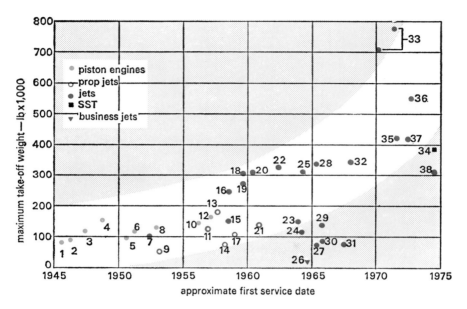

Figure 2.1   Increase of weight over the years.

Key to Figures 2.1 and 2.2

1 York	11 Britannia 102	21 Vanguard	31 Boeing 737-100
2 DC4	12 L1649	22 Boeing 707-320B	32 DC8-63F
3 L749A	13 Britannia 312	23 Boeing 727-100	33 Boeing 747
4 Boeing 377	14 V810	24 Trident 1	34 Concorde
5 Hermes	15 Comet 4	25 VC10	35 DC10-10
6 DC6B	16 Boeing 707-120	26 Business Jets	36 DC10-20
7 Comet 1	17 Electra	27 BAC 1-11-200	37 L1011
8 L1049	18 Boeing 707-320	28 Super VC10	38 A300B
9 V700	19 DC8-10	29 Trident 1E	
10 DC7C	20 DC8-40	30 DC9-10	

It is therefore clear that transport aircraft should fly either at the highest subsonic speed possible before compressibility drag rise becomes excessive (Mach 0.8 to 0.9), or at a supersonic speed sufficiently high for the economic advantages of speed to offset the supersonic drag penalties (Mach 2.0 and above).

14

It is clearly cheaper to use one large aeroplane than two small ones to carry a given number of passengers at the same time. As the potential traffic on any particular route grows so will the optimum size of aeroplane for that route increase. Thus there will always be a tendency for aircraft to become larger until the full traffic potential is realised. This makes the case for large, fast aeroplanes, and figures 2.1 and 2.2 show how weight and speed have increased with time.

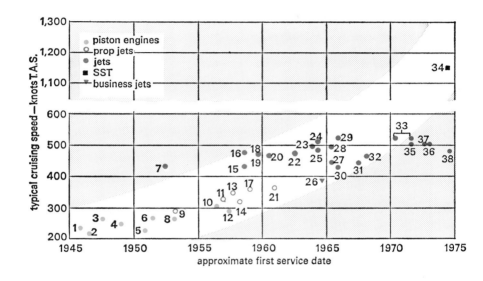

Figure 2.2   Increase in speed over the years.

The engine qualities for a large fast aeroplane can best be highlighted by identifying the more important of the particular qualities required and comparing the piston engine with the jet engine in each case. In order to keep this to a reasonable length and in balance with the other parts of this chapter some fairly general statements will be made, and substantiated later in the introduction to Chapter Four. The required engine qualities, not necessarily in order of importance, would appear to be as follows:—

(a) **High total power output**   Only a jet engine can produce the enormous power (say 7,500 thrust horsepower) required under the particular operating conditions required (high altitude and high speed); the best piston engine produced much less than 1,000 thrust horsepower under the same conditions because of propeller compressibility losses.

15

(b) **High output per single unit** Because of the optimum number of power units required for a given task the piston engine again failed to produce the high power required in a single unit, whereas the jet engine succeeds.

(c) **Low weight** The piston engine at best produced 2 lb. of thrust for every 1 lb. weight; the jet engine at worst produces 4 lb. of thrust for every 1 lb. weight. This ratio is improving rapidly with more recent jet engines.

(d) **Small frontal area** The piston engine at best produced 425 lb. of thrust per square foot of frontal area; the jet engine at worst produces 690 lb. of thrust per square foot of frontal area.

(e) **Low fuel consumption** For some years the jet engine, in terms of S.F.C., used twice as much fuel as a piston engine. This ratio is now decreasing significantly, to the advantage of the jet engine. Furthermore, when the jet engine fuel consumption is related to better utilisation, higher operating speeds, increased passenger capacity and lower fuel costs, all of which stand in favour of the jet aircraft, the jet engine is more economical overall than was the piston engine.

(f) **High efficiency** The jet's propulsive (Froude) efficiency rises as cruising speed increases, particularly as by-pass ratios increase; its 'conversion' efficiency remains substantially constant over a wide-speed range, unlike propeller efficiency which falls off rapidly due to compressibility trouble above about Mach 0.5. Therefore its overall efficiency is greater than that of the piston engine.

(g) **Efficient cooling** The jet engine, in terms of drag and fuel consumed, is less expensive to cool than was the piston engine.

(h) **Good reliability** The jet engine is already about four times more reliable than was the piston engine and several jet engines have approved overhaul lives which are more than double those of the best piston engines. Jet engine reliability does not deteriorate with size, unlike the piston engine where the reliability varies (roughly) inversely as the number of cylinders.

To summarise we can say that the piston engine and the propeller have been rendered obsolete by the increase in size and operating speed of the modern transport aircraft. Only a turbine engine can meet all the requirements in the critical parameters discussed above.

Faster

Within reason it is not too difficult to design any vehicle to accomplish its primary task, whether it is a submarine, a large earth mover or a vehicle for crawling across the surface of the moon.   The degree of difficulty will depend on just what the primary task is in relation to the state of the art and material capability at the time.   In the case of air travel that task is to travel quickly.

Apart from the natural evolution of air transport producing higher speeds (this is common to all forms of passenger transport) increased speed of travel can be defended on two grounds:—

(a) the sociological one of travelling time being unproductive, possibly boring and merely a hindrance to the early completion of the task at the destination.

(b) the economic one of production capability against time; for more or less fixed overheads the faster the aeroplane the greater its productive capacity in any time period.

The need for greater speed having been established the remainder of the explanation lies in the technical field.

A simple graph of cruising speed against time shows steady progression over the years except for two significant hesitations in the upward trend. The first came as a result of propulsion rather than airframe limitations. The necessary increases in engine power became more difficult to obtain; the jet engine removed this problem, although it had to do it in two stages — firstly the small increase provided by the prop-jet, and secondly the larger increase provided by the pure jet.

The second hesitation, which is still with us, comes mainly as a result of the airframe problems involved in exceeding Mach 1.   Although there are problems in adapting the jet engine to supersonic flight, it will remain an efficient source of power in this regime.

The needs to fly fast and high are very closely related; having discussed the basic reasons for flying faster the remainder of the argument will be covered under the next sub-chapter.

Higher

The primary reason for operating a jet transport at high altitudes is to make coincident the best operating conditions of the engine with the best operating conditions of the airframe.

On the airframe side this is because total drag varies with speed in the manner shown in figure 2.3.   Induced drag decreasing with speed and profile drag increasing with speed produce a characteristic curve with a minimum value somewhere around 1.4 Vs (but see caption to figure 2.3).   This minimum drag speed is used only for maximum endurance, for example when holding; for maximum range the optimum speed is classically $1.3V_{IMD}$. This is explained in detail under the headings 'Endurance' and 'Range' in Chapter 4.

The optimum speed for maximum range varies with altitude; it is somewhat higher at low altitudes and lower at high altitudes. If the lower speeds are used, however, greater care is necessary to avoid the consequences of reducing speed stability and possibly reducing oscillatory stability which will more than negate the advantage gained from the reduced speed. Since drag, in terms of speed, varies only with EAS, and since TAS in relation to EAS increases with altitude, it follows that the higher the altitude the higher the TAS for a given EAS and drag (and in fact the higher the TAS even for a reducing EAS, within reason). Hence more miles are covered for the fuel expenditure necessary to produce the thrust to equal the drag.

On the engine side it can be said that for best SFC the engine needs to be operated at its design optimum condition which, in very broad terms, is around say 90% r.p.m. Since for a given r.p.m. thrust falls with altitude (the jet engine being 'unsupercharged'), it follows that only at high altitude will the thrust be low enough to equal the required thrust at normal cruising r.p.m.

Now we have the coincidence of the engine operating at its optimum condition (and producing just the required amount of thrust to equal the drag of the airframe at its reasonable minimum) at an EAS giving a high TAS. Thus there is a need to fly high.

It scarcely needs saying that, having designed an airframe and engines to be at their best at certain flight conditions, then some deterioration must be accepted for significant departures from the optimum; but it is perhaps worth detailing the reasons for not operating at other points in the speed/altitude envelope.

At high altitude any lower speed might involve stability and control difficulties; divergent dutch roll, certainly a reduction in speed stability, reduced manoeuvre capability and a move away from best SFC r.p.m. Any higher speed will result in increased drag compounded by the increase in drag with Mach number, reduced speed margins and again a move away from best SFC r.p.m.

At low altitude and low speed SFC will rise markedly because of the poor performance of the jet engine under throttled conditions. Any attempt to run the engine efficiently at high r.p.m. will produce so much thrust that the resulting speed will incur high drag penalties and quite easily exceed the permitted maximum speed.

Referring once again to figure 2.3 and considering the engine thrust against altitude curve, it can be seen that at low altitudes engine thrust decreases with speed because of the increasing engine internal drag with increasing aircraft speed. At high altitudes there is a restoration of this loss with increased speed due to the ram effect at higher Mach numbers. In figure 2.6 the speed versus altitude curve has a 'Best Speed' altitude band; the specific range versus

18

altitude curve (figure 2.4) has a 'Best Economy' altitude band. These show that for best cruise speed relatively low cruise altitudes are required and that for best range relatively high cruise altitudes are required.

The fuel flow versus altitude curve (figure 2.5) reflects the reducing fuel flow associated with the reducing thrust required at altitude.

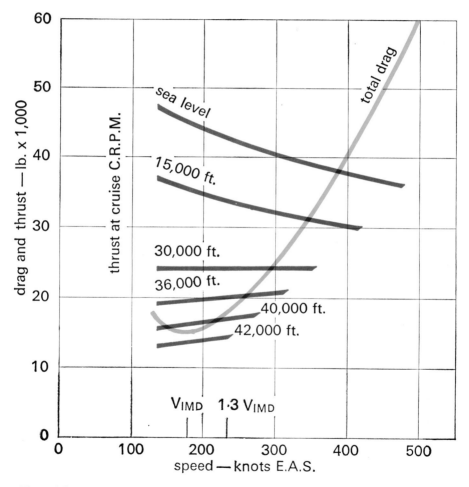

Figure 2.3   Variation of drag and thrust with altitude.   (Note: These data are taken from one of the earlier jet transports, which is why V_{IMD} is as low as 1.4Vs. V_{IMD}, on current jet transports, in the clean configuration, is much higher—in the range 1.6Vs to 1.7Vs.)

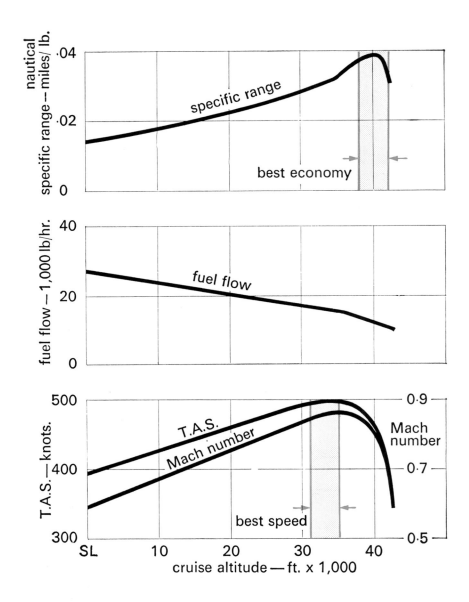

Figure 2.4 Variation of specific range with altitude.

Figure 2.5 Variation of fuel flow with altitude.

Figure 2.6 Variation of true speed with altitude.

3 The consequences of increased size and weight

Momentum

As we remember from our elementary mechanics, the momentum of a body is the product of the mass of the body and its velocity. It is a vector quantity having both magnitude and direction and if m is the mass and v the velocity the momentum is therefore mv; if m is in lbs. and v in ft./sec. then the momentum is mv lb.ft. units of momentum. As an illustration of these rather basic facts consider the following examples:—

(a) A piston-engined aircraft of 80,000 lb. weight climbing at 160 knots at 10,000 ft. has a momentum along its flight path of 24.8 millions lb.ft. units.

(b) a jet aircraft of 300,000 lb. weight climbing at 280 knots at 10,000 ft. has a momentum along its flight path of 162 millions lb.ft. units.

The momentum of the jet aircraft is approximately $6\frac{1}{2}$ times that of the piston-engined aircraft and this is quite simply because of the increases in weight and speed.

If we now draw two simple diagrams (figure 3.1) representing momentum by lengths we can see the effect of the application of the same unit force for the same time on each aircraft.

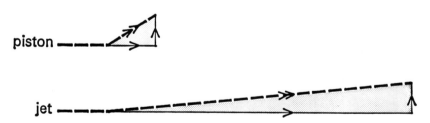

Figure 3.1   Comparison of momentums by vector diagrams.

Assuming that the flight path deviations considered are small it is apparent that the jet aircraft will change direction by approximately only one-sixth of the angle turned by the piston-engined aircraft — compare the left-hand base angle in both diagrams.

Admittedly the jet aircraft has been designed to exert greater control forces, but the example does illustrate the principles involved and the significance of mass and speed.

The matter of momentum is most important in the handling of jet aircraft. When we think back to our flying days on light and comparatively slow aeroplanes we remember how quickly we could change the projected flight path over both small and large angles and this remained true even if control effectiveness was not to a high order. This handling quality is, however, reduced with the traditional piston-engined transport and is lowered still further on the jets, to the extent that it is no longer safe enough to correct a significant error only after it has developed sufficiently to become apparent to an insensitive pilot. Intelligent anticipation is now necessary to stop unwanted excursions developing to a significant extent. Let us define two terms which we need to understand:—

(a) The *projected flight path* of an aeroplane is the path it will follow through the air as a result of its motion at any moment in time if it is not further disturbed.

(b) The *required flight path* is, obviously, the path through the air which is necessary to satisfy the pilot's immediate task.

It is not difficult to visualise the projected flight path; one has only to extrapolate the motion of the aeroplane ahead in time and one has a pretty good idea of what the achieved flight path will be. It should be to a high order of accuracy over the few seconds immediately ahead, then to a decreasing order of accuracy as the future time increases.

The required flight path can be long term or short term. A good example of a long term required flight path is that part of an approach from joining the glide slope to reaching the threshold, where it can be described broadly as an average 3° descending flight path. A good example of a short term required flight path is the flight path necessary to regain the correct approach slope having realised a one dot error half way down the approach. It is with the short term required flight path that we are primarily concerned.

An aeroplane possessing greater momentum will tend to go on diverging longer from its required flight path after a given initial disturbance and will require more time for correction for a given restoring force, or a higher force for the same time for the same correction value. It follows that, if a divergence is allowed to develop to a comparatively large extent before it is appreciated, there will be a further unavoidable divergence, albeit of decreasing magnitude if a restoring force has been applied, before the flight path can be changed to the required converging one. All this means that in real life the flight path of a jet transport needs to be controlled more closely than can be done by the comparatively ignorant method of correcting divergences only after they have become really noticeable. There is a need, at the subconscious level, while the conscious mind is actively engaged on another task altogether, to monitor the present flight path, extrapolate it into the projected flight path and satisfy oneself that this projected flight path matches the required flight path. If they match, things are going well and there is no need to do anything; but if they show a projected divergence then action must be taken immediately. By 'immediately' is meant not an unthinking brutal control input but rather a smooth gentle correction which will stop the divergence, start the aeroplane back on to a smooth interception path and finally bring it nicely on to the required flight path.

After a little experience it will be found that this continuous subconscious monitoring of the present, projected and required flight paths comes quite easily; what requires further practice is the need to anticipate the control actions necessary in order to produce a significant change in the achieved flight path which will match very closely any significant change in the required flight path. In this way changes can be made in a smooth and controlled manner without over or undershooting the targets of altitude, speed, attitude or power.

Let us take one typical example; the change from the initial steep, full power climb to the reduced power drift-out segment at, say, 2,000 ft., of a noise abatement departure procedure. We pick up the flight at, say, 1,000 ft. by which time the pilot has the aeroplane nicely trimmed out. Now — if he just sits there until nearly 2,000 ft. is indicated he is bound to overshoot the altitude and have to apply a gross down elevator movement in order to try to regain 2,000 ft. He might even fail to reduce power in time and, as a result, finds himself approaching the flap limiting speed while still struggling to achieve the required altitude and speed; generally making life very difficult for himself.

While this example is perhaps a little exaggerated it is not too far divorced from the sort of untidy mess that can result. On the other hand, with a bit of practice, some intelligent anticipation and, in particular, some fore-knowledge of the attitude and power necessary for steady flight in the next segment of the flight, the manoeuvre can be made in a smooth and polished manner and can also be made very simple. Doing it well will, incidentally, give a lot of confidence to the other flight crew members and provide a smooth ride for the passengers in the cabin.

The drill should be as follows. At about 1,700 ft., depending on the rate of climb, start easing the control column forward, so as to bring down the rate of climb, and begin to reduce power smoothly. Armed with a knowledge of the attitude and power required for the drift-out segment, continue the interception manoeuvre and power reduction so that the aeroplane arrives at 2,000 ft. in almost exactly the right attitude and at the right power to continue the next segment. It will then seem as though the aeroplane had been steady under the required flight conditions for some minutes instead of having just arrived there.

The amount of trim change required for this change in the flight path should also be known, and this should have been applied progressively throughout the manoeuvre. This will prevent the otherwise out-of-trim condition causing an immediate divergence should the pilot relax moment-arily at the completion of the manoeuvre. None of this is exaggerated; with a bit of practice this sort of manoeuvre can be flown time and time again to a very high level of accuracy, even in turbulence.

Only this one example has been elaborated in detail. There are many more, such as achieving cleared flight levels from a descent, configuration and speed changes on the initial approach, correcting displacement errors on an ILS approach and indeed the landing and overshoot themselves. All should be flown with fore-knowledge of the attitude and power required in the next stage and a continuous sub-conscious matching of the projected flight path against the required flight path. Remember that if you wait for the aeroplane to make it perfectly clear to you that you should be doing something different you have already left it a bit late.

Powered controls

On a very small aeroplane, which flies slowly, it is possible to hinge a control surface at its leading edge and expect the pilot to be strong enough to deflect the surface against the air forces. On larger aeroplanes, however, it is found that the forces required to move such a control surface are beyond the strength of the pilot. The control force required increases with increased control angle at constant speed and with a given control angle at increased speed. The control forces, therefore, have to be made lighter and this is done by balancing the control surface. Control balance is achieved in a variety of ways; set back hinge, horn balance, trailing edge balance tabs and so on. In this way the pilot supplies a proportion of the force required and the balance supplies the rest.

On even larger aeroplanes the balancing itself becomes a problem. On big aeroplanes, which fly faster, the controls are required to handle reasonably well under all flight conditions, and the balance required varies with deflec-tion, speed and configuration changes. If the control is underbalanced it will be too heavy; if it is overbalanced it will be too light. In extreme cases it will lock on at full travel. Towards the end of the development of the piston-engined aircraft control balance was causing a great deal of difficulty in spite of the most sophisticated aerodynamic devices and refuge was taken, in some instances, in power boosting; that is, reducing the balance to avoid over-balance problems and making up the operating force with power assistance.

With the advent of the big jet transport three things occurred to make life even more difficult. The size of the aeroplane increased enormously, the speed of the aeroplane increased enormously and, with increased altitude capability, the speed increase difficulty was compounded by Mach number effects which caused pitch changes on the aeroplane, upset the pressure distribution over the control surfaces and brought about unwanted changes

24

in hinge moments. It was about this time that the design of the pure aerodynamic control was seen to be, perhaps not impossible, but certainly very difficult, costly and time consuming. Something was needed to remove the problems — and the answer lay in operating the control surface by pure power.

In fairness to some design teams it must be pointed out that their early jet transports would fly all the way to 0.95 TMN on a manual elevator; this, for its day, was a great achievement. But the limitations of a manual elevator under upset conditions at very high Mach numbers are now becoming known and this philosophy is not likely to be repeated on future designs.

With a pure power operated control the pilot merely signals the control angle required and a mighty hydraulic muscle puts the surface to that position. The need for some balancing is not removed entirely because the hinge moments still have to be kept within the strength of the structure; but the balancing problem is, in general, no longer critical.

So we now have a powered control surface which is not too sensitive to the air loads acting on it and will always go to the required angle of deflection. (This statement will be qualified later.)

There are many types of power operated control arrangement. For example, some aeroplanes have power on all three surfaces while others have powered elevators and rudders, manual ailerons and powered spoilers. A combination of manual elevators, powered tailplanes, powered rudders and spoilers and manual ailerons is yet another type.

The system philosophy also varies between the following:— single surfaces with two or three sources of hydraulic supply, split surfaces each with its own hydraulic supply, and power supported by manual in each axis. For example we may have a manual elevator with powered tailplane, manual ailerons with powered spoilers, or powered rudder with manual reversion.

This explanation of the development of powered controls has been longer than was originally intended; but it is considered to have been worthwhile because, in common with the design problems of the wing, control design is one of the most important aspects of any aeroplane. It is one of the roots of the two main handling qualities — stability and controllability. A pilot may believe, for example, that he will rarely be concerned with the stall qualities designed into his aeroplane, but he cannot ignore the design qualities of stability and control because they play a part in every moment of his airborne life.

Turning now to the consequences of flying an aeroplane with powered controls and their associated systems, it is quite a relief to be able to say immediately that, under normal circumstances, there are simply none which need specific elaboration. The aeroplane has been properly designed and built, and certificated, and it is handed over to airline pilots as a perfectly conventional flying machine which is not in any way odd in normal operation.

There is one qualification: in order that the aeroplane shall be handled in the manner proposed by the designer and accepted by the certification authority *it is essential* that the failure and emergency cases are fully understood by the operating pilots. For a given degree of failure there will be a reduced level of controllability which must be fully appreciated. The more significant the failure the more remote must be the possibility of its occurrence from a reliability point of view.

It has already been indicated that there are too many variations of powered control arrangements to be dealt with individually, but some of the more common cases of failure can be discussed. It must first be said that if the control is pure power operated, without any manual reversion, then the complete failure case is not entertained; the design must be such that the possibility of this failure occurring is extremely remote. Secondly, if the control of an aeroplane is significantly reduced by a failure then the remainder of the flight should be programmed in such a manner as to avoid the need for any large or rapid control application. This is not difficult, and, if the failure is a really significant one, the pilot in command has every right to expect full co-operation from the air traffic controllers. Significant turbulence must be avoided.

Failure in pitch can be a degraded elevator or a stuck tail. The latter will be covered later in the sub-chapter dealing with variable incidence tailplanes. With a less effective elevator manoeuvrability in pitch will be limited. Several things can be done, however, to improve matters. If it is possible, by fuel management or passenger movement, to get the C.G. aft rather than forward, then do so. This will reduce the need for large elevator angles. You can also make configuration changes, gear and flaps, earlier than usual to give time to sort out the aeroplane before the next change has to be made. Finally, so long as distance is not limiting, it is advisable to restrict the flap angle for landing in order to reduce the flare demand.

Failure in yaw can only be a degraded rudder. Most aircraft can be handled perfectly well without the rudder at all, provided that all engines remain operating and the landing is substantially into wind. If the cross wind component does not exceed, say, about 10 knots, this is one time when the pilot is quite entitled to take advantage of the strength of the gear and put the aeroplane down with drift on. If the cross wind component exceeds about 10 knots a diversion to a runway more into wind should be made. Those types which can suffer a degraded rudder have to show acceptable handling qualities in combination with engine failure: this usually results in increased values of V_{MCL} for landing.

Failure in roll can be degraded ailerons or spoilers. As a very broad generalisation it can be said that roll control is about equally shared between ailerons and spoilers. Failure of one should not be too much of an embarrassment, therefore, and cross wind components of up to, say, 15 knots should present no undue difficulty for landing. Values above this should suggest a diversion to a runway more into wind.

It must be repeated now that the failure cases quoted have been discussed only in the most general terms. There are some jet transports flying which do not fit some of the above cases and it is emphasised that your particular aeroplane control system must be fully understood; you must be quite familiar, and well practised, with the procedures for particular failures.

It was mentioned earlier that one advantage of pure power operation was that the control surface would always go to the angle signalled by the pilot. This is not true in some remote cases. Some examples are as follows:—

(a) The power of a power control unit can be deliberately limited to prevent the pilot applying excessive hinge moments which might cause structural damage, or to prevent excessive control angles imposing too high a load on the structure generally.

(b) The same effect is sometimes achieved, in the rudder control for example, by fitting a collapsible spring strut in the rudder bar system so that excessive foot forces, while they deflect the rudder bar further, do not produce increased rudder angles. This is a protection for the fin and rudder in otherwise excessive yaw manoeuvres.

(c) A power control unit can be limited to a value which will not be destructive in the event of a runaway. This is only found in the split surfaces designs.

(d) Really rapid and excessive control movements, such as applying full opposite aileron to reverse a highly developed rate of roll, can occasionally result in a temporary stall of the power control units.

These limitations on power control system designs appear for good reason and are there for the protection of the aircraft. Some of them can quite easily be demonstrated in flight but they are really only of academic interest. None of them compromises the required manoeuvrability of the aeroplane under normal operating conditions.

Artificial feel

A power operated flying control surface, by its very nature, is irreversible; it doesn't feed back to the pilot any information about how hard it is working and what air forces it is coping with. There is a need, therefore, to give this information to the pilot so that he is aware of the control angles being applied and their effect on the aircraft. In its simplest form this can be a plain spring. Some aeroplanes fly with a plain spring in the ailerons and in the rudder.

While this can be justified to some extent in these applications, obviously in the elevator a spring would not be satisfactory because the chosen spring rate could give an ideal control feel at only one speed. If correct at low speed it would be uncomfortably light at high speed and invite the real danger of overstressing the aeroplane (unless it is protected by 'q' stops for example); if set for good feel at high speed it would be unacceptably heavy at low speed.

To meet the requirements of progressive feel against control surface deflection at constant speed, and against a constant angle at varying speeds, an artificial feel system based on 'q' was developed. 'q' is our familiar friend $\frac{1}{2}\rho V^2$. There are many variations of this system but substantially they all sense static and pitot pressures and feed into the control system a force characteristic which duplicates fairly closely the normal feel which would be obtained from a conventional aerodynamic control working under ideal conditions. Because the device is artificial the actual V law can be changed for the appropriate control surface. An elevator for example is often proportional to $V^{2.2}$ while the rudder, because it has to protect the fin at high speed, is often V^3.

To those who haven't yet handled power operated controls with 'q' feel and perhaps view them with a bit of a jaundiced eye, let this be said: a good powered control is so good that the pilot has no indication that there is a servo system between him and the surface; the feel and response of the control is absolutely natural and there is nothing to suggest that it is other than a good old fashioned control.

Failure of the artificial feel on a pure powered control can be a most significant failure. For this reason the feel system is usually duplicated, either in such a manner that failure of one system results in no reduction of feel forces, or in such a way that one failure reduces the feel forces by half, both systems needing to fail before the control is reduced to the no-feel case.

Whenever the feel on a control is significantly reduced great care must be exercised in its use; the control must be moved slowly and smoothly over the minimum angles required for control of the flight path. Significant turbulence must be avoided. Large control angles must not be applied because of the danger of overstressing the structure. If the failure is in the elevator feel system, and some degree of C.G. shift can be exercised by non-standard fuel usage or passenger movement, the C.G. should be brought forward to increase the natural stability of the aircraft and render the pitch control less sensitive.

Having now recommended a different C.G. shift for each of two different failure cases let us repeat them to make sure they are never confused:—

(a) For a *degraded elevator* (*or stuck stabiliser, to be covered later*) you can lessen the need for large pitch control demands by getting the C.G. *aft*.

(b) For a *reduction in elevator feel or total feel failure* the aircraft should be made less responsive to small elevator movements by getting the C.G. *forward*.

In the rare event of total feel failure it will be only the basic control circuit friction which will hold the control in any selected position and the greatest care must be exercised in the use of the control. Such a failure is a most remote possibility. Everything which was said about the partial feel failure case must be said again — but with greater emphasis. It cannot be over emphasised that only a few pounds pull on the elevator control will be more than enough to take the structure way beyond its safe limits.

It is hardly worth making any distinctions in criticality in the event of a total feel failure but — just for the record — it is more critical at aft C.G. and at high altitude. Great care must be exercised when trimming the aeroplane and the trim should be such as to keep the elevator substantially in the middle of its range at all times. As nearly all the world's autopilots rely on the aeroplane's control feel for correct functioning, and for protection in the malfunctioning cases, then the autopilot must not be used. Only a very advanced autopilot, with lots of redundancy capability (and not in any way needing the aircraft control feel as part of its normal functioning), may be used in the event of a total feel failure.

Large weight range

As mentioned earlier, jet aircraft are generally much bigger, much heavier and have a far greater range than the old piston-engined aircraft. They are designed to offer a large payload and to carry a lot of fuel. Very large weight changes, due to fuel consumed, are therefore possible on any one flight. Even larger changes can occur between different flights due to variations in payload.

Let us take a look at some typical values:—

	Piston-engined	Jet
Max. take-off weight	107,000 lb.	335,000 lb.
Max. landing weight	88,000 lb.	234,000 lb.
APS weight	59,000 lb.	153,000 lb.
Weight of full fuel	33,000 lb.	155,000 lb.
Full payload weight	25,000 lb.	55,000 lb.

By a little simple arithmetic we can also arrive at the following:—

Fuel weight with max. payload	23,000 lb.	127,000 lb.
Payload with max. fuel	15,000 lb.	27,000 lb.

If we now reserve 7,000 lb. fuel for the piston aircraft and 14,000 lb. fuel for the jet we obtain the following figures:—

Minimum practicable flying weight	66,000 lb.	167,000 lb.

Now, to go on a little further, we get the following results:—

'Same flight' max. weight	107 000 lb.	335,000 lb.
'Same flight' min. weight	81,000 lb.	194,000 lb.
'Same flight' difference	26,000 lb.	141,000 lb.
Max. possible change in weight	41,000 lb.	168,000 lb.
'Same flight' max./min. weight ratio	1.32 to 1	1.73 to 1
'Any flight' max./min. weight ratio	1.62 to 1	2.00 to 1

4

In the examples quoted the maximum zero fuel weight limitations are assumed to be not limiting.

So much for the numbers. Now let us consider some rather startling facts which can be drawn from the values quoted for the jet aircraft:—

(a) It can carry more than its own weight in fuel, i.e. the fuel can weigh more than the aeroplane itself.

(b) The difference between take-off weight and landing weight on the same flight can be as much as 141,000 lb.

(c) Allowing for payload changes the maximum flying weight can be double the minimum flying weight.

(d) A simple calculation based on thrust/weight ratios suggests that at an extremely light take-off weight, a take-off could be made using only two of the four engines. (This is not a suggestion — merely an observation!)

These large weight changes are very important. They reflect on the momentum of the aeroplane in flight — a phase which has been discussed — and also on the ground, a phase to be covered later. They significantly change the performance level of the aeroplane and this can be significant in both directions, as it were. If one normally flies at middling weights and only occasionally at a very high weight, then, on the heavy weight flight the general performance level will not only feel, but actually be, comparatively low. Some finesse will be necessary to realise, for example, the correct take-off distance. Equally, if one is used to very heavy weights, but has occasionally to position a very light aircraft, then again some care will be necessary on the light weight flight to keep the high level of performance, and the generally very eager aircraft, properly subdued and under full control.

Buffet boundaries, optimum cruising levels, aerodynamic and performance ceilings and all reference speeds are absolutely dependent on weight and it is essential that the weight of the aeroplane is known.

Knowing the weight of the aircraft

In en route flight a weight error of 10,000 lb. equates very broadly to a 4 knots change in stall speed; and there will be small associated changes in buffet boundaries and expected cruising speed against altitude. These changes will not be all that significant, particularly as few flights are scheduled right up to the limits of the aeroplane's handling and performance capability. Any larger error, however, tends to lead to sloppy weight control and is bad for crew discipline generally. It is suggested, therefore, that the captain should know in which 10,000 lb. weight slot he is flying; that is, that his true weight is within 10,000 lb. of the calculated weight.

For take-off and landing the weight should be known to within 5,000 lb; this equates to a 2 knots change in stall speed and all reference speeds which are based on Vs. While 2 knots doesn't sound much the effect on distances is probably double the straight effect of a 2 knot change in stall speed. On take-off, for example, if the aeroplane is actually 5,000 lb. heavier than the calculated weight there will be the small increase in take-off distance due to the wrong V_R having been chosen and flown to, plus the increase in take-off distance due to the actual extra 5,000 lb. weight. While all scheduled speeds for take-off and landing are capable of some abuse the amount of abuse permissible is limited and based on accurate weights. If the weights are in error and the speeds abused somewhat then significant changes in take-off and landing distances will occur.

So know your weight to within 10,000 lb. en route and to within 5,000 lb., or better, for take-off and landing. These recommendations apply to the big jets with fuel capacities of around 155,000 lb. Obviously on a little executive jet one should work to roughly pro rata values. In the case of an aeroplane with a total fuel capacity of say 8,200 lb. the take-off and landing weights should be known within 500 lb. and the en route weight to within 1,000 lb.

Large changes in reference speeds

The term 'reference speed' in the context of this sub-chapter is taken to mean the fundamental stall speed and also any scheduled operating speed such as the take-off safety speed V_2 or the landing threshold speed V_{AT} for which the stall speed Vs can be a limitation.

Stall speeds vary with a number of parameters but for any given aeroplane the two most significant are weight and configuration. For a given configuration the stall speed increases with weight in the relationship.

$\dfrac{V_{S_1}}{V_{S_2}} \propto \sqrt{\dfrac{W_1}{W_2}}$; and, for a given weight, the stall speed varies with

configuration because of the change in effective wing area and maximum lift coefficient with the extension of trailing edge flaps and leading edge high lift devices. Just to make sure that we understand the expression

$\dfrac{V_{S_1}}{V_{S_2}} \propto \sqrt{\dfrac{W_1}{W_2}}$ let us work a simple example. If the stall speed (V_{S_1}) at

100,000 lb. weight (W_1) is 100 knots, the stall speed (V_{S_2}) at 144,000 lb. weight (W_2) will be:—

$$100 \times \sqrt{\dfrac{144000}{100000}}$$
$$= \quad 100 \times 1.2$$
$$= \quad 120 \text{ knots.}$$

It has been shown by comparison that piston-engined aeroplanes could experience only small weight changes whereas a jet aeroplane can experience very large weight changes. The wing of a piston-engined aeroplane, since

31

the aeroplane was not designed to fly very fast, produced reasonably good lift at low speeds and the flaps were therefore not required to produce a lot of extra lift. But the efficient high speed wing of the jet aeroplane produces very poor lift at low speeds in the clean configuration. The flaps are therefore required to produce a lot of extra lift; and on the more advanced designs they are supported by quite sophisticated wing leading edge high lift devices.

For this reason the stall speed variation with weight and configuration is much larger on a jet than on a piston-engined aeroplane. Since nearly all scheduled operational speeds are basically functions of stall speeds it follows that there are also very large variations in these reference speeds on jet aeroplanes. Just how large the variations are, and how they compare with those of the piston-engined aeroplane, can be seen from figures 3.2 and 3.3. Just as we compared weights earlier we can now compare speeds.

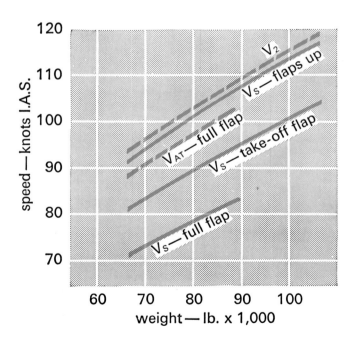

Figure 3.2   Variation in reference speeds — piston.

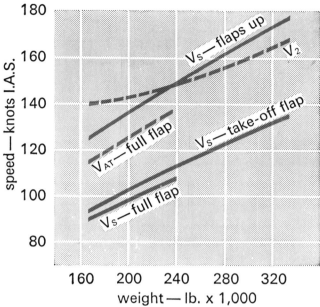

Figure 3.3   Variation in reference speeds — jet.

	Piston	Jet
		(knots IAS)
In any one flight, maximum change:—		
(a) in flaps up stall speed	15	44
(b) in safety speed	15	26
(c) in threshold speed	13	22
(d) in stall speed between flaps up and flaps take-off at maximum landing weight	12	36
Over a number of flights, maximum possible change:—		
(a) in flaps up stall speed	25	54
(b) in take-off safety speed	25	29
(c) in landing threshold speed	13	22

The highlights of the jet aircraft values appear to be:—
(a) The difference in the 'flaps up' stall speed from 177 knots at top weight to 123 knots at minimum weight; a change of no less than 54 knots.
(b) The change in stall speed at say maximum landing weight between 'flaps up' and 'flaps take-off' of 36 knots.   (Note this particularly.)
(c) The difference in safety speeds at maximum and minimum weights of nearly 30 knots.
(d) The difference in target threshold speeds at maximum and minimum weights of 22 knots.

33

Take-off and landing speeds are most important. Handling qualities generally, performance in particular and indeed the whole safety of the flight are very closely associated with the accuracy of achieving these speeds. This is not to say that they will not bear some abuse; in critical areas ±5 knots is assumed to occur anyway. But when the accuracy falls to about ±10 knots then, in some particular instances, the safety of the manoeuvre begins to be compromised. Field performance is particularly sensitive to speed. On take-off ±10 knots can significantly affect distances and obstacle clearance; on landing excess speed can extend landing distances and a shortage of speed can result in handling difficulties. Away from the ground the aeroplane is more tolerant of speed divergences but, in critical areas like turbulence or engine-out climbs, it is still important to stick as closely as possible to the scheduled speeds in order to enjoy the full performance and handling protection provided.

It follows, therefore, that it is really quite essential that pilots know the weight of their aeroplanes; approximately, all of the time, and accurately, at critical times such as take-off and landing, so that the correct reference speeds can be extracted and used.

Finally, to ram the point of this sub-chapter fully home, consider the following example. If ever there is a need to fly a heavy jet transport slowly in the flaps-up configuration for a protracted period of time, for example in a holding pattern or for fuel dumping, the minimum speed should not be less than about 1.5 Vs; this will give a typical airspeed of about 240 knots.

Remember that this is a minimum speed and reflect on the fact that some of the older piston-engined transports would never approach this speed under normal operating conditions, even in the high speed(!) cruise or descent.

Large C.G. range

All civil transports need a reasonable range of C.G. positions in order to cater for the loading of passengers and freight. On a piston-engined aeroplane, because of its straight wing, fuel loading is not normally a limiting parameter in establishing C.G. travel. On a jet aeroplane, however, there are two factors demanding a larger C.G. range than previously. Firstly, the use of fuel from the wing results in a large change in the C.G. position; because of the sweep of the wing, the C.G. moves forward as the fuel is consumed. (Use of fuel from the centre tank, which is usually a little forward, will however cause the C.G. to move aft.) Secondly, because of extremely long passenger compartments the effects of freight and indiscriminate passenger loading are exaggerated.

The effects of extreme C.G. positions are the same in a jet as they are in a piston-engined aeroplane. They are felt primarily in the stability and controllability qualities in the longitudinal plane. In the majority of aeroplanes at a very forward C.G. the stability of the aeroplane is increased and the static and manoeuvre margins are large. Stick forces for manoeuvring are relatively high, larger stick movements are required for a given manoeuvre and larger trim changes are necessary to produce, for example, a given speed change. Generally the aeroplane is heavy and less responsive to handle in flight and larger and heavier control forces are necessary for take-off and landing. At a very aft C.G. the stability of the aeroplane is decreased and the static and manoeuvre margins are smaller. Stick forces are comparatively light, stick movements are smaller, and a smaller amount of trim is necessary for any given change. Generally the aeroplane is lighter and more responsive.

All aeroplanes have acceptable handling qualities throughout the certificated C.G. range and no special briefing should be necessary. In any case, because of the domestic limits inside the certificated limits which most operators prudently impose, it is rarely that an airline pilot experiences the changes in handling qualities which go with extremes of C.G. positions. It is, however, worth highlighting the high stick forces which can be required to flare at forward C.G. and the comparative delicacy with which the elevator control should be used at aft C.G. It is particularly important not to overtrim longitudinally when manoeuvring on aft C.G. at high speeds.

Finally, when making an aft C.G. landing some jet aeroplanes tend to pitch nose up on application of the spoilers and sometimes even with reverse thrust. If this tendency is not guarded against the aeroplane will leave the ground and this leads to a few hectic seconds spent sorting things out. The correct drill (and this applies to quite moderate aft C.G.s) is as follows. As the main gear touches the runway, push the control column smoothly and positively right forward and hold it there while the spoilers are pulled and reverse thrust selected. Do not release it until the aeroplane makes it quite clear that it intends to stay on the deck. Because of the need to exercise lateral control on the ground this is really a three-arm task: if the first pilot wishes to keep control of the column the co-pilot should pull spoilers and reverse; if the first pilot wishes to handle spoilers and reverse the co-pilot should assist with forward pressure on the control column.

Variable incidence tailplanes

There are basically four reasons for employing a variable incidence tailplane:—

(a) The requirement of a large C.G. range.

(b) the need to cover a large speed range.

(c) the need to cope with possibly large trim changes due to wing leading and trailing edge high lift devices without limiting the amount of elevator remaining.

(d) The need to reduce trim drag to a minimum.

Compared with piston-engined aircraft jet aircraft need a larger C.G. range and certainly have a much larger speed range. Where V_{NE} on a representative piston-engined aircraft might have been, say, 280 knots, something like $V_{MO} = 380$ knots is quite usual on a jet aircraft. While any one of the above requirements in isolation might not demand a variable incidence tailplane, in combination they certainly do; particularly as some demand more upward movement and the others more downward movement from the tail. Once the need has been established, say by (a) and (b), then advantages accrue in the other areas, (c) and (d).

Large C.G. range

The fixed tail/elevator configuration can become rather limited when having to deal with a very large C.G. range. Ideally, for an aeroplane in balance

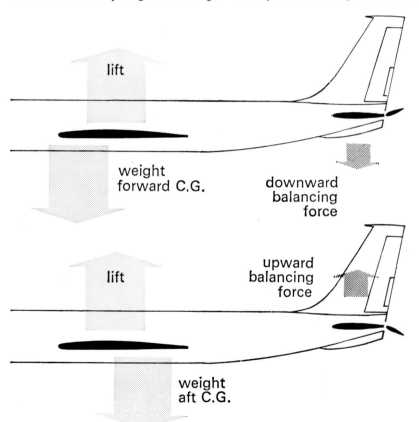

lift

weight
forward C.G.

downward
balancing
force

upward
balancing
force

lift

weight
aft C.G.

Figure 3.4 Balancing contribution by trimmable elevator.

longitudinally in cruising flight, the weight acts downwards through the same point as the lift acts upwards on the wing and the tail is not called upon to provide any balancing force. If the C.G. is now moved a long way forward there will be a nose down tendency which has to be counteracted by up elevator producing the required downward balancing force from the tailplane. If the C.G. is moved a long way aft there will be a nose up tendency which has to be counteracted by down elevator producing the required upward balancing force from the tailplane. For very large changes of C.G. position a condition could be arrived at in which the elevator would be fully deflected and no further control in the pitching sense would be available.

Figure 3.4 illustrates change of elevator angle against change of C.G. position for steady state conditions.

Life would become very difficult, long before full elevator angle was necessary just to hold a steady state condition, because manoeuvrability in pitch would have been lost.

With a variable incidence tail, however, as the C.G. is moved over comparatively large distances, the incidence of the tail is altered to provide a balancing force and the elevator remains in the streamlined position. Because the tail area is much larger than the elevator area the tail can be moved through a smaller angle to produce the required balancing force; and the elevator, always being 'neutral' to the tailplane, remains available over its full range at all times. This large increase in balancing forces available from a variable incidence tailplane, together with good pitch control from an unrestricted elevator, makes a large C.G. range a practicable proposition.

Figure 3.5 illustrates the much smaller angles through which a movable stabiliser is effective in producing the required balancing forces and shows how full elevator movement is available, up and down, even at extreme trim positions.

Stall speeds and C.G. position   While we have this simple diagram before us let us explain how stall speed changes with C.G. position.   It isn't perhaps sufficiently well known that, all other factors remaining constant, stall speed increases with forward C.G. movement and that a typical EAS change between aft and forward C.G. is 5 knots.   The diagram shows why.   At aft C.G. the tail has to produce an upward force which balances a small portion of the total weight of the aeroplane.   Therefore, that part of the weight being supported by the wing is reduced.   At forward C.G. the tail produces a downward force which increases the weight supported by the wing.   Hence the stall speeds are higher at forward C.G.'s.

Large speed range

Speed has an effect similar to C.G. in terms of tailplane balancing forces. On a fixed tail/trimmable elevator aeroplane low speed needs up elevator and high speed needs, speaking very simply, down elevator.   If the speed range is

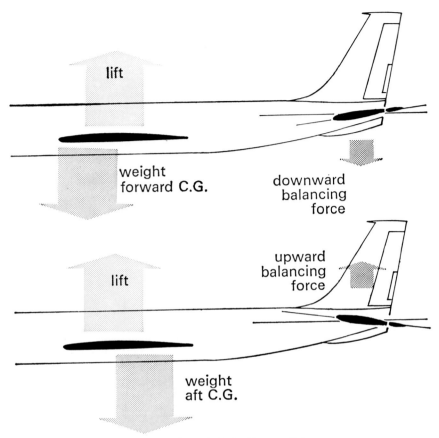

lift

weight
forward **C.G.**

downward
balancing
force

upward
balancing
force

lift

weight
aft **C.G.**

Figure 3.5   Balancing contribution by variable incidence tailplane.

extended considerably elevator deflection becomes very marked for trimmed out steady state conditions.   In combination with variable C.G. positions this effect is made much worse.   The variable incidence tailplane eases the speed range problem in the same manner as it eases the C.G. range problem.

Large trim changes

Large trim changes on a fixed tail aeroplane need large elevator deflections. At these large deflections little further elevator movement remains in the same direction.   A variable incidence tail, however, can be set to take out the trim change — and being larger than the elevator it does not need to be moved through such a large angle — thus leaving the elevator streamlining the tailplane with full range of movement remaining up and down.

38

Trim drag

In practice a fixed tail carries a small download in the cruise in order to counteract the pitching moment of the wing (very rarely does $C_{mo} = 0$) and in order not to limit the amount of up elevator required to make, for example, a forward C.G. landing. A fixed tail also requires a deflected elevator to trim out the aeroplane, and the drag of the deflected elevator can be quite high. With a variable incidence tailplane, however, cruise drag is reduced by setting the tailplane at the required incidence and thus keeping the elevator slipstreaming the tailplane.

Summary

In dealing with the consequences of having a variable incidence tailplane one basic fact must be kept in mind — *it is very powerful*. Because the elevator, when in trim, is always slipstreaming the tail it remains available over its full range and can be smaller than the elevator on a fixed tail aircraft. This is simply because the stabiliser can be set to handle the bulk of the demand and the elevator remains to look after the rest of the demand. On a variable incidence tailplane aeroplane, therefore, the elevator is smaller, and consequently less effective in isolation than it is on a fixed tailplane aeroplane.

This enormous power in a variable incidence tailplane can be a good servant when required but an impossible master when not required. Normal manoeuvres should be carried out on the elevator alone and the tail trimmed to remove the residual stick force after the manoeuvre has been completed. If, in an extreme case, the tail is needed to assist in a manoeuvre it should be used slowly and carefully and its effect on the aeroplane monitored all the time. A variable incidence tailplane should be used only in short bursts, particularly at very high speeds, and the full effect should be appreciated before any more tail change is made.

If a variable incidence tailplane should be grossly mis-set, before take-off for example, there is every likelihood that, not only would the resulting stick forces be too high to hold but, even if they could be held, full elevator deflection would be insufficient to control the aeroplane. For take-off it is essential that the stabiliser be set very closely to the proper setting according to the C.G. position.

In fairness to some designers a distinction must now be drawn. The design which will produce the above difficulties is the one which has a manual elevator behind a powered stabiliser. A manual elevator can be extremely heavy at large angles and suffers a lot of control circuit stretch. As a result the powerful tail completely dominates the degraded manual elevator. (The same sort of degradation can also exist on a manual elevator at very high Mach numbers.) The powered elevator on the other hand can be moved to a large deflection by a reasonable control force and is more effective because it can achieve large angles. A mistrimmed take-off with a powered elevator aeroplane, while it isn't all that good, is a much more manageable affair. It is possible to take-off at the 'wrong end' of the approved stabiliser take-off setting range and not need two hands on the control column until the aeroplane is accelerating through two hundred feet after take-off.

The failure cases

We now turn to the disadvantages of a variable incidence tailplane (stabiliser). These are, of course, the failure cases. A stabiliser can fail in four ways:—

(a) A normal operating system failure is, comparatively, no trouble. Some aeroplanes have provision for hand winding or slow standby electrical operation of a failed power system to the tail. In this case it is only necessary to make changes of configuration, power and speed in plenty of time to allow for the very slow rate of tailplane change.

(b) A simple stuck stabiliser On those aeroplanes where no such provision is made, and in a real stuck tail condition, life is a little more difficult, but not impossibly difficult so long as you know what to do. If you enjoy the facility of splittable flaps or spoilers to alter the basic pitch of the aeroplane take advantage of them. If not, remember that *so long as you maintain the speed at which the tail stuck you will remain substantially in trim.* This should be sufficient reason to declare an emergency and fly the remainder of the flight as closely as possible to this original speed. Plan for a long final and reduce the speed as late as prudently possible in order to keep to a minimum the length of time for which high stick forces will have to be held. They can be extremely high on the approach, so get the co-pilot to relieve you beforehand so as to conserve your strength for the approach and landing. Use a reduced flap setting or a higher speed for landing if distance is not at all limiting. Guard against the tendency to come below the glide path because of a subconscious relaxing of the high pull forces involved over an appreciable length of time. With a tail stuck within the normal flight settings there should be no lack of elevator available for the landing. It is also possible to vary the C.G. of the aeroplane in order to make life easier. If the tail stuck in the cruise any speed reduction will need a pull force on the control column. This can be alleviated by getting the C.G. further aft, either by moving the passengers (if this is possible) and/or a non-standard fuel usage. Although this manoeuvre can involve very high loads in the last stages of the flight it is quite predictable and within the capabilities of average pilots; it just requires a lot of beef.

(c) A runaway stabiliser must be stopped as soon as possible. There are approved drills for this emergency for every aeroplane. If the runaway is arrested, either handwind back, or use the stuck stabiliser drill above. If the runaway is not arrested life is going to be very difficult. The fact that some aeroplanes can be flown under some conditions of configuration and speed with a full runaway tail is of academic interest only. If this should occur at high speed the aeroplane is bound to be in severe trouble; the only hope is to get the speed off. There is not much point in taking this analysis any further. The design of aeroplanes is such that the possibility of this failure (that is, the failure to stop the runaway) occurring is extremely remote, so if the tail starts off on its own or does not stop moving when the input is removed, take the required emergency action immediately.

A gentler kind of runaway (perhaps a walkaway would be a better term) occurs when an autopilot lock (height, for example) causes the auto-trim to change the tail setting significantly in long term vertical draughts. This isn't strictly a fault condition but it is most undesirable that this should be allowed to persist. Take out the autopilot and be prepared for the stick force as the autopilot comes out.

(d) A stalled stabiliser drive can occur on some types where it is possible, with a very high elevator hinge moment, to apply a load on the tailplane so high that the drive mechanism is completely defeated and fails to produce any movement. It is unlikely that this will ever occur with the aeroplane in trim since a pilot is most unlikely ever to require a manoeuvre involving such large elevator angles and high stick forces. In an upset of some kind, however, where the stabiliser has achieved a gross out-of-trim condition, this position can arise. In turbulence, for example, a pilot might have run the stabiliser rather a long way away from the trimmed condition, a large and rapid change in speed could produce a very high stick force or the autopilot height lock in a long draught could have run the stabiliser a long way. All these could result in a grossly out-of-trim stabiliser setting with the immediate need of a very high stick force to keep control of the flight path.

While it is obviously disturbing to find that the trim will not run when signalled to relieve a high stick force, very recent tests by the author have shown that recovery from this condition is comparatively simple. Just sitting there and pulling a very high load, while it is the instinctive reaction in order to produce the required flight path, only compounds the difficulty. The stabiliser will not run until the hinge moment is relieved. So, keeping the trim button engaged, slowly ease off the stick force. The aeroplane will not react very strongly because you are not doing much trade with all that force anyway. As the force falls through the critical value (actually, about 120 lb. pull on the type tested — although you won't know this, of course) the stabiliser will run and the aeroplane will come back under control.

Some aeroplanes with powered stabilisers and manual elevators have been cleared against a full aircraft nose down runaway stabiliser condition from a simulated jet upset manoeuvre, but only after the maximum nose down stabiliser range has been restricted. Tests in a particular case showed that, provided the proper drill was followed, the aeroplane could be recovered although not, of course, within its normal speed limitations. The dive having been entered and speed brakes pulled, both pilots had to hold maximum up-elevator forces. The aeroplane stabilised at 0.93 true Mach number in the dive and held this condition for a comparatively long period of time.

As the EAS increased at constant Mach number with decreasing altitude the stability of the aeroplane returned very slowly, the elevator began to take effect and very slowly the Mach number started to fall. Once this occurred it could be seen that the recovery would be made. As the Mach number decreased the full elevator effect returned, pitch attitude decreased and the speed began to fall. The recovery rapidly improved in quality thereafter, although very high stick forces had to be maintained until level flight was established at a much lower altitude.

Power was not reduced from the cruise setting during the whole of this manoeuvre because containment of the initial dive angle was so marginal that nothing, but nothing, was allowed to add any nose down pitching moment — which is just what reducing power would have done. It should be pointed out that this manoeuvre was flown on a type where it had been proved that the stabiliser drive could not be stalled in the presence of very high stick forces.

How this rather hairy manoeuvre will be regarded by an airline pilot is not known, but it must be of some comfort to know that there is a drill which will provide a recovery, although at the expense of a large height loss. Remember that this is for a stabiliser *stuck* at full nose down, a most unlikely event. For the more likely (but still improbable, of course) case of a stalled drive just remember the drill described earlier: keep the trim switch selected and ease off the high load on the stick. When the stabiliser starts running again ease off the stick force progressively and stop trimming when the stick force is down to a low value.

Again, in order to be fair to the designers it must be pointed out that originally there were no requirements relating to stabiliser drive stalling, although, in some cases, an arbitrary figure of about 100 lb. stick force was used. In the light of more recent experience, requirements in this area are being applied. This is always difficult to handle retrospectively: the easiest way out has been simply to limit the maximum amount of aircraft nose down stabiliser range under power.

All-flying tailplanes

This development is one in which the normal longitudinal control and the trimming control are incorporated together in the one surface, the whole of which moves. This represents perhaps the most efficient form of longitudinal control in that the smallest surface area is required for a given power. This is particularly so with a design which has the aft portion hinged to increase the surface camber at large angles of displacement.

42

The design of such a control involves complex engineering to combine the pitch and trim facilities. The reliability has to be to an extremely high order so as to make the total failure case sufficiently remote.

In terms of flying qualities only three points need to be made:—

(a) The tail is very effective at all times and gives the aeroplane very good controllability under extreme operating conditions.

(b) Because it is difficult to get control system resolution down to the very fine limits required for precise flying, the control column centering devices have to be rather dominant; this leads to an irritating notch effect and a reversion to flying on the trimmers.

(c) At large angles of trim settings some limitation of stick movement is imposed; i.e. trim nose down imposes a small restriction on nose up pitching ability.

Long wheelbase

The location of the main gear is dictated by its primary task of supporting almost the entire weight of the aeroplane, the range of static balance combinations on the ground, the need to route the ground reaction loads up into primary structure and finally elevator effectiveness in terms of rotation capability. The nose wheel is then located so that it carries its correct proportion of the loads, and provides reasonably small turning circles.

On an aeroplane with a very long fuselage this results in the main gear being well aft, about two-thirds of the fuselage length behind the pilot. The nose wheel is also some significant distance behind the pilot.

In manoeuvring on the ground the location of the gear must be constantly kept in mind; it is only too easy on a turn to forget momentarily and find the inside wheels off the hard surface. When going round a corner go deep into the corner before coming round on the steering. On very restricted taxyways don't be afraid to lose sight of the edge of the concrete for example; the nose wheel is still behind you. Aim to take full advantage of this so as to give as big a clearance for the main gear as possible.

If in doubt, stop—and stay stopped until you've decided what to do next. If you decide to proceed for some good reason then risk bogging the nose wheel rather than the main gear. It makes the subsequent work much easier for the ground crews.

Where this very long wheelbase shows up most is probably on approaching the active runway at right angles and then getting lined up on the centre line first time without losing what is possibly valuable distance by wriggling forward to correct a large error. Remember where the inside main gear is. Go well across the centre line, about half your fuselage length, then come around and you will find yourself on the centre line. Remember also to straighten up the nose wheel before actually stopping.

There is a further effect of the very long wheelbase—that of attitude on lift-off and touch-down. Long wheelbase isn't quite the right term in this context. What is significant is the distance between the flight deck and the main gear. For reasons which will be explained later, swept wing aeroplanes need a higher incidence for a given lift than do straight wing aeroplanes. Rotation before lift off is therefore through a larger angle and the main gear is a long way aft and a long way below the pilot. This should not be forgotten on the day that an engine is lost on a WAT limiting take-off in terms of obstacle clearance after unstick.

Similarly on landing. Some, but not all, swept wing jets come in with a comparatively high nose up attitude and it must be remembered that the main gear can be as much as 30 ft. below the pilot's eye level. Close-in obstructions, like blast fences, must be given plenty of clearance.

4 The flight handling significance of turbine engines

Introduction

Before attempting to discuss the flight handling significance of turbine engines it will help if a little basic theory is covered first.

Engine cycle

As both piston and turbine engines are internal combustion engines, they have a similar basic cycle of operations; that is, induction, compression, combustion, expansion, exhaust.

Air is taken in and compressed, and fuel is injected and burnt. The hot gases then expand, providing a surplus of power over that required for compression, and are finally exhausted.

In both cases the thermal efficiency of the cycle improves with increasing compression ratio, while the power output increases with the amount of fuel burnt, which is proportional to the airflow and the fuel/air ratio.

Figure 4.1 illustrates the principle of the simplest type of gas turbine, i.e. the simple jet engine.

| Induction | compression | combustion | expansion | exhaust |

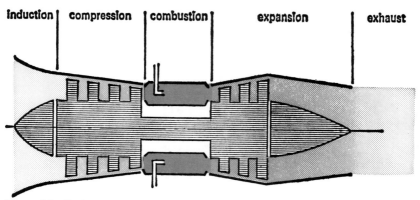

Figure 4.1   Basic cycle of operation.

Part of the expansion takes place in the turbine providing sufficient power to drive the compressor, while the remainder takes place in the nozzle in order to accelerate the gas to a high velocity jet.

Now let us consider the major difference between the piston engine and the gas turbine. In the piston engine, part or all of the compression, combustion and expansion processes takes place in the same component, the cylinder. This imposes severe practical limitations which are discussed later, and also dictates that nearly all the power in excess of that required for compression is taken out in the shaft. Hence a propeller is necessary.

In contrast the separate components of the gas turbine may each be of the optimum design for the process and their particular duties. Furthermore, the use of separate components gives great flexibility in design. By adding turbine stages to the simple jet engine and reducing the acceleration in the nozzle the jet velocity can be lowered, and extra shaft power obtained, either to drive a conventional propeller or to compress extra air to provide more jet flow, as in ducted-fan and by-pass engines.

Propulsion

The thrust of an aircraft propulsive system is the reaction to the force required to accelerate a mass of air through the system, and is manifested as pressure forces on the propeller blades in the case of a propeller, or on all internal surfaces in the case of a jet engine. The major difference between propellers and jets is in the relation between the values of mass and acceleration in the equation: force = mass × acceleration.

The acceleration through a conventional propeller is comparatively small, and can be increased only within small limits. Thus the thrust can be increased only by increasing the mass; this in turn is difficult because of the difficulty of accommodating extremely large propellers.

The jet engine produces thrust by giving a comparatively small mass of air a very much larger acceleration. The mass flow is limited by engine size, which can only become embarrassing in terms of installation if the by-pass ratio is extremely high.

The influence of jet velocity on the efficiency of propulsion is discussed later.

The economics of speed and size

So much for basic theory. We can now consider in rather more detail how the jet engine compares with the piston engine in meeting the performance and economic requirements of the transport aeroplane. To do this it is best to refer once more to the most important of the qualities demanded. These were mentioned briefly in Chapter Two, but as a reminder they are high total power, high output per single unit, low weight, small frontal area, low fuel consumption, overall efficiency, efficient cooling and reliability. Let us look at them individually.

(a) **High total power output** The typical drag of a jet transport in a high altitude cruise, at 240,000 lb. weight, 40,000 ft. and 0.85 true Mach number is 20,000 lb. On a four-engined aeroplane this means that each engine must be delivering 5,000 lb. of thrust; and under these conditions 5,000 lb. of thrust is equivalent to nearly 7,500 thrust horse power. This is clearly beyond the capabilities of even the most advanced piston-engines — approximately 3,400 shaft horse power at sea level — which were capable of delivering about 1,000 shaft horse power at 40,000 ft. (and considerably less thrust horse power since a 0.85 true Mach number cruise would result in large propeller compressibility losses with current designs).

(b) High output per single unit   There is an optimum number of power units for a given task.   The number is arrived at by stating the thrust required for take-off, assuming one engine failure, and catering for the one, and two, engine failures en route as a function of stage length and flight over water.   There is, of course, a lot of background in terms of engine failure probabilities and airworthiness requirements but the final analysis would appear to suggest that two engines are 'right' for short range, three for medium range and four for long range aeroplanes.

An important parameter of power is air mass flow in unit time. The piston engine is limited in the amount of air it can handle.

On the engine side this is because of the limitations of individual combustion chamber size and boost pressures due to flame propagation difficulties, and the difficulty of multiplexing cylinders due to simple geometric limitations, crankshaft design and cooling problems.

The law of diminishing returns would show eventually that compounding radial banks of cylinders, or in-line rows of cylinders with the freedom to use more than one primary crankshaft, would reduce the mechanical efficiency and increase the weight to a prohibitive extent.

On the propeller side there is the difficulty of accommodating large propellers and the excessive losses due to compressibility effects at the very high tip speeds of large propellers at forward speeds above 0.5 aircraft Mach number.   These limitations apply equally to the propeller gas turbine.

Taking now the figures quoted in the preceding section on 'high total power output' and assuming, rather generously, that 0.85 true Mach number could be achieved using a propeller with an efficiency of 85% at 40,000 ft., a simple calculation will show that, to produce the required total power from piston engines of 3,400 sea level horse power, we would need about nine engines. Propellers are more efficient at low Mach number, but if the calculation were done again for a take-off condition, assuming 2.6 lb. of static propeller thrust per shaft horse power, there would still be a need for at least six engines.   The next generation of jet transports will probably gross 700,000 lb. all up weight with four engines producing a total of 180,000 lb. thrust equating to over 60,000 shaft horse power in the take-off condition.   For the same power to weight ratio this aircraft would need eighteen piston engines producing 3,500 shaft horsepower per unit. These numbers are far removed from the optimum, quite apart from the problems of installation.

To meet the requirements of high total power and the optimum number of power units for a given task, therefore, there is obviously a need for a high output per single unit which the piston engine cannot provide.

The jet engine on the other hand shows no sign of any parameter which will limit its growth. First generation jet aircraft were powered by 5,000 lb. thrust engines, present aircraft by 20,000 lb. thrust engines and the projected jumbo-jet will have 45,000 lb. thrust engines. The limit has not yet been reached.

(c) **Low weight**   The requirement for lowest weight and highest power does not really need any elaboration.

The piston engine needs a lot of beef in its carcass to provide the strength to cope with the high loads which are produced in the engine by the heavy reciprocating masses.

A typical piston/propeller combination weighs 4,500 lb., produces 3,400 shaft horsepower and, at an assumed 2.6 lb. static thrust per shaft horsepower, gives approximately 2 lb. thrust per 1 lb. weight of engine.

The turbine engine can be lighter because its main assembly is a continuously rotating one, although precautions must be taken in the design to safeguard the engine and surrounding structure from failures which might release the enormous energy locked up in this rotating machinery. A typical large jet engine weighs 5,200 lb. and produces 21,000 lb. of static thrust, giving a value of 4 lb. thrust per 1 lb. weight of engine. This comparison has been drawn under conditions most favourable to the piston-propeller combination; under more representative cruise conditions the ratio will improve much more to the advantage of the jet engine. As for the propeller turbine, the weight of a propeller and reduction gear militates against their use in combination with a turbine unless very high efficiency at low forward speeds is required.

(d) **Small frontal area**   All excrescences are of course expensive in terms of profile drag. For an optimum bore/stroke ratio the diameter of a radial piston engine is proportional to its capacity; for an in-line engine, as compromised by cooling and crankshaft design problems, the same holds good. A typical piston engine (excluding the propeller in this case, because with power on there is no drag from it) grosses about 20 square feet of frontal area including the nacelle. Taking the values previously assumed this results in 425 lb. of thrust per square foot of frontal area.

In a jet engine, while as a first approximation its frontal area is proportional to mass air flow, the power can be increased by increasing the cycle temperature while the mass air flow remains constant. The fuel consumption will be improved by higher component efficiencies and high pressure ratios which, over the years, have also tended to produce lower frontal areas due to the employment and development of the axial compressor. The development has been substantially lengthwise and not radially, which would have been penalising in terms of profile drag. A typical large jet engine, including nacelle, grosses about 29 square feet of frontal area — rather larger than the piston engine considered above but able to deliver a much higher thrust, 690 lb. per square foot of frontal area, at altitudes at which the piston engine propeller combination is no longer effective. Again, the jet engine would improve its showing were the comparison drawn for more realistic operating conditions.

The fan type of jet engine will, however, have a larger frontal area than a simple jet of the same thrust and the cowl design becomes increasingly important as the by-pass ratio is increased.

(e) Low fuel consumption Hand in hand with the demand for higher powers and better power to weight ratios goes the quest for lower and lower fuel consumption. In terms of specific fuel consumption (lb. fuel/lb. thrust/hour), the ratio of cruise values for the jet engine relative to the piston engine which, a year or so ago, was of the order of 2 to 1, is now decreasing significantly. This is particularly true at low power and low altitude due to higher turbine temperatures and the better low speed propulsive efficiency of the by-pass engine. But these fuel consumptions, must be considered in conjunction with better utilisation, higher operating speeds, larger passenger capacity, and lower fuel costs, all of which stand in favour of the jet aircraft. It then becomes obvious that the jet aircraft is more economical overall than is the piston-engined aircraft.

True airspeed can be increased considerably at the higher altitudes possible with jet aircraft. Fuel consumption in terms of lb. per hour is proportional to thrust, which is equal to drag, which is proportional to indicated airspeed. Thus, if the true airspeed can be increased for a constant indicated airspeed, by increasing altitude, the fuel consumed for a given distance will be less. This is a most important factor and is the only one over which the pilot has control.

Fuel consumption in isolation is not enough: there must be compatibility of fuel economy with typical cruise conditions which are, in the case of the jet, high speed at high altitude. Faced with its own modest speed and altitude targets the piston engine didn't do a bad job in terms of fuel economy — as indeed could reasonably be expected after about fifty years of development. But the targets have changed.

It is now necessary to fly high and fast; and, as already explained, the piston engine is incapable of providing the power required under the operating conditions of speed and altitude.

(f) Overall efficiency The overall efficiency of an aero engine is the product of the thermal and propulsive efficiencies. The thermal efficiency of both the piston and turbine engine can be increased by increasing the pressure ratio. The pressure ratio of the piston engine is now limited by flame propagation considerations (e.g. detonation) but the gas turbine has not yet reached a limit.

The propulsive efficiency is made up of the Froude efficiency and the losses associated with the conversion (in turbine, fans and propellers) of gas power to jet or slipstream velocity. The Froude efficiency (the thrust power produced divided by the kinetic energy added to the air) is given by:—

$$\frac{2U}{V + U}$$

where U is the speed of the aircraft and V is the jet or propeller efflux velocity relative to the aircraft. This efficiency is low when V is much higher than U and rises to 100% when the two velocities are equal, i.e. when there is no acceleration and hence no thrust! Figure 4.2 compares the propulsive efficiency of the various systems. The propeller with its high mass flow and small acceleration has a high Froude efficiency, but because of its high tip speed becomes affected by compressibility losses at considerably lower forward Mach numbers than the aeroplane itself.

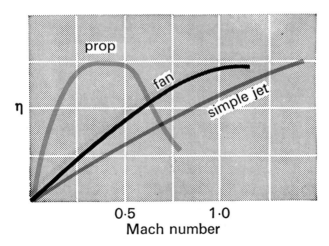

Figure 4.2 Comparison of efficiencies.

The simple jet with its high velocity becomes competitively efficient only at very high forward speeds. In the Mach 0.8 to 0.9 region it is only moderately efficient, and will become less so as turbine entry temperature (and hence jet velocity) is increased. At these Mach numbers the lower jet velocities of the by-pass and ducted fan engines offer improved efficiencies at the expense of an increase in mass flow for a given thrust.

It is clear that, at the high speeds currently required of transport aircraft, the conventional propeller is quite unsuitable, leaving the field clear for the jet engine, with increasing emphasis on the fan types of jet at the high subsonic speeds.

Finally, a comparison of mechanical efficiencies stands very much in favour of the turbine engine: in a turbine engine all the primary moving parts are continuously rotating with a mechanical efficiency approaching 100%; in a piston engine mechanical losses are, comparatively, high due to the weight of the reciprocating parts.

(g) Efficient cooling The cooling of a piston engine can be expensive in terms of drag because a radial must be exposed to the airflow and an in-line needs a radiator exposed to the airflow. This drag is increased under high power conditions when the cooling air exit flaps are extended. Careful design of engine or radiator cowling is necessary or this heat loss becomes a sheer loss in terms of B.T.U.s contained in the fuel which were expended in passing this heat away to atmosphere. The fuel/air ratio in a piston engine is increased under high power conditions to provide fuel for cooling purposes in the combustion chamber, which is expensive in fuel.

In the turbine engine the only cooling losses arise from the use of some of the compressed air for cooling instead of in the combustion and expansion processes. This of course is reflected in the efficiency of the cycle.

(h) Reliability There is a need in any propulsive system to be able to draw a high power continuously. In a piston engine, due to the limitations of exhaust valve material and the high level of internal stresses, the maximum cruising power is restricted to about 50% of the maximum available in order to provide an acceptable engine life. A jet engine is limited in a similar manner by the turbine blade material but in this case the typical maximum cruising power is 75% of the maximum available.

The jet engine is basically a simpler engine and very much more reliable. The absence of the highly stressed mechanism of the variable pitch propeller and associated reduction gear gives the turbine engine an added advantage; some jet engines have approved overhaul lives which are more than double those of the best piston engines.

The only real threat to the jet engine's life is excessive turbine temperature. The maximum temperature at the turbine is critical and a number of jet engine types spend a lot of time near this limit. If the limit is exceeded grossly on start-up the engine will undoubtedly be damaged; if the cruise limit is exceeded only slightly, but for prolonged periods, the engine life will be shortened.

To summarise, we can say that the piston engine and the propeller have been rendered obsolete by the increase in size and operating speed of transport aircraft. Only a turbine engine can meet all the requirements in the critical parameters discussed above.

The development of the turbine engine

Without going into too much detail on this subject it is worth taking a look at figures 4.3 to 4.9, which show line drawings of the various types of engines, and attempting to summarise the reasons for their development. It is a difficult thing to do since the state of the designer's art — both engines and airframes — at the particular date of the development was a significant factor, as were various commercial and political factors.

Jet engines come in a variety of types, from the original simple centrifugal compressor type to the large turbofans proposed for the jumbo-jets.

The centrifugal compressor engine

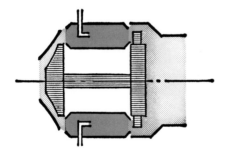

Figure 4.3   Centrifugal compressor engine.

The use of the centrifugal compressor enabled the extensive background of development of superchargers, for piston engines, to be applied directly to the turbine engine, thus hastening the advent of a reliable engine of adequate performance.

52

The axial compressor engine

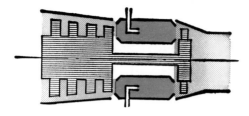

Figure 4.4   Axial compressor engine.

The axial compressor replaced the centrifugal compressor because of the need for greater economy and minimum frontal area.   Economy requires higher pressure ratios and better efficiencies; the axial compressor with its straight-through flow and ability to accommodate a number of stages in the same casing was clearly preferable in principle, and considerable improvement in performance became possible as a result of aerodynamic research.

The twin spool engine

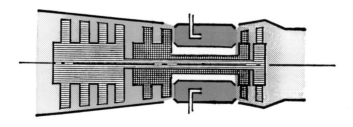

Figure 4.5   Twin spool engine.

The twin spool engine tended to replace the single spool engine, as pressure ratios increased, because the handling and part load performance of high pressure ratio engines could be improved without the need for automatic blade angle variation and the associated complex control system.

The by-pass engine

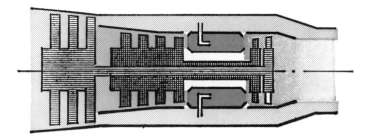

Figure 4.6   By-pass engine.

The by-pass engine was developed in order to permit the use of higher turbine temperatures to obtain higher thrusts, without a corresponding increase in jet velocity and reduction in propulsive efficiency leading to higher specific fuel consumption.   The term 'by-pass' is normally restricted to layouts with mixing of the hot and cold flows: without this restriction there is no essential difference between the by-pass engine and the front fan engine described below.

The fan engines

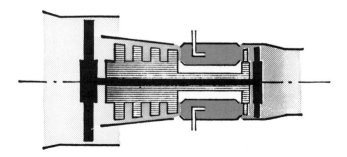

Figure 4.7   Front fan engine.

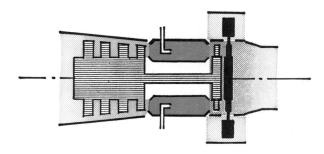

Figure 4.8　Aft fan engine.

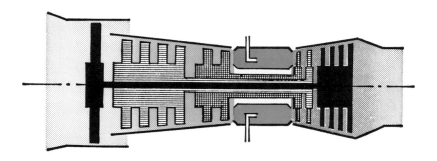

Figure 4.9　Three spool front fan engine.

The fan engine, an extension of the by-pass principle without hot and cold flow mixing, may be regarded as an intermediate stage between the turbojet and the turboprop, but does not suffer from the compressibility effects of the latter due to the control of the airflow by the surrounding ducting.　Higher ratios of fan air flow to engine flow are used and increased advantages of the type given for the by-pass engine are obtained.　The design of the nacelle has an increasingly powerful influence on the available thrust at these by-pass ratios and some variability may be necessary to reconcile the conflicting requirements of cruise and take-off operation.

Future trends

As has been said earlier, the steps in development have been influenced by current technology as well as political and commercial pressures. However, the objectives of development have remained broadly the same:—

Improved specific fuel consumption

Increased thrust-weight ratio

Improved reliability

Better control

Reduction of noise level.

The first two items in particular have demanded higher component efficiencies (e.g. compressor efficiency), higher compression ratios and turbine temperatures and increases in by-pass ratios.

As far as controllability is concerned the properly designed engine should not present handling difficulties whatever its form.

With the development of turbofan engines from present values of by-pass ratios of 1:1 and 2:1 up to projected values of 8:1 and 12:1 and beyond, different arrangements will result. The 3-spool turbofan is an example. Greater control flexibility and ability to vary the fan speed to reduce noise levels under approach and landing conditions are two of the advantages claimed for this type.

The following points regarding multispool engines are also of interest and may be significant in certain cases. Engines of this type may be more flexible due to the better aerodynamic matching at part load and the lower inertias of the rotating components. Multispool engines may be easier to start since only one spool needs to be turned by the starter.

Thrust to thrust lever relationship

Thrust in a piston/propeller combination is proportional to r.p.m., manifold pressure and propeller blade angle; of these, manifold pressure is the most dominant. More thrust variation can be produced at a constant r.p.m. by varying manifold pressure, and therefore blade angle, than can be produced at constant manifold pressure by varying r.p.m. However, as r.p.m. is selected in steps in sympathy with manifold pressure, it is broadly true as a rough approximation that thrust is proportional to throttle (and r.p.m. lever) position. At a constant r.p.m. typical of an approach setting then thrust is proportional to throttle lever position.

On a jet engine, however, thrust is proportional to r.p.m. (mass flow) and temperature (fuel/air ratio). These are matched and a further variation comes from the efficiency of the compressor at varying r.p.m. The whole operating cycle and the gas flow through the engine are designed to be at their most efficient at high r.p.m. where the engine is designed to spend most of its time. As r.p.m. rises, mass flow, temperature and efficiency all increase and a lot more thrust is produced per, say, 100 r.p.m. near the top of the range than near the bottom.

Figure 4.10 shows quite simply thrust lever position against thrust, from full ahead to full astern, for both a piston propeller installation and a pure jet installation. These diagrams do not represent particular installations and the characteristics have been deliberately exaggerated in order to accentuate the differences. The following facts are all important in terms of flight handling qualities:—

(a) Thrust is more or less proportional to throttle position in a propeller installation (note the straight line), but quite disproportional in a jet (note the curve steepening sharply at high r.p.m.). An inch of throttle movement on a propeller is worth say 700 horse power wherever the throttle might be. On a jet an inch of thrust lever movement at low r.p.m. might be worth only 500 lb. thrust, but at high r.p.m. will be worth more like 5,000 lb. of thrust. This is why, if significantly more power is needed from a low thrust lever setting, it is no good inching the lever up a bit — if the power is needed, give it a handful. This doesn't mean to say that it is necessary to be rough with the levers at all times; if they are at a typical approach power setting then only small changes need be made.

(b) Throttle closed on a propeller installation produces drag — note the continuance of the thrust line to below zero in the forward range. Thrust lever at idle on a jet still leaves some forward thrust on — notice there is about 1,000 lb. of forward thrust at flight idle. This gives a free wheeling effect which is the reason for the development of thrust reversing and better brakes. Residual thrust, in company with the lack of aerodynamic drag of an aeroplane with a tricycle undercarriage, leads to an extremely slow rate of speed reduction on a landing roll. In the event of a total brake failure (not possible on a properly designed aeroplane of course but equivalent to a very icy runway surface) the aeroplane would simply go on and on and on. There is incidentally an advantage from not having the disturbed flow from a windmilling propeller. This flow often reduces elevator effect and produces, for example, in the case of a forward C.G. landing when the throttles are closed at the threshold, an inability to flare the aeroplane and a subsequent heavy landing. There is none of this elevator degradation on a jet aeroplane; elevator effect remains constant, power-on and power-off.

(c) The net change in thrust between forward idle and reverse idle on a propeller is very large — notice the steepness of the line. As the propeller reverses the drag, really builds up and at reverse idle the propeller is

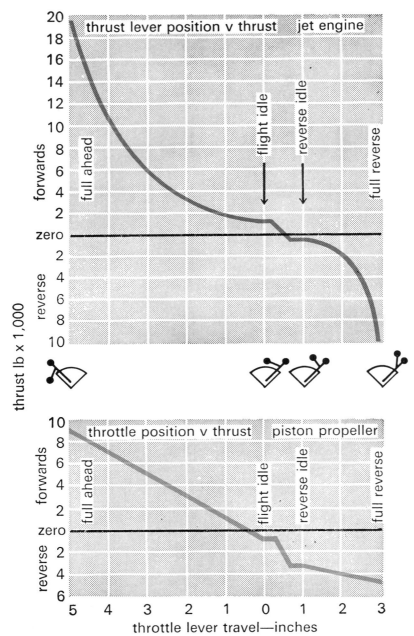

Figure 4.10   Relationship between power lever position and thrust.

already producing about 60% of its maximum possible drag at full power — the remainder being achieved by opening up in reverse. This is why it is dangerous to reverse a propeller before the aircraft is firmly on the ground; not only is the drag enormous but the lift is destroyed over a large part of the wing and elevator effect is very much reduced. On a jet engine, however, the net change in thrust between forward idle and reverse idle is very small; with a reverser efficiency of 50% the net change will be from 1,000 lb. forwards to 500 lb. reverse. This is why, provided the aeroplane is flight cleared, it is comparatively innocuous to reverse a jet engine in flight. This argument also shows up the need for not dwelling any longer than is necessary at reverse idle on a landing; very little drag is being produced and, to get full value from the reversers, the engine must be opened up to full reverse power as soon as possible, particularly as reverse thrust is much more effective at high forward speeds.

On reflection it is rather surprising that power lever position in relation to thrust on a turbine engine has been allowed to have been so mis-matched for so long; mis-matched from the pilot's point of view that is. Control systems presently under development can be arranged to provide almost any relationship of power lever to thrust required. The fact that they might be, for example, electric controls (for other reasons) makes the provision of this elaboration very easy. However, sub-stantially the same facility could have been provided on present turbine engines by a fairly simple variable mechanical gearing in the power lever control system which would alter the present linear fuel valve opening to one related to thrust.

Acceleration times

In a propeller installation the constant speeding ability of the propeller keeps the engine turning at an r.p.m. which is a compromise between the approach and baulked landing power conditions and power is altered by varying the boost pressure. To increase power quickly the boost is increased, the propeller coarsens off and the demanded thrust is supplied quickly. 'Quickly' in this context means about 3 to 4 seconds because of the propeller momentary overspeed tendency which is not acceptable to a pilot with any sympathy for mechanical engineering devices. Incidentally, on a propeller installation thrust can be reduced just as quickly (and reduced to the point where drag is produced) because the constant speed control unit can no longer fine-off the blade angle.

It has already been explained that efficiency in a jet engine is highest at high r.p.m. where the compressor is working closest to its optimum conditions of gas flow, etc. At low r.p.m. the operating cycle is generally inefficient. If a sudden demand is made for more thrust from an r.p.m. equivalent to a normal approach r.p.m. the engine will respond immediately and full thrust can be achieved in about 2 secs. From a lower r.p.m., however, a sudden demand for maximum thrust will tend to overfuel the engine and cause it to overheat or surge. To prevent this various limiters are contained in the fuel control unit and these serve to restrict the engine until it is at an r.p.m. at which it can respond to a rapid acceleration demand without distress. This critical r.p.m. is most noticeable when doing a slam acceleration from an idle thrust setting. Acceleration initially is very slow indeed but then changes to very quick as the r.p.m. rises through this significant value. From idle thrust to substantially full thrust at a typical approach speed takes about 6 secs. on average. Some engine types are better than others, but there is also a scatter between individual engines of the same type; so occasionally the full 8 secs. permitted by the requirements is needed.

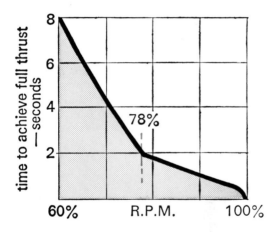

Figure 4.11   Engine acceleration times.

Notice, in figure 4.11, the kink in the curve of time to achieve full thrust against r.p.m. at about 78%. The engine is struggling up to this point but beyond it responds very rapidly. Notice also the limiter which cuts in just before maximum r.p.m. — depending on which parameter is limiting at the time. This is a little sophistication of no great interest in terms of flying qualities because there is already enough thrust to meet the baulked landing climb requirements as far as airworthiness is concerned.

This acceleration time delay is most important in the approach, landing and overshoot stages of the flight. While small thrust changes can be made sufficiently quickly to modulate a nicely controlled final approach, if ever there is a demand for a lot of thrust quickly then the r.p.m. from which it is demanded must be borne in mind. If the r.p.m. is low, say following a high and fast excursion above the glide slope at its lower end leading to the need to overshoot, then up to 8 secs. can be required before full thrust is being delivered. It is important to emphasise that there is very little increase in thrust for perhaps the first five seconds following thrust lever movement. Under properly controlled conditions this delay can be tolerated but, in an emergency, where a lot of thrust is needed instantly, this delay can be fatal. There are many good reasons on a jet aircraft why there can be a sudden demand for a rapid increase in thrust (about which a lot more will be said later). So, until the need for a sudden large increase in thrust has been completely removed, don't let the engines run down below the rapid acceleration r.p.m. value. This value varies from engine to engine but most engines seem to come out at about 5% below a typical approach r.p.m. — say in the upper seventies as a percentage of maximum r.p.m.

Absence of propeller slipstream

A propeller produces thrust by accelerating a large mass of air rearwards and this air passes over a comparatively large percentage of the wing area. Remembering the V term in the basic lift formula it is clear that the lift on a propeller aeroplane wing is the sum of the lift generated by the wing area not in the wake of the propellers (as a result of aircraft speed) and the lift generated by the wing area which is influenced by propeller slipstream. By varying the speed of the slipstream air, therefore, it is possible to vary the total lift on a wing at constant aircraft speed. In the past this simple fact has turned a number of potential accidents into incidents. Many a too low, too slow approach has been salvaged by a quick blast of power. Apart from increasing the lift at constant airspeed the stalling speed itself is also depressed; with a typical approach power setting a normal power-off stall speed of say 90 knots can be reduced by about 10 knots, and even more at full power.

A jet engine also produces thrust by accelerating a large mass of air rearwards but this air is largely discharged clear astern and does not pass over the wings. There is, therefore, no lift bonus at increased power at constant airspeed and no significant depression of the power-on stall speed. In practice there is a small reduction, worth perhaps two or three knots, due to (a) some entrainment of the air by the jet efflux and (b) the vertical component of thrust at high nose up attitudes effectively reducing the weight of the aeroplane.

So in not having propellers the jet aeroplane pilot has lost out in two ways:—

(a) It is not possible to produce increased lift instantly by simply increasing power.

(b) It is not possible to depress the stall speed by simply increasing power. The hidden margin of say, in very round figures, 10 knots (the difference between power-off and power-on stall speed on a propeller aeroplane for a given configuration), is lost.

Now add the poor acceleration response of the jet engine already discussed and we have three ways in which the pilot of a jet aeroplane is worse off than his piston/propeller counterpart. These three reasons all stem directly from having jet engines and no propellers. Later will be added three further qualities from the airframe design side.

For these reasons there is a marked difference between — and here let us take the most significant area — the approach qualities of a piston-engined aircraft and a jet aircraft. In the former there is some room for error; speed is not too critical and a burst of power will salvage an increasing rate of sink. In the latter there is little room for error. If an increasing sink rate should start to develop remember two points in their correct sequence. Firstly, increased lift can be gained only by accelerating the airflow over the wings (this will be qualified in a later sub-chapter) and this can be done only by accelerating the whole aeroplane. Secondly, the aeroplane can be accelerated, assuming a height loss cannot be afforded, only by a rapid increase in thrust from the engines, which are known to be slow in response from low r.p.m. values.

The salvaging of an increasing sink rate on the approach can be a very difficult manoeuvre and more will be said of this later when basic airframe matters have been covered. Let us content ourselves for the moment with the knowledge we have of the engine side and bear these three factors in mind. In order not to be presented with a salvage operation you must at all times, and particularly on an approach, maintain the approach speed, keep the engine r.p.m. up and act very early if either of these controlling parameters starts wandering towards its limit. You are now being asked not only to imagine your projected flight path but also the way in which it can be modulated with the tools at your disposal; and to do this you must be aware of the capability of these tools and their limitations.

Absence of propeller drag

When the throttles are closed to idle on a piston-engined aeroplane the propeller produces drag, that is, negative thrust. The zero thrust position at approach speed would approximate to a setting of about 1,800 r.p.m. and 12 in. boost. The amount of drag produced by a windmilling propeller is also a function of its rotational speed and blade pitch angle; with the propeller on its fine pitch stops, therefore at fixed pitch, the higher the r.p.m. the higher the drag. This ability to produce drag from the propeller is useful, because, just as it is necessary to accelerate quickly under some conditions of flight, so is it equally necessary to be able to lose speed quickly, too.

On a jet engine, however, when the thrust levers are closed to idle the engine still produces forward thrust, up to 1,000 lb. on a 20,000 lb. rated engine. Like everything else this has advantages and disadvantages. The main advantage is that the pilot can no longer be faced with the appalling drag penalty of a runaway propeller or a reversed propeller (a reversed propeller in flight can equate to a solid disc, which, for a 14 ft. diameter, produces about 4,000 lb. of drag). The disadvantage is the 'free-wheeling' effect it has on the aeroplane; while this can occasionally be used to advantage (for example in a long descent) it is an embarrassment when it is necessary to lose speed quickly, when entering a terminal area say, or on the landing flare.

This basic deficiency is made up by the provision of other means of producing drag. Speed brakes are used on nearly all aeroplanes, the main gear is used quite often and — although on two types only to date — reverse thrust in flight is also employed. While these devices are there to be used they need not be used in an ignorant manner. With a little bit of anticipation it is quite possible to control the flight path of the aeroplane so as to reduce the need for these drag producing devices to a minimum. Their use nearly always produces noise or buffeting and the more considerate pilot will use them only when he has to.

This free-wheeling effect of significant forward thrust at idle compounds the momentum problem of a large, fast, clean aeroplane. Having said earlier that, because of poor acceleration qualities, the thrust levers should never be unthinkingly retarded, and now emphasising the free-wheeling qualities at idle thrust, a reader could well be forgiven for thinking that the progress of a jet aeroplane along its flight path in terms of speed is not an exact state of affairs. Quite so — this is just the case. But it is not difficult to control in practice. This is typical of those things which can be demonstrated in a few minutes in flight but take a lot longer to put down on paper.

A propeller aeroplane is more or less locked in its longitudinal flight path by the helix action of the propeller, rather like the way in which a mountain railway engine is locked to its track by the rack and pinion. Power variations on a propeller aeroplane will accelerate and decelerate the aeroplane in a predictable fashion. The jet, however, is not 'locked' to anything, and its progress longitudinally must be modulated by an intelligent awareness of the delay in response to increased and decreased thrust and an appreciation of the forward thrust which remains at the idle setting.

In holding a speed on the approach you should not wait for a clear indication of the need for more thrust — the power levers should have already been advanced a crack to compensate for the first suggestion of a speed decay. Similarly, if a comparatively large thrust increase has been necessary for a rapid loss of speed don't leave it on too long or the aeroplane will rapidly get too fast again. Back most of it off fairly soon and you will see the speed stabilise nicely.

High consumption at low altitude

It has already been stated that fuel consumption in terms of lb./hour varies with IAS and thus the larger the difference between IAS and TAS the more miles per gallon can be achieved. This, to a large extent, explains the title of this sub-chapter. However, it is worth going into it in slightly more detail. In so doing endurance and range will be considered separately.

Endurance

In this case, where the need is to stay airborne as long as possible on a given quanitity of fuel, the lowest fuel consumption in lb./hour is required. Since,

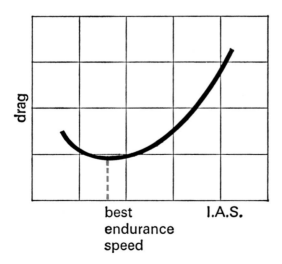

Figure 4.12   Deduction of best endurance speed.

for a jet engine, fuel consumption in lb./hour is approximately proportional to thrust, minimum thrust and minimum drag are required.

64

Figure 4.12 shows the classic graph of total drag against IAS, and the best endurance speed is obviously that at which the drag is least. Broadly, this speed remains constant with altitude, but in practice it is (a) usually increased slightly to improve handling qualities and to avoid small reductions in speed which would allow the aeroplane to slip up the 'wrong' side of the drag curve and (b) reduced slightly at high altitudes to avoid extra drag from increasing Mach number effect. Fuel consumption remains more or less constant with height because the drag and thrust are constant. Again, in practice, fuel consumption decreases slightly at high altitude because of the higher propulsive efficiency due to the higher TAS, and because the higher r.p.m. necessary to maintain the required thrust (remember that a jet engine basically is 'unsupercharged' and at any given setting its power falls off with altitude) brings the engine nearer the lowest SFC operating condition. This lowest SFC operating condition is a function of the internal aerodynamic design and reflects the optimisation of the engine generally to be at its best — best SFC — under the conditions where it will spend most of its operating life, i.e. high altitude high speed conditions at a comparatively high power setting.

So, other operational considerations not being overriding, if you need to extract maximum time from the fuel remaining, in a long hold for example, fly, within reason, as high as possible. If you are forced to accept lower

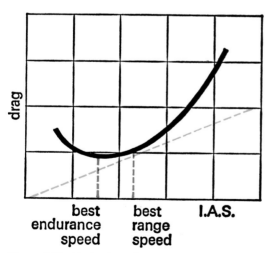

Figure 4.13   Deduction of best range speed.

altitudes there is no great cause for concern because the fuel penalty is not exorbitant.

Range

In this case the need is to fly as far as possible on a given quantity of fuel and therefore extract maximum air miles per gallon. Figure 4.13 shows the same basic graph of drag against IAS, but now drawn with a tangent from the point of origin to the curve. This gives, at the point where the tangent touches the curve, the highest IAS for the least drag, or thrust, or fuel consumption and thus the greatest air miles per gallon. Notice that this speed is higher than the best endurance speed.

Again, theoretically, this IAS is constant at all heights but in practice it is (a) increased slightly at low altitudes (the improvement effected by bringing the r.p.m. up nearer the best SFC point more than outweighs the slightly higher drag) and (b) decreased slightly at high altitudes to avoid excessive Mach number drag. It now becomes obvious that the higher the altitude the more miles per gallon will be achieved. IAS, drag and fuel consumption remain more or less constant while TAS, and thus distance covered, increase. This effect is most important. For example, a typical jet transport will go about 65% further at 40,000 ft. than it will at sea level on the same amount of fuel.

So the rule for best range is: the higher the better. Just how high of course will depend on many other factors. Two of the most important are winds at different levels and sector length. The influence of these two factors does not really need any elaboration.

With the way in which fleets of jet transports are now operated, where a lot of planning is done by specialist departments who themselves are expected to know traffic densities at varying flight levels, there should not be many occasions on which a pilot has to do any basic thinking in terms of range and endurance flying. But when the need does arise remember that you cannot go wrong if you remain as high as possible as long as possible. This applies so long as there are no marked variations of winds at different altitudes. A lot of sculling around at low altitude is expensive in terms of fuel consumed and distance covered. The rate at which a big jet transport uses up fuel, in, for example, a couple of abortive attempts to land at a declared destination due to weather can be quite frightening; a prudent decision to divert earlier from a high cruising level leads to a much more peaceful existence.

Noise abatement techniques

Jet engines make an awful lot of noise. The noise is caused by the shear effect at the boundary of the jet efflux; the higher the power, the faster the speed of the jet efflux, the more the shear effect, the greater the noise. The really distressing noise comes from the exhaust at maximum thrust, but on the

66

approach some engines radiate compressor or fan noise forwards along the flight path and this noise can be just as distressing. Noise suppressors are devices fitted to the jet pipe which mix the boundary layer at the periphery of the jet efflux so as to produce a velocity gradient across the mixing layer. This reduces the shear and, therefore, the noise. There is, of course, a small performance loss with the fitting of noise suppressors. The noise is sufficiently high to cause a real nuisance to residents living near aerodromes and there is now an obligation on operating companies to adopt procedures which will keep the noise to a reasonable minimum consistent with safety. The permitted maximum noise levels for day and night periods are published by National Authorities and are measured over listening posts which are situated some distance out from each departure runway.

Of the many parameters affecting noise only two are really dominant and capable of being handled in practice. Firstly, the noise is proportional to the power being developed by the engine and, secondly, the noise is an inverse function of the distance between the noise source and the listener. In order to reduce noise, therefore, only these two freedoms can be exercised. We must reduce power and get as far away from the noise sensitive area as possible, as quickly as possible. Because noise sensitive areas generally completely surround an airport there is not much freedom in the selection of departure tracks — although where this is possible it is done — therefore all the work necessary has to be carried out in the vertical plane.

The following basic technique, adopted world wide, is the only one which can be used. There is no alternative foreseen at this time. After leaving the runway the technique is split into two separate parts:—

(a) *The noise abatement first segment* in which is adopted as steep a climb as is properly safe, at full power, so as to gain as much height as possible, either within or close to the boundaries of the airport. Just before the listening posts, which themselves are just short of the noise sensitive areas, the flightpath is changed to —

(b) *the noise abatement second segment* in which the engines are throttled so as to leave the aeroplane in a gentle climb condition. This drift out and up is continued until either a declared height has been reached or the noise sensitive area has been cleared when climb power is restored, the aircraft accelerated, cleaned up and established in the normal en route climb condition.

The first segment meets the requirement of getting as much distance between the noise source and the listener as possible and the second segment meets the requirement of keeping the power as low as possible. The end of the first segment is usually defined by the elapse of a standard time interval from brakes off at the start of the take-off run.

There are obviously two very important factors of this noise abatement technique; the speed chosen for the first segment and the amount of power reduction for the second segment. In all other respects the procedures are quite straightforward. Most jet transports retain the take-off flap setting throughout the second segment.

The speed in the first segment is chosen to meet all of the following requirements:—

(a) To result in a climb gradient all engines at a speed which does not embarrass the assumed engine-out flight path at V_2 in terms of obstacle clearance.

(b) To ensure adequate controllability in the event of engine failure, remembering that this procedure is regarded as an everyday occurrence.

(c) To ensure adequate stability in the spiral mode (this will be explained in a later chapter).

(d) To maintain pitch attitudes, including a reasonable allowance for mishandling, which are within the range of the flight instruments.

The speed which normally comes out of all this is constant for all weights up to a fairly high weight (this speed normally being based on the pitch attitude requirements); and a speed from this weight up to top weight of $V_2 + 15$ knots (this to meet the climb gradient requirement). The other requirements are not normally limiting.

The amount of power reduction in the second segment is based quite simply on a performance requirement of a flat 2% gross gradient (say 400 ft. per minute rate of climb) under the most adverse conditions of weight, altitude and temperature. Because of the need to keep these drills as simple as possible, on some aeroplanes a unique value of r.p.m. is selected for all second segments; under more favourable combinations of weight, altitude and temperature the indicated rate of climb in the second segment will of course be far higher. On aeroplanes which cannot tolerate this broad brush treatment the second segment r.p.m. is varied with weight and temperature in simple steps. The 2% minimum gradient was chosen to ensure that, under combinations of variables such as normal piloting ability, weather and performance scatter between aeroplanes, the actual climb performance of the aeroplane would never be negative.

There are variations in these techniques between aircraft types; in the use of flaps for example, and speed for the second segment, which is normally the same as the first, but can be slightly faster. For particular drills see the approved Flight Manuals.

68

Figure 4.14 shows a typical noise abatement departure profile. The sequence of operations is as follows:—

(1) First segment — gear-up, take-off flap, full power, $V_2 + 15$ knots.

A. Change to second segment — simply throttle back to reduced power.

(2) Second segment — take-off flap, reduced power, $V_2 + 15$ knots.

B. End of need for noise abatement. Restore climb power.

(3) Third phase — accelerate and clean up.

C. Achieve all engines en route climb speed.

(4) Fourth phase — en route climb.

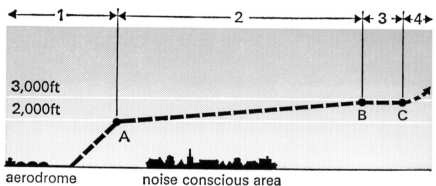

Figure 4.14   Typical noise abatement departure profile.

Having explained the reason for noise abatement techniques, and elaborated on the structure of these techniques, let us now turn to the consequences in terms of flying the aeroplane. It is immediately necessary to state that, contrary to opinions which were circulating some time ago, there is nothing exceptionally demanding or difficult in the performance of these techniques and that the average pilot is certainly well able to fly to the required degree of accuracy and cope with the problems involved. This is not to say that it is all very easy; the noise abatement departure procedures are certainly a little more demanding than the old departure procedures. But with a bit of practice, full knowledge of the facts and some accuracy in control of the flight path, it turns out to be not so difficult as it might appear at first sight.

There are only a few points which need to be made specifically on noise abatement techniques. In order to get smoothly, quickly and accurately into the first segment after lift-off it helps enormously to know in advance the approximate pitch attitude required in the first segment as modulated by the level of performance obtaining at the time. Let us assume that we know that 15° pitch attitude will be required in the first segment: then after gear retraction and a satisfactory rate of increasing airspeed pull up smoothly and gently to 15° pitch attitude, stop at 15° and hold it there. The airspeed will then settle pretty close to the required airspeed and further slight adjustments in pitch and airspeed can be made subsequently. If one should shoot for airspeed as the first parameter the flight path will be less stable because of the lag in airspeed inherent in its reflection of pitch attitude. Having made this suggestion it must again immediately be said that one must not simply fly attitude to the exclusion of all else. While pitch attitude is recommended as the primary parameter it is assumed that the normal and close monitoring of airspeed, altitude and vertical speed will support the information being drawn from the horizon.

The change from the first to the second segment needs to be made smoothly and progressively, as elaborated earlier under the broad heading of Momentum. You should know the pitch attitude required in the second segment. Shoot for this as the power is reduced, then keep your eye on the VSI. Keep the aeroplane climbing gently and monitor the airspeed. Now, just drift out in comparative peace and quiet. Your next task will be to clean up. Increase power first, then, at the approved airspeed, select flaps up. Watch the pitch attitude during flap retraction — don't let the aeroplane go downhill. Keep the nose up, trim out at the en route climb speed and you are away.

One particular type, which has a high buffet speed flaps up, needs a slight pitch down after flap retraction selection in order to accelerate quickly to the speed for flaps fully retracted under high altitude and high temperature operating conditions. In this manoeuvre only just enough height should be traded for the required rate of acceleration.

It has been established that, if by sticking to a noise abatement procedure the pilot feels that the overall safety of the flight is being hazarded in some way, then he is fully entitled to depart from the procedure and fly as he considers best in view of the circumstances existing at the time. This needs emphasising. If, for reasons such as unexpected turbulence or engine malfunction, adherence to the noise abatement procedure involves a lowering of the safety level or a greater demand on your skill than you are confident of producing then — don't hesitate — throw noise abatement away and do whatever you consider best. You might ring the bell in the process and you will be required to explain this later. But don't worry; a genuine decision on these grounds will of course be upheld.

The recent trend towards reduced thrust take-offs also has noise implications. A take-off and climb out at reduced thrust will result in the aeroplane being lower than normal and, although the reduced thrust will make very slightly less noise, this improvement is more than balanced by the effect of lower altitude. So if you have a noise problem don't use reduced thrust, that is unless the noise margin you have to play with is capable of taking a little abuse without causing annoyance.

The whole of this sub-chapter has dealt only with the reduction of noise on take-off. The problem of reducing noise on the approach is now receiving attention but is proving more difficult to resolve. Steeper glide path angles involve much more flying hazard than is justified by the small reduction in noise achieved. Similarly, the two segment approach procedure (up to 6° approach path down to, say, 1,500 ft., then intercept the standard 2½° or 3° glide slope to the threshold) is still in its early research stage and the problems it poses are quite large. As of this time there are no specific approach noise abatement procedures other than the avoidance of a low altitude drag across a populated area. Glide slopes should therefore be joined at 2,500 ft. or 3,000 ft. rather than 1,500 ft.

Approach noise can of course be reduced by late selection of gear and flaps and by not using auto-throttle; it is a pity that these two variations of technique are in opposition to the present requirement, which is for as many auto approaches as possible in good conditions in order to build confidence for the future clearance of automatics in low weather conditions.

Engine locations

The problems of installation of a piston-propeller combination rather limited the airframe designer in his choice of power plant location. Apart from cooling problems there was the need to provide adequate propeller clearance; from other propellers, from the structure and, not least, from the ground. Although propellers have been mounted in a variety of places over the years they finally finished up across the span and ahead of the wing on large transport aeroplanes. While this had advantages in wing bending relief and slipstream effect it was not good in terms of asymmetric yawing moments and undercarriage design.

Jet engines though, primarily due to the absence of the propeller, lend themselves to a comparatively wide choice of location on civil transport aeroplanes; although air intake distribution can give rise to problems of performance and handling during the development stages due to the enormous air consumption, the jet engine presents the designer with greater installation freedom than he ever had in the piston-propeller case.

Jet engines are mounted in three primary positions and these are:—

(a) Buried in the wing fairly close to the root.

(b) Mounted in pods underslung across the wing.

(c) Mounted in, or in pods on, the rear fuselage.

Each position has its advantages and disadvantages, and while there is little a pilot can do about controlling the latter, it is worth summarising the respective features so that a better understanding can be achieved of the total airframe and engine qualities, limitations and consequences.

(a) Buried in the wing root

Advantages:

1 Asymmetric yawing moment due to failure is smaller because the thrust line is close to the fuselage centre-line; other parameters not being dominant rudder design is, therefore, less demanding and critical speeds are, comparatively, lower.

2 The engines are mounted near the C.G. of the aircraft; this effectively keeps the wing itself forward and, for a given tail arm, enables a smaller tail to be employed with less overall drag.

3 Since there are no pods the drag is again reduced.

Disadvantages:

1 Structural problems occur due to the need for cut-outs for intake and exhaust passages in the spars and structure generally.

2 The containment of a disintegrating engine can be costly in terms of installation weight.

3 The passenger cabin tends to be noisy.

4 Thrust reverser design is limited by the impingement of the reversed flow on the fuselage.

5 Acoustic damage can occur to structure within the area of the noise pattern from the exhaust.

6 Having a common intake for two or more engines with a short splitter can lead to a one engine break-up affecting neighbouring engines due to blades, etc., going forwards initially then down into the other engines.

7 The hot parts are a bit close to the fuel in the event of a crash.

(b) Mounted in underslung wing pods

Advantages:

1 Depending on geometry and design cruise Mach number, installation (interference) drag is minimised.

2 Intake efficiency is rarely compromised by interference flows.

3 The engines provide bending relief thus reducing wing structure weight.

4 The wing profile is not compromised.

5 At high incidence (and, by careful design, at other times) the pylons tend to act in a way similar to fences by controlling spanwise flow.

6   There is less acoustic damage to the airframe.

7   Thrust reverser design is comparatively uninhibited.

8   Engine accessibility is good.

9   There will be less overall damage in the event of a gear-up landing.

Disadvantages:

1   Unless the engines are mounted well inboard (which itself would spoil the wing bending relief provided by more generous spacing) the asymmetric yawing moment following failure is high: this demands good rudder control and inflicts, comparatively, higher critical speeds.

2   With pods below the wing, roll freedom on the ground is limited.

3   A low thrust line can have an adverse effect on longitudinal control (the nose down pitch on reducing thrust).

4   On a swept wing four-engined type, the reversed thrust flow from the inners upsets the intake flow on the outers; this necessitates early cancellation of reverse on the inners.

5   The low mounted engines encourage ingestion from the runway surface.

(c) Mounted in, or in pods on, the rear fuselage

Advantages:

1   The passenger cabin can benefit markedly from the reduction in engine noise.

2   The asymmetric yawing moment following failure is small because the thrust lines are close to the centre-line.

3   The wing design, freed from the restriction of engine mountings, can be optimised in terms of lift and drag throughout the flight envelope.

4   An odd number of engines can be accommodated.

Disadvantages:

1   Passenger accommodation is reduced for a given fuselage length.

2   Engine malfunctions are more likely due to the disturbed flow from the wing at high incidences.

3   Care has to be exercised in the routeing and the protection of the fuel lines from the wing to the engines.

4   The engines are well behind the C.G.; this gives the unloaded aircraft a very aft C.G. and in order to get the left near the C.G. the wing has

to be set well aft: this in turn (for a given tail arm requirement) requires a larger tail.

5   The basic structure weight is higher because the wing itself has to be stronger (without the bending relief provided by wing mounted engines) and the rear fuselage has to be strengthened, both to support the engines and to take out through the fin structure the tail loads from the high set tail.

6   The tailplane usually has to be set high up to be clear of the engines involving, in some cases, severe problems in terms of stall qualities.

7   Where a third engine is centre-line mounted in the rear fuselage there can be difficulties in intake design, difficulties in reverse thrust design and no inherent warning to the pilot of engine failure.   This puts a premium on good instrumentation and proper engine monitoring.

Of the disadvantages outlined above there is little the pilot can do about the majority of them, but some can be handled in a sensible anticipatory manner.   The following techniques are worth remembering:—

(a) Where the engines are mounted in pods across the wing the swing following engine failure on take-off is likely to be quite severe.   As a very large fin (which is the best cure) has penalties elsewhere there will have been some pressure during certification to have demonstrated the lowest safe value of V_{MCG}.   Again, as the operating rules permit minimum V_1 to equal V_{MCG} the effect of both these quite proper optimum scheduling rules is . . . . no fat.   There is little comfort to be drawn from the alternative of an accelerate/stop; an aborted take-off can be more untidy in terms of lateral displacement and rolling tendencies than a continued take-off.   (This statement simply emphasises the fact that most aeroplanes need to take full advantage of some particular requirement during certification.   An aeroplane with this engine layout needs to go as close to the V_{MCG} requirement as possible.   A simple solution would perhaps be to factor minimum V_1 to not less than $1.05 \times V_{MCG}$.   As, however, an engine failure, at V_1, on a limiting runway, is 'sufficiently remote' the factor cannot be shown to be necessary on a probability basis.)   So, on the day you are making a light weight take-off from a short field where V_1 equals V_{MCG}, keep on the ball.   Be psychologically prepared, and mentally practised, for an abort until V_1 has gone by; be prepared after V_1 to make a smooth co-ordinated take-off in the event of a failure, not neglecting (and this often happens) to rotate at V_R and hit the screen speed at the screen height, in spite of the difficulty you might still be having with the rudder and aileron controls.

(b) On any installation where two engines are mounted very close together keep an eye on both of them in the event of one suffering a strike or

74

showing signs of breaking up; there is the remote possibility that bits from one can damage the other.

(c) With wing pod engines roll freedom can be quite limiting on or close to the ground. Wing tips and flaps also are quite close to the ground on a swept wing. Take care to maintain lateral level on cross wind take-offs and when pushing (not kicking) off drift on a crosswind landing.

(d) When using reverse thrust on landing with a four-engined wing pod installation remember that, depending on cross wind, full reverse held to a low speed will cause the outer intakes to be upset by the reversed exhaust from the inners and they will surge. Don't, however, do the obvious thing and cancel reverse on all engines — you are throwing away good and effective reverse on the outers. At about 80 knots in a head wind, or slightly higher in a cross wind, gently reduce the inners so as to be at idle reverse by say 60 knots, then progressively reduce the outers to reverse idle. In this manner you won't risk damage to the engines yet you will draw maximum use from reverse thrust.

(e) Particular care should be taken to monitor those engines which give little or no notice of failure on take-off due to lack of an inherent swing. This is obviously true of the middle engine of a three-engined aeroplane and is still fairly true of an inner engine failure on a four engine rear-mounted installation. Take-off field factors are tied very closely to a quick recognition of engine failure, and a run down engine, not recognised, could completely upset either the accelerate/stop distance or obstacle clearance after take-off.

Many of the items discussed in this sub-chapter are design problems. By the time the aircraft type is certificated any snag inherent in the design will have been fixed and it is important to emphasise that, by the time of certification, all types, regardless of engine layout, will have reached an acceptable level of flying qualities. The author has chosen to discuss these design matters because he believes that a pilot should be aware of them. Then, if he is ever exposed to extraordinary operating conditions in which some of these items could have a bearing, he will have the necessary background information on which to base a command decision.

Auto-ignition and fuel dippers

Jet engines started life as very simple bits of machinery; even the burner pressure gauge was dropped at an early stage of development and the total engine control and instrumentation was then two levers and two gauges — a power lever and fuel shut off, an r.p.m. gauge and a jet pipe temperature gauge. A great deal was quite properly made of the simplicity of operation of the jet engine in comparison with an advanced piston-engined installation. There then followed a period of natural development with the engine being required to work much closer to its limitations, and an increase in the numbers of controls and instruments resulted. Fortunately, this progression was arrested and the present-day jet engine remains, comparatively, a simple piece of machinery to control and monitor. However, one or two ancillaries, the reasons for which might not be immediately clear, do exist and these are worth some explanation.

Auto-ignition

The normal ignition system is used for ordinary functions such as starting, inflight relighting and to maintain combustion when taking-off from, or landing on, contaminated runways when it is selected to manual override. On some aeroplanes there is one special use of the ignition system when it functions automatically and it is as follows.

It has been pointed out that a jet engine is sensitive to the flow characteristics in the intake. So long as the flow is substantially normal the engine continues to run quite happily. However, where the engines are mounted in pods on the rear fuselage some abnormal flight manoeuvres, and even some nearly normal ones, give the engine every excuse to get upset. Some rear-mounted engine installations are ideally placed to catch any disturbed flow which might be shed from the wing. This disturbed flow is generated when the flow pattern on the wing begins to break down at high incidences in more or less steady flight (pre-stall buffet), and again in high 'g' manoeuvres at altitude where Mach effect produces a flow breakdown.

Under these conditions the disturbed air passes from the wing and goes down the engine intakes. This completely upsets the engine running conditions, puts the fire out and causes the engine, or engines, to run down.

This of course is basically unacceptable. A stall or a steep turn, for example, should be only a stall or a steep turn, and it would be compounding the pilot's difficulties if these manoeuvres also involved the loss of one or more engines. Now, it so happens that those aeroplanes which tend to suffer this problem also tend to suffer stall warning and stall quality problems (about which more later) and are, therefore, equipped with incidence sensing systems to operate stick shakers and stick pushers. An additional pick-off is used to operate the ignition systems at a particular value of incidence, usually less than the stick shaker value, so that the ignition is switched on before a disturbed airflow is generated by the wing and swallowed by the engines. This ensures that in the event of the aeroplane being taken to a high incidence at least the engines continue to run, although in some cases they might surge a little. This will be indicated by variations in r.p.m. and TGT.

It is not difficult on some aeroplanes to achieve comparatively high incidence values without fully realising it. For example, imagine a low take-off flap limiting speed combined with an early buffet threshold in the clean configuration. In this case, it is quite possible, in the flap retraction segment after take-off, to achieve, with only slight mishandling, incidence values sufficient to bring on the auto-ignition warning lights. Apart from being an extra early reminder of an increase in incidence this is nothing alarming; auto-ignition is one of those devices which can do only good and never, within reason, any harm. The life of igniters is good and it is of little consequence if they are allowed to run for a duration of minutes on occasions. Some pilots in fact actually use the auto-ignition lights on one particular aeroplane as a form of monitoring the flap retraction flight path under performance limiting conditions; it is hard to frown on a technique which makes full use, in a knowledgeable manner, of the equipment provided.

This breakdown in intake flow producing the need for auto-ignition occurs mostly in the longitudinal high incidence sense. There are, however, some jet transports which are capable of achieving very high values of slip in an extreme sideslip condition. This can produce the same end result. The angle of intake flow exceeds the design capability of the intake mouth, the flow breaks down over the lips and the engine gets upset. As these extreme slip cases are most unlikely anyway, and additionally not likely to be held for more than a moment or two, there is no provision in the auto-ignition sensing circuits for large angles of sideslip.

Another time when an engine may surge — and this time in an effectively nose down attitude — is on those aeroplanes which tend to roll very fast with yaw following engine failure in the low speed high power conditions. Assume that number four fails and the pilot is slow in taking control. The aeroplane will roll hard right and the number one intake on the other side is faced with a momentarily stalled intake tendency, from the top lip this time because the relative airflow is coming effectively from above. Again, this condition should last only for a moment or two.

Fuel dipper

Drawing on the information discussed under auto-ignition we now go one step further. There are some jet engines which get upset in a different fashion if the intake flow pattern should be significantly disturbed. The breakdown in flow in the intake upsets the fuel control system which leads to a rapid rise in TGT.

In a critical situation this rise is sufficiently large and fast to result in damage to the back end of the engine and, just as it was unacceptable to permit the run down of an engine in a stall or steep turn, so is it just as unacceptable to burn off the back of an engine under the same conditions. The fix in this case is the fuel dipper.

Dippers are fairly new in civil aviation but they have been used in fighters

7

for some time to prevent, for example, engine misbehaviour during gun-firing. A dipper is simply a device for rapidly reducing fuel flow on receipt of an over-temperature warning. As the upset occurs and TGT begins to rise a tempera-ture sensitive signal causes a bleed in the fuel supply line to open and this reduces fuel flow to a value very similar to that for flight idling r.p.m. at altitude, so that the engine simply runs down to idle. This signal is held on for about 5 secs. (during which time the pilot is assumed to have recovered the aeroplane to a more normal attitude) after which the bleed closes and the engine accelerates to, and settles at, the condition selected before the upset occurred. The thrust lever does not of course move from its setting through-out this sequence. In this way an engine with susceptibility to overheating is protected during a stall or similar manoeuvre. The fact that idle thrust is imposed for a period of 5 seconds is of little consequence; just as soon as the pilot is in a position to start flying again the engine is back at its originally selected thrust value.

Some fuel dip systems are comparatively innocuous in their fault conditions so that even a dip runaway on take-off causes only a $1\frac{1}{2}\%$ r.p.m. drop, which is very small. Other dip systems, however, can cause virtually a total loss of thrust if a runaway should occur during take-off. Systems of this type are engineered in such a manner that they are selected off for take-off and landing and on for flight. Between ground level and a few hundred feet a stall deep enough to overtemperature an engine with fuel dip inoperative would cause a damaged engine to be only of academic interest.

So much for auto-ignition and fuel dipping. There is not too much a pilot needs to do about them except understand them and handle the controls in the approved manner. They are fitted to restore the flying qualities of certain jet transports to the level which was properly enjoyed before these rather intricate patterns of misbehaviour were identified. They are there for your protection so don't put them inoperative without good reason.

General operation

The seven second — order items stemming from turbine engines are sufficient-ly significant in their own right to warrant special sub-chapters. There remain a handful of items which are slightly less important, or less likely to be significant in service. These can conveniently be discussed under the heading of general operation. They are fuel, engine operation, susceptibility to damage by ingestion, intake stalling and restarting.

Fuel

In the civil field there are basically two types of fuel available, JP1 and JP4. There is little difference in engine performance; some engines will accept either fuel with no adjustment, others require a minor resetting of the fuel control unit and occasionally a resetting of the fuel contents gauge system. Fuel temperature, however, is important in three respects:—

(a) Inlet temperature should be kept above $+10°C$ in order to avoid icing of the filters.

(b) Inlet temperature at the engine driven pump should be kept below $+90°C$ continuously or below any higher value for a shorter period in order to avoid pump cavitation and damage to seals, etc.

(c) If tank fuel temperatures fall below $-40°C$ down to $-60°C$ (depending on the grade of fuel) there will be a risk of solidifying lumps forming.

Inlet temperatures are normally controlled automatically. If tank temperatures fall below minimum, altitude must be reduced to achieve a higher outside air temperature.

Kerosene has a higher flash point than petrol but little comfort should be drawn from this knowledge in the event of a ground incident causing a rupture of any part of the fuel system.

Engine operation

In terms of simplicity of operation the jet engine is very much better than the piston engine. Compare, on the jet engine, the thrust lever, HP cock and possibly top temperature control with the forest of levers and knobs which we remember on a large piston engine.

The importance of not overtemperaturing the engine has already been emphasised. One important point in relation to maximum permitted power needs to be made. Some jet engines are 'full throttle' engines; the thrust levers can be advanced to their maximum travel and various limiters in the engine control system will control the engine so that it does not produce more than the maximum declared thrust. Other engines are not 'full throttle' engines and maximum thrust must be selected, typically, on the EPR gauge. If the power lever should be advanced fully, under conditions of low altitude and low temperature, a lot more than maximum thrust will be delivered. For example, a nominally 18,000 lb. ISA sea level static thrust engine, at sea level at $-40°C$, would give 22,000 lb. thrust. While this is not immediately destructive occasionally, it completely compromises the certification of the aeroplane. Engine-out critical speeds such as V_{MCG} for take-off and V_{MCL} for landing (overshoots) are based on yawing moments associated with maximum declared thrusts. If significantly more thrust is produced during a one-engine-out overshoot when the airspeed is at the recommended minimum, the controllability of the aeroplane will be degraded, possibly to an extent where control will be lost unless power is immediately reduced or speed increased. EPR limits are analogous to boost pressure (manifold

79

pressure) on a supercharged piston engine without an automatic boost control system.

Susceptibility to damage by ingestion

Within reason a piston-propeller combination is not normally upset by any material which might strike it; the most usual cause of damage is chipping of the propeller blades by stones picked up during the use of reverse pitch on loose surfaces. A turbine engine, however, is intended to take in air, and air only, through its intake. Anything else is likely to damage it or upset its functioning in some way. The flow attraction in front of the intake, even at idle thrust, is very strong and the engine is eager to suck in anything which comes within range. This includes people, so ground staff should be advised to keep well clear. The following four classifications are worth highlighting:—

Water in the form of precipitation when airborne is usually innocuous but standing water on a runway, in the form of a bow wave from the nosewheel, can be ingested in sufficient quantity to cause flame out. It is important to observe the Flight Manual limitation on water depth and use engine ignition for take-off and landing.

Birds are a significant hazard. One big one or a handful of little ones may be sufficient to cause serious malfunctioning or a complete loss of power. In some ways a lot of little ones are the greater hazard because they can affect more than one engine. If a bird strike is suspected monitor the engine instruments carefully, particularly the vibration indicators, and be prepared to shut down immediately. It is not suggested that the aeroplane can be manoeuvred so as to avoid a strike but there are ways in which strikes can be made less likely. There are publications dealing with the places and times when bird strikes are more likely and visual observation during taxying out can be helpful.

Ice from the intake in large lumps is of course damaging. The bleed air for intake anti-icing is not too significant in terms of power decrement in flight and intake anti-icing should be used whenever there is a suspicion of ice formation. This will prevent ice being built-up and subsequently shed, possibly in large lumps, when the de-icing is finally switched on. On take-off (and for the overshoot), however, engine ice protection bleeds can be very significant in terms of reduced performance and this loss must be taken into account when planning limiting operations. Note that on those aeroplanes with rear fuselage mounted engines the same sequence can occur if the wing anti-icing is selected late. If intake anti-icing operation should have been delayed until a significant amount of ice exists then don't make the mistake of selecting all engines anti-ice on together because, in a bad set of circumstances, this could involve more than one engine flaming out. Select one or two engines on at a time with a delay between each sufficient to give reasonable assurance that they will continue to run.

Foreign objects can mean almost anything; stones, pieces of clothing, tools, cleaning rags, etc. etc. The inlet guide vanes and compressor blades are easily damaged by foreign objects and such damage can lead to severe out-of-balance forces which are rapidly destructive. Engine damage from foreign object ingestion occurs far more frequently than most pilots imagine. It is good basic airmanship, as you approach your aeroplane, to check the ground ahead, and the intakes, to make sure there is nothing which can be ingested on start up. Avoid high power ground running on loose surfaces. In particular avoid, if possible, the use of reverse thrust at very low speeds on surfaces suspected of being loose. If distance is not limiting on landing cancel reverse earlier than usual (but note other qualifications in this respect elsewhere in this book). Loose snow is not harmful to the engine (although in reverse thrust at low speeds it can reduce visibility to zero of course), but sand is. Since you are checking the ground in front of your aeroplane as you go out to it check also the ground behind it. From a difficult parking stand a fair bit of thrust can be required to move off, particularly in a turn. Jet blast is very powerful and can cause damage to people, vehicles and other aeroplanes. Observe this before you enter the aeroplane and if you don't like the look of something then do something about it. Get it moved or have the aeroplane moved.

Intake stalling

A jet intake is designed to take in its air over a reasonable variation of angles of incidence and slip. It is difficult to be precise, but up to about 20° of slip and incidence the flow pattern in the intake should be good. Beyond these values, however, the flow can stall over the intake and upset the flow through the compressor causing surging. If this is only mild it is not immediately dangerous, although the exhaust gas temperature will rise and the r.p.m. will fluctuate. In a bad case the engine will be completely upset, substantially all thrust will be lost and the back end might get very hot. Aircraft with rear fuselage mounted engines are more critical to intake stalling than wing mounted engines. At angles of incidence approaching the stall the flow pattern on the wing breaks down and lumps of jagged air are shot down the engine air intakes, which are in fact ideally placed to receive them. This again leads to intake stalling and its associated problems. It is fixed by the automatic switching on of the auto-ignition system triggered from the stall warning sensing system. This at least stops the engine running down while the aeroplane is being recovered to a more reasonable attitude.

Restarting

To restart a piston engine it is necessary only to supply fuel and ignition and then turn the engine by unfeathering the propeller. The drill on a jet engine is roughly the same except that the engine is already turning. Shutting off the fuel to a jet leaves the engine windmilling at about, very roughly, 10% to 25% r.p.m., depending of course only on true airspeed. To relight, therefore, it is only necessary, with the power lever fully closed, to switch on the ignition and then turn on the fuel. Some jet engines, however, will not relight at very high speeds and most will not relight at very low speeds or very high altitudes. This is because, at these extreme limits, it is not possible to offer the engine the correct proportions of air and fuel for the speed at which the engine is windmilling. For these reasons there is, in the Flight Manual, an approved relight envelope of speed against height. This should normally be observed.

In an emergency, however, there are some alternatives. You can attempt a relight outside the approved envelope. This is acceptable so long as the fuel is not left on longer than the approved time without a relight and the exhaust gas temperature remains within limits during the relight. If a relight is needed instantly simply switch on the ignition but monitor exhaust gas temperature carefully. If the attempted relight fails, close the power lever and try again. If this fails the fuel must be shut off and the regular drill used.

5 Flying faster

Low drag

In spite of the risk of being labelled a pedant it can only be said in introduction to this sub-chapter that a jet transport has low drag because it is designed to fly fast; it has comparatively thin wings, a streamlined shape and all the devices and design philosophies necessary to keep all forms of drag to a reasonable minimum, consistent with other associated qualities.

All the consequences of having a low drag aeroplane are important and there are none which can be dismissed in a few words; they will be discussed in the appropriate sub-chapters which follow.

However, somewhere in this book there should appear a brief discussion on the qualities of the high speed, low drag wing. As this is the first place in which it may logically be introduced let us consider the problem now. On re-reading the derivations in the Table of Differences it becomes clear that the table could have been arranged in many other ways, as was admitted earlier. For example, many of the features of jet handling qualities read right back to the fact that it has a high speed, low drag wing which brings with it all sorts of complications. Pilots generally tend to crticise some handling qualities in isolation without recognising or acknowledging that the design of a wing is a compromise in which an improvement in one area has to be weighed carefully against a certain deterioration in another area. So, to do justice to our designers, let us consider some of their problems.

A digression on the problem of designing the wing

In designing the wing of a jet transport the designer is faced with requirements from lots of different directions, most of which conflict in some way. There are three major areas to be considered:—

(a) The requirement for economical high speed performance in the cruise configuration.

(b) The need to keep airfield performance within acceptable limits.

(c) The need to give the structural people a reasonable task.

There are seven main areas in which the designer has freedom to manoeuvre in order to attain his objective. The first four decide the wing planform and the last three the performance of that planform. These areas are as follows:—

1   **Area**   Remembering the basic lift formula of $\frac{1}{2}\rho V^2 S C_L$ the optimum area for the design wing loading is dictated by the C_L appropriate to the peak

of the L/D curve shown in figure 5.1. A smaller than optimum area will spoil airfield performance for a given degree of sophistication of slats and flaps; a larger wing area will increase drag.

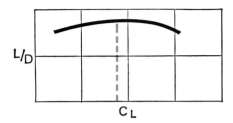

Figure 5.1 Variation of C_L with lift/drag ratio.

2 **Aspect ratio** The drag of an aeroplane is made up of the profile drag, which is proportional to the wetted area, and the induced drag, which is inversely proportional to the aspect ratio; at the best lift/drag ratio each of these drags contributes more or less equally to the total drag. Although the higher the aspect ratio the less the induced drag a very extreme aspect ratio becomes limited by structure weight and a very demanding cantilever ratio, i.e. structure depth at the root sufficient to support a long semi-span. Too low an aspect ratio, as stated, produces a high induced drag.

3 **Sweep** The sweep angle is chosen to permit a cruise at the design Mach number. Too little sweep will cause an early drag rise because the wing is sensitive only to the airspeed vector normal to the wing leading edge (the less the sweep the higher the chordwise vector for a given free stream velocity). Too much sweep produces poor oscillatory stability and a tendency for the tip to stall, causing pitch up. A combination of too much sweep and too high an aspect ratio can give marked pitch up because the tip is further aft and has a higher moment.

4 **Taper ratio** This is the ratio of the root chord to the tip chord. A ratio of about $2\frac{1}{2}$ to 1 gives approximately the optimum lift across the span, i.e. elliptical loading (each section of the wing producing the correct proportion of the total lift of the wing). Any change from the optimum taper ratio simply results in an upset of the lift across the span. If the ratio is grossly too small, say 1 to 1, then there is again incurred a penalty in structure weight; if the ratio is grossly too large, i.e. too small a tip, high local C_L's are produced which lead to a tendency to stall the tips.

5 **Section** It should perhaps be explained that the following exposition on wing section is in the realm of opinion rather than fact. There are

84

basically two types of section, 'Roof Top' and 'Peaky', which are said to have the following qualities:—

(a) *Roof Top* (figure 5.3)   This produces lift over a significant proportion of the chord.   It controls the accelerated air so as to ensure that the local flow does not go supersonic and hence remains shock free.

(b) *Peaky* (figure 5.3)   This distribution of lift induces a high value at the leading edge, but the velocity is made to fall very rapidly to attain a region of shock-free supersonic flow.

Other things being equal the Peaky section can produce a higher cruise Mach number before a significant drag rise sets in, although it appears to

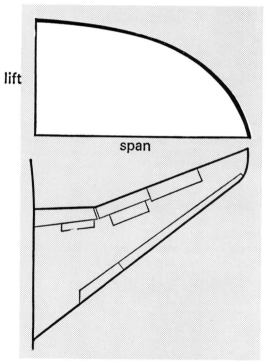

Figure 5.2   Variation of lift across the span.

carry with it a slightly higher value of drag at lower Mach numbers. The Roof Top section appears to be more predictable probably because a great deal is known about the behaviour of the type.   The Peaky section is not so forgiving of errors, is less well substantiated by basic research and is very dependent on nose profiles.

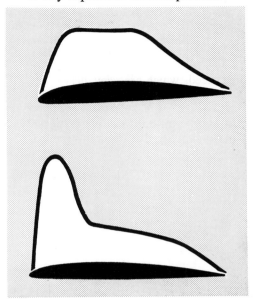

Figure 5.3   Variation of upper surface pressure distribution across the chord for different sections. Roof top (above), peaky (below).

6   **Twist and camber**   These again are used to ensure the distribution of the lift in an optimum manner across the span.   Wash-out produces a lower incidence at the tip and helps to avoid tip stalling.   Simple twist and camber have long since been left behind and the sophistications of these two parameters are now aimed at balancing conditions for lowest cruise drag against the clean stall qualities (all other stall configurations generally being looked after by the design of the slats and flaps).

7   **Thickness/chord ratio**   This parameter appears to be a straight fight between aerodynamics and structures.   The aerodynamics people require thin wings for highest cruise Mach numbers, or less sweep for the same required Mach number; the structures people require a comparatively thick wing to make their job of providing accommodation for gear, fuel, etc. easier and to make the structural work no more demanding than it needs to be.

By these simple discussions of the seven major parameters of wing design it has been shown that life can be very difficult.   In a civil transport no one parameter can be allowed to become dominant at the expense of other qualities. The final wing design of any jet transport is a masterly compromise between all these conflicting qualities.

Speed margins

Speed margins have always existed to provide for the occasion when an aeroplane is forced beyond its normal maximum permitted speed. In the piston-engined aircraft there are three speeds which are relevant:—

V_{NO}, which is the normal maximum permitted speed.

V_{NE}, which is the higher limiting speed authorised for use on special occasions, at the discretion of the pilot, with due regard to the existing circumstances.

V_{DF}, which is the maximum demonstrated flight diving speed used in the design and certification trials.

Speed margins in general are not too significant on piston-engined aeroplanes because the aeroplane has very little overspeed tendency. This is, firstly, because at the low cruise powers which can be drawn continuously as a percentage of the maximum available (around 55%), the associated cruising speed is normally a long way below V_{NO}; and, secondly, because the drag generally, and propeller effect particularly, form effective barriers to inadvertent speed increases. Most of these aeroplanes have to be driven downhill in a determined manner in order to get anywhere near V_{DF}.

With the jet transport, however, speed margins are a problem. First let us define the new nomenclature:—

V_{MO} and M_{MO} are the maximum indicated speeds in knots and Mach number at which the aeroplane should be flown intentionally and at which the normal strength and normal level of handling qualities are provided.

V_{DF} and M_{DF} are the maximum demonstrated speeds in knots and Mach number used during certification testing and at which there are reduced strength and quite often a lower level of handling qualities.

A jet transport can very easily eat into its speed margin because of its low drag in the en route configuration and the enormous power available from the engines. This is particularly true at the lower altitudes. At around 15,000 ft., for example, there is more than enough power available on some types to achieve the V_{DF} value without exceeding maximum continuous power, and in a gentle climb at that. At high altitudes, while M_{DF} is not normally achievable even at maximum continuous power in level flight, there may still be enough power to take the aeroplane well beyond the M_{MO} value. In any significant descent, even at cruise power, speed builds up very rapidly indeed and the aeroplane could go out beyond M_{DF} and, at the lower altitudes, way beyond V_{DF}.

To give some life to these rather abstract terms let us look at some typical values for a jet transport.

$$V_{MO} = 380 \text{ knots IAS} \qquad V_{DF} = 450 \text{ knots IAS}$$
$$M_{MO} = 0.88 \text{ IMN} \qquad M_{DF} = 0.95 \text{ IMN}$$

Piston-engined aircraft enjoyed a relatively large speed margin between V_{NO} and V_{DF}. A margin of the same size could not be afforded on jet transports because it would have resulted in either an uneconomically low maximum permitted speed or a requirement for transonic capability. To make up for the smaller speed margin it has been necessary to justify the value in more detail and this has been done by means of a defined, fairly rational, upset manoeuvre, although within admittedly arbitrarily established limits. To take account of the relative ease with which jet transports can exceed their limiting speeds four things have been done:—

(a) Aural high Mach/high airspeed warnings have been introduced to warn of speeds in excess of the maxima.

(b) The old V_{NE} philosophy has been dropped and there is now only one maximum speed V_{MO}. Effectively the old V_{NE} has been reduced to V_{NO} and relabelled V_{MO}. Note that the old suffix was an $-N$ and the new suffix is an $-M$.

(c) As an acknowledgement of the fact that handling qualities can change significantly above M_{MO} due to high Mach number effects a crew-training M_{MO} (and V_{MO} where necessary) has been established and is quoted in Flight Manuals. This is the indicated Mach value of the true Mach number which is half-way between M_{MO} and M_{DF}. Pilots are encouraged to become familiar with the flying qualities of their aeroplanes up to these speeds so that they are practised in the technique for recovery from an overspeed condition.

(d) Requirements relating to stability and controllability have been spelled out to be met at the V_{DF} and M_{DF} values. These are naturally to a standard lower than those applicable at V_{MO} and M_{MO}, reflecting the less frequent occasions on which they are needed, but an adequate level of handling qualities is provided.

In any speed excursion, where nothing else is involved (severe weather will be discussed separately), the recovery should be tailored to the amount of excess speed and to the probable maximum speed which it is estimated will be reached in the recovery. For a small error it is only necessary to reduce thrust for a short while, or to reduce pitch attitude in a descent; but for a large error, which looks like getting larger still, prompt action should be taken to reduce the speed quickly. If it is an IAS overspeed at fairly low altitude, reduce the thrust and extend the speed brakes. If it is an excursion in terms of Mach number, extend the speed brakes but don't apply too much up elevator initially. The amount of 'g' which can be pulled before buffet is experienced can be quite small at altitude and the recovery may be compromised by pronounced buffeting. If necessary, balance a small degree of buffet against the required rate of speed reduction. Reduce thrust only if (a) the dive angle is small, (b) the maximum likely Mach number is not much above M_{MO} and (c) *you are confident of your elevator capability at high Mach number.*

If a very high indicated airspeed is ever achieved be prepared to exert large forces on the control column. The approximate V^2 law which is fed into the feel system produces high stick forces at very high speeds, but unless these forces become unmanageable avoid using the tail trim. Tail trim gearing, like everything else, is a compromise. At very high speeds a normal blip's worth of trim will produce a large pitch change on the aeroplane with the real possibility of overstressing; so if you are forced to use trim do so in short bursts and allow each change to take effect before you apply more.

Poor lift at low speeds

A wing designed primarily for efficient high speed flight with low drag has poor lift at low speed.

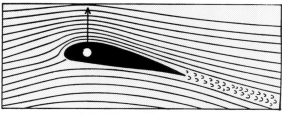

thick, high lift section

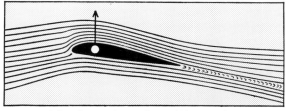

thin, low drag, low lift section

Figure 5.4   Airflow around different aerofoil sections.

It has been mentioned earlier that one of the basic parameters of wing design is area; a required area can be achieved with widely varying values of aspect ratio. Reflecting back to our gliding days we remember that, in isolation, the higher the aspect ratio the less the induced drag and the better the lift/drag ratio. A jet aeroplane with a very high aspect ratio wing, however, is not really feasible because of the structural and handling

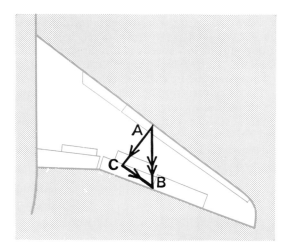

Figure 5.5   Effect of wing sweep on airflow normal to the leading edge.

problems involved.   So, from the very outset, in a pure sense as it were, we have already lost some potential lift.

The next item of significance is thickness/chord ratio.   The thick wing which we associated with piston-engined aircraft was obviously a good lifter; the section imposed a wide difference between the upper and lower stream speeds therefore the lift vector was large.   But the thick wing also produced a lot of drag at high speed and this conflicts with the design requirement for a jet transport, so a much thinner wing section had to be employed. With a smaller difference in stream speeds less lift is produced, so away goes some more lift.

The last important item is the effect of sweep.   It will be explained later that sweep is necessary to achieve lower drag at high Mach numbers, but at the moment our concern is with the lift qualities of a swept wing.   As a swept wing is in general responsive only to the airspeed vector normal to the wing leading edge (the spanwise vector being simply washed out because it does not affect the pressure distribution) it is clear that, in relation to the speed term in the basic lift formula, the swept wing suffers a reduced effective chordwise component of flow and therefore suffers a loss in lift for a given airspeed at a given incidence.

In figure 5.5 the free stream resultant AB is felt by the wing as a velocity vector normal to the leading edge AC and a washed out spanwise vector CB.

As AC is less than AB the apparent airspeed is lower than the real airspeed and there is a corresponding reduction in lift. (A corollary of this fact of course is that for a given amount of lift a swept wing needs to be flown at a higher incidence than an unswept wing). So sweep removes some more basic lift.

For these reasons the jet transport wing is a poor producer of lift at low speeds in its clean configuration.

The first real consequence of poor lift at low speeds is a high stall speed. Illustrations have been given earlier of just how high the stall speed can be in the clean configuration on a jet transport compared with a piston-engined transport. A value of 177 knots was quoted for the stall speed on the jet aeroplane at maximum weight. If this is factored to take account of the increase in stall speed due to 'g' in a pull-up or a turn, and then a margin added to provide some freedom of manoeuvre between the flying speed and the pre-stall buffet speed, it will be seen just how fast one has to fly in order to overcome the poor lift qualities of the jet transport wing at low speed in its clean configuration.

The second consequence of poor lift at low speeds is the manner in which lift and drag vary with speed in the lower ranges.

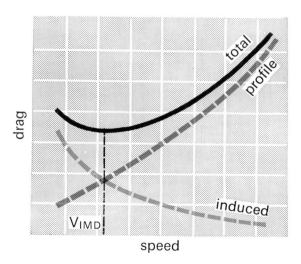

Figure 5.6   Variation of drag with speed.

Figure 5.6 shows how the reduction of induced drag with speed (because of the smaller energy losses in the smaller tip trailing vortices at lower angles of incidence) combines with the increase in profile drag with speed (where P.Drag $= \frac{1}{2}\rho V^2 S C_D$) to produce the characteristic total drag picture. This

91

shows a reduction down to a fairly low speed then an increase with further reduction in speed. The bottom point is V$_{\text{IMD}}$, the speed for minimum drag.

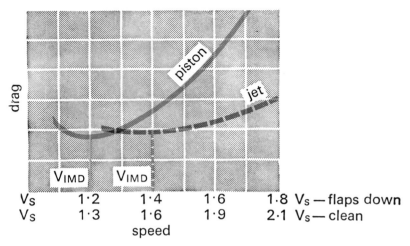

| V$_s$ | 1·2 | 1·4 | 1·6 | 1·8 V$_s$ — flaps down |
| V$_s$ | 1·3 | 1·6 | 1·9 | 2·1 V$_s$ — clean |

Figure 5.7 Comparison of total drag values.

In figure 5.7 the total drag curves have been plotted against speed for both a piston-engined and a jet aircraft. The two speed scales at the bottom show the relative changes, as a function of stall speed, with configuration. The illustration is deliberately exaggerated to show the difference arising from the jet's relatively lower profile drag and higher induced drag. Vertical locations of the curves are not correct in terms of absolute values in relation to each other.

Notice the V$_{\text{IMD}}$, with the flaps down, of 1.2Vs for the piston; this is typical. On the jet, however, V$_{\text{IMD}}$ is much higher at around 1.4Vs; this is typical of the latest jets, although earlier models were nearer 1.3Vs. In the clean configuration V$_{\text{IMD}}$ at 1.3Vs is typical for a piston. But now notice V$_{\text{IMD}}$ as high as 1.6Vs for the jet, flaps up; this is most important. Flight below V$_{\text{IMD}}$ on a piston-engined aeroplane is quite well identified by the steepness of the drag curve; in flight, as well as on paper! But the relative flatness of the drag curve around V$_{\text{IMD}}$ for the jet does not produce any noticeable changes in flying qualities (other than a vague and irritating lack of speed stability), and all this is a bit of a trap.

All this means that when, for example, holding in the clean configuration in a jet transport at high altitude, with a speed in the neighbourhood of 1.5 to 1.6Vs, care is necessary to avoid any decrease in airspeed; if this should occur the aeroplane will quietly slide up the back end of the drag curve. Although at the higher lift coefficients associated with lower speeds some extra lift is

92

Plates 1 and 2   Bigger and heavier

The photograph below illustrates the family history of a typical big jet, the Douglas DC-8. Here the DC-8 is compared with earlier Douglas aeroplanes (reading upwards):—DC-3, DC-4, DC-6 and DC-7). Plate 2 (overleaf) shows a view of the biggest and heaviest civil jet transport now operating, the Boeing 747. It is 230 feet long, has a span of 195 feet and grosses around 710,000 lb., 322,000 kg. It is a *very big* aeroplane.

Photographs: McDonnell Douglas and BOAC

Plate 3 Engine locations

Typical layouts: from top to bottom a Comet with wing root buried engines, a 707 with wing pod mounted engines and a VC10 with rear fuselage mounted engines. It is worth considering the advantages and disadvantages of each (as listed on pages 71-75) and relating them to the photographs.

Photographs: Hawker Siddeley, The Boeing Company and British Aircraft Corporation

The Pratt and Whitney JT3D (right, above) produces around 18,000 lb. thrust. This is the engine which powers the majority of DC-8s and 707s. The JT9D (left, above) produces around 45,000 lb. thrust. Four of these power the Boeing 747. It would be

[...]ing is instead the number of highest power piston engines required for a 747. Depending on the conversion factors used and the assumed propeller efficiency it could be as many as eighteen for take-off and vastly more to sustain it in a typical cruise condition! The picture below shows the

[...]compactness and accessibility of the Rolls-Royce Conway Co10's fitted to the BAC Super VC10. Appearances can be deceptive—each engine produces nearly ten tons of thrust at take-off.

Photographs: Pratt and Whitney Aircraft and Rolls-Royce

Plate 6   Scramble!

An illustration of the sort of performance level which can be enjoyed
on a modern high performance jet aeroplane under favourable
thrust/weight ratio conditions. This sort of overshoot climb angle is
not likely to be needed under normal operating conditions but it is
comforting to know that it is available if required.

Photograph: The Boeing Company

produced, the drag increases faster than the lift increases, the L/D ratio deteriorates and the net result is a steepening of the flight path. So the aeroplane begins to sink.

This sinking tendency can be salvaged in two ways:—

(a) The nose can be put down to reduce incidence and allow the aeroplane to accelerate to a speed above V_{IMD}, when steady flight conditions can be again established, but as this always involves a height loss it can rarely be used.

(b) The thrust can be increased to accelerate the aeroplane to a value above V_{IMD} to establish steady flight conditions again. It is important to emphasise that the amount of thrust required is quite large. Not only has the thrust to accelerate the aeroplane and regain the lost altitude but, if the penetration has been a long way up the back end of the drag curve, the drag will be very high and a lot of thrust will be required to overcome this high drag.

So, if you suspect that this is what is occurring, don't play around with small increments of thrust hoping to sort the thing out without making it obvious that something has gone wrong — give it a handful. Fly the aeroplane with some determination and get it re-established in a steady flight condition as soon as possible.

So much for the poor lifting qualities of the jet aeroplane wing at low speeds. The fact that the drag increases more rapidly than the lift, causing a sinking flight path, is one of the most important aspects of jet aircraft flying qualities. We are going to need this information again in the sub-chapters dealing with, for example, speed stability and approach techniques. So, if you have rather skimmed this explanation because of a few pictures and a few technical terms, for your own sake go back and read it again. This is really important.

High lift devices

As already explained, a wing designed for low drag at high speeds doesn't produce much lift at low speeds and therefore imposes a high stall speed. The high stall speed that results in the clean configuration can be lived with by careful choice of speed factors and operating techniques generally, but could not possibly be acceptable in terms of field performance, that is, take-off and landing distances. High lift devices are therefore fitted to reduce stall speeds and their associated take-off and landing speeds. This naturally reduces take-off and landing distances.

Let us take one more look at the lift formula $\frac{1}{2}\rho V^2 S C_L$ and remember that S = effective wing area and C_L = lift coefficient.

The use of trailing edge flaps is well understood. With the exception of the simple plain and split flaps these increase lift by:—

(a) Extending chordwise, thus effectively increasing wing area (that is, upping the S term).

(b) Increasing the camber of the overall wing section (that is, upping the C_L value). Increased camber deflects the air downwards more rapidly, thus increasing lift.

Flap design can be quite sophisticated in terms of double and even triple slotted arrangements which are all designed to produce a highly cambered section and to keep the flow attached properly at high angles of wing incidence. The slots are to ensure the adherence of the upper surface flow and thus prevent separation.

With the advent of the developed jet transport the need for a good high speed wing became even more pressing in order to serve the combined needs of economic operation at very high cruise speeds and good field performance; but in spite of further elaboration in trailing edge flap design stall speeds remained high and something further was needed. Quite logically the wing leading edge came in for attention and high lift devices were fitted to it. These originally were simple drooped leading edges but more recently have become slatted leading edges or leading edge flaps. They work in the same way as trailing edge flaps, that is they (a) slightly increase wing area in most instances, (b) further camber the total profile and (c) increase the efficiency of the basic wing section by persuading it to retain its airflow to higher incidences, preventing flow separation and hence providing higher maximum lift coefficients.

The difference in overall section between the en route configuration and the landing configuration can be seen in figure 5.8.

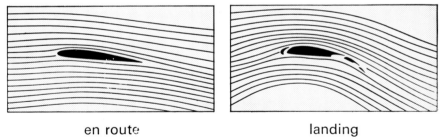

en route   landing

Figure 5.8   Change of lift with configuration.

In this way a low drag, high speed wing en route can be turned into a very high lift wing for take-off and landing.

Most of that which needs to be said about the consequences of having high lift devices is pretty elementary stuff and can soon be identified by a little bit of basic thinking. Perhaps the following four conditions should be specially highlighted.

Extra lift

In the initial approach procedure, when the take-off configuration is selected from the en route configuration, a lot of extra lift is generated. If the attitude of the aeroplane is not changed height will be gained. The speed effect is a little academic because the extra drag will soon re-establish an appropriately lower speed after the transient condition has passed. The overall change of trim can be significant and care should be taken to avoid the height increase in the interests of precision instrument flying.

Too-early retraction

If the devices are retracted after take-off at too low an airspeed the aeroplane will be left much too close to its clean stall speed, with the additional complication of the high drag penalty associated with flight below V_{IMD}. A lot of thrust will be needed to salvage both these complications. If maximum thrust is already being used a height loss is almost inevitable during recovery. Those who are aware of the predicted flying qualities of supersonic transports will appreciate that this equates to flight below the zero rate of climb speed, recovery from which is possible only with a reduction in altitude. The effect of early flap retraction will be worsened if this occurs in a turn because of the increased stall speed inherent in turning flight.

So before you select flaps-up after take-off make sure that you have a satisfactory speed for the clean configuration. If the rate of flap retraction is slow, which it often is, then balance the known rate of flap retraction against the expected rate of acceleration so as to arrive at an acceptable speed just as the flaps run fully home. If you are in any doubt about raising the flaps for any reason then . . . . . . don't; leave them down and continue the climb until both you and the aeroplane are more settled.

Partial failure case

The design philosophy and reliability of the leading and trailing edge flaps will establish the frequency of one or the other failing to extend. On most aeroplanes with which the author is familiar any flap is better than no flap; as much of the devices as can be extended should be used, but only symmetrically of course. With these unusual configurations go possibly poorer but still safe stall qualities (for example) and certainly higher approach speeds for the landing. Flying qualities remain substantially normal except that the attitude on final approach will be a lot more nose up if the trailing edge flaps have failed to extend. *Note that some jet transports will not tolerate trailing edge flap extension without the leading edge devices, or vice versa.* A failure of either, therefore, involves a clean landing. Make sure that you know the drills for your particular aeroplane.

Complete failure case

In the rare event of an unrelated double failure denying the pilot all his high lift devices the aeroplane will be committed to a clean approach and landing.

This is no trouble. Certainly the approach speed will be very high, but there is no magic in speed in isolation (but see below) and the approach is flown exactly as was a typical flapless approach on a piston-engined aeroplane. Some relevant points can be made, however:—

(a) Weight should be reduced as much as prudent so as to lower the required approach speed and avoid exceeding any tyre ground speed limit.

(b) Low weather conditions should be avoided. This is one of the areas where speed in isolation is important because the time available to correct a lateral displacement between breaking out and getting lined up with the runway decreases as the speed increases, for any given contact height.

(c) The landing distance required is likely to be very long. This varies with the type of aircraft of course and the variation is very large. On one type it is not much longer than normal because, in such an emergency, full reverse thrust can be applied just before touch-down. On those types with leading edge high lift devices and no reverse thrust until after touch down it is something like 9,000 ft. *gross* (without any margins) from the threshold height at threshold speed to a stop in zero wind.

(d) Fly a low, flat final approach. On four-engined types speed control is improved by idling the outers and flying the approach on the inners only (on a three-engined type idle the centre engine). As the drag is so low there will be plenty of thrust available and larger thrust lever movements are possible without upsetting the speed.

(e) Do not flare too much for the landing or you might strike the rear fuselage. When close to the ground just fly it on, after having reduced the sink rate initially with a little up elevator.

(f) After touch-down get on with the job of stopping the aeroplane. Extend the spoilers and pull full reverse thrust on all engines immediately. Hold full reverse until it is perfectly clear that the aeroplane is not going to overrun. Let the reverse thrust do the work for the first few seconds to ensure that the aeroplane is firmly on three points, then smoothly bring the braking pressure up to maximum and hold it there. Modern brakes are pretty capable and the amount of energy absorption required in this manoeuvre is less than that associated with a maximum V_1 stop at maximum take-off weight.

So, for a clean landing, divert if necessary to a long runway with good approaches and reasonable weather. The rest is not difficult.

Sweep

A wing produces lift by accelerating the air which passes over the top surface to a higher speed than that which passes under the bottom surface. The greater the difference between these two speeds the higher the difference in pressure, hence the larger the lift vector.

Because the local speed of the upper surface air is higher than the free stream speed — a good bit higher where the camber is marked — it is clear that this airstream will become sonic before the free stream reaches the sonic value. At this airspeed local shock waves are formed on the wing and compressibility effects become apparent; the drag increases, buffeting is felt and changes in lift and the position of the centre of pressure occur which, at a fixed tail angle, are reflected as changes in pitch. The Mach number at which these compressibility effects first become apparent is the critical Mach number; all other parameters aside, this can be quite low for a straight wing, around 0.7 Mach number.

By sweeping a wing significantly, it will be remembered, the velocity vector normal to the leading edge is made less than the chordwise resultant.

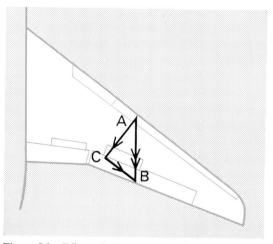

Figure 5.9   Effect of wing sweep on airflow normal to the leading edge.

In figure 5.9 AC is shorter than AB. As the wing is responsive only to the velocity vector normal to the leading edge, for a given Mach number the effective chordwise velocity is reduced (in effect the wing is persuaded to believe that it is flying slower than it really is). This means that the airspeed can be increased before the effective chordwise component becomes sonic and thus the critical Mach number is raised. This is why a high speed aeroplane has a swept wing. As the thickness/chord ratio defines the amount of acceleration imposed on the upper surface stream it follows that the thinner the wing, the lower the acceleration, and the higher will be the airspeed before, for this reason alone, the upper flow becomes sonic. This is why a high speed aeroplane has a *thin* swept wing.

97

Wing sweep carries with it a lot of significant consequences. A glance at the Table of Differences will show the number of qualities which stem from sweep. All these are sufficiently important to merit their own sub-chapters; of the remaining effects of sweep only two need to be elaborated here.

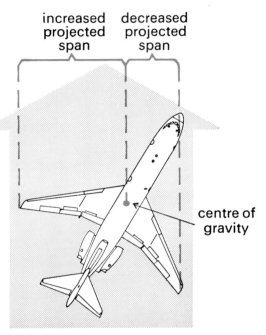

increased projected span   decreased projected span

centre of gravity

Figure 5.10   Change in effective aspect ratio with yaw.

As sweep involves an apparently lower sensed airspeed it follows that, if all other parameters are kept constant, the swept wing will produce less lift than a straight wing for a given airspeed. This lift is restored by increasing the angle of incidence which accounts for the rather nose high attitude which some swept wing jet transports demonstrate on the approach. This doesn't mean that the swept wing aeroplane is flying any nearer its stalling incidence than the straight wing aeroplane; both are at the correct airspeed of say 1.3Vs but the swept wing realises its max. C_L at a higher incidence than the straight wing aeroplane. The proof of this last statement lies somewhere in the rather deeper field of the total flow pattern around wings of different planforms. The upflow ahead of a swept wing is less vigorous than that ahead of a straight wing and a higher incidence can be achieved before max. C_L is arrived at.

When a straight winged aeroplane is yawing it also rolls. This is because the inside wing is effectively slowed down and the outside wing is effectively speeded up, thus unbalancing the V terms in the lift formulae for each wing taken separately. The lift is unbalanced and the aeroplane rolls. On a swept wing aeroplane this effect is compounded because the angle of slip effectively alters the sweep of the two wings. The faster (outside) wing becomes less swept and generates increased lift at a constant incidence because of the increase in effective aspect ratio. This is because the projected span of that wing is increased. The slower (inside) wing becomes even more swept and loses lift at a constant incidence for the same basic reason. This further unbalances the lift and the rolling tendency is markedly increased. Reference to figure 5.10 shows that the outside wing has a much greater effective aspect ratio than the inside wing, and is also travelling faster. Thus, for each wing separately, in the formula $\frac{1}{2}\rho V^2 S C_L$ the outside wing enjoys a higher value of V^2 and C_L while the inside wing suffers depressed values of these two quantities. This imposes a very marked roll on the aeroplane. Note that during the actual dynamic manoeuvre of *yawing* both the contributions to roll are present; when however a steady state of sideslip is achieved the contribution of asymmetric V^2 disappears and only the change in effective aspect ratio remains. This marked roll with yawing is very significant in terms of flying qualities and its various consequences will be discussed in detail in their appropriate sub-chapters.

Dutch roll

If you fly a piston-engined aeroplane in a properly trimmed-out (including the rudder and aileron trimmers) cruise condition and then abandon all the controls, the aeroplane will continue in its steady flight condition because it is stable about all axes. Now take hold of the aileron control and roll the aeroplane smoothly to, say, 15° of left bank then 15° of right bank — and keep on doing it. This, basically, is what a dutch roll feels like on a jet aeroplane. Next let the aeroplane settle down and this time push left rudder, then right rudder — and keep on doing it for a while. The same sort of motion will develop as that which developed when using ailerons alone; the yaw in one direction **will** cause the aeroplane to roll (as explained in an earlier sub-chapter), then the yaw in the other direction will cause the roll to reverse. We are now much closer to what a dutch roll actually is, as well as to what it feels like, on a jet aeroplane.

A dutch roll is this combination of yawing and rolling motions; the yaw is not too significant, but the roll is much more noticeable and the aeroplane proceeds with a continuously reversing roll action. Not until the motion becomes very exaggerated is there any disturbance in pitch.

A more correct term for dutch roll is oscillatory stability. There is an associated quality known as spiral stability which needs to be mentioned here; it will be explained later, although the term itself is almost self-explanatory.

There are several factors which dictate the directional and lateral qualities of an aeroplane; they are all inter-related and cannot be handled separately. On one hand we have the effects of dihedral and sweep which basically dictate the lateral qualities and on the other hand fin and rudder size and effectiveness which basically dictate the directional qualities. On the relationship of these two qualities rest the spiral and oscillatory qualities of the aeroplane, and they are always in conflict. If the lateral qualities are dominant the aeroplane tends to be spirally stable and oscillatorily unstable; if the directional qualities are dominant the aeroplane tends to be spirally unstable but oscillatorily stable. Other factors influence the aeroplane's behaviour of course but the end result, as always, is a fair compromise between these two stability requirements.

Oscillatory stability, that is stable dutch roll, can now be defined as the tendency of an aeroplane when disturbed, either directionally or laterally, to damp out the ensuing yawing/rolling motion and return to steady flight.

Before we work out just why all this happens remember that with a swept wing there is a marked rolling tendency with yaw; this has been explained in detail in the previous sub-chapter.

When an aeroplane is yawed it rolls. The fin and rudder then oppose the yaw, slow it down and stop it, and return the aircraft towards straight flight. If the fin and rudder are big enough, the second yaw and roll are less than the first and each excursion gets progressively smaller until the motion damps right out. If, however, the fin and rudder are too small (but, please note, only 'too small' in this particular context) the second yaw and roll are bigger than the first, each overswing gets progressively larger and the motion becomes divergent, i.e. unstable. Although the initial yaw is the trigger for

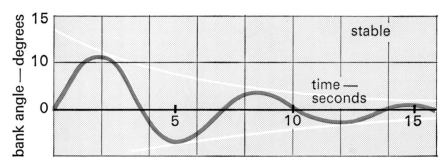

Figure 5.11   Stable dutch roll.

this misbehaviour it is the rolling motion, in most aeroplanes, which is most noticeable to the pilot; this is why the rolling behaviour is used as the main parameter in measuring dutch roll.

Like any other form of stability, oscillatory stability can be positive,

100

neutral or negative, which is to say the dutch roll can be stable, neutral or unstable. A dutch roll is measured by plotting bank angle against time. The stable case is illustrated in figure 5.11.

Positive stability is basically safe because the aeroplane, left alone, will,

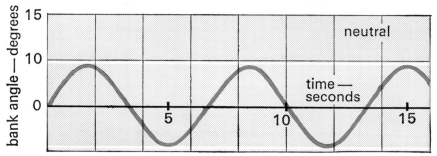

Figure 5.12   Neutral dutch roll.

either quickly or more slowly, finally bring itself under control.   Figure 5.12 illustrates neutral stability.   Neutral stability is safe (enough) because it won't get worse, but undesirable because, if the amplitude is large, or the frequency is small, the aeroplane is tiring and tedious to fly.

Figure 5.13 illustrates negative stability.   Negative stability is potentially dangerous because sooner or later, depending on the rate of divergence, the aeroplane will either get out of hand or demand a constant very high level of skill and attention to maintain control.

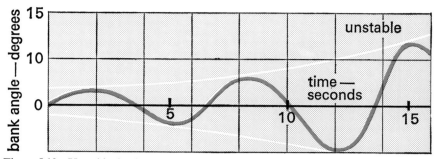

Figure 5.13   Unstable dutch roll.

The unstable case, however, needs to be qualified in this way: if the divergence is rapid the aeroplane is obviously unacceptable, but if the divergence is very slow then it can be tolerated.   To the pilot there is no significant difference between a dutch roll which is only very, very slowly divergent and one which is truly neutral. They feel substantially the same over a fairly short period of time and a much longer period is needed to prove that the unstable case is actually unstable. In the same way a dutch roll which is only very, very slowly convergent will feel the same as a neutral dutch roll over a short period of time. Time, therefore, is important, and the convention is to use the time period taken to reach double amplitude (in the unstable case) or half amplitude (in the stable case) as a means of expressing the degree of stability.

The requirements in this field have not yet been finally agreed, although a lot of work has been done for the supersonic transport and it is likely that this will be read back to the subsonic jet transport. It is known that times to double amplitude down to around 50 secs. can be considered substantially to equate to neutral stability; it is also known that times up to 15 secs. constitute marked instability. It would appear that a level could eventually be drawn around the 35 to 40 secs. mark. Time to double amplitude, however, is not the whole story. Frequency is very important; if this falls to somewhere below 3 secs. the roll is fast enough to make it difficult for a pilot to keep in phase with his recovery on the ailerons and there is the possibility of the motion being made worse.

Dutch roll qualities vary with aircraft configuration, for a given configuration with altitude and for a given altitude with lift coefficient. The dutch roll, therefore, gets worse with increased altitude and usually, but not always, with reduced speed at constant weight or increased weight at constant speed.

The control of a divergent dutch roll is not difficult so long as it is handled properly. Let us assume that your aeroplane develops a diverging dutch roll. The first thing to do is nothing — repeat *nothing*. Too many pilots have grabbed the aeroplane in a rush, done the wrong thing and made matters a lot worse. Don't worry about a few seconds delay because it won't get much worse in this time. Just watch the rolling motion and get the pattern fixed in your mind. Then, when you are good and ready, give one firm but gentle correction on the aileron control against the upcoming wing. Don't hold it on too long — just in and out — or you will spoil the effect. You have then, in one smooth controlled action, killed the biggest part of the roll. You will be left with a residual wriggle, which you can take out, still on ailerons alone, in your own time.

Don't attempt to correct the manoeuvre with rudder; as explained, the yaw is very often suppressed and it is difficult to work out which way to apply the rudder at what particular moment and there is a good chance that the wrong rudder will be applied which will aggravate things very quickly. It is not difficult, however, to apply the correct aileron control. Further, don't attempt to squash the dutch roll flat in one fell swoop but be content with taking out a big bite first time then sorting out the remainder next time. In a dutch roll in a turn aim for recovery at the bank angle appropriate to the turn. Don't attempt to deal with the dutch roll and the return to level flight simultaneously; fix the dutch roll first then, if necessary, recover from the turn.

The drama which surrounded the dutch roll some years ago was not really earned by the aeroplanes but was engendered perhaps more by a lack of knowledge of the subject and possibly an over-exuberance on the part of the pilots. It is a comfort to be able to say now that there are no civil jet transports flying which need be the slightest bit demanding in terms of oscillatory stability and control; most have a raw dutch roll which is only slowly unstable when there is any instability and the others are adequately protected in other ways (see the following sub-chapter on yaw and roll dampers).

The recommended drill for correction of dutch roll on ailerons alone holds good for all subsonic jet transports. As a matter of interest it is already known that this technique might prove very difficult on a supersonic jet transport because of the yaw produced by the lateral control; but this will be resolved in due time so don't let it influence you on your present aircraft.

Yaw and roll dampers

When an aeroplane has a significant dutch roll, that is anything less stable than a reasonably quickly damped variation, some assistance is necessary to avoid a tedious and demanding task for the pilot. It has previously been pointed out that the basic cause of a dutch rolling tendency (apart from wing sweep of course) is lack of effective fin and rudder area; the point has also been made that too large a fin area is detrimental to spiral stability qualities. The final choice of fin and rudder area, therefore, is a compromise, as always. If because of this the size of the fin cannot be increased the effective fin area must be increased in some other way.

On some early jet transports with manually operated rudders, the rudder tended to trail downwind in a sideslip, at least over small angles; this decreased the effect of the fin and made the oscillatory stability worse. Boosting the rudder from zero angle resulted in the rudder remaining central in a slip thus increasing fin size and this materially improved the dutch roll. On aeroplanes with power operated rudders (which now means most of them) the obvious step is to apply rudder against the yaw to prevent the slip starting or building up. This is exactly what a yaw damper does.

A yaw damper is a gyro system sensitive to changes in yaw which feeds a signal into the rudder which then applies rudder to oppose the yaw. With this device a dutch roll will not develop because the yaw which triggers it all off is not allowed to develop. If a dutch roll has developed with the damper off then switching it on will result in the aeroplane being brought under control. Under normal operation the damper cannot make a mistake, but applies the rudder in the correct direction and in the correct amount, thus reducing the slip angle to zero and stopping all rolling tendency.

The number of dampers required is a function of the dutch roll qualities of the naked aeroplane and the philosophy of the power control system design. If the roll is merely tedious in its demand normally only one damper is required; it is accepted that, for a damper failure en route, it is not a great hardship to continue to the destination. If the dutch roll is significantly unstable then two dampers are required so that the failure of one en route still leaves the aeroplane with some protection. In the case of marked dutch roll instability three dampers can be fitted. While it is generally true to say that the number of dampers is a reflection of the degree of instability this is not always so — some constructors fit more than the minimum demanded by the requirements so as to cater for allowable deficiencies, for example. If the power operated rudder is of the split surface design, then naturally each portion should have its own damper.

Basically there are two types of yaw damper. The early one was hooked into the rudder control circuit so that it applied rudder control through the same control run as did the pilot and its activity was reflected in rudder bar activity. While this was a comforting reassurance of its serviceability it did increase rudder control loads. To prevent this making matters worse in the event of an engine failure on take-off or a cross-wind landing the damper was switched out for take-off and landing. As this damper effectively paralleled the pilot's actions it has come to be known as a parallel yaw damper. The later type of yaw damper is known as a series yaw damper. This hooks into the rudder control circuit effectively right at the back of the aeroplane in such a way that it does its job of moving the rudder without moving the pilot's rudder control circuit. As foot forces are not increased with the series yaw damper operative it may be used for take-off and landing.

Some aeroplanes have, additionally, a roll damper; this does substantially the same job as a yaw damper but works through the aileron controls instead. Where this is done it is not necessarily for dutch roll damping; it can be purely for roll damping in turbulence on a type where the rolling inertias are such that this sort of damping is needed. It will of course control a dutch roll through the ailerons and can thus be equated with a yaw damper.

So ends the lesson on dutch roll and yaw dampers. It has been spelled out in some detail to emphasise the fact that with knowledge, practice and a measure of prudence there is really not much to it. The prudence bit needs to be underlined; with sweep angles increasing and the design of jet aeroplanes being stretched all the time it is likely that oscillatory stability will get worse with a heavier reliance on stability augmentation in general.

As training involves, quite rightly, a proper understanding of the basic flying qualities of the type it follows that a training captain and a pilot under training can be exposed to flight conditions where oscillatory stability is markedly negative. To make this sort of operation safe the excitation of a dutch roll should be made gently and with care, and it is essential that the capture capability of each yaw damper, where more than one is fitted, is known with a fair degree of accuracy. On one type presently flying, the

Flight Manual drills are quite explicit and cover the extension of air brakes and an immediate reduction in altitude if the recovery of a diverging dutch roll looks like being delayed, or looks like achieving large angles of roll with associated high angles of sideslip.

Take the trouble to know your aeroplane in detail and keep in practice in dutch roll recovery if it is one of those which has a significant dutch roll; a dark and dirty night when you have a load of passengers is no time to find out whether you or the aeroplane is master of the situation.

Directional and lateral trim

A number of flying qualities are sensitive to sideslip and in order to realise the level of handling qualities and performance declared for the type it is important that the aeroplane should be flown without significant slip. Some of the qualities affected are:—

(a) Spiral stability; if mistrimmed this will be better in one direction but worse in the other.

(b) Stall qualities; a bit academic perhaps but the stall qualities are only true for substantially straight flight at the stall — if any slip exists an otherwise straight nose-dropper can turn into a roller at a slightly higher speed.

(c) Performance; slip creates drag in its own right but if the slip is sufficient to cause enough aileron trim to be applied to crack the spoilers open on one side then the drag penalty will be compounded — this can be significant in terms of fuel consumption and range on a long sector.

(d) The flight path following autopilot disconnect; this is a most important one because if the autopilot drop-out should be missed for some reason, and the aeroplane is out of trim, it will quietly react to the mistrim and, in all probability, gently roll and slowly enter a spiral dive.

It is appreciated that there is no choice of directional and lateral trim for take-off — the rudder and aileron trimmers are normally set at neutral. As soon as reasonably possible after take-off, however, an accurate trim should be picked up and thereafter maintained. It should be rechecked occasionally even if the flight condition hasn't changed and it should certainly be checked after changes in speed, power and configuration. Changes in altitude also calls for attention because power decreases with altitude. Rather than turn this need into a chore it should become second nature to check the directional and lateral trim state, even when flying on autopilot, because the effect of the aeroplane being mistrimmed is very significant.

To trim an aeroplane accurately start from zero on both trimmers; there is a good chance that the final trims will not be too far divorced from zero anyway. Holding the aircraft laterally level on ailerons, and with the rudder substantially free or only lightly held, move the rudder trimmer as necessary to stop any turning tendency and to ensure that a constant compass heading is being maintained. This is always the first task: select a rudder trim which maintains a constant compass heading. Do not use the turn and slip indicator for this, it is not sufficiently accurate. Now slowly take out the residual aileron load, if any, on the aileron trimmer. Having done this there is sometimes the need to make a further adjustment one way or the other to the rudder trim to ensure that the heading is being maintained and that there is not a very slow residual turning tendency. In the all engines configuration an accurate trim has now been established and, when pitch trim is also satisfactory, the autopilot can be engaged. If the autopilot should subsequently drop out the aeroplane will be substantially in trim and should maintain its flight path within reasonable limits.

In an engine-out condition (excepting V_2 at full power where the requirements permit a residual foot force at full rudder trim of up to 50 lb.) the same basic philosophy applies. Holding lateral level on the aileron control, and having achieved the rudder angle necessary to fly a substantially constant compass heading, trim the rudder to remove the foot load. Having done this now trim the ailerons so as to remove the residual aileron load, in the meantime allowing the aeroplane to pick up a bank angle sufficient to balance the asymmetric thrust (about 3° in a climb and 1° in a cruise); again finally check that with all control loads released a constant compass heading is being maintained. On those types with manual ailerons it is only rarely that the ailerons can be left for any significant period of time without the aeroplane slowly rolling off. On those types where ailerons are supplemented with spoilers for lateral control it is best to trim the rudder so as to achieve a substantially level aileron spectacle setting; this avoids having the spoilers cracked open on one side and keeps the drag to a minimum although the net result is a slightly higher residual sideslip angle (this is less penalising in terms of overall drag). If the autopilot can cope in this condition it can now be engaged. This will result in wings levelling and a lateral drift which should be compensated by a heading change towards the higher thrust side so as to maintain track. Remember that, in the engine-out case, changes in thrust have a marked effect on the required directional trim and that it is just as important to wind the trim off as power is reduced as it is to increase the rudder trim as power is increased.

Lastly, it is a recommended drill, in the final stages of an engine-out approach, say below 300 ft., to get the co-pilot slowly to wind off the rudder trim maintained during the approach so that when all thrust is reduced for the landing the aeroplane is in trim directionally; if this is not done a surprisingly high force has to be applied to the 'other' rudder pedal to keep the aeroplane straight.

Spiral stability

Several references have already been made to this subject. It is not a new subject of course since all aeroplanes have spiral qualities, but it is much more

106

significant on a jet transport than it was on a piston-engined aircraft. This is because of the jet's generally much higher level of performance, its ability to cover a lot more sky in a given period of time and its need to depart from aerodromes in, relatively, steep climbing attitudes.

Spiral stability is defined as the tendency for an aeroplane, in a properly co-ordinated turn, to return to laterally level flight on release of the ailerons. It is not to be confused with lateral stability, which is the tendency to return to laterally level flight on release of the ailerons in a sideslip. The essential difference is that, in a sideslip, the rolling moment due to sideslip assists the aeroplane to recover (the increased dihedral effect of the leading wing, etc.), whereas in a properly co-ordinated turn there is effectively no slip to produce this righting moment.

After release of the ailerons in a steady turn the spiral stability is positive if the bank angle decreases, neutral if the bank angle remains constant, or negative if the bank angle increases.

If the stability is markedly negative the bank increases fairly quickly, the nose falls into the turn and the aeroplane quickly enters a spiral dive.

It has been stated previously that spiral stability is worsened by too large a fin area (but again, only 'too large' in this context). What happens is simply that, as the aeroplane just starts to slip into the turn on release of the ailerons, and before the rolling moment due to sideslip can take effect, the rather dominant fin jumps into play and insists on straightening the aeroplane up directionally. This accelerates the outer (upper) wing and causes an increased bank; the increased bank angle causes another slip which the fin again straightens. This sequence repeats and the turn is thus made steeper.

Once the bank angle exceeds say 30° the nose falls into the turn and the speed increases as the roll increases and the aeroplane enters a steep spiral dive. Let us assume the aeroplane is longitudinally stable (which it ought to be). When the speed is sufficiently displaced from the trimmed speed there will then be a nose up pitch in the longitudinal sense; but as the bank angle by this time can be very large this only serves to tighten the spiral.

The relationship between oscillatory and spiral stability can now be better understood, and it can be seen that they are in conflict because what is good for one is bad for the other in terms of fin and rudder size and effect; a large fin improves oscillatory stability but degrades spiral stability. The choice facing the designer is a difficult one because in fixing the size of the fin there are many more factors involved than just spiral and oscillatory stabilities: the larger the fin the less the rudder angle for a given V_{MC} (minimum control speed engine out); the better the aileron centring over small angles the less the need for good spiral qualities from other sources, and so on.

Yet again it all ends up as a masterly compromise, and just as the deficiency in dutch roll damping, for example, is made up by a yaw damper, so a deficiency in spiral qualities can also be made up artificially by taking a term from the yaw damper and feeding this back into the powered rudder control system. This ensures that a positive aileron angle is always needed to maintain a turn. When this occurs the spiral stability is bound to be improved because when the ailerons are released they centre and naturally the aeroplane recovers from the turn. In this case there is a small penalty in aileron control loads when initiating and holding a turn.

Like oscillatory stability, spiral stability and instability are measured by the time taken to halve or double the bank angle, and again small degrees of positive or negative stability are generally considered to be substantially neutral. The bank angle must double in less than about 20 secs. before the spiral stability feels qualitatively negative.

The general level of spiral stability can be assessed by evaluating the aileron load which is being held in the turn. If the ailerons have to be held on to maintain the turn, then, on release, they will centre and the spiral stability should be good; if bank has to be held off the ailerons will apply themselves a little further on release and the aeroplane is bound to roll further over. If substantially no load is being applied, which is quite often the case, then the aeroplane survives or does not survive on its basic balance of lateral and directional qualities. This puts a premium on good aileron self-centring qualities over small angles.

Spiral stability varies with configuration and airspeed and can be greatly compromised by the accuracy of the directional and lateral trim selected. An aeroplane with rather weak spiral stability (as demonstrated in an accurate directional and lateral trim condition) can, if only slightly mis-trimmed, particularly directionally, be, say, quite stable to the left but quite unstable to the right. The difficulty is that the zero settings normally selected for take-off can quite easily be not the absolutely correct ones; this means that the true spiral qualities of the aeroplane are not likely to be realised during the climb after take-off.

The significance of all this is the degree of attention required to fly the aircraft. In spite of sweep improving the rolling moment due to sideslip because of the increase in C_L of the leading wing, the spiral stability of most jet transports is substantially neutral and great care has to be exercised in trimming the rudder and ailerons to prove that it is not negative. If your aeroplane really is spirally stable then, having established a turn, you can relax a little with the comforting knowledge that even if you are distracted it will, by itself, return to laterally level flight. If on the other hand your aeroplane is not stable spirally you simply must watch it like a hawk, particularly in IMC where visual clues are absent and particularly at low altitudes where neglect could lead to a spiral dive into the ground or into a condition from which recovery will need to be quite violent to avoid striking the ground. Because this monitoring needs to be a conscious one you must consciously watch your bank angles during turns, particularly at low altitudes.

If you have to make a turn during the steep climb part of the noise abatement departure procedure, roll into a gentle turn with say 15° bank and take

108

Plate 7 Large flying control surfaces

Anyone who has ever carried a large sheet of hardboard in a high wind can imagine the task of attempting to handle surfaces of this size without some assistance. The VC10 tail unit illustrated, which has a rudder area of 100 square feet, an elevator area of 144 square feet and a total tailplane area of 638 square feet, employs full hydraulic power actuation on all control surfaces.

Photograph: BOAC

Plate 8   Variable incidence tailplanes

The 'all-flying' tail of the Hawker Siddeley Trident. Notice how the elevator (trailing edge portion) is deflected in the lower photograph, thus increasing the effect of the tail angle. The range through which the tailplane operates (and therefore the enormous power in terms of pitch control contained in it) can be seen by studying the relationship between the tailplane leading edge and the bullet.

Photographs: Hawker Siddeley

Leaving aerodynamics aside for a moment let us consider the basic simplicity of this design. There is a fuselage containing the payload, a wing to support it in flight, four engines to push it along, tail surfaces to control it—and not much else. We can also use

this picture to illustrate zero fuel weights and wing bending relief. If most of the fuel weight were in the fuselage and only a small amount of the total were in the wings the upward bending of the wings at the fuselage joint would be very marked. By keeping a better

balance this upward bending force is relieved. Even so, the depth required at the wing root to provide the necessary strength is considerable.

Photograph: BOAC

Plate 10 Long wheelbase

This photograph of a Super VC10 rotating illustrates two important points: (a) the distance of the main gear aft of the pilot's station (76.5 feet) and (b) the distance of the nose gear aft of the pilot's station (10.7 feet). When taxying aeroplanes of this size and layout, no attempt should be made to cut the corners. It is essential to go in deep before coming around on the steering.

Plate 11 Long body

An impressive shot of the 747 undergoing high attitude take-off tests with the tail scraping the runway. The position of the main gears shows that the aeroplane is just about 100% airborne. Take care not to repeat this trick in line service; elevator forces for rotation are quite light.

Photograph: The Boeing Company

Plate 12 Flight at high altitude

It is difficult to express in a photograph the almost ethereal quality of flight at very high altitudes—the silence, the loneliness and the total divorce from an earth-bound environment. In this picture, however, the photo-

grapher has managed to capture something of the atmosphere found at 35,000 feet. On a more practical level one should bear in mind the effect of this rarified atmosphere, which is to reduce aerodynamic damping.

Because of this the pilot must be gentle with the aeroplane when manoeuvring.

Photograph: BOAC

care to stop the roll at 15° of bank; then hold it there accurately throughout the turn and don't relax until the turn is completed and the aeroplane is back to laterally level flight. Ideally, there should be no turns in the initial steep climb, but if they have to be accepted they should not be started below 500 ft.

The rather weak spiral stability of some jet transport aircraft highlights the need for careful monitoring of bank angles during turning flight and accurate directional and lateral trimming.

Stalling

Stalling is one of the major areas which always come up for discussion whenever responsible pilots get together. Unlike its current twin problem of flight techniques through severe weather, where there is broad agreement, stalling appears to drive even the most rational of pilots to completely opposing points of view. Opinions vary from those who claim that 'Pilots just don't stall so why not forget the problem and simply rely on good stall warning' to those who say 'Pilots do stall sufficiently often for it to matter. It is a real problem and should be tackled in a thoroughly responsible manner.' Somewhere within this scatter lies the truth, at least the truth in the opinion of the author. In deliberating the design philosophy and flying qualities of an aeroplane there are three categories of pilots involved: the constructor's pilots, the certification authorities' pilots and the operators' pilots. And while all these pilots shoot for the same broad target — safety — each leans slightly so as to favour, in areas which are strictly matters of opinion, his loyalty to his employer. This is perfectly understandable, and indeed proper, human behaviour pattern in the real world in which we all live. This is, therefore, an admission that the line of reasoning which follows in parts of this sub-chapter is quite openly 'The stalling problem and its solution as seen from the certification pilot's point of view.'

Before we can get down to the simple task of answering the question 'Why do some of the later jet transports stall differently from piston-engined air-craft and what do we do about it?', it is necessary to cover some background material. In particular we must study the philosophy of the requirements because they have a most significant impact on the design of an aeroplane. We shall, therefore, explain the stall requirements and review the stall qualities of the post-war aeroplanes as introductory material, then proceed to the stalling qualities of jet transports, the super-stall and factors affecting the stall.

An explanation of the U.K. stall requirements

The significance of any problem has first to be established before it can properly be evaluated. The degree of protection required against a risk must be related to the probability of its occurrence. The latter of course is the foundation stone of rational performance requirements. It is necessary, therefore, to know just how often aeroplanes actually are stalled in service.

If they are never stalled the problem can be dismissed; if they are stalled sufficiently frequently the problem must be faced.

Those people whose job it is to survey incidents and accidents records and draw sensible conclusions from flight recorder traces claim that the illustration given in figure 5.14 is approximately true. Without being able to prove or disprove it, it looks fairly acceptable, particularly when, crew loyalties being understandably what they are, it is known that a significant number of stall incidents are not reported.

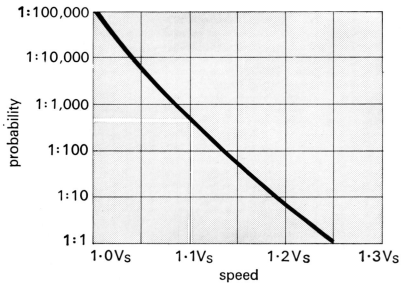

Figure 5.14   Stall probability curve.

The figure illustrates the probability of achieving a given speed, as a function of stall speed, against numbers of flights. It can be seen that $1.25V_s$ is of course achieved on every flight; that $1.1V_s$, the assumed stall warning speed, is achieved somewhere between 1 in 100 and 1 in 1,000 flights; and that the stall speed is achieved around the 1 in 100,000 flights.

To help you to go along with these values let us compare them with something better documented — the rates for engine shutdown. These are approximately 1 in every 1,000 flights for a shutdown en route and 1 in every 100,000 take-offs for a failure near to V_1 on take-off.

This begins to show the size of the stalling problem. As pilots are properly grateful for the care which is taken to ensure their survival in the event of engine failure, the same broad conclusions can be read across to the stall problem.

Since it has been established that stalls occur sufficiently often for them to

110

be taken into account and, since it is known that a stall is a potentially hazardous manoeuvre involving loss of height and loss of control, it is now necessary to state the degree of protection required against a risk of such magnitude. Without quoting the requirements in detail it is reasonable to say that three specific things are required:—warning, identification and survival capability. A significant hazard demands these three simple qualities. Just think about it for a moment and draw some elementary parallels in other fields of human activity and the simplicity and accuracy of the basic thinking will be seen to be true.

Stall warning For something as potentially hazardous as a stall there must be clear and distinctive warning sufficiently in advance of the stall for the stall itself to be averted. The warning may be furnished by aerodynamic qualities or by a suitable device of sufficient reliability to give unmistakable warning under all normal conditions of operation.

This is provided by aerodynamic buffet so long as it really is clear and unmistakable and to a level where it cannot be compromised by turbulence. The warning should occur at a speed normally not less than 10% EAS above the stall speed.

In all cases where natural warning is absent a suitable device must be fitted. (To date a stick shaker appears to be the best device.)

Stall identification Until recently, that is immediately preceding those jet transports possessing a super-stall capability, it was assumed that the stall qualities themselves would be recognised immediately by the pilot as the stall, and for conventionally stalling aircraft this assumption remains valid. For aircraft where the 'stall' speed is identified artificially, because there is either no 'traditional' stall or Max. C_L can be exceeded without a nose down pitch (this might develop into a pitch up), then something clear and unmistakable is needed; notice particularly that the attainment of Max.C_L in isolation simply won't do unless it is accompanied by something the pilot cannot miss. Further, as flight at or near the stall occurs mostly as a result of matters outside the pilot's control, or as a result of irrational behaviour on the part of the pilot, it is unreasonable to expect the pilot to react in a rational fashion to a simple visual or aural stimulus. It is believed that in these circumstances the recovery of the aeroplane should be automatic. Hence, on aeroplanes capable of super-stalling, the 'stall' speed needs to be positively identified by a completely unmistakable, sharp, forward movement of the control column causing the aeroplane immediately to pitch down and reduce its incidence. (See subsequent discussion on the super-stall and stick pushers for a more detailed treatment of this most contentious area.)

Stall qualities On the older aeroplanes the requirements called, quite simply, for a straight nose drop at the stall, with some relaxation in terms of roll angles in the turning flight cases. The requirements still call for basically the same qualities regardless of the pure aerodynamic stall qualities of even the most advanced aeroplane. This is undoubtedly correct in principle because the aeroplane then naturally recovers from the stalled condition and helps itself to return to unstalled flight; it does what the pilot himself should have done a few seconds earlier. Leaving aside any directional misbehaviour at the stall because of its spin inducing tendency and the whole question of pitch up (as opposed to pitch down), which is potentially very hazardous and forbidden by the stability requirements anyway, the only freedom left is a disturbance in roll before the nose down pitch. While an argument can be made to support this philosophy, at least over moderate angles, its weakness lies in the fact that it would not necessarily be a self-unstalling tendency and could lead to directional troubles.

Summary This completes the bones of the requirements and their interpretations. It is appreciated that there are many arguments which can be raised against the philosophy expounded here. There is a great deal of safety and comfort to be had from everything which we have enjoyed in the past in terms of stall qualities generally and there is a danger in tossing some basic qualities away and horse-trading one quality for another; aeroplanes might have changed but pilots haven't.

Finally, there is no agreement with that body of pilots which claims that aeroplanes are not stalled; if only it were true then the airworthiness authorities could drop their stall requirements. Neither is there any agreement with that other body of pilot opinion which claims that adequate stall warning will always prevent the stall. Even aeroplanes with lots of good natural buffet figure in the stalling records and it is not generally realised just how quickly, particularly in the accelerated cases, the speed can be reduced from the stall warning speed to the stall speed. It can, in fact, be less than *2 seconds* in a severe case and there would be no hope of the pilot reacting in time to avoid the stall.

The requirements, therefore, still demand stall warning, unmistakable stall identification and a substantially straight nose drop at the stall. In this way the safety level of past practice is continued and the pilot, in a time of distress and irrational behaviour, is not required to perform with the touch of a master. It may be that the absence of this master touch was partially responsible for his arriving at the stall speed anyway.

A review of the stalling qualities of post-war aeroplanes

It just so happens that nearly all post-war aeroplanes fall into four distinct categories within each of which is a remarkable similarity in stalling qualities and between each of which is a well-defined change in stall qualities. There are naturally the exceptions, which will be known to some pilots, but the following general summary is broadly true.

Category	Stall quality
Traditional piston-engined transports.	Traditional: i.e. good natural stall warning by buffet and a substantially straight nose drop at the stall.
Propeller turbine transports.	Somewhat degraded: stick shakers needed for warning and a tendency to roll coincident with the nose drop, particularly with power on.
First generation jet transports.	Surprisingly, very good: plenty of natural stall warning and an immaculate nose drop at the stall.
Second generation jet transports.	Not good: the true natural stall being disastrous in some cases; devices needed both for warning and qualities.

Before we go any further, two important items must be noted. Firstly, some aeroplanes were, or are, out of character, i.e. much worse or much better than the generalised treatment given above. Secondly, a definition of the difference between a first and second generation jet transport is needed. For the purposes of this book, a first generation jet is an early design jet transport with a comparatively undeveloped wing and the engines mounted elsewhere than on the rear fuselage; a second generation jet is a developed first generation or a new design having either a highly developed wing in terms of lifting ability and/or rear fuselage mounted engines with a high set tailplane.

Traditional piston-engined transports It is assumed that the reader is familiar with these stall qualities. They can be broadly summarised as: good natural stall warning by buffet from the early flow separation on the wing due to its comparatively high camber and lack of design to avoid early separation; a substantially straight nose drop at the stall because of a good pitching moment/incidence characteristic and progressive and non-critical equal loss of lift on both wings.

Propeller turbine transports During the design and development of this class of aeroplane two things occurred which resulted in poorer stall qualities overall:—

(a) The wing section was developed in the move towards increased overall efficiency (i.e. better lift/drag ratio) at the higher speeds possible with the new power plant. Subsequently, it was found necessary to develop higher lift trailing edge flaps. As a result, flow separation, both in the clean and flapped configurations, was delayed until a much higher incidence at lower speed. This lost the natural stall warning which had to be replaced with a stick shaker.

(b) It was found that, because of these high lift capabilities (particularly in the power on cases where the slipstream wetted area of the wing was very large), when the flow separated it would let go suddenly, and unless both wings went exactly together of course the aeroplane would roll. A lot of work went into keeping the tips flying at high angles of incidence and/or tuning inboard leading edge spoilers (the fixed leading edge disrupter type) so as to achieve a symmetrical inboard stall causing a nose down pitch. This was in general finally achieved, although, as the stall qualities of this type are naturally sensitive to sideslip it follows that a sharp roll can just precede the nose drop if the stall should be reached with some slip on.

First generation jet transports Some of the early first generation jet transports earned a bad reputation for some of their handling qualities. It is a great pity that these aeroplanes were never given full credit for their excellent stall qualities. Not only did they meet the requirements handsomely but their behaviour really was, and is, immaculate (it isn't true, *sine qua non*, that in meeting requirements one necessarily produces a good aeroplane!). The wing section and the trailing edge flap design were sufficiently under-developed to allow a flow separation early enough to provide stall warning by good natural buffet; in some cases the buffet rose to quite high values just before the stall. Also, without too much wing leading edge lift development, the pitching moment/incidence relationship remained stable right up to Max. C_L and, combined with a centre section stall before a tip stall (necessary on a swept wing to avoid pitch up), resulted in a good positive nose down pitch at the stall.

The power-on stall which gave trouble on the prop-jets was avoided on the pure-jet because, in the power-on condition, there was no increase in lift due to slipstream taking the aeroplane to higher incidences and very high pitch attitudes. The power-on almost equated to the power-off condition, the only difference being a slight increase in pitch attitude and a slight reduction in stall speed due to (a) the vertical component of the thrust efflux reducing the effective weight slightly and (b) slight entrainment of air over the wings by the jet effluxes.

Second generation jet transports These types can be subdivided into three groups:—

(a) Those which stall like first generation jets, i.e. have generally good qualities.

(b) Those capable of a super-stall.

(c) Those which have a pitch up preceding a good nose-down stall quality.

Group (a) has already been covered. Group (b) will be covered under the heading of the super-stall, but Group (c) needs some explanation. This is

114

the jet transport which doesn't have a high set tail but does have a fairly highly developed wing in the form of either fixed or movable leading edge and trailing edge devices. If high lift wing leading edge development is carried too far inboard on a swept wing, in order, for example, to achieve a very high Max. C_L for very best field performance, the inboard part of the wing hangs on to its lift to a very late stage, even after the rest of the wing has started to let go, and produces a pitch up tendency.

While the subsequent true stall can be an immaculate nose down pitch (the wing tips never stalling), the initial pitch up tendency is nevertheless quite unacceptable in principle because it represents longitudinal instability and leads to a tendency for the aircraft to self-stall from speeds below which the pitch up starts. Where this occurs it is sometimes necessary to fit a stability augmenter to operate just before the stall. This is not in any way a stick pusher and cannot strictly have any effect on pitch up, which is a function only of pitching moment/incidence and total tail angle (stabiliser and elevator) to stall, if the pilot insists on stalling the aircraft. This stability augmenter introduces only a small force into the elevator circuit which imposes positive stick free stability and removes the otherwise self-stalling tendency. The augmenter having been mentioned it should also be stated that, as its input is so small, all the runaway cases are completely innocuous.

The super-stall

The most significant thing, in terms of stalling qualities, of most (but not all) of the second generation jet transports is the super-stall. Any title, such as super-stall, deep stall or a locked-in condition, is acceptable because they all refer broadly to the same thing; the only point to be made is that the locked-in description should be applied only to those types on which recovery is not possible.

Before we tackle the aerodynamics of the super-stall let us make sure that we fully understand the stall on a conventional aeroplane. In order to do so we must high-light the two areas from whence spring the reasons for an aeroplane having a super-stall. These are:—

(a) The basic pitching tendency of the aeroplane at the stall.

(b) Tail effectiveness in recovery from the stall.

On a conventional straight wing, low tailplane aeroplane, trimmed at say 1.4 Vs, the forces acting on the aeroplane in the pitching plane are illustrated in figure 5.15. The weight acting downwards, forward of the lift acting upwards, produces the need for a balancing force acting downwards from the tailplane. The elevator trim has been set to reduce the stick force to zero. (Some aeroplanes in some configurations at aft C.G. might require an upward balancing force from the tail, in which case the picture needs to be redrawn with the weight aft of the lift on the wing and an upward force from the tail. Speed reduction is then achieved by up elevator reducing the upload from the tail.) As speed is reduced by gentle up elevator deflection the static stability

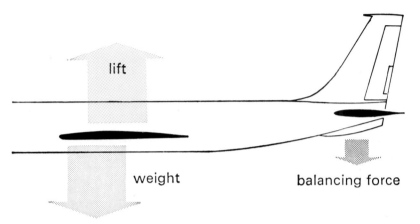

Figure 5.15   Distribution of forces in the pitching plane.

of the aeroplane comes into play and causes a nose down tendency.   This has to be resisted by further up elevator to keep the nose coming up, and in this progression an increasing pull force is necessary to continue the speed reduction.   The low set tail soon finds itself in the wing wake, which is slightly turbulent, lower energy air.   This reduces the efficiency of the tail.

At the stall two distinct things happen.   The conventional straight wing aeroplane obeys the traditional nose down pitching tendency at the stall and gives the whole aeroplane a fairly pronounced nose down pitch.   Also, at the moment of stall the wing wake passes more or less straight aft and goes *above* the low set tail.   This leaves the tail working in crisp, high energy air where it experiences a sharp increase in positive incidence causing upwards lift.   This lift then assists the nose down pitch of the whole aeroplane.

Therefore, in terms of the two qualities referred to earlier, the low tail conventional aeroplane (a) possesses a wing-tail combination producing a nose down pitch at the stall and (b) moves its tailplane from disturbed flow to clean flow below the wing wake at the stall, which assists the overall nose down pitch.   Figure 5.16 illustrates this quite clearly.

So much for the stalling aerodynamics of the straight wing, low tail, conventional aeroplane; an increasing pull force all the way to the stall and a good nose down pitch at the stall.

Now let us turn to the swept wing jet transport with rear fuselage mounted engines and a high set tailplane.   There are only two qualities which are different from those of the older aeroplane and which lead to a super-stall;

116

these are the pitching tendency of the aeroplane as the stall develops and the loss of tailplane effectiveness at the stall.

Let us start from the trimmed 1.4Vs condition again. From this point down to the stall, handling qualities are much the same as on the older aeroplane except that the high set tail remains clear of the wing wake and retains its effectiveness during the speed reduction towards the stall. (This is put to good effect when a stick pusher is fitted, as the good elevator response produces a crisp nose down pitch change following the stick push.) Continued speed reduction is, therefore, more likely because the wing wake has not yet reduced the effectiveness of the tail.

At the stall, again two distinct things happen. The rear-engined high tail aeroplane tends to suffer a marked nose up pitch after the stall (this will be explained in detail later) and the wing wake, which has now become low energy turbulent air, passes aft and immerses the high set tail which is in just about the right position to catch it. This greatly reduces the tail effectiveness and makes it incapable of combating the nose up pitch and the aeroplane continues to pitch up. This pitch up just after the stall is worsened by greatly reduced lift and greatly increased drag which cause a rapidly increasing descent path, thus compounding the rate of increase of incidence. The

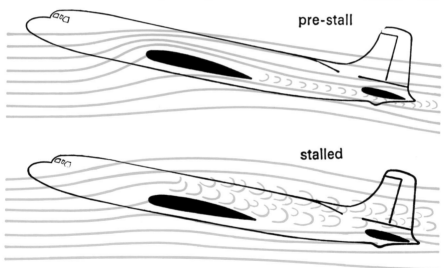

Figure 5.16   Influence of wing wake at the stall—typical piston-engined aeroplane.

aeroplane is thus well on its way to extreme angles of incidence and a deep stall.

Therefore, in terms of the two qualities referred to earlier, the rear-engined, high tail aeroplane (a) suffers a nose up pitch after the stall and (b) puts its

117

tail into the wing wake after the stall thus losing the pitching capability required for recovery. Figure 5.17 illustrates this.

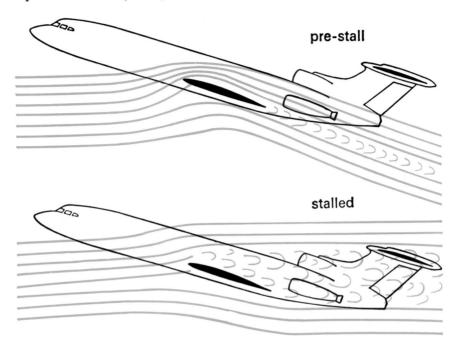

Figure 5.17   Influence of wing wake at the stall—T-tail jet transport.

So these are the stalling aerodynamics of the swept wing, high tail aeroplane: an increasing pull force down to the stall and a marked nose up pitch after the stall with a severely reduced tail effectiveness in recovery.

We must now explain the nose up pitch following the stall. This needs to be taken in three parts:—

(a) **The effect of the wing section characteristics**   The section characteristics of most wings are such as to cause a nose down pitch, if the whole wing could be stalled at the same instant spanwise. As the stall is approached the rather roof-top pressure distribution, which is favoured for good high Mach number qualities in the cruise, changes to an increasingly leading edge peaky pattern because of the enormous suction developed by the nose profile. At the stall this peak collapses, the pressure distribution pattern changes, and the result is usually a nose down pitch. (Figure 5.18.) The basic section characteristics however are usually much less important than the three-dimensional effects (i.e. sweep and taper) of the complete wing.

118

(b) **The effect of the wing planform characteristics (sweep)** In practice the whole wing does not stall at the same instant. A simple swept and tapered wing will tend to stall at the tips first because the high loading outboard, due to taper, is aggravated by sweep back. The boundary layer outflow also resulting from sweep reduces the lift capability near the tips and further worsens the situation. This causes a loss of lift outboard (and therefore aft) which produces pitch up. A lot of design sophistication is needed, including the use of camber and twist, leading edge breaker strips, fences, etc., to suppress this raw quality and get an inboard section stalled first so that the initial pitching tendency is nose down. However, when a highly developed swept wing is taken beyond its initial stalling incidence the tips may still become fully stalled before the inner wing in spite of the initial separation occurring inboard. The wing will then, therefore, pitch up. (Figure 5.19.)

(c) **The effect of the fuselage** On a modern aircraft the forward fuselage makes a more significant contribution to the aerodynamics than in the case of a piston-engined aircraft because of its increased forward overhang and relative size. The forward fuselage lift, which usually continues to increase with incidence until well past the stall, has a significant destabilising effect contributing to the nose up pitching tendency as the incidence exceeds the stalling incidence.

So, for these reasons, a swept-wing high tail aeroplane tends to pitch nose up after the stall.

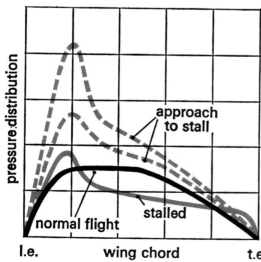

Figure 5.18   Change in pressure distribution through the stall.

119

Many explanations of the super-stall invoke the term 'downwash' and suggest that changes in downwash on the tail have some effect on super-stall qualities. This is not true. A change in downwash angle alone in the approach to the stall does not produce any nose up pitching tendency from the tail. Although the tail experiences an increasing negative incidence with increase in attitude this increase is always 'beaten' by the decreasing negative incidence due to the physical change in attitude. If this were not true then the aeroplane would be unstable in the stall approach, which it

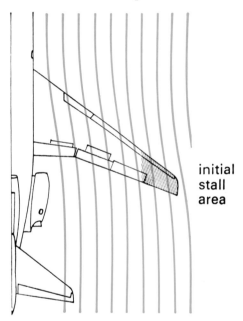

initial
stall
area

Figure 5.19   Initial stall area on swept wing.

is not. For those for whom a simple expression is worth a hundred words the following perhaps makes this clear:—

$$\alpha_T = (\alpha - \varepsilon) + \alpha_0;$$

and $\alpha - \varepsilon$ always increases as α increases

where α_T = tailplane incidence

            α = main wing incidence

            ε = downwash angle

            α_0 = angle between tail and wing

Having explained the elements of the deep-stall let us now look at the complete picture. Figure 5.20 illustrates pitching moment and lift coefficient against angle of incidence. This shows that as incidence is increased towards the stall there is a stable nose down pitching tendency. Notice particularly the increase in stable slope of Cm just before the stall. This is typical of some aircraft types and reflects the success of the designer in achieving an inboard stall first, thus producing a nose down tendency. After the stall, however, the aeroplane pitches up at increasing angles of incidence until it reaches a more or less stable state at around say 30°. So far so good, for a purely academic illustration. In real life, however, the manoeuvre is more treacherous than the illustration suggests, for two reasons stemming from the same source. It has been explained previously that below, say roughly, 1.4 Vs, an increase in incidence causes drag to increase faster than lift and thus the aeroplane tends to sink. It is most important to realise that this increasing sinking tendency, *at a constant pitch attitude,* results in a rapid increase in incidence as the flight path becomes deflected downwards. Furthermore, once the stall has developed and a lot of lift has been lost, the aeroplane will start to sink rapidly and this is accompanied by a rapid increase in incidence.

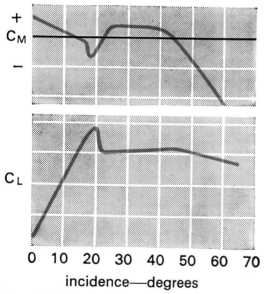

Figure 5.20   Pitching moment and lift coefficient against angle of incidence.

This matter of a downwards inclining flight path producing rapid increases in incidence compounds the entry to, and the progression of, the super-stall. It must be emphasised again that this can occur without the need for an excessively nose high pitch attitude. It can happen on some types at an apparently not abnormal pitch attitude, and it is this quality that can mislead the pilot because it looks very similar to the beginning of a normal recovery.

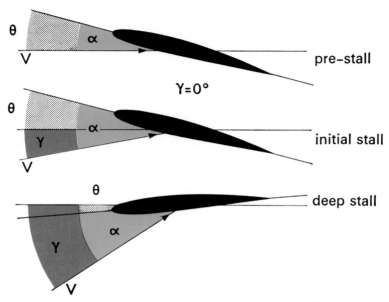

Figure 5.21   The lack of relationship between attitude and incidence.

Recovery from a super-stall should not really have a place in this book since the book is written for airline pilots who have every right to say that they have no interest in an aeroplane which can achieve a super-stalled condition.   However, just to complete the technical treatment of the whole subject let us take a look at it.

In figure 5.22 an illustration of Cm and C_L against α (incidence) is repeated, but this time with the addition of a line illustrating the maximum available nose down pitching moment from full forward elevator control movement. So long as this line stops below the axis of zero pitching moment, recovery is academically possible; if the elevator control line should rise into the positive pitching moment area, then recovery is not possible.   The fight between aircraft nose up pitch and elevator nose down pitch has been lost and the aeroplane will win.   There is no point in discussing the irrecoverable case any further, except perhaps to say that those aeroplanes which have been lost in such manoeuvres finally reached the ground substantially level laterally, having defied all efforts to roll or spin them out of the stabilised condition; only slightly nose down in pitch, with little or no forward speed; at an extremely high incidence; rotating only very slowly in yaw; with (in one case) all the engines flamed out because of being exposed to such massive angles of incidence; and finally with an enormous vertical velocity.

The recoverable case is still rather academic in more ways than one. At one time it was thought that an attempt to roll or spin the aeroplane would offer the best chance. This idea has now been withdrawn because, even assuming that this upset could be achieved, the resulting very steep nose down attitude, the lack of proof of spin recovery capability, the very high rate of descent and the large height range required for recovery makes it unlikely that this method offers any advantage at all.

Where a super-stalled aeroplane is claimed to have some recovery capability the best recovery technique is now considered to be as follows. Persist in full forward elevator control, put the flaps to the position recommended by the manufacturer (which will be where the aeroplane's overall pitching moment quality is most favourable of course) and wait for the aeroplane to pitch down and recover from the stall.

It is important once again to realise that pitch attitude is not enough guide to the recovery. Too early a recovery, from a gentle dive following

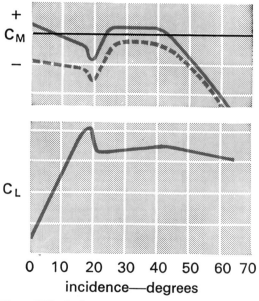

Figure 5.22   Stall recovery capability.

assumed recovery from the super-stall, will again increase incidence and ensure that the aeroplane remains locked in. It is necessary to persist with full forward elevator control until the aeroplane is quite steeply nose down *with*

123

a rapidly increasing airspeed which then indicates that stall recovery has been achieved. Some finesse is then necessary during the dive recovery to strike a proper balance between excessive height loss and speed gain and too fast a recovery once again leading to excessive angles of incidence.

It is more productive to talk about avoidance of entry into a super-stall than to discuss recovery from it. It must be emphasised that we are still in the rather academic field because an aeroplane capable of super-stalling would not, of course, be certificated without adequate protection. Firstly, it must be said that conventional instrumentation is not adequate for flight in the vicinity of the stall; pitch attitude can be most misleading, airspeed and altitude and vertical speed are only component parts of the one parameter which is all important — incidence — and in isolation, and indeed even in sensible combination, these individual parameters can be either misleading or nearly valueless. The only valuable parameter is *incidence*. This is what dictates the behaviour of the aeroplane and this is what needs to be presented to the pilot.

The installation for giving this information is comparatively simple. Vanes or probes are mounted in an inviolate position on each side of the fuselage (to balance the sideslip case) and they are calibrated in fuselage incidence values; the relationship to wing incidence is fixed and known, of course, so that there is no special significance in the fact that it is fuselage incidence. These duplicated gauges then serve the essential purpose of indicating to the pilot not only the incidence value being achieved but the equally important value of rate of change of incidence.

Let us have a few moments on this rate of change of incidence — it is important. In a very slow approach to a stall the incidence can be controlled very accurately, and in this steady slow approach condition, from an initial trimmed-out steady state descent, incidence bears a fixed relationship to airspeed. *But only under these strictly defined conditions.* If anything at all should disturb the flight path then the assumed relationship between airspeed and incidence is lost. If, for example, at say 1.2Vs, the stick is momentarily eased forwards then back, the progression can be regained on airspeed but, having imposed a steepening in the flight path, the remainder of the approach to the stall will obviously be at a higher datum incidence. In a fast approach to a stall the rate of change of incidence will be a lot greater than the rate of decay of airspeed, particularly when very close to the stall. Additionally, a large aeroplane being rotated in pitch will, due to high pitching inertia, possess high pitching momentum. This pitching momentum makes it very difficult to stop a stall penetration at a given angle of incidence. The aeroplane will overswing in pitch to a value which is related to the speed of full down elevator application and the amount of pitching inertia.

Great care has to be exercised in the investigation of accelerated stall cases in experimental flying because the harder the aeroplane is rotated into the stall the further will it overswing against full corrective elevator application.

Although down elevator can be applied at an instantaneous 'safe' value of incidence the aeroplane may still pitch up a further 6° to 8° which might be enough to get it over the maximum safe incidence and on its way to a deep stall.

This discussion of the super-stall has rather drifted into the field of experimental test flying, which isn't directly related to the everyday duties of an airline pilot. However, all extra knowledge is a good thing and without this drift into test-flying it wouldn't have been possible to have covered a lot of this ground. The airline pilot should be presented with either an aeroplane which has no possibility of a super-stall in its basic state however much it should be mishandled (there is, of course, a top limit to the assumed degree of mishandling which will be covered later), or an aeroplane capable of a super-stall but suitably and properly protected. The protection is provided by the stick shaker and stick pusher.

So much for the basic elements of the super-stall. Having covered it in so much detail let us finish off with a few reminders:—

1. A super-stall is one where very large angles of incidence are developed after the stalling incidence has been exceeded.

2. A super-stall is caused by the basic wing nose up pitching moment at the stall being compounded by the effect of the wing wake, which destroys the effectiveness of the high tail in a recovery.

3. In the pre-stall and immediate post-stall regimes, the lift/drag qualities of the aeroplane can cause an increasingly descending flight path *with no change in pitch*, which is a further encouragement to super-stall entry.

4. A super-stall can be recoverable or irrecoverable depending on the particular qualities of the aeroplane.

5. Where recovery is possible an extremely large height loss is involved and a further height loss is involved in recovery from the subsequent steep dive.

6. The best recovery action known at this time is to maintain full down elevator control until a rapidly increasing airspeed is seen at a fairly steep nose down attitude.

7. Without incidence information, a nose down pitch with an increasing speed is no guarantee that recovery has been effected and an up elevator movement at this stage merely serves to keep the aircraft stalled.

8. *Suspected entry to a super-stall must always be countered by immediate and full down elevator application which must be held until it is quite clear that the stall has been avoided.*

Factors affecting the stall

The stall qualities of jet transport aircraft are overlaid with the other characteristics of the aeroplane and its environment. These need elaborating in this context:—

(a) The increasing sink rate before the stall has already been mentioned several times.

(b) The effect of momentum in the stall recovery needs elaboration. If a very heavy aeroplane should be stalled, it is no good, the nose having dropped, simply pulling the nose up again and expecting an immediate return to unstalled flight. When the stall occurs the aeroplane begins to sink fast and the initial sink rate is almost independent of pitch attitude. After the nose has been lowered to reduce incidence the recovery flight path must be programmed in such a way that a recovery to level flight is made with the minimum loss of height, and without again producing a high incidence leading to repeated stall warning and in extreme cases a second stall. Therefore, keep the nose down initially, apply power and 'fly' the aeroplane around the recovery path. It is much better to use a little extra height on the first attempt than to stall again.

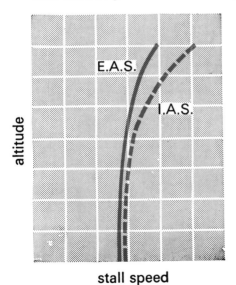

Figure 5.23 Variation of stall speeds with altitude.

(c) Since a wing always stalls at the same incidence, and the aeroplane is only interested in EAS, the stall will occur at a fairly constant EAS. However, at the very high altitudes of which the jet transport is capable, the

126

indicated stall speed increases. This is due to two things. Firstly, the compressibility correction, which forms part of the difference between ASIR and EAS (the other parts being instrument error and position error), is larger in the EAS to ASIR direction due to the effect of Mach number. Secondly, the actual EAS stall speed increases due to Mach number effect on the wing. At very high altitude the EAS stall speed occurs at a significant Mach number (180 knots = 0.61 Mach number, for example); the pressure pattern is disturbed and a higher stall speed results.

(d) Stall speed varies with weight.

$$\frac{V_{S_1}}{V_{S_2}} \propto \sqrt{\frac{W_1}{W_2}}$$

where weight in this context means effective weight. The effective weight of an aeroplane can be increased by a straight pull up or by rolling into a correctly co-ordinated turn, both of which produce increments of 'g'.

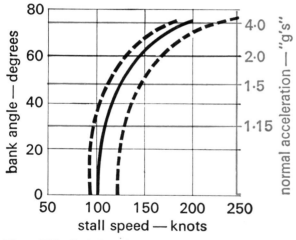

Figure 5.24   Variation of stall speeds with bank angle and acceleration.

Figure 5.24 illustrates the variation of stall speed at three different weights (180,000 lb., 220,000 lb. and 300,000 lb.) for steady 1g flight at 90 knots, 100 knots and 118 knots.   The three curves are then plotted against 'g' and the associated bank angle for a steady turn.   (In a balanced turn the 'g' for a given bank angle is fixed; it is independent of aircraft type, height or speed.)   Taking the 220,000 lb. line, which is representative of maximum landing weight on a big jet aeroplane, the stall speed is 100 knots in steady level flight.   In a 1g increment, 2g total, pull out of a dive the stall speed would be around 140 knots, because the effective weight has been doubled. It can also be seen that the same effect can be achieved in a 60° banked turn. This simple example, of course, involves a manoeuvre well beyond that occurring in normal passenger flying. Take a look at some more examples, more reasonable and less reasonable:—

(i) A 30° banked turn (= 1.15g) produces 6 knots increase in stall speed.

(ii) A 45° banked turn (= 1.4g) produces 18 knots increase in stall speed.

(iii) A 60° banked turn (= 2.0g) produces 40 knots increase in stall speed.

(iv) A 63° banked turn (= 2.25g) produces 50 knots increase in stall speed.

The significance of the last, rather odd, value of 63° bank is that it imposes 50% increase in stall speed.

This very large increase in stall speed possible in manoeuvring flight is an important subject. We need to consider it later when discussing flight through severe weather.

There has been a lot of explanation of why some jet aeroplanes stall as they do. When we come to the second part of this sub-chapter, in which there should be advice on what to do about stalling, there is only one thing that can be said — don't! The constructors and airworthiness authorities have played their part to see that you have an adequate degree of protection but this is not proof against a really ham-handed manoeuvre. If ever the day should come when you are faced with a choice of stalling, or doing something else, choose the alternative. It cannot be put too strongly. Whatever you do, *don't stall the aeroplane.*

Stick shakers

The requirements quite properly require stall warning. In the case of the older aeroplanes this was provided by the wings which did not hang on to the airflow up to high angles of incidence; the flow separated comparatively early and this separation provided the traditional aerodynamic buffet by shaking the wing and by buffeting the tailplane (which buffet, it should be noted, was transmitted up the elevator control runs and thus shook the control column).

As wing design became more sophisticated, the flow was encouraged to hang on up to a higher incidence and the aerodynamic stall warning was either absent altogether or occurred too late to serve as an adequate warning.

Hence the stick shaker was used, and its fitting was a significant precedent in that it was one of the first examples of a lack of natural qualities being replaced by an artificial device.

In the field of warning stimuli one can only 'get at' a human being through one of his senses. Of the five senses, two — smell and taste — cannot be used in flying, or at least they haven't been yet. Of the remainder there is a definite order of preference — tactile, aural and visual. A pilot is always receptive to a tactile warning (a thump on the shoulder from an agitated flight engineer, say) and indeed an aural warning (perhaps a shout from an equally agitated co-pilot), but a visual warning pre-supposes the pilot to be looking in the area of the warning, and this cannot be relied upon.

In this context, therefore, a stick shaker is a good device in that it most nearly represents that which it is replacing; it shakes the stick and is tactile in its stimulus. There are times, however, when even the best stick shaker is inadequate. Such a time is when stall warning is required and the pilot's hands are not on the control column: when the aeroplane is on autopilot, for example, and particularly when on height lock. Under these conditions a very quiet stick shaker could not function as a stall warning and something else is needed to intrude on the aural sense. If the shaker happens to be noisy in its operation the noise serves as the aural warning. Some shakers, however, are very quiet indeed and in these cases a stick knocker is added in parallel to serve as the aural warning.

Stick shakers get their signal from a detector which is one of three types: a simple vane on the wing leading edge which is sensitive to the movement of the stagnation point around the leading edge close to the stall; a pressure differential system sensing substantially the same parameter; or an incidence measuring probe or vane mounted on the side of the fuselage. All of these sense incidence and, therefore, automatically take care of changes in all-up-weight; the better systems also compute rate of change of incidence and give earlier warning in the faster rates of approach to the stall. The detectors are sited either where they are not influenced by configuration changes or are datum compensated for configuration changes. They are always heated or anti-iced. The better systems have sensors on both sides to take out sideslip effect. All except the pressure differential type — and the rate term of all types — can be reasonably simply pre-flight tested, and this includes the electrical circuits. The stick shaker itself is a simple motor with an out-of-balance weight clamped to the pilot's control column. When this starts up it shakes the stick. There is a 'best' combination of frequency and amplitude which depends on the dynamics of the control column assembly. Too low a frequency fails to provide a sufficient stimulus even if the amplitude is comparatively large; too high a frequency merely results in a 'buzz' with no significant amplitude. To date, the optimum frequency has appeared to be between 10 to 30 c.p.s. with sufficient amplitude actually to move the yoke. Some care is taken during certification testing to adjust the frequency and amplitude of the shake so that it is clear and unmistakable and not compromised by turbulence or the high stick forces involved in manoeuvring on the forward C.G. Like everything else, the qualities required of stick shakers have changed over the years; some which were accepted years ago now feel too weak for words. A modern shaker really shakes (and knocks) the control column, properly reflecting the importance attached to stall warning.

As both pilots of a modern jet transport are supposed to enjoy equal facilities in flying the aeroplane, separate shakers (and knockers) should be fitted for each. Among other advantages this allows some flexibility in allowable deficiencies, particularly where knockers are fitted separately from the shakers. It is essential, for example in the design where one pilot's devices can be unserviceable as a despatch deficiency, that the other pilot's devices should be clearly felt and heard across the flight deck.

That just about covers stick shakers. They are not really new — they have been fitted to propeller turbine-engined aeroplanes for at least fourteen years. They have become accepted and pilot resistance to them has long since subsided. There is little briefing necessary on stick shakers; they work well, they are reliable and they warn of the approach to the stall under all flight conditions. They are a first-class example of the way in which a good reliable device can adequately replace a natural deficiency. Don't put the stick shakers inoperative without good reason, or take-off knowing them to be unserviceable. Remember that without stall warning your aeroplane's Certificate of Airworthiness is invalid.

Stick pushers

The subject of stick pushers is known to be rather a controversial one with some pilots at this time. While it is unfair of them to criticise something without full knowledge of the facts, it is equally unfair to expect operating pilots to accept a new philosophy without some explanation, in spite of the confidence which they are assumed to have in the constructors' test pilots, the certification test pilots and their own development or engineering pilots. Let us, therefore, look quietly at the facts and see what comes out in the wash.

Let it first be admitted that aeroplanes are fitted with stick pushers only when they have failed to meet the stalling requirements by normal aerodynamic means — and no-one pretends otherwise. This, however, is not quite so damaging as that rather naked statement implies. Just consider the facts.

There are several precedents for using an artificial device to make up for a natural deficiency. For example, we can mention yaw dampers to counter dutch roll, Mach trimmers to counter longitudinal instability and stick shakers to provide stall warning.

There is, therefore, nothing intrinsically wrong in using a stick pusher to

130

replace the stall artificially. It is only a logical extension of the philosophy. Additionally the pusher is required to work only when the wing arrives at its 'stalling' incidence which, in normal operation, will not be as often as the need to operate some of the other devices. These can be required to work on every flight, and not only required to work on every flight, but in some instances, work continuously. Some aircraft cruise in the range where the Mach trimmer is active and others fly for long periods when the yaw dampers are working full time. It is no good beefing about these devices. The very qualities of jet transports demand them, and it would be a positive handicap to the development of the high speed high altitude aeroplane to insist that acceptable levels of handling qualities be provided by natural means. It can't be done, and to progress we must have these devices.

All this philosophy is conditional upon the qualification imposed that the device must be sufficiently reliable. Now 'sufficiently reliable' in this case is defined as:—

(a) **On failing to operate when required to operate** The stall probability rate of 1 in 100,000 $\times$ the per flight failure rate of 1 in 100 flights = 1 in 10 million; which is the same rate as that assumed for failure in a blind landing. Expressed more simply this means that, 99 times out of a 100 occasions on which the aeroplane is stalled (which is once in every hundred thousand flights), the pusher will push and recover the aeroplane; on the hundredth occasion the pusher is assumed to have failed and the aeroplane possibly suffers a catastrophe. But this will occur only once in 10 million flights. However much you might object to this possibility, it is an acceptable level (because it is extremely remote) and one on which are based a lot of the other risks which are run in civil airline operation.

(b) **On operating when not required to operate (the runaway case)** For a modest upset, 1 in 100,000 flights; for a severe upset, 1 in 10 million flights. (A modest upset is defined as not worse than zero 'g'. A severe upset is defined as significantly negative 'g' but not beyond proof negative. These values are closely related to autopilot certification which even the stoutest opponent of stick pushers never seems to question.)

These values have been proven to have been met on present stick pusher installations, and the argument should now proceed on the assumption that the reliability is to the required standard. This having been established then it really doesn't matter whether the stalling requirements are met naturally or artificially.

If a stick pusher is used to meet the stall requirements it must provide two qualities: clear and unmistakable identification of the stall, by a sharp positive forward movement of the control column, and an adequate nose down pitch by the aircraft.

The sharpness of the push is necessary to identify the stall instantly because a slowish sort of push might allow a pilot to pull too far into the deeper area. The amount and duration of the push are tailored to give a good positive recovery manoeuvre under all configurations, all C.G. positions and for varying rates of entry to the stall. The push is cancelled at a lower safe incidence when the stick returns to its previous position. The push is frequently cancelled as the shake is cancelled so that when stall recovery is complete all the devices cancel together.

It is obvious that those constructors forced to use stick pusher installations did so because they either found that their natural stall was quite unacceptable, or were not prepared to investigate the aeroplane's qualities beyond Max. C_L by other than a small margin, or decided that some part of their structure could not take the hammering in the violent buffet before the nose drop.

It follows from all these considerations, therefore, that the stick pusher must always prevent the natural stall being reached in service. To cater for this some rate sensitive phase advance system must be provided to look after the cases where the stall is approached in accelerated flight conditions.

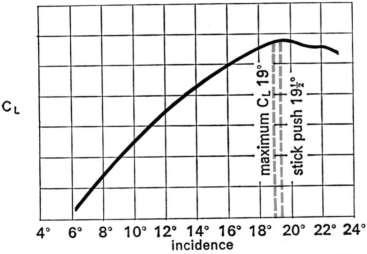

C_L

maximum C_L 19°

stick push $19\frac{1}{2}$°

4° 6° 8° 10° 12° 14° 16° 18° 20° 22° 24°
incidence

Figure 5.25   Relationship between stick pusher firing incidence and Max. C_L incidence.

Because the lift curves on some second generation jets are typically rather flat-topped the pusher is set to operate just after Max. C_L so that the wing is allowed to develop its maximum lift even when the device operates at the earliest edge of its tolerance. In a slow straight stall approach, therefore, the pusher will never operate before the wing has developed its maximum lift. In order to cater for configuration changes there are datum adjustments which automatically reset as flaps and slats are extended and retracted.

The accelerated stall approach cases are looked after by the phase advance sub-system which operates the pusher earlier by an amount proportional to the rate of change of the value being measured, so that the pitching momentum in the aeroplane never takes the wing significantly beyond Max. C_L. The pusher pushes early, and the overswing due to momentum does not take the aeroplane beyond a safe incidence value. This phase advance, however, is not allowed to inhibit the manoeuvre capability of the aeroplane. The 'g' increments at low speeds which flight recorder results show to be necessary in normal operation are retained; for example, a demonstration of 0.4g increment at V_2 is required. Early phase advance systems were based on rate of change of pitch using a twin rate gyro system. These systems have definite limitations in that rate of change of pitch bears only an assumed relationship to the really significant parameter, which is incidence. These systems expose the aeroplane to the remoter cases of a rapid rate of change of incidence at small rates of change of pitch where the phase advance sub-system cannot be active. Later designs employ rate of change of incidence so that the device can never be fooled.

The force of the push is typically about 80 lb.; this is high enough to stop the pilot strangling it when it operates, yet not too high to hold in the runaway condition. Provision is made to dump the entire system in the event of a runaway or a potential fault condition. There are the usual associated flight deck instrumentation and pre-flight testing facilities.

The incidence at which the device operates also gives the speeds used for performance scheduling purposes, and advantage can be taken of the V_{MS} philosophy so that a stick push stall speed equates exactly to a natural stall speed.

Certification pilots are no different from any other pilots, except that their loyalties lie in a direction which causes them to examine their technical consciences most closely sometimes. This is not suggesting in any way that constructors' and operators' pilots take their responsibilities lightly. But in the last analysis, particularly when only opinions can be called upon in the absence of positive proof, there is a tendency for everyone to lean rather heavily on the certification pilot. His is the ultimate responsibility, and he weighs matters very carefully indeed before coming to a decision which could have far-reaching effect in all sorts of directions and ramifications in the light of subsequent experience. The certification pilot is in a stronger position than other pilots, and he realises that he must exercise his authority with the judgement almost of a Solomon.

The initial certification of stick pushers was one such case. Present any pilot with a device instead of a natural quality and he will look sideways at it until it is proved to his satisfaction. In accepting a device instead of a natural quality there is a very human desire to make the device prove itself absolutely and, on stick pushing aeroplanes, the stall requirements have been applied more fiercely than ever before. Accelerated stalls have been done at very high rates of change of incidence equating to a 0.8g increment and speed reductions of up to 8 knots per second in some configurations. This is a lot fiercer than anything done on aeroplanes without stick pushers. There are many older aeroplanes flying which will not look at any stall requirements under manoeuvres of this severity.

So much for stick pushers in stall manoeuvres. Now what about the runaway cases, which are perhaps a more important matter to those pilots who cannot stand the thought of a stick pusher. The runaway cases have been investigated and they are much milder than was at first thought. A simulated push soon after take-off merely results in a reduction from, say, an indicated 3,000 f.p.m. rate of climb to an indicated 2,000 f.p.m. rate of climb over a two second delay period, and the disturbance to the flight path is quite small. Similarly on the approach. The aeroplane dips below the glide slope by about a hundred feet and is fairly easily recovered. A runaway in the holding pattern at 200 knots also loses less than 100 feet over a good two second delay period.

The high speed runaway cases are protected in different ways on different types. For example, one has a limited travel push; the push is always distinct enough to properly identify the stall, yet just not disturbing enough to qualify as a severe upset. This pusher can run away at V_{MO} and M_{MO} and not exceed 1g increment. Because of its limited stroke this pusher can also run away on any part of the take-off and landing without hazarding the aeroplane. Another type has a speed cut-out at about 250 knots. Up to this speed the pusher will push in a stall; above this speed the pusher is inactive because a stall would involve load factors exceeding proof 'g' or be equiv-alent to a gust in excess of the assumed maximum gust for stressing cases of 66 ft. per second. Yet another variation has no protection against a high speed runaway push because the feel system and the PCU blow-off values are such that they prevent a significant amount of elevator being applied. Remember that a stick pusher exerts a force only and does not apply a defined elevator angle.

Accept then that a stick push runaway, while certainly a surprise, is no great hazard. It approximates very broadly to the older autopilot runaways, which never stopped pilots using the autopilot.

There is one exception to these generalised statements. On those types where the pusher pushes the stick full stroke, it is true that the aeroplane can be hazarded by a pusher runaway at some low height on the approach. Down to, say, about 120 ft. and again below, say, 10 ft. there should be no trouble. The first case might lead to a baulk and the second to a hard landing. The defence for this case is in two parts:—

(a) Between 120 ft. and 10 ft. it can be assumed that the pilot is alert and has his hands on the control column. Consequently he should be able to counter a runaway in less than 2 seconds thus reducing the critical height band to a much smaller value.

(b) In the remaining height band one simply has to live on the improbability of its occurrence. It has been stated that a modest upset must not occur more frequently than 1 in 100,000 flights, but it should be noted that the aeroplane is only at risk for a few seconds per flight. To get at the real risk, therefore, one must multiply 1 in 100,000 by the number of seconds it takes to traverse this critical height band in a typical flight. As pushers are fitted to short range and long range aeroplanes let us take one hour as the typical flight and 10 seconds as the time at risk; we then arrive at 1 in 100,000 × 360 = 1 in 36 million occasions.

This we just have to live with. The problem is far less than the normal risk of an accident resulting from any single cause.

Well now, where do we stand? Stick pushers have been very carefully designed and very thoroughly tested. Those pilots who have considerable experience of them have long since 'bought' them with a completely clear conscience, and this includes some of the toughest nuts who were quite violently opposed to stick pushers before they got their hands on them. Stick pushers protect aeroplanes from hazardous flight conditions and give them virtually immaculate stalling qualities. Their behaviour in extreme turbulence has been checked in simulators and is predicted to be just as reliable — every time that wing gets up to maximum incidence the pusher will operate and immediately reduce incidence. When the pilot is fully extended, it will act long before the pilot himself would, and will do in advance what he might possibly leave a little late, i.e. reduce incidence.

There is little more to say except to repeat the conclusions which appeared under stick shakers. Stick pushers work well, are reliable and confer immaculate stall qualities. They are another good example of a device adequately replacing a natural deficiency. Get to know what the push feels like during training. The training technique is fully written up in Flight Manuals. Do not deactivate the pusher without good reason. Remember that without the pusher a full stall is likely to be a most hazardous manoeuvre.

The design and requirement philosophy of stick pushers

It is not intended to go deeply into this subject. Most of the required qualities of a stick pusher system have already been covered. The handling qualities, reliability standard and runaway cases certainly have. On the reliability side there is a good bonus in real life. When a designer is asked to meet a failure to push rate of not worse than 1 in 100, in making absolutely sure that he does meet it he produces a system which is at least an order better, and the likely failure rate is more like 1 in 1,000. The detailed engineering design of these systems is such that several unrelated failures need to occur before a spurious push can occur. One system requires three separate failures in a defined sequence before the pusher will give a false push. The

135

probability of this occurring is extremely remote. One or perhaps two of these failures merely result in a 'lock out', which is indicated by a warning light signifying that part of the push circuit has become active but has been immediately cancelled by a safety circuit. Because of the difference in reliability levels required, the design is heavily biased towards not pushing when not required rather than making sure of a push when required.

The push is cancelled at an angle of incidence related to a good recovery incidence. This often equates to the incidence required for stick shake so that, after stall recovery is complete, the push and shake cancel together. A small lag of up to one-fifth of a second is employed in the push circuit to give protection against unnecessary operation of the stick pusher in sharp-edge turbulence. The pusher does not have to be armed; it is active all the time that electrical power is on the aeroplane. Complete instrumentation is provided to indicate its correct functioning and failure cases. Lights are specifically provided to warn of and indicate the arming of any part of the pusher circuit. A dump system is provided which will completely deactivate the push, and the dump lever is conspicuous when in the dumped position. Once having been dumped it cannot normally be reset in flight.

With the need for stick shake, stick push and auto-ignition all relating to incidence it was a logical move to integrate all these systems with one comprehensive stall protection system. Some of the latest jet transports have comprehensive stall protection systems which look after auto-ignition, stick shake and stick push. Complete duplication is provided by separate incidence detectors for warning and identification on both sides of the fuselage. Both pilots have their own shakers and, where necessary, knockers. Additionally there is a warning horn, a rather strident klaxon, in parallel with each pusher circuit. There is a high degree of protection; a simple failure loses only a very small part of the overall system. The stick push jack is the only unduplicated part. It is a very simple and very reliable piece of engineering. Its required level of reliability of course is not all that high (a minimum of 1 in 100), and in its inactive position it is not tied to the control column directly.

The general design and the reliability standard of the stall protection system of a modern jet transport properly reflect its importance in the overall certification of the aeroplane.

A typical stick pusher installation

It will be appreciated that in order to meet the requirements a fairly comprehensive stick pusher system is required. In practice it has been found to be logical to combine the stick pusher system with the well established stall warning system and to inter-relate them for improved safety. Judged by modern standards the resulting system, although complicated, is not unduly so. For ease of understanding the following description has been simplified, but nevertheless it contains the significant features of the systems now in service.

A line diagram of the system (figure 5.26) is included and the following description is best read in conjunction with this diagram. A study of the diagram should make the operation of the system fairly clear.

Basic signals The system has been designed to operate from signals initiated by the airflow relative to the wing, thus maintaining a direct relationship with incidence, the main stalling parameter. These signals pass through the main body of the system and out to operate the stick shake and stick pusher units. Additionally, a signal is fed out to an auto-ignition device, as it has been found that pre-stall buffeting can cause engine malfunctioning, particularly with rear mounted engines.

The signal sensing system The measurement of incidence is made by probes or vanes trailing in the airstream. These are fitted at the fuselage side. The incidence taken up by these vanes initiates a signal at a predetermined value, this value also being varied according to the rate of change of incidence. The latter refinement is necessary to cover the dynamic stall case whereby the aircraft might overswing beyond a safe incidence. Once the aircraft incidence has been reduced to below a set value the signal is cut off.

There are two vanes per side of the aircraft which, in the interests of reliability, operate two virtually separate systems. A further sub-division is that one vane per side operates the stick shaker and auto-ignition, the other operating the stick pusher. As a safeguard against false stick pushes, it has been arranged that a stick shake signal is necessary before a stick push signal can pass right through the system.

The auto-ignition signal is set off at the lowest incidence of the three settings used, i.e. auto-ignition, stick shake, and stick push. No rate of change of incidence factor is fed into this signal as it is set well in advance of the other two, and also before the value at which engine malfunctioning occurs. The signal goes virtually directly to the auto-ignition device.

Stick shake signalling is initiated next, and in order to maintain the pre-stall margin it incorporates the rate of change of incidence factor. The signal passes to a unit where any configuration bias, i.e. flap setting, is fed in and then passes to a priority unit. The function of this unit is to hold one signal in reserve and pass the other on should signals from each side of the aircraft be received simultaneously. The passed signal then goes on to the stick shakers and to prime the stick push system.

The highest incidence setting of the three initiates the stick push sequence. Rate of change of incidence, configuration bias, priority checks, etc. are applied as for stick shake, and provided that the system has been primed by a stick shake signal, the stick push signal is allowed to pass to the final stage.

137

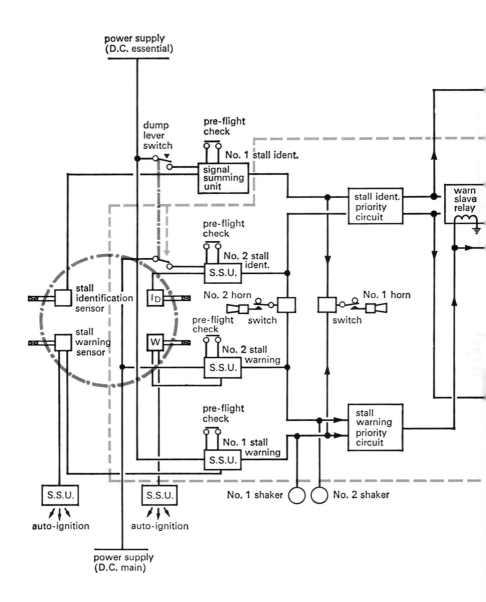

Figure 5.26 A typical stick pusher system.

138

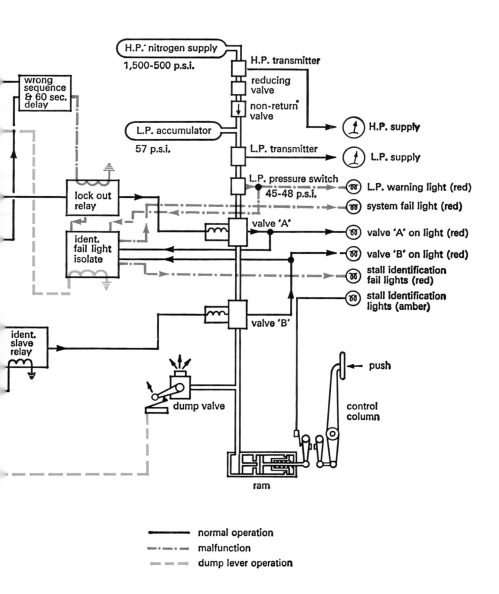

wrong sequence & 60 sec. delay

H.P. nitrogen supply
1,500-500 p.s.i.

H.P. transmitter

reducing valve

non-return valve

H.P. supply

L.P. accumulator
57 p.s.i.

L.P. transmitter

L.P. supply

lock out relay

L.P. pressure switch
45-48 p.s.i.

L.P. warning light (red)

system fail light (red)

ident. fail light isolate

valve 'A'

valve 'A' on light (red)

valve 'B' on light (red)

stall identification fail lights (red)

stall identification lights (amber)

ident. slave relay

valve 'B'

dump valve

push

control column

ram

———— normal operation

—·—·— malfunction

— — — dump lever operation

139

Before a stick push signal is allowed to reach the operating unit further safeguards are now involved. Typical of those used in systems already in service are incorrect sequence lock outs, time delays to avoid nuisance pushes in turbulence, and time limiters. The first two are self explanatory. The last is desirable to lock out a stick push signal if the push signal does not follow the shake signal in an appropriate period of time.

The nature of the system lends itself to electrical circuits and power for all functions right from the incidence vanes to the stick push opening jack. The jack itself is operated by a pneumatic system. Auto-ignition and stick shake are electrically operated. All parts of the system exposed to extreme atmospheric conditions are suitably protected to ensure satisfactory functioning.

The pneumatic system to the stick push jack This system is comparatively straightforward. High pressure nitrogen is supplied from a bottle through various valves and a low pressure accumulator to Valve A and Valve B. When these valves are opened by the signal sensing circuit the supply reaches the ram and pushes the control column. The dump valve when operated immediately exhausts the air from the stick push ram.

Indicators The system operates completely automatically, but as an aid to trouble shooting, pre-flight checking and inflight information, a system of warnings and indicators is provided. It is not intended to go into detail here, but ample indication is available to pre-flight check each part of the system. Also, any inflight malfunction will be indicated well before the aircraft can be affected.

The system described is similar in broad principles to those now in service on several types of modern aircraft. An increasing amount of operational experience is being gathered on the maintenance and reliability of these systems, and this to a great extent has supported the original thinking on the matter.

Speed stability

This may be defined as the behaviour of the speed following a speed disturbance, without considering any interaction from stability in pitch, at a fixed power setting. Perhaps this isn't the world's most elegant definition of speed stability, but it will do, so far as speed alone can be isolated. The speed is stable if an increase in speed leads to an increase in drag; this tends to return the speed to its original value. Similarly, a decrease in speed leading to a decrease in drag will again tend to return the speed to its original value. The speed is unstable if a decrease in speed leads to an *increase* in drag which therefore leads to a further decrease in speed and hence a speed divergence. Similarly, if an increase in speed leads to a *decrease* in drag speed stability will again be negative.

While the problems of speed stability exists in all configurations let us limit ourselves to the approach case, because this is the most critical area. It will be remembered that the total drag of an aeroplane is the sum of the induced drag and the profile drag which vary with speed as indicated in figure 5.27. For an aeroplane at constant weight in steady flight (either level or on a 3° glide slope for example) the picture can be redrawn plotting power required against speed.

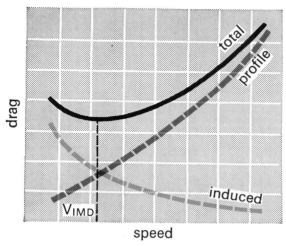

Figure 5.27   Variation of drag with speed.

Figures 5.28 and 5.29 show the essential differences between a piston-engined transport and a jet transport.   These are firstly the different shapes of the power required curve for the piston-engined aircraft and the drag curve of the jet aircraft and secondly the relationship of the 1.3Vs (recommended threshold speed) point with the V_{IMP} or V_{IMD} (speeds for minimum power or minimum drag respectively) points on the curves.   The graphs do not represent any particular aeroplanes and are deliberately exaggerated to highlight the differences.

The piston picture shows that the recommended speed lies above the minimum power speed and that the aeroplane is flying in the speed stable area; that is, less speed requires less power and so on.   The jet picture, however, shows that, due to the comparative flatness of the drag curve over a range of speeds, the recommended speed is in the speed 'neutral' area and that it is difficult to select an exact power for the speed required.   Additionally, 1.3Vs is actually lower than V_{IMD}, so if the speed should be further reduced then the aeroplane is already speed unstable in that for a reduced speed *more* power is required.   This is because the aeroplane is now sliding up the back end of the power required curve where power is required is increasing with reducing speed.   This means that, although at the higher lift coefficient associated with lower speeds more lift is produced, the drag increases faster than the lift increases, the lift/drag ratio degrades and the net result is a tendency to go on losing speed and, of course, to enter a sinking flight path profile.

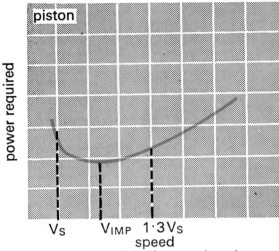

Figure 5.28 Location of significant speeds on the power required curve-piston.

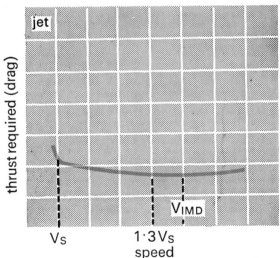

Figure 5.29 Location of significant speeds on the drag curve-jet.

Figure 5.29 illustrates a worst case for a jet-engined aircraft with a 1.3Vs value *below* the V_{IMD} point; this is only true of some aeroplanes. There are

142

many with the 1.3Vs value above V$_{IMD}$, in which case the aeroplane has slight but positive speed stability.

The problem so far has been argued only in terms of power required in the case of the piston-engined aeroplane and thrust required in that of the jet-engined aeroplane. This approach was chosen because, as a first approximation, with changing airspeed power tends to stay constant for a piston/propeller combination whereas thrust tends to stay constant for a jet. In a piston/propeller combination, thrust changes with speed in a fashion which improves the speed stability of the aeroplane, i.e. thrust tends to decrease with increased speed and increase with decreased speed, and these tendencies assist the aeroplane to return to the original steady speed condition. The explanation is simply that if we assume that the power remains constant at a fixed manifold pressure and r.p.m., and that propeller efficiency does not change significantly with small changes in airspeed, then the rate of doing work remains constant. If, therefore, the speed is decreased, then the thrust must be increased, and similarly if the speed is increased then the thrust must be decreased, i.e. rate of doing work (power) = a constant × velocity × thrust. In the case of the jet aircraft, thrust remains substantially constant with small changes in speed. The jet picture, therefore, is not complicated by changes in thrust with speed, and the speed stability qualities of the aeroplane are a function only of the variation of airframe drag with speed as already explained.

Compared with the piston-engined aeroplane, the jet aircraft's speed stability qualities are poorer because of (a) its variation of drag with speed tending to be in the unstable relationship range and (b) the absence of thrust changes with speed which were stabilising in the case of the piston-engined aircraft.

Aeroplanes with good speed stability (and a number of modern jets come in this category) can be flown on the approach with never any need to look at the power gauges. It is broadly true to say that wherever one sets and leaves the thrust levers always seems to be just about the 'right' place for them to be. An aeroplane with neutral or negative speed stability however (and there are some about) is difficult and irritating to fly on the approach. It is not possible, instinctively, to make a power selection and have confidence that the setting will do for the next minute or so. One soon has to make a power alteration, then another, and another, and eventually the power selected gets a long way away from where it ought to be. One has then to go back to the datum thrust setting for the approach and start all over again, but this time making deliberate, calculated changes in r.p.m. values related to the airspeed trends and allowing sufficient time between changes to assess the effect on airspeed.

A falling airspeed trend on the approach on a speed unstable aeroplane needs more power than you might at first imagine to counteract it. A little power fails to stop the speed falling further, a little more might just hold the speed constant at its lower level, but none of this is good enough. Your need is to get back to your target airspeed. So apply a fair bit of extra thrust and

143

get your airspeed back, but then immediately revert to a power setting just a little above your original value. Excess thrust left on too long will quickly produce excess speed which is difficult to lose quickly without yet another large change in the thrust setting.

To watch, as an academic exercise, a pilot struggling with speed instability, without full knowledge of the problems he is having to struggle with, is to see a typically divergent pattern of behaviour building up. Power lever movements get larger and larger, speed divergences get bigger and bigger and finally, the whole thing gets substantially out of control.

This is the worst that can happen, and it is not suggested that present-day jet transports are anything like as bad as this. Some, however, are speed unstable on the approach and that divergent tendency is there. With a bit of care and practice there should be no difficulty in handling this problem. Get used to monitoring your airspeed and particularly your airspeed trends very closely. Pick up the trends before they become significant and put them right, either by a movement of the elevator control (if the vertical component of the flight path will accept it), or by a calculated alteration in engine power. Then see the effect of the change and make a further, smaller correction when necessary. In this manner a very smooth approach can be flown with apparently no effort, and anyone watching would not believe that there was such a thing as poor speed stability.

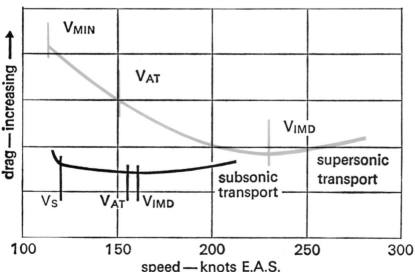

Figure 5.30 Comparison of subsonic and supersonic aircraft drag curves.

Finally, a word about the probable speed stability of a slender-delta supersonic transport. Figure 5.30, plotted in similar values, compares

144

one typical subsonic jet with the forecast qualities of an SST. With the knowledge that the reader now has, the picture really tells its own story. Notice how far up the back end of the drag curve the threshold speed is compared with the speed for minimum drag. There are some present-day delta planform jet fighters flying which have roughly the same shape drag against speed curves. They can be flown and landed without any stability augmentation and with manual power lever control; but they are difficult to handle and need a high degree of skill and concentration.

SST designers have already accepted the fact that this level of flying quality has no place in the civil air transport world. Stability augmentation and a proper auto-throttle system (one which puts in speed stability artificially — not merely auto-throttle for speed holding) are both coming along as part of the basic design. While we have this SST picture in front of us let us introduce a short digression. The point marked V_{MIN} is likely to be the lowest speed demonstrated in testing, approximately equating to the stall speed on a subsonic aeroplane. However, at a speed higher than this there will occur a condition where the drag is so high that full power on all engines will only just maintain the aeroplane in level flight (and at yet a higher speed of course in the engine out case). This speed is known as the 'zero rate of climb speed'. Opinion is hardening towards the philosophy of equating *this* speed to the stall speed for performance and handling certification purposes because the two speeds are very similar in their qualities. That is, recovery cannot be effected without a loss of height.

Spoilers

The case for spoilers is a little involved. They are fitted for several reasons, but all eventually lead back to the fact that the aeroplane flies at high speed.

Firstly, the ailerons on a jet transport are limited in size because as much of the trailing edge of the wing as possible is needed for flaps. This is because the lifting ability of the wing section is poor at low speeds because it is designed to fly fast. Secondly, large ailerons on a thin swept high speed wing would twist the wing too much and produce aileron reversal effects. Thirdly, ailerons tend to lose effectiveness at very high Mach numbers, and very large ailerons can cause a large adverse yaw. Fourthly, a swept high speed wing causes a strong roll with yaw and therefore additional roll control is needed. Fifthly, there is a need for high drag devices because the aeroplane itself has low drag. Sixthly, there is a need to dump the lift off the wing and on to the wheels on landing because the aeroplane has high ground speed. Basically all these considerations arise because the aeroplane is designed to fly fast.

To make up for the necessarily small ailerons, the spoilers provide additional roll control. Spoilers are opening panels in the top surface of the wing arranged spanwise between the inboard end of the ailerons and the fuselage. They vary in number, are power operated because the operating force required is beyond the strength of the pilot, are connected to the normal aileron control and work in unison with the ailerons for lateral control. When used for roll control they open on the side of the upgoing aileron, spoil the lift on that side and help drive that wing down.   They are also connected to the speed brake control and work symmetrically across the aeroplane for producing drag and also for dumping lift off the wing on landing.

Spoilers, when already extended as speed brakes, are still operative in terms of lateral control.   There are two significantly different designs.   *Non-differential* spoilers will extend on one side in response to a roll demand *but will not retract on the other side.   Differential* spoilers are slightly more sophisticated and will extend on one side in response to a roll demand *and will retract on the other side.*   The following table shows spoiler behaviour in a typical manoeuvre — a roll to the right from a laterally level condition.

	Non-differential	Differential
Speed brake fully retracted	Right spoilers extend Left spoilers remain retracted	Right spoilers extend Left spoilers remain retracted
Speed brake fully extended	Right spoilers remain extended Left spoilers remain extended	Right spoilers remain extended *Left spoilers retract*
Speed brake half extended	Right spoilers extend further Left spoilers do not move	Right spoilers extend further *Left spoilers retract*

There are two points which should be noted particularly as they will be needed later.   In the differential type, roll response varies with speed brake extension and is at its highest with half speed brake selected; this is because *both* spoilers respond to the roll demand.   In the non-differential type, the spoilers *do not* supplement the ailerons in roll control when the speed brakes are fully extended.

Spoilers generally do a lot of trade in terms of lateral control and can be capable of producing up to half of the total rolling power in the aeroplane.

In normal operation spoilers form a part of the lateral control and work quite normally; if used sharply, however, they usually cause momentary buffet as the flow breaks down behind them.   For several reasons, it is worth knowing the spectacle angle at which they start to crack open.   Firstly because if care is not taken to trim the aeroplane accurately they can be cracked open on one side only, which will cause unnecessary drag; and secondly, because of the discontinuity in the roll response rate, which occurs as the spoilers start to supplement the ailerons if the spoiler initiation angle is more than a few degrees from the zero roll control angle.

Failure cases are worth a little thought.   If they all fail, the remaining lateral control is normally quite adequate for a continued flight to the destination, although control loads will naturally be higher for a given response.   Also, it would obviously be wise not to accept too high a cross-wind component for the landing.   You will of course be denied their use as speed brakes and lift dumpers.   The spoilers are normally split in pairs, and

146

a single failure results in the loss of only a proportion of the spoilers. The reduction in lateral control is then proportional to the loss. If one spoiler section should fail extended, the aeroplane will suffer a rolling tendency; the solution is to deactivate the part of the system supplying that particular spoiler.

There is one difficulty with spoiler design worth special mention. It is clearly true that an aeroplane designed to use spoilers for lateral control will suffer reduced rolling ability if the use of the spoilers should be denied to the pilot (and here we are excluding any *failure* of the spoiler systems). Unfortunately this condition did arise (with a fully serviceable aeroplane) on a number of types of jet transport aircraft. The problem arose like this. At very high speeds, the spoilers, when selected fully out symmetrically as speed brakes naturally blew back some way under the high air loads (they are designed to do just this). The fact that the spoilers blew back on a non-differential design was of no significance, because the spoilers were not designed to operate for roll control when already selected fully out as speed brakes. But it was a disappointment to find that the differential design also gave trouble. Despite the fact that the spoilers should have retracted on one side in response to a roll demand, this did not occur. It so happened that the retracting differential spoilers had a design minimum retraction angle of 15° extended. The difficulty arose because the blow back angle at high speed was already *less than* 15°; so the retraction signal could not be effective. So with both designs we ended up with exactly the same difficulty — no roll control from the spoilers when fully extended. This meant that the ailerons had to do all the work.

This wouldn't have been so bad if the ailerons had continued to work at high speeds, but that didn't happen either. Ailerons lose effect at high speeds due to wing twisting, excessive control loads combined with circuit stretch and Mach number effect. Where these effects are marked, aileron effectiveness can reduce to zero. The net result was that, with the brakes out, at the coincidence of M_{DF} with V_{DF} (typically, around 19,000 to 22,000 ft.) there was just no lateral control at all.

The position was further worsened by the fact that, at very high Mach numbers, these types (in common with most jet transports) suffered a reversed rolling moment due to sideslip. In simple terms, pushing left rudder caused a roll to the *right* instead of to the left. Where this reversal was significant control difficulties were compounded.

While all this was of absorbing interest to test pilots, there was a very real read across to the every day operation of the aeroplane in terms of the 'jet upset' type of incident. The sort of behaviour described does not of course occur up to the normal maximum speed approved for service use, i.e. M_{MO}/V_{MO}, but it could and did occur at the design limits of V_{DF}/M_{DF} and was obviously worse where these two values coincided.

'Jet upsets' usually result in a high speed dive with the strong probability of a large bank angle. Having appreciated his flight condition the pilot

147

naturally extends the speed brakes. With the spoiler design limitations described there was nothing left to assist the ailerons. On finding no rolling power remaining by means of the normal lateral control, he would then apply rudder to assist a turn, only to discover that the aeroplane rolled further the wrong way. Not a very happy state of affairs!

On three different aeroplanes the problem was solved in three different ways:—

(a) On the type with differential spoilers the design Mach limits were arbitrarily lowered so that, at the original value of V_{DF}, but with a reduced M_{DF}, adequate roll rates were achieved with the speed brakes out. To make this more than just a change on paper M_{MO} was reduced proportionally to provide substantially the same speed margins. None of this 'hurt' the aeroplane operationally because even the reduced M_{MO} was still comfortably higher than the highest likely cruise Mach number.

(b) One of the non-differential spoiler designs was fixed by restricting the maximum spoiler angle in the speed brake mode (in flight) to a value *below* the blow back angle. This then always provided some upgoing spoiler movement in response to a lateral control demand. Although the amount was not much it was sufficient, at these high speeds, to provide an adequate rate of roll. The restriction in this instance was effected by the manual operation of a collar on the speed brake lever. Operated after take-off and before landing it restricted the in-flight angle, yet permitted full spoiler extension on the ground.

(c) The other non-differential spoiler design was also fixed by restricting speed brake angle; but this time, automatically, as a function of speed. A speed sensitive device, operating at about V_{MO} + 15 knots, served two functions. It restricted maximum angle if the brakes were selected above V_{MO} + 15k.; it also automatically retracted the brakes from full extension to the restricted angle if the brakes had been fully extended below V_{MO} and the aeroplane then accelerated to a speed above V_{MO} + 15 knots. Again, the restricted angle always allowed some upgoing spoiler to provide adequate roll rates.

All three types now have adequate rates of roll, at all combinations of speed, Mach number and altitude, up to the design limits of V_{DF} and M_{DF}.

This development story explains speed brake restricting devices on some types. They are there for good reason, so don't override them unless you know exactly what you are doing and why you are doing it. Just to complete the story for those who see the 'loose end' it should be stated that, where reversed rudder effect exists at high Mach number, the roll rate to be demonstrated *includes* this 'wrong' rudder effect. So that if, instinctively, a pilot should apply rudder to help (!) himself he can comparatively easily overpower the reversed rudder effect and still achieve adequate controllability on the lateral control.

148

6 Flying higher

High mach number

Stability

As discussed under the heading of sweep, there is a Mach number at which the airflow over the wing becomes sonic and the wing experiences shock wave effect. This has three distinct consequences:—

(a) The shock wave on the upper surface upsets the lift distribution chordwise and causes a rearwards shift in the centre of lift.

(b) The swept wing tends to experience shock wave effect at the thick root end first causing a loss of lift inboard and therefore forwards.

(c) The shock waves cause a reduction in downwash over the tail.

All three effects cause the aeroplane to pitch nose down. In the case of (a) this is obvious. In the case of (b) it is because the tips maintain lift aft of the mean centre of lift and in the case of (c) because the balancing force exerted by the tail is reduced (unless countered by up elevator). The aeroplane thus becomes increasingly unstable at increasing Mach number.

In a few cases, as the Mach number is further increased, the stability tends to return. This is due partly to the upper and lower shock waves, which were out of line (the lower shock being forward of the upper shock), moving aft and lining up and thus shifting the centre of lift forwards again; and partly to the shock wave effect spreading towards the tip from the root end thus re-balancing the lift across the span. The reverse applies of course as the aeroplane is decelerated from a very high Mach number to a lower Mach number. This tendency for the stability to return at very high Mach number is usually found on those types which have an M_{DF} in the region of 0.95 TMN. Slower types, with an M_{DF} around 0.85, usually terminate their high Mach runs at 0.85 still in an increasingly unstable condition.

The easiest way to illustrate this is to plot a graph of elevator stick force to maintain a range of Mach numbers over the critical Mach range from an initial trimmed condition. A typical graph from 0.8 to 0.95 IMN looks something like figure 6.1.

This shows that for an intended high Mach run you are required to push gently up to 0.86, because the stability is positive, but that this push force reduces to zero at around 0.88 (neutral stability). The aeroplane then goes nose down and you have to hold an increasing pull force to stop it running away; at something like 0.92 (where the instability is at its worst) you are holding a 60 lb. pull force. This pull force then decreases until at 0.95 it is again zero and the aeroplane is back in trim. The whole process repeats in reverse during recovery back to 0.8 IMN.

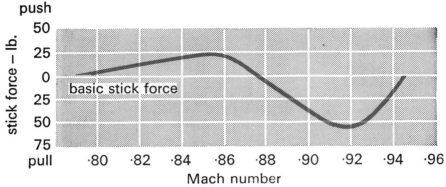

Figure 6.1   Stick force against Mach number.

This picture is typical of some jet transport aircraft.   The demand on the pilot is not so very high in terms of high Mach number demonstrations under good flying conditions; sixty pounds is not such a high stick force when compared with the stick force required to flare on some of the older piston-engined transports.   In service, however, this instability is quite unaccept-able because a small lack of attention could result in the aeroplane slipping quietly away to very high Mach numbers well beyond the permitted maximum.

Very high Mach numbers are normally accompanied by two other charac-teristics — marked increase in drag and the onset of aircraft buffet.   Not too much comfort can be drawn, however, from either of these.   In the first case, although it is true that drag increasing because of the breakdown in flow will result in a stick free stabilised Mach number maybe not exceeding M_{DF} at very high altitudes, at lower altitudes, in seeking the same stabilised speed in terms of Mach number, the aeroplane would go way beyond its V_{DF} limit in terms of EAS.   In the second case, while it is true again that buffet sets in at very high Mach numbers, it is also true that on many aero-planes it is impossible, subjectively, for the pilot to distinguish between high Mach number buffet and pre-stall buffet, particularly at very high altitudes where the actual speeds at which these occur are not too far divorced.   At the absolute aerodynamic ceiling of the aeroplane these speeds are coincident.

So, while it is true that high Mach number stability investigated under good crew training conditions can be made to look rather innocuous, in terms of real life flying it is much more significant.

The constructor is now left with the choice of limiting the operation of the aeroplane to a margin below the onset of the instability (as agreed with the

150

certification authority) or fixing the instability. The first alternative is operationally unacceptable and, since the difficulty by its very nature cannot be fixed aerodynamically, it is fixed artificially (see the next sub-chapter on Mach trimmers).

Controllability

Apart from stability, high Mach numbers can reduce controllability about all axes. Reference has been made earlier to some of these cases. Let us now just summarise them briefly:—

Directional This is the reversed rolling moment due to sideslip which causes the aeroplane to roll the wrong way in response to applied rudder. The application of right rudder, for example, certainly accelerates the left wing but, instead of picking up lift, it is driven deeper into compressibility, loses lift and so rolls the aeroplane the wrong way. This is potentially dangerous when in combination with reduced rolling ability. As nearly all jet transports suffer a reduction in rudder effectiveness at very high Mach numbers, if not actual reversal, it is safest to keep the rudder central and effect recovery to level flight on the roll control alone.

Lateral All control surfaces (except perhaps spoilers) tend to lose effectiveness at high Mach numbers and this is true whether the surface is manually operated or power operated. If very high hinge moments are experienced additionally, then the manual control becomes very heavy to operate and the powered control, depending on its system design, may suffer jack stalling. This will be felt either as a sudden solid stop or as an ability to apply further control, without much of an increase in force, accompanied by no further response from the control.

Compounding the reduction in aileron effect can be loss of roll rate due to spoiler system limitations. Where high speeds are achieved in combination with high Mach numbers spoiler blow back can completely defeat their attempt to operate and the net result is that, in very bad cases, absolutely no roll control is left in the aeroplane via ailerons or spoilers.

Where this occurs the M_{DF} value is reduced until adequate roll capability is achieved and a corresponding reduction is made in M_{MO} so as to preserve the operating speed margins. Alternatively, maximum spoiler deflection, in the speed brake mode, is restricted to something below the blow back angle so that some up going spoiler will always be available to supplement the ailerons. In the first case, however, there is no guarantee that a really violent upset will not drive the aeroplane to a Mach number above the reduced M_{DF} when roll control difficulties will be met. In an extreme circumstance like this, the aeroplane must be recovered laterally before it is recovered longitudinally. So close the speed brakes, suffer the increase in speed while rolling the aeroplane back to level flight, then open the speed brakes again.

Longitudinal At very high Mach number the elevator loses effectiveness for a given angle of deflection as well as, in the manual case, losing deflection range because the high operating loads cause excessive control circuit stretch. Both these effects reduce the manoeuvrability.

The stabiliser tends to retain its effectiveness at very high Mach numbers and for this reason should be used most carefully to avoid overloading the aeroplane. A difficulty on some types is that a very high elevator hinge moment will cause the stabiliser drive motor to stall. The harder up elevator is pulled, the more sure is the motor's stalled condition. If this should occur in a steep high speed dive it is suggested that a good choice of action is as follows. If you are in a type with an M_{DF} around 0.95 TMN and you estimate that you look like containing the manoeuvre on full up elevator alone, then hang on to full up elevator, with help from the co-pilot, and wait for the recovery. If things look like getting rapidly worse however, or if you are in a type with an M_{DF} around 0.86, then you would be better served by adopting the procedure of momentarily relaxing the pull force and regaining control of the stabiliser in short bursts. You do not have to, and indeed should not, run the stabiliser very far back before it becomes obvious that you have regained pitch control of the aeroplane. As soon as you feel you have regained control, complete the manoeuvre on the elevator alone. Do not use the stabiliser any more than is necessary or the aeroplane might pitch very hard nose up, particularly as the Mach number decreases.

Mach meter position errors

At very high Mach numbers the position error in the Mach meter system tends to get larger and perhaps change sign. This is because of the changes in the pressure field around the pitot and static sources with increasing Mach number. It is because of this that 'round number' true Mach numbers assumed in the design of the aeroplane come out to perhaps three rather strange places of decimals in terms of indicated Mach number. Thus 0.88 true might be 0.887 indicated.

It is generally true that the position errors up to M_{MO} are small; the requirements in fact insist that they be small. At speeds up to M_{DF}, however, quite large variations in position error occur. So long as the error causes the Mach meter to over-read this is an error in a safe direction; but if the error causes the Mach meter to under-read this is an error in a potentially unsafe direction. It is not a requirement that M_{DF}, either in true or indicated values, be placarded on the flight deck because it is strictly a flight test figure and not supposed to be of interest to airline pilots. With the occasional jet upset leading to very high Mach numbers perhaps this policy should be revised, although a defence can properly be made that if an airline pilot finds himself above M_{MO} it is only necessary to let him know this because his line of action is to slow down to below M_{MO} again. To every defence there is of course a counter defence. If a pilot should find himself above M_{MO} then the amount by which he is above should govern the rate at which he takes action to slow down. It is therefore worth knowing for the type you fly the true and indicated values of M_{DF}.

Most of the later jet transports have a high Mach position error arranged to over-read at M_{DF}. For example, 0.94 true = 0.955 indicated and 0.95 true = 0.97 indicated. This is comparatively easy to arrange where an Air Data Computer (ADC) is installed; a specially profiled cam is used to ensure that the indicated Mach reading expands in advance of true Mach values. Some of the older jet transports, however, have high Mach position errors which cause the Mach meter to under-read — and under-read more and more as Mach number increases. One particular installation reads only from 0.9 to 0.92 between 0.9 and 0.93 true Mach number and thereafter, from 0.93 to 0.95 true Mach number, *does not increase its indicated reading at all*.

In view of the fact that you should condition your overspeed recovery actions to the amount by which you are too fast, you should know the value of M_{DF} in indicated Mach number. Aeroplanes actually are quite strong and well capable of being manoeuvred at speeds up to M_{DF}. You are not likely to bust anything through applying high control forces to the elevator and ailerons on most types. But remember to leave the rudder alone and, *if you have to use the stabiliser, do so in very short bursts, evaluating the effect of one burst before putting in another.*

Well, so much for flight at very high Mach numbers. Stability deteriorates and controllability can become very limiting under some circumstances on certain types of jet transports. They all have satisfactory stability and control up to their scheduled M_{MO} values but some get into trouble on the way to M_{DF}. So take care to avoid flight above M_{MO}. Pay attention to the high Mach warning and do not fly with the device unserviceable. Some of the later aircraft have been proved to be not actually unstable at high Mach number and therefore were not required to be fitted with Mach trimmers, but this does not mean they are stable. They are in fact neutral, which means that a given tail setting will suffice for a range of Mach numbers and there is no stability, stick free, to return the aeroplane to a lower Mach number if it should start to get too fast. High speed warnings are usually duplicated on this sort of aeroplane because the aural warning is the only indication of an overspeed condition available until the overspeed has reached gross proportions.

Mach trimmers

As the characteristics which cause longitudinal instability at high Mach number are inherently associated with the design for high speed flight they are difficult to alter by aerodynamic means and the deficiency in stability must be made up by a device. This deficiency in stability does not always exist; there are some swept wing jet transports flying which do not need stability augmentation.

The philosophy of the acceptance of devices in place of natural qualities has already been covered in principle in the sub-chapter dealing with stick pushers.

The device which artificially corrects or compensates for longitudinal instability at high Mach number is the Mach trimmer. This is a device which is sensitive to Mach number and is programmed to feed into the elevator, or variable incidence stabiliser, a signal proportional to Mach number so that the stability remains positive throughout the range up to MDF. With this ability to select artificially a level of stability the opportunity is usually taken to put in a reasonably high level of stability so as to give added protection in this area.

Referring back to figure 6.1 in the sub-chapter on high Mach number it will be seen that the stick force against Mach number relationship is unstable between 0.88 and 0.95 IMN. Refer now to figure 6.2 where, laid on top of the basic stick force curve is the Mach trim input. The resultant is a nicely stable stick force gradient all the way from 0.86 to 0.95 IMN.

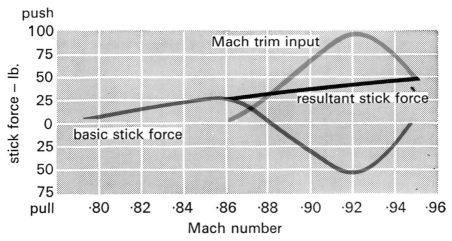

Figure 6.2   Stick force against Mach number as corrected by Mach trimmer.

With the Mach trim operative therefore the aeroplane is stable up to MDF, needing an increasing push force all the way. If this push force is relaxed, or if the aircraft is forced to a higher Mach number than that at which it is trimmed, by a gust for example, the positive stability will exert itself and start to return the aeroplane towards the trimmed condition.

For crew training purposes there is an increased MMO so that pilots may become familiar with their aircraft's handling qualities in the range between the normal MMO and MDF. For the chosen values of 0.88 and 0.95 a

154

typical crew training M_{MO} would be something like 0.92 IMN. It is essential that all pilots are familiar with the aeroplane in this range, both with and without the Mach trimmer operating. It is essential also that the pilot should know the approximate Mach number at which the Mach trimmer should start to work. A Mach trimmer can become active in any one of three speed bands:—

(a) Above M_{MO}, in which case it will operate only when the aeroplane is forced into an overspeed condition.

(b) Below M_{MO} but above the normal maximum cruise Mach number, in which case it will operate more frequently, particularly if a high cruise Mach number is chosen.

(c) Within the normal cruise Mach range, in which case it will be active most of the time.

Mach trim operation in normal conditions will not be shown up by the behaviour of the aeroplane (it is designed to do just the opposite) but will, depending on the installation, activate the trim wheel and/or illuminate the activity light. You must be conscious of these indications so that you can satisfy yourself that the device works when it should, stops working when it should stop and doesn't work when it shouldn't. This simply means that, almost subconsciously, Mach trim operation should be checked against indicated Mach number for any significant change in the flight condition.

In the event of Mach trimmer unserviceability there is usually imposed a reduced value of M_{MO} so that a margin is retained between the cruising Mach number and the Mach number at the onset of instability. It is important to note that the onset of instability usually occurs in a sneaky sort of way and, if the pilot is not paying too much attention to control of the flight path, the next occurrence is the high speed warning, which is set just above the normal M_{MO}. So the aeroplane is too fast already, probably gaining speed quickly and as a result comparatively high stick forces will need to be applied for the recovery. As the 'g' increment increases the aircraft will enter the buffet boundary and further upset the pilot. So, watch it all the time.

The Mach trim runaway is also important. It has been suggested that the pilot should be monitoring, subconsciously, the behaviour of the Mach trimmer at all times. If the Mach trim starts to work for no apparent reason, or if it runs on longer than normal, suspect a runaway at once. Do not ditch it immediately because it might be coping with a demand of which you are not aware, but don't give it too long. As soon as you are sure that it is not operating normally — *stop it*. There are, in one particular installation which comes to mind, at least five different ways in which a runaway stabiliser due to Mach trim can be stopped. The captain should immediately go through the approved drill, at the same time getting the other crew members

155

on to their back-up drills. This is vital, particularly as on some types of jet transport it has recently been confirmed that from a gross overspeed condition with the aeroplane out of trim nose down (which is what one type of Mach trim runaway can impose on the aeroplane) the resulting recovery can be marginal. This situation has been covered in detail in the sub-chapter headed Variable Incidence Tailplanes.

Finally, to summarise the foregoing discussion, you should:—

(a) Know the qualities of your aeroplane with Mach trim operative and inoperative.

(b) Monitor Mach trimmer activity against indicated Mach number.

(c) Reduce speed if the device is known to be unserviceable.

(d) Mentally rehearse the trim runaway procedure on every flight.

(e) Stop a trim runaway immediately you really suspect one.

Emergency descents

An emergency descent procedure is necessary only because the jet aeroplane flies high. The effect of lack of cabin pressure and lack of oxygen on passengers and crew should be well understood by pilots of jet transports. A sudden and complete failure of cabin pressure at a typical maximum permitted ceiling of 43,000 ft. will render the average person unconscious within fifteen seconds and reduce the crew's ability sooner than this. While the time quoted is an average it must be remembered that there is a large scatter about the average and some occupants of the aeroplane could be seriously distressed in a much shorter time. In the event of the need arising, therefore, the emergency descent procedure must be initiated immediately.

The drills vary between aircraft types but they all involve reduction to idle thrust, operation of the high drag devices and a steep descent, at least initially, with a target speed of M_{MO} where the aeroplane is Mach limited and V_{MO} when the aeroplane becomes speed limited at lower altitudes. There are some aeroplanes fitted with a never-exceed speed needle on the airspeed indicator; this is datumed to M_{MO} at high altitude and V_{MO} at lower altitude and on this device it is necessary only to fly to the needle at all altitudes.

Whether or not the aeroplane is cruising at M_{MO}, reducing thrust and operating the high drag devices will immediately cause a speed loss which will not be held by the initial pushover because this must be made in a prudent fashion. The initial dive angle will therefore be fairly steep in order to get back to M_{MO}, then there will be a need to reduce the dive angle in order not to overshoot M_{MO}. When the aircraft approaches the altitude at which $M_{MO} = V_{MO}$ (say, 0.88 IMN = 380 knots which, on a standard day will be equivalent to 24,500 ft.) it is necessary to reduce the dive angle again otherwise the aeroplane will exceed V_{MO}, possibly by a significant amount. This is particularly so where a never-exceed needle ASI is fitted. As the initial dive is made at constant Mach, the maximum permitted speed needle will be moving up; this reflects the increasing IAS permitted for constant Mach number with reduction in altitude. At the M_{MO}/V_{MO} coincident altitude it will of course stop increasing and remain at V_{MO}. On some aircraft the needle might also be programmed to indicate a changing V_{MO} below this altitude, in which case the needle may move downwards a little with further reduction in altitude.

The change from the cruise to the stabilised emergency descent usually involves a nose up trim change which is quite strong in some aeroplanes. If the stick load becomes very high trim some of it out, but *don't trim all of it out* otherwise you might be left with a very high pull force when you

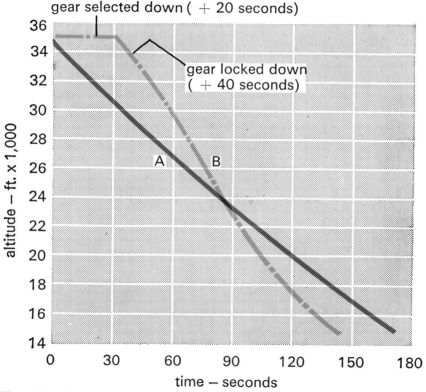

Figure 6.3   Alternative emergency descent profiles.

wish to terminate the procedure. An altitude of 15,000 ft. is generally accepted as the bottom of the procedure, when a return can be made to level flight, although on some routes the minimum terrain clearance altitude might impose a higher value.   Remember that some aeroplanes will achieve descent rates of up to 14,000 ft. per minute, and 9,000 ft. per minute is quite common. These are very high rates and care must be taken to reduce the rate of descent as the target altitude is approached so as to make a smooth intercept on to it and not undershoot it.

Figure 6.3 illustrates the difference in total time required to reach 15,000 ft. between an immediate descent at M_{MO} with speed brakes out and an initial delay in order to lower the gear where the maximum gear operating speed is significantly below the cruising speed.   Assuming that the initial conditions are: 290 knots, 0.86 Mach number at 35,000 ft., that the gear limit speed is 250 knots for selection, and M_{MO}/V_{MO} is permitted after the gear is locked down; descent profile (A) will give 7,060 ft. per minute overall and 7,500 ft. per minute average rate of descent while descent profile (B) gives 8,570 ft. per minute overall and 11,330 ft. per minute average rate of descent when established. While the overall rates of descent are finally near enough the same, the important thing is that in descent (B) valuable time is wasted at high altitude, where it matters most, in order to slow down the aeroplane to the gear limiting speed.   Some aeroplanes are not limited in this way; where normal cruise is 0.82 IMN and the gear speed is 0.82 IMN the gear can be operated with the speed brakes and the descent commenced immediately (don't, however, exceed the gear limit speed until the gear is down and locked and the door lights out).

Where a significant speed reduction has to be made before the gear can be selected, don't bother about it; leave the gear up and get on with the descent. Knocking off those top few thousands of feet is much more important than hoping to pick up a steeper gradient of descent later on.   The graph shows that 30 secs. and 60 secs. after initiation of the descent procedure the immediate descent technique will bring the aeroplane significantly lower than the wait-for-the-gear technique, although the with-gear technique produces a steeper gradient eventually.

Like any other sudden emergency the need for a rapid descent can catch out a crew and there is a danger that both pilots will start into action and neither will start breathing oxygen.   To avoid this, above 20,000 ft. both pilots should have their oxygen gear instantly available (except for the drop-out type which meets the same basic requirement) and whichever pilot is in control of the aircraft at the time should initiate the descent while the other pilot gets firmly established on 100% oxygen and *re-establishes his intercom and communications facilities*. He can then take control of the aeroplane while the other pilot gets on to oxygen and communications facilities. Again, as in other emergencies, don't rush and make a hash of things — take a little more time and do it properly first time.

A sudden and complete decompression at altitude fills the cabin with cloud; this is due to the reduction in pressure condensing out the water vapour in the cabin air.   This tends to look like smoke, but it won't confuse and alarm you if you are expecting it. If the descent has to be made through significant turbulence, descend at the rough-air Mach number initially, then at the rough-air speed (M_{RA} and V_{RA}).

The above drills all relate to the full emergency descent procedure. There are many occasions when a precautionary descent becomes necessary due, for example, to difficulty in coping with the pressurisation system. In these cases only a hold on the climb, or a precautionary descent, is necessary and then as much or as little of the full procedure should be adopted as is necessary according to the level of the difficulty being experienced. On aircraft where cabin pressure is supplied by engine bleed air the thrust levers should not be fully closed unless it is essential; keeping some power on will keep some cabin air supply going. Most systems will support quite a significant leak rate. On aircraft employing cabin blowers it is usually true that the thrust levers can be fully closed while still leaving an adequate supply of air to cope with an increased leak rate.

One last point. The buffet with speed brakes extended on some aircraft is quite small, particularly at lower speeds; having completed a descent with speed brakes out remember to retract them.

High drag devices

Jet transport aircraft generally have high momentum and low drag in the clean configuration and there is no increase in drag when the thrust levers are closed to idle. This low drag characteristic can be a severe embarrassment whenever it is necessary to slow down quickly or descend quickly. For this reason high drag devices are provided for use in three separate areas; in flight for rapid descent from high altitude and for quick speed and height reductions for air traffic control purposes, on the landing approach to improve handling qualities and on the ground after landing and for the rejected take-off.

The following high drag devices are used either singly or in combination:—

(a) Speed brakes; that is, the spoilers used symmetrically or the gear (or possibly main legs only).

(b) Reverse thrust.

(c) Braking parachute.

(d) A flap setting behind the normal landing setting.

There are never (or should never be) any speed restrictions on the use of spoilers as speed brakes and they are normally cleared for use right up to M_{DF} and V_{DF}; at increasingly higher speeds they blow back progressively. If they tend to operate asymmetrically they cause a rolling tendency. They usually produce buffet at high speeds but often very little buffet at low speeds, so don't forget to retract them. Spoilers, perhaps surprisingly, have little influence on the 1g stall; they might increase the buffet a little and might increase the stall speed somewhat, but they don't normally affect the stall qualities. They are designed to produce either no pitch change at all or possibly a small nose up pitch change. There is at least one type where the selection of spoilers symmetrically as lift dumpers on landing (particularly on an aft C.G.) causes the aeroplane to pitch up sufficiently to leave the ground again for a short distance. When selecting lift dump therefore push the elevator control smoothly but firmly forwards to hold the nose down and keep the aeroplane on the ground. Spoilers and flaps should not be used in combination because they produce marked buffet and very high sink rates. A number of aircraft types have a high drag aural warning for this case.

The main gear, when used as a speed brake, usually has a speed limitation for extension, but when locked down is then cleared up to M_{MO} and V_{MO}. Actual values, and whether the speed limitation includes the nosewheel or not, vary between types. *Particular care must be taken where a lower limit is again imposed for retraction.* Because of a lower level of buffet the gear is preferable to speed brakes in terms of passenger comfort where only an expedited descent is required.

The second high drag device, reverse thrust, will be dealt with fully in a later chapter on take-off and landing.

The braking parachute is used on the ground only. It is normally very effective and its reliability is now to a more reasonable standard. It is very useful on a runway surface which is known to be slippery. In crosswind conditions, however, its use is normally restricted to a component significantly lower than the component for the clean aeroplane because, regardless of trail length, the parachute flies down wind and exerts a strong weather cocking tendency on the aeroplane. If directional control problems are encountered due to this the parachute should be jettisoned.

With the combination of a strong crosswind and a slippery surface the parachute will cause the aeroplane to drift towards the downwind side of the runway. This drift is aggravated by the use of wheel brakes because they use some of what little adhesion is available. So, if a drift starts, ease off the brakes; if the drift continues, jettison the 'chute to prevent running off the side of the runway and accept the reduced deceleration. It is invariably preferable to run straight off the end of the runway, slowly, than to run off the side, in a drift, at high speed.

Trailing edge flaps themselves are high drag as well as high lift devices. The dangers of a slow approach speed will be emphasised later. Bear in mind the contribution made by the high drag flaps and keep both the thrust and the speed up, particularly in the last stages of the engine(s) out procedures where full flap has finally been selected after the projected landing has been assessed as 'guaranteed'. The aeroplane will lose speed extremely quickly if the thrust is reduced too early so don't be afraid of keeping the power on right down to touchdown if necessary. A 'lift dump' flap setting, for use on the ground only, is generally handled in the same fashion as spoilers.

160

Having discussed the consequences of high drag devices it is worth spending a moment or two on the absence of high drag where it is normally enjoyed. In a flapless approach, or, more significantly still, in an approach where both the trailing edge flaps and leading edge devices are inoperative, the drag of the aeroplane will be very low. Rather than use all four thrust levers together and suffer the need for minute movements if speed excursions are to be kept within reasonable values, it is much easier to idle a pair of engines (or the centre one on a three engined installation) and set up the remaining pair at a higher power to compensate. Further power alterations will then be only half as critical. There will still be plenty of power available to baulk, flapless on two, at landing weights, if necessary.

High altitude characteristics

Flight at high altitude in a typical modern jet transport incurs at least four penalties in the field of flying qualities in comparison with the medium altitude capability of the older piston-engined aircraft. These are reduced aerodynamic damping, reduced stability, restricted operating speed range and reduced manoeuvrability. The subject of absolute performance and manoeuvre ceiling, although rather academic, is also discussed under this heading. Finally, there is a note on the use of flaps at high altitude.

Reduced aerodynamic damping at altitude

Oscillations can always occur in a situation where a displacement from a neutral position gives rise to a restoring force.

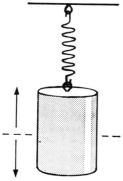

Figure 6.4   Illustration of simple damping.

As a simple example consider a weight hanging on a spring as in figure 6.4. There is a neutral position about which the weight will oscillate if disturbed. The restoring force due to the spring always acts towards the neutral position and is proportional to the displacement from the neutral position.

161

Another example is an aircraft in yaw (figure 6.5). In this case the centering force is provided by the 'lift' on the fin due to its incidence which always acts towards the neutral position and is proportional to the displacement from the neutral position for small angles.

If we imagine the test on the spring and weight being conducted in a vacuum then the system, once disturbed, could go on oscillating for ever (this is not strictly true because losses in the system which do not concern the present argument would eventually bring the system to rest). If, however, we let air into the vacuum then the system would be slowed down by the

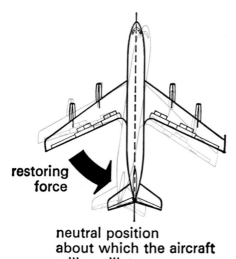

restoring
force

neutral position
about which the aircraft
will oscillate

Figure 6.5 Damping effect of vertical tail in yaw.

airloads *due to the motion*. These airloads always oppose the motion, i.e. when the weight is moving downwards the airloads on it are upwards. It is this aerodynamic force opposing the motion which provides the damping. Obviously, the larger the aerodynamic force the more heavily damped the oscillation.

Now return to the aeroplane and consider an instant during a yawing oscillation when the sideslip is zero (that is, when the aircraft is passing through the neutral position), and see what is happening to the fin (figure 6.6).

At the instant considered the aircraft has a rate of yaw to port due to the oscillation, and the fin therefore has a velocity to starboard. So the relative velocity of the air is from starboard to port. This sideways velocity compounded with the forward velocity gives the fin an incidence and hence a sideways force *opposing the motion*. The size of this force depends on the

162

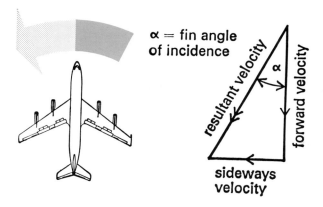

α = fin angle
of incidence

resultant velocity

α

forward velocity

sideways
velocity

Figure 6.6 Fin angle of incidence in yaw.

fin area, q$(=\frac{1}{2}\rho V^2)$, and the incidence, and the greater the force the heavier the damping.

To see the effect of altitude on the damping think of the same aeroplane flying at the same indicated airspeed, i.e. the same 'q', at two different altitudes. The aerodynamicists can prove that the frequency of the oscillation is independent of altitude and in practice this is found to be true. So for a given amplitude of disturbance the fin will have the same sideways velocity when passing through the neutral position, at both altitudes. But if we look at the vector diagram which compounds the forward velocity with the sideways velocity to give the fin incidence (figure 6.7), then we immediately see a difference.

The higher the altitude, the higher the forward speed, since 'q' is constant, and therefore the smaller the incidence and so the smaller the damping force, all other factors being constant. It should be added here that the restoring force which causes the oscillation and the damping force which opposes the oscillation, once it exists, both come from the aerodynamic forces on the fin. The two forces are, of course, superimposed, so that at any instant there is only one resultant force acting on the fin.

This simple explanation has been made using the aeroplane in yaw. Exactly the same conditions apply to the aeroplane in pitch. In the case of pure roll, however, at least over small angles and small time periods, there is no restoring moment and hence the response is just a subsidence (or divergence) instead of a damped (or undamped) oscillation. In the oscillatory mode, however, where yaw is the primary parameter and the roll a second order effect (although it is the more noticeable result), the reduced damping in yaw does apply and hence the deterioration in dutch roll damping with altitude. Damping decreases with altitude, therefore the time to half amplitude increases. As the period of the motion doesn't vary with altitude the cycles to half amplitude increase. This deterioration of damping with

163

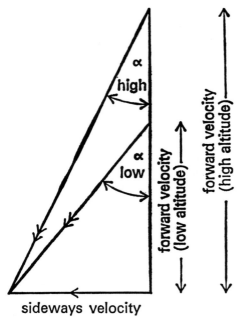

Figure 6.7   Effect of altitude on fin angle of incidence at constant IAS.

altitude can be quite marked; where oscillatory stability is positive at 18,000 ft., it can be neutral at 22,000 ft. and measurably negative at 25,000 ft. Similarly a landing configuration dutch roll can be stable at 1,000 ft. and unstable at 8,000 ft.   Both these changes in stability occur for a height gain of only 7,000 ft.

Reduced stability at altitude

Reference has been made in this book to five modes of stability (if we ignore speed stability).   These are stick free static longitudinal stability, static lateral stability, directional stability, oscillatory stability and spiral stability.

Altitude as an isolated parameter has little effect on the first three in terms of their steady state results but, as aerodynamic damping decreases with altitude, the aeroplane will feel much less stable in dynamic manoeuvres. Additionally the longitudinal stability is compromised by high Mach number effect so that most jet transports either suffer a reduction or actually become unstable in terms of stick free static stability, as previously explained.   It has also been explained, as perhaps the best example of the effect of reduced damping at altitude, that oscillatory stability degrades quite rapidly.   So far we seem to have lost out every time!   Spiral stability, however, which always opposes oscillatory stability, maintains its independence and improves with

164

altitude, while oscillatory stability deteriorates with altitude. This is because, for a given IAS, the fin suffers a smaller incidence at altitude, therefore a smaller restoring force. The fin is less dominant in its stabilising effect directionally and causes less roll because it is more reluctant to reduce the side-slip angle. This maintained level of spiral stability at altitude, however, is only of some comfort in the area of long-term manoeuvre behaviour; it is of comparatively little consequence in the area of short term manoeuvre behaviour.

The effect of this general reduction in stability and damping at high altitudes is a reduction in the qualitative feel of the aeroplane in terms of its dynamic stability; the aeroplane feels, and is, less stable. It will diverge further for a given disturbing force, due to the higher TAS and will take longer to settle after a disturbance. There are also two further effects which aggravate the difficulty:—

(a) The basic control circuit friction values are likely to go up due to the effect of the very low ambient air temperature in sliding seals in pressure bulkheads, on the efficiency of cables around pulleys and on the viscosity of lubricating greases in general. Any increase in control circuit friction puts up the value of the friction range of trim and destroys the stick free stability within this range.

(b) The friction range of trim itself becomes much more significant. At low altitudes the $\pm 10\%$ of the requirement at say 280 knots permits a speed spread of ± 28 knots for zero stick force (although most aeroplanes do a lot better than this). But at high altitudes a friction band this large, at a cruise Mach number of 0.82 at 40,000 ft., would, in terms of Mach number, equate to ± 0.08. Thus there could be no start of a positive stick force gradient over a range of 0.16 Mach number; say, from 0.74 to 0.9 IMN. (Clearly this is undesirable. The latest requirements in fact are calling for a maximum friction range of trim of ± 0.03 Mach number.)

So be gentle with the aeroplane at high altitude. Make control movements slowly and smoothly and recover from divergences in the same manner.

Restricted operating speed range

The bottom end of the achievable speed range is the stall; the top end is V_{DF} or M_{DF}. These are absolute minimum and maximum values and are not available or permitted for normal operation. Within each limit there is a more prudent limit; the lower one can be taken as pre-stall buffet or a defined margin above the stall and the upper one as V_{MO} or M_{MO}. Stall speed increases with altitude as previously explained and increases with weight. So, therefore, will any function of stall speed. The lines of V_{MO} and M_{MO} and V_{DF} and M_{DF} do not vary with weight. We can now draw some pictures to illustrate these points.

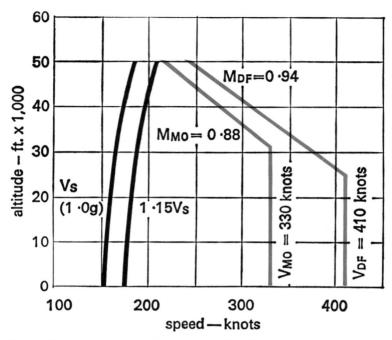

Figure 6.8   Variation of significant speeds with altitude.

Figure 6.8 is drawn for a mid-weight, say 250,000 lb. If 1.15 Vs is acceptable as a minimum speed and V_{MO}/M_{MO} must be accepted as the maximum speed then the size of the permitted speed range at any altitude can be read off. Notice how it gets smaller with altitude above 30,000 ft. due to the limiting Mach number bringing down the airspeed.

Now let us repeat the picture ignoring the absolute limits of Vs and V_{DF}/M_{DF} but including the effect of weight (figure 6.9). Notice that at light weight there is a comparatively much bigger speed band available, due to the suppression of the stall speed.   Because piston-engined aeroplanes did not, in general, have a high altitude capability or a large weight range they had a substantially constant speed range, from clean stall, or function of stall, to V_{NE}.   It can be seen, however, that a large jet aircraft has a permitted speed range which varies with weight and particularly with altitude.   It can be as much as 200 knots at light weight and low altitude or as little as 50 knots at medium weight and high altitude.

Pilots need little urging to keep away from the stall.   Some care must also be taken not to exceed the maximum permitted speeds because of the reduced strength factors involved as well as quite likely reductions in handling qualities.   With fixed values of V_{MO} and M_{MO}, which are additionally

166

marked on the instruments, these are easily remembered and identified maximum speed values. Occasionally a particular type of aeroplane will have a V_{MO} varying with altitude. Many of the latest aeroplanes have a maximum speed needle on the airspeed indicator which records V_{MO} (whether varying or not) up to the height at which $V_{MO} = M_{MO}$ when it is then datumed to M_{MO} and reduces progressively as altitude is increased. This maximum speed needle will always indicate maximum permitted airspeed in knots at all altitudes. To high-light the undesirability of exceeding maximum speeds in a

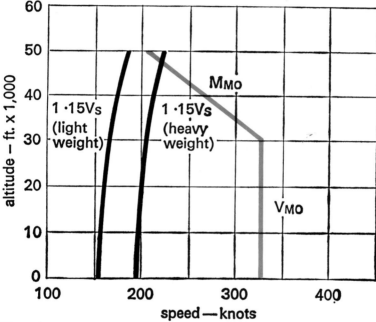

Figure 6.9   Variation of significant speeds with altitude and weight.

jet transport there is also an aural high speed warning, which is usually duplicated. This is set to sound off between 6 and 12 knots above V_{MO} and about 0.01 Mach number above M_{MO}, with small tolerances on both settings.

Some care has been taken to make you conscious of maximum permitted airspeeds and Mach numbers and this is for good reasons. Observe these speeds carefully. It is not difficult under good flying conditions. Operation in severe weather will be covered, in detail, later.

Reduced manoeuvrability

This heading does not refer to the reduction in control application due to systems limitation, nor the loss of control effectiveness at high Mach number,

167

both of which have been covered separately. We are now concerned with the reduced manoeuvrability of any jet aeroplane due to its high altitude environment.

Ignoring straight 'g' factors at low altitude, where a 1g excess can be considered the prudent upper limit to the required amount of manoeuvre capability, manoeuvres in the pitching plane, and speed excursions, are normally limited by the following:—

(a) At the low speed end, either pre-stall buffet or a chosen function of the stall.

(b) At the high speed end, either a maximum permitted speed restriction or high Mach number buffet.

Figure 6.10 illustrates this.

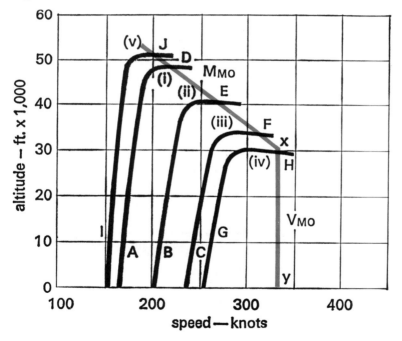

Figure 6.10   Buffet boundaries.

Consider figure 6.10 *and assume, for the moment, one weight only,* say 250,000 lb. Line A is the 1g buffet speed increasing with altitude then curving over and becoming a Mach buffet line. Line B is the 1.5g curve of the same values and Line C is the 2g value. For 1g flight, therefore, the buffet

168

boundary/speed envelope is defined by the shape ADXY, for 1.5g by BEXY and for 2g by CFXY.

The highest altitude point on each line may also be called the manoeuvre ceiling of the aeroplane. Hence point (i) is the manoeuvre ceiling for 1g flight, point (ii) the manoeuvre ceiling for 1.5g flight and point (iii) that for 2g.

The same picture can be used to illustrate the effect of changes in aeroplane weight. *If we assume 1g flight only for the moment,* then the upper boundary (ADXY) becomes the buffet boundary/speed envelope for medium weight, the middle boundary (BEXY) that for a higher weight and the lower (CFXY) that for maximum weight. If we now add a new curve GH for heavy weight flight at 2g we can put in point (iv) which is the 2g manoeuvre ceiling of the aeroplane at maximum weight. Similarly we can add a final curve IJ for light weight flight at 1g and put in point (v) which is the 1g manoeuvre ceiling of the aeroplane at light weight.

Depending therefore on the weight of the aeroplane and the amount of 'g' pulled, the usable speed range changes quite significantly at any given altitude as does the manoeuvre ceiling; in the example used the 1g light weight ceiling is around 51,000 ft. while the 2g heavy weight ceiling is as low as 30,000 ft.

Absolute performance and manoeuvre ceilings

The example chosen of a 1g absolute manoeuvre ceiling at light weight of around 51,000 ft. is a long way beyond the performance capability of a modern jet aeroplane, due to its lack of thrust. Similarly at heavy weight the 1g buffet ceiling of approximately 40,000 ft. is again beyond the performance capability of the aeroplane. These altitudes are out of reach, and not only because of lack of thrust. Even if thrust were not limiting, any divergence from the best climb speed (V_{IMD}) will result in failure to make height. Too low a speed will increase drag and hit the stall buffet too early; too high a speed will hit Mach buffet too early and again put up the drag.

In other words, just as piston-engined aircraft were limited by performance so is the modern civil jet aircraft. The old days of coffin corner went out with the over-powered, low Mach number limited designs.

So now we know that we cannot, and also why we cannot, be too carefree with our jet transports at high altitudes. Because of reduced damping and reduced stability the aeroplane needs to be handled with some precision. Because of the closing-in of limits at both ends our speed range contracts with altitude. Finally, our manoeuvrability becomes increasingly restricted as altitude increases. None of this is any bother if the weather is good, but in severe weather all these things are of the greatest importance. A proper understanding of them is necessary if you are to fly the best possible flight path under these demanding circumstances.

169

Use of flaps at high altitude

It would appear that in recent years pilots have developed the habit of using their flaps at high altitude, presumably for holding or descent purposes. This rather indiscriminate use of flaps has caused some concern. While the captain of an aeroplane can of course take any action he considers justifiable under a special set of operational conditions, there are good reasons for not using flaps in other than the normal circumstances.

Firstly, flap design is based on the assumption that the flaps will be used for take-off and climb, and approach and landing, and that they will be retracted for the rest of the flight. On this assumption are based the strength and fatigue calculations of the flaps. If they are used at other times then the original design assumptions are compromised. Secondly, there is a lower level of proof strength with the flaps extended; this is quite often $+1$g increment instead of the $+1\frac{1}{2}$g increment in the flaps retracted case. Lastly, on some of those types fitted with stick shakers and stick pushers, the design of these systems is such that, with the flaps extended above certain altitudes, the shake and the push will not function in the correct fashion and the aeroplane will be denied some of its normal stall protection (in the clean configuration stall protection is provided at very high altitude by the marked pre-stall buffet due to Mach number effect, regardless of the point at which the stick shaker operates).

In this last instance specific limitations on the use of flaps above certain altitudes will be found in the Flight Manual. They are there for good reasons, so observe them. Unless there are specific operational reasons the use of flaps should be confined to the normal low altitude function. While you are about it, do try to stay within the speed limitations; flight recorder results show far too many occasions on which the flap speeds have been exceeded, in some cases by large margins.

7 Take-off and landing

High sink rates on the approach

In discussing high sink rates on the approach there is a very strong temptation to wander away from the problem in isolation and get on to landing techniques in general. However, because the high sink rate is a unique problem in itself let us tackle it here and keep the remainder of the associated problems for discussion later.

High sink rates on the approach stem from two separate areas; the dynamics of the aeroplane in terms of the second by second resolution of its flight path and the wider related influences which bear on the pilot.

The dynamics of the aeroplane on the approach

Having taken some care in the arrangement of this book the author and the reader may now enjoy the same benefit. All the elements of this problem of high sink rates on the approach have been covered individually; this is where we bring them together. There are six ways in which a jet transport is worse off than a piston-engined transport in making an approach and in correcting errors on the approach.

They are:—

1. The absence of the propeller slipstream in producing immediate extra lift at constant airspeed.
2. The absence of the propeller slipstream in significantly lowering the power-on stall speed.
3. The poor acceleration response of the jet engine from low r.p.m.
4. The increased momentum of the jet aircraft making sudden changes in the flight path impossible.
5. The lack of good speed stability being an inducement to a low speed condition.
6. Drag increasing faster than lift producing a high sink rate at low speeds.

These are the facts of the dynamics of the aeroplane, but let us keep the problem in perspective; the fact that six isolated reasons have been dredged up to show you that life is potentially more difficult shouldn't cause you to overrate the difficulty of making an approach in a jet aircraft or in correcting errors on the approach. With a proper understanding of the facts and a modicum of flying ability neither of these tasks is difficult.

Let us now go through the operational application of the above parameters — when the whole approach is properly controlled and when something has gone wrong or can be seen to be going wrong.

If in isolation you can see the need for more lift you can get it in two ways:—

(a) By increasing incidence — but only if your airspeed and sink rate are otherwise acceptable. In this case you must then increase thrust to counter the drag from the extra incidence or the resulting sink rate will be higher.

(b) By increasing airspeed. This is obtained, keeping all other parameters substantially constant, by increasing the thrust. A heavy aeroplane takes a lot of accelerating so if this option is exercised a lot of thrust will be needed.

If you can see the need for more thrust for any reason apply enough of it in good time, bearing in mind the poor engine response from low r.p.m. and the comparatively small amounts of thrust produced for a given power lever movement in the lower ranges of power settings. With experience you will be able to spot the very first tendency of a falling airspeed trend and a small increase in thrust at that time will put matters right. If you delay you will need a lot more thrust which will subsequently have to be reduced in order to stabilise at the regained speed.

Remember the dominant influence of high momentum. This is effective in two ways:—

(a) Fore and aft in terms of speed. It takes a lot of power and time to increase speed. It takes a lot of time to reduce speed because of the limited amount by which thrust can — and should — be reduced.

(b) Downwards in terms of sink rate. A high sink rate takes a lot of stopping. Assuming that all other parameters are near enough right, a high sink rate must be countered by increased incidence coincidentally protected by an increase in thrust to counter the extra drag. Depending on the amount by which the sink rate needs to be trimmed will be the amount and rate of corrective action. For small amounts, smooth and gentle, almost anticipatory, corrections will be sufficient; for gross divergences really drastic corrective actions will be required. The salvation of, for example, a very high sink rate close to the ground is the immediate application of full thrust on all engines and the selection of a required flight path which will give the best compromise between (i) hitting the ground with the nose down and (ii) hitting the ground with the nose up or even stalling in an unnecessarily fierce attempt to recover the aeroplane without taking advantage of the height available. The solution of a high sink rate very close to the ground is a short application of high thrust. Rely only on the thrust to cut the sink rate and *don't rotate the aeroplane nose up*, in spite of the temptation: a sharp rotation very close to the ground will only drive the gear on harder. This is because over a very short period of time sudden up elevator merely lowers the tail, causing the gear to hit the ground before the increased incidence has had time to produce increased lift.

Beware of poor speed stability leading to a low speed condition with its attendant risk of high drag increasing the sink rate. Beware particularly of an increasing sink rate and remember that an apparently normal pitch attitude is no guarantee of a normal incidence value or sink rate.

It is difficult to detail the achievement of a proper approach path in all respects, by number, as it were. Enough has been said to illustrate the potential danger of allowing any one parameter to start diverging. Enough has also been said to show the interdependence of all the related parameters. Quite early in this book there was a fairly lengthy discussion on projected flight paths and required flight paths. Here the whole lot come together, and in one of the most critical areas of flight — the approach to land. Remember, you cannot reasonably expect to make a good landing off a bad approach.

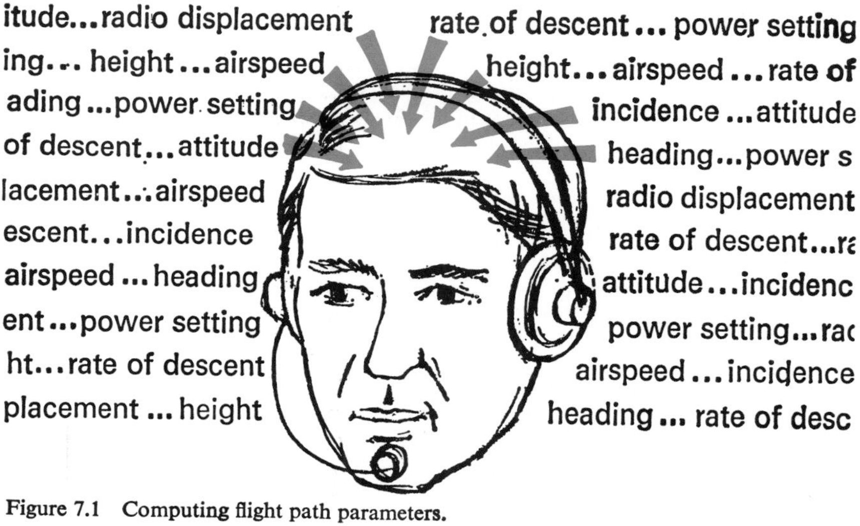

itude...radio displacement   **rate.of descent ... power setting**
ing... height ... airspeed   **height... airspeed ... rate of**
ading ...power setting   **incidence ...attitude**
of descent...attitude   **heading...power s**
lacement...airspeed   **radio displacement**
escent...incidence   **rate of descent...ra**
airspeed ...heading   **attitude...incidenc**
ent...power setting   **power setting...rac**
ht...rate of descent   **airspeed ...incidence**
placement ... height   **heading ... rate of desc**

Figure 7.1 Computing flight path parameters.

In making an approach in a jet aeroplane the subconscious mind of the pilot (it is still insisted that control of the flight path is primarily a subconscious workload as there are other things to be done with the conscious mind) should look a bit like the illustration in figure 7.1. All the eight parameters listed affect the aeroplane's flight path, and the pilot's subconscious mind should be constantly monitoring these parameters and also their rates of change. These signals are fed into his brain which computes all the values, their rates of change, their effects on each other and the effects of a range of corrective actions. The most advanced computer possible with loads of memory capability! The answer comes out as signals to the hands and feet which make the required corrective actions. These are then closely monitored to make sure that the aeroplane responds in the required fashion so as to follow an intercepting flight path back to the required flight path. It is essential that these corrective actions serve two purposes, not only to stop a divergence and to start it back the right way but also to lead to the regaining of the previously lost stable condition. Any corrective action applied in a gross and unthinking fashion will lead to a divergence on the other side. In correcting a low speed condition, for example, too much thrust for too long will rapidly lead to an overspeed condition.

Well now, this is an awful lot of words to explain something which most pilots know already. Making an approach in a piston-engined aeroplane is the same sort of problem, but different in that changes to the flight path can be made much more quickly and with more immediate effect. In the case of a jet aeroplane there will be delays before control inputs become effective. You simply have to make allowances for the delays, as well as for the fact that the behaviour of the aeroplane over the next few seconds will be dictated more by what it was doing a few seconds ago than by what you yourself did one second ago.

There are other factors which influence the approach path. These are wind gradients, gusts, glide path angle and lack of glide slope guidance. It is worth considering each of them in detail.

Wind gradients

Wind speed tends to decrease close to the ground. This is due to the surface friction effect of the ground on the wind. It is rather academic even to quote the standard assumed wind shear with height — even if there is an agreed standard — because local effects will always change the shear ratio significantly. Reported wind speeds in relation to actual surface wind speed vary because of the differing heights at which they are measured at different airports although it is claimed that reported winds are 'corrected' to the standard 10 metre height. While temperature changes and convective sources play a part, by far the most significant influence is the local terrain — not only geographical contours but also upstanding obstructions like tall trees and buildings. All these things produce wind shears and affect the height above the surface at which their effects first become significant. As a generalisation therefore it can be said that, depending on the locality and the strength of the wind, there can be significant wind shear effects on the approach.

An aeroplane is sensitive to changes in wind speed. A sudden loss of 10 knots in wind speed is almost exactly equivalent to a sudden loss of 10 knots in airspeed, with the expected results. This is because the indicated airspeed decreases much faster than the speed of the aeroplane over the ground in still air can be increased — and this is more significant in a turbine-engined aeroplane than a piston-engined aeroplane. Not only does the jet aircraft take longer to accelerate but there is no added protection from a substantially reducing stall speed with increasing power.

In making an approach with a suspected wind gradient problem, some

174

protection has to be built-in in advance and this is done by flying the approach at a higher airspeed. There are various rules of thumb, the most common of which is to add a half of the reported windspeed to the otherwise chosen airspeed. This may normally be done up to a maximum increment of 15 knots. Only in exceptionally demanding cases, such as when there is a need to consider gusts additionally, should this be exceeded.

Gusts

As wind speed increases so does potential gustiness. Gusts are as much the result of upstanding obstructions causing turbulence downwind across the runway approach path as the general choppiness at low level on a rough day. Unlike straight wind shear, which usually results in a lower wind speed at lower levels, gustiness is pretty random, and can cause disturbances in speed, height and altitude. The rule of thumb increase in approach speed due to wind shear will normally be sufficient to look after a proportionate amount of gustiness, but if gustiness alone is considered to be more important than shear effect then some extra allowance has to be made. Moderate increments for shear may be increased to take account of gusts where, again, the rule is to add half the gust value.

Where shear and gust increments need to be added cumulatively they may be, up to a maximum of 20 knots above the approach speed chosen for calm conditions. These two effects together therefore give a maximum increment of +15 knots for wind shear plus another 5 knots for gusts. This speed increment of 20 knots total should provide adequate controllability for all except really appalling approach conditions. As in many other absolutely extreme conditions the captain is then authorised to take whatever decision he considers prudent under the prevailing circumstances.

Glide slope angle

The optimum glide slope angle for a modern jet transport is somewhere between $2\frac{1}{2}°$ and $3°$. For an aeroplane with a target threshold speed of 140 knots maintaining 150 knots on the approach under still air conditions, these represent descent rates of exactly 662 f.p.m. and 797 f.p.m. respectively. Average these and round them off and we can say that in still air for approach slopes of $2\frac{1}{2}°$ to $3°$ *the rate of descent should be just over 700 f.p.m.* Now remember this figure; when all else fails it is a good number to remember.

Let us now go one step further. Assuming that correct heights are flown this magic number will change only as a function of ground speed. If ground speed is low, due for example to a strong head wind, the required rate of descent will be *less*; if ground speed is high, due to a tail wind, the required rate of descent will be *more*. The lower the ground speed the smaller the rate of descent; the higher the ground speed the greater the rate of descent. A simple rule of thumb based on ground speed is given later.

A steep glide slope involves higher rates of descent which is just what we want to avoid in the approach with a jet transport aircraft for all the reasons already elaborated.

A much shallower than normal approach is also undesirable, not only because of the noise problem, but particularly because its extension towards the threshold can lead to an early touchdown. This will be discussed later.

Lack of glide slope guidance

It is now becoming accepted that a simple visual approach can be a difficult manoeuvre in a jet transport aeroplane. This is particularly true of a night visual approach and a long straight-in final approach in daylight. This is because visual assessment of height above the ground, particularly with a featureless surface, and visual assessment of distance out from the threshold are difficult. In the old days where it was normal practice to fly a circuit before landing the circuit procedure made it possible for the pilot to select a position in space of known height and distance out from which to fly a traditional approach path. But modern air traffic procedures are far removed from circuit philosophy and a pilot is often .faced with a very long final approach. Where there is guidance, ILS, VASIs or GCA for example, there is no difficulty because there is in effect a railway line correctly aligned in space and all he has to do is to get on to it, fly down it and it will lead him safely to the threshold provided that he is capable of controlling his airspeed. In the absence of a railway line, however, the pilot is poorly placed because not only does he not have guidance down the slope but he also lacks guidance as to where he should join the slope. Having been conditioned by a flight at very high altitude and speed it is often difficult to rearrange one's computing mechanism and start resolving heights, time and distances at low level. With the performance capability and flying qualities of a modern jet transport large excursions in height, speed and rate of descent can take place unless the projected flight path is very closely monitored and adjusted so as to achieve the required flight path especially under conditions where outside visual references are *apparently good*.

In view of the potential difficulties of the pure visual approach, VASIs should be the minimum standard fit at all airfields. These have the added advantage that they serve to continue guidance right down to the threshold at heights below which many ILS glide slopes are unreliable.

If you should be denied all approach slope guidance then fall back on some simple arithmetic and make use of any aid (NDB or DME) which will give distance out from the threshold. With distance out and an assumed 3° glide slope, height required can be calculated; if you multiply the distance from the threshold in miles by 3 you get the height in hundreds of feet you should be at for a glide slope approximating to 3°. For example:—

(a) 3 miles out × 3 = 900 feet.

(b) 10 miles out × 3 = 3,000 feet.

176

Alternatively, for those with ground speed read-out, the rate of descent for a 3° glide slope is:—

feet/min. required = 5 × ground speed in knots.

This then is broadly how you get around lack of glide slope guidance. Without overstating the case it is true to say that even very experienced pilots sometimes make a hash of a visual approach. At say three miles out they suddenly realise they are a lot too low, or at two miles out they suddenly realise they are a lot too high.

Some of these errors can be difficult to salvage. So make an attempt to programme the approach and fly it with some accuracy. Achieve the correct height at the appropriate distance out (even if you just have to estimate distance out) then thereafter fly a mean rate of descent of just over 700 feet/min. and you won't go far wrong. At least the really gross errors will be avoided.

Note that the whole of this sub-chapter has been concerned with the approach only; techniques related to the flight path approaching the threshold will be covered later.

Reduced roll freedom on the ground

On a straight wing aeroplane the wing tips, engines and flaps all remain at about the same height above the runway as the aeroplane is rotated for take-off and flared for landing; the static roll clearance which exists before a wing tip touches the ground can therefore be enjoyed at all times.

On a swept wing aeroplane, however, the ground clearance is less, even in the three point attitude. This is due to the absence of propellers and low engine pods (where they are wing mounted), less dihedral and very extended trailing edge flaps. This reduced clearance is further compromised when the aircraft is in a nose high attitude, which is higher than normal because of the greater incidence required to produce lift on a swept wing. During the rotation on the ground, the outer part of a swept wing, because it is aft of the main gear (which is the pivot of the manoeuvre), rotates closer to the ground and the wing tips and flaps can get very close indeed. Under these conditions only a few degrees of roll freedom may exist before something scrapes the runway.

Life is more complicated yet, because it must also be remembered that swept wing aeroplanes roll hard with yaw. The control of this roll has to be nicely matched by the lateral control, bearing in mind the possible dis-continuity in roll against lateral control application when the spoilers start to take effect.

So take care when operating in cross winds. On take-off, set in a little into-wind aileron control quite early in the take-off run whether or not you feel it necessary; this will stop the down wind roll which will otherwise occur just before lift-off. Then, throughout the rotation and lift-off, make sure you keep the aeroplane substantially level laterally. On landing, don't get too active on the ailerons close to the ground. Apply enough but not too much and bear in mind the approximate spectacle angle at which the spoilers start to augment roll control. Avoid the divergent lateral oscillations which can develop and eat up your roll clearance in no time.

If you look like getting into trouble put the ailerons back into the middle, let the aeroplane settle down and start again. When taking out the drift angle just before touch down *don't kick it off* — rather, *push it off*. Feed in the rudder smoothly and match it with the required amount of aileron control.

Some types of jet transports tend to lift the into-wind wing during a cross wind landing, *some time after touch-down*. Be prepared for this and continue to maintain lateral level until quite a low speed has been reached.

When landing in a maximum crosswind component on a gusty day in a type with non-differential spoilers (those which go up but never down in response to an aileron signal) remember that the selection of full spoiler after touch-down will leave you on ailerons alone for lateral control. In these circumstances it is wise to pull only half spoiler angle thus leaving some further up spoiler movement to assist the ailerons in maintaining lateral control.

Again, take care on a continued take-off following engine failure. While on some types you must get the rudder in immediately, try not to overdo it on the ailerons otherwise you will roll too far and scrape something. Apply rudder in a controlled manner as the change in heading demands it and match the aileron control so as to maintain lateral level.

High ground speeds

As has already been discussed, the designer, when choosing the values which dictate his wing design, is faced with a number of conflicting requirements and the final outcome is a compromise which retains most of the best qualities and trims the poorer qualities to within reasonable limits. This results in a wing which is best in high speed cruise condition but has poor lift values at low speeds; to a certain extent the lift remains a bit of a disappointment in spite of the most sophisticated trailing and leading edge devices. Wing loadings have also increased over the years and this carries an increase in stalling speed. The net result is that stalling speeds remain high and therefore the take-off and landing speeds are high.

The consequences of high ground speeds are most significant and the more important problems are discussed at some length later.

These aside, there are three other basic points which need to be made:—

(a) A high ground speed means that a lot of distance is being covered every second; a piston-engined aeroplane's V_1 of 90 knots = 150 feet/sec., while a jet's V_1 of 140 knots = 233 feet/sec. While the scheduled performance of the aircraft automatically looks after these higher speeds it must be emphasised that any delays due to indecision on the part of the pilot prove very expensive in terms of distance. Take the decision to abort a take-off for example. This is always a psychological shock when it actually happens and it is well worth while, in the minute or two before you start the take-off, to rehearse the abort drill mentally; then, when it does happen, you are fully prepared for it and can go into the drill quickly and crisply — power off, brakes, spoilers open, reverse, and *keep it straight*.

(b) A reduction from a high ground speed to a lower speed can lead to the impression that the aeroplane is travelling quite slowly, whereas it can still be moving quite fast. From a touch-down at 130 knots, deceleration to 90 knots can give an impression of a significant reduction in speed. But 90 knots is still a fair speed, and a lot remains to be done before the landing can be considered finished. So do not fall into the trap of thinking that the landing is as good as done merely because the ASI has come below 100 knots. A lot remains to be done; persist with reverse thrust, modulate your braking according to the distance remaining and don't relax until you are down to taxying speed.

(c) Most tyres have maximum ground speed limitations; the normal limit is 200 m.p.h. (174 knots). However, under certain operating conditions (high altitude, high temperature take-offs at high weight, particularly when a reduced take-off flap setting is used for better climb gradients after take-off), the maximum true ground speed can exceed 200 m.p.h. Under these conditions special high speed tyres cleared to 225 m.p.h. (195 knots) must be used.

Tyre and brake temperatures

Because jet transports are very heavy a high load is imposed on each individual wheel and tyre. The brakes too, although they are designed for their job, can have enormous energy absorption imposed on them; this results in very high temperatures. A large jet taxying out at say 316,000 lb. can have as much as 17 tons bearing on each wheel and tyre and a rejected take-off from a high V_1 involving heavy braking can produce brake temperatures of 900°C and above.

It is widely known that, on any aircraft, one prolonged high demand on the brakes will raise them to high temperatures. It is also known that continual small demands on the brakes will produce elevated temperatures over a period of time. What is not sufficiently well appreciated, however, is that, on a very heavy aeroplane, just simple taxying over a long period, with comparatively little use of the brakes, is sufficient in itself to get the tyres and brakes quite hot. This results in temperatures, when finally lined up for take-off, high enough to compromise the assumed design energy absorption capability of the brakes. Significant use of the brakes during a prolonged taxi out from the ramp will quite definitely result in temperatures which invalidate the design performance of the braking system. A rejected take-off from what might appear to be a comparatively low speed (say 80 knsts) takes a great deal out of the brakes and a further take-off must not be made until the brakes have had time to cool. This waiting time is a lot longer than is usually imagined.

There are generally two limiting design cases for brakes:—

(a) The maximum landing weight case at a high touch down speed. This is usually factored by 1.5.

(b) The maximum take-off weight case for a rejected take-off at the highest scheduled V_1. This is not usually factored. This means that on the very rare occasions when the need arises the manoeuvre will terminate with the brakes having absorbed their design maximum energy; they will be extremely hot with the possibility of welding on.

In order to achieve these design maximum performances it is assumed that the brake temperatures are below certain values before the manoeuvre starts. These temperatures, therefore, must not be compromised by the possible abuses quoted above. Care must be taken to keep the work imposed on all elements of the gear to a reasonable minimum. Few jet transports are fitted with brake temperature gauges. In their absence, guidance is given in the Flight Manual on cooling periods to be observed after significant use of the brakes before the aeroplane can again be exposed to the possibility of another high demand on the brakes. These periods must be observed. The guidance appears in rather generalised statements and it is left to the pilot in command to interpret them, in a prudent manner, for the particular set of circumstances he comes up against. Be very prudent in this matter — it is important. Be conscious of what you are putting into the tyres and brakes, particularly in relation to possible subsequent demands which you might make.

If you suspect that you might have got the tyres hot, leave the gear down after take-off for a while in order to cool down the assemblies. Do not commit yourself to a landing (for some other good reason) very soon after take-off until you are satisfied that the gear has had time to cool off. In crew training, do not make consecutive touch and go landings without interspersing them with a few extended circuits with the gear down to cool off.

Fusible plugs are fitted to the wheel rims of most jet transports. These are temperature sensitive plugs which will blow at their design value and deflate the tyre before it bursts. A tyre explosion in a wheel well can be a pretty serious occurrence. While fusible plugs now avoid this, one shouldn't 'lean' on these plugs, because a landing on deflated tyres is also a hazard. Remember also that fusible plugs give protection only against overpressures due to high wheel temperatures resulting from excessive use of the brakes; they do not give protection against tyres bursting due to excessive carcase temperatures caused by prolonged taxying at high weights.

If it is known that the brakes and tyres have been used hard with associated high temperatures, take the following precautions:—

180

(a) After take-off leave the gear down, for up to twenty minutes, to cool right off before retraction.

(b) After landing clear the runway if possible, then stop, vacate the aircraft and be prepared to deal with a possible brake fire. If the brake use has been high, but not excessive, keep rolling gently to the ramp (checking the brakes for effect before turning in to a restricted manoeuvring area), get the aircraft chocked as quickly as possible, and release the brakes, otherwise they might weld on.

(c) After a rejected take-off, if the brake demand really was low, hold out of the way for the recommended period of time before making a second take-off; use just enough brake pressure to keep the aeroplane stationary. If the brake demand was at all high, return to the ramp and shut down for the recommended time period.

In pointing out the dangers which can exist in many areas there is always the possibility of shaking the pilot's confidence in the particular item under discussion. One needs to be able to see the whole picture and keep all these things in correct balance and perspective. So long as, in this case, the brakes and tyres have not been abused, have confidence in them and use them as you require them. Any reasonable demand you are likely to make has been taken account of in the design. But, to be fair to the designers and others who are responsible for the scheduled operation of your aeroplane, you must not hack away the foundations on which their work is built. In this case, if you keep tyre and brake temperatures below the published values before you make a high demand on them, then they will perform properly and not let you down.

Mishandled rotations

The very first type of flying accident specifically related to civil jet transport aircraft was the take-off accident in which, due to an error in rotation, the aeroplane failed to leave the ground in the distance available. The reason for this is now well understood and almost ancient history, and a lot of work has been done, and requirements written, to guard against it in the future. But the basic danger still exists, though in a slightly less critical fashion, and the importance of a correct rotation technique cannot be overrated.

The early jet transport had a rather symmetrical wing section designed primarily for good high speed qualities. This section was a critical producer of lift, even with the trailing edge flaps at the take-off setting, because the rather sharp nose profile caused the wing to stall at an incidence which could be reached on the ground if the aeroplane were rotated to too high an angle. This critical incidence occurred before the tail grounding limited the maximum achievable incidence. A significant contribution to this condition was the absence of propeller slipstream. Had there been four large propellers producing a lot of increased lift and a much lower power-on stalling speed it is probable that the aeroplane would have lifted-off during the rotation manoeuvre; but without the propeller slipstream the wing had to be accelerated to the right speed and set at the right incidence for lift-off.

Since that time both the requirements and the design of the aeroplanes have been changed so as to lessen the possibility of a ground stall. The aeroplanes have been improved in that the wing leading edge profile (either the wing leading edge itself or, where extensible high lift devices are fitted, the devices) has been drooped so as to make it retain its lifting ability at higher incidences. The requirements have been changed to make it possible to lift-off and climb out initially in the declared VMU attitude without undue hazard and without exceeding a defined increase in take-off distance. This applies to all aeroplanes. On those on which a tail drag has been demonstrated, or which are accepted as being geometry or elevator power limited, a 5% margin over VMU is applied to the VR speed. On those on which a tail drag has not been demonstrated, or which are not geometry or elevator power limited, a 10% margin over VMU is applied to the VR speed in order to achieve an equivalent level of safety. It is important to realise that rotation to a value exceeding the demonstrated VMU attitude can result in a stalled wing and complete inability to lift-off.

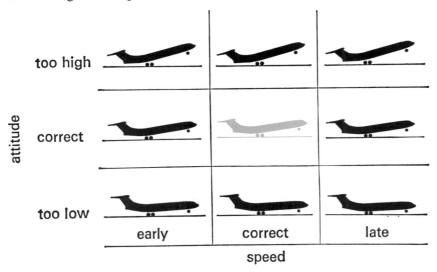

Figure 7.2   Rotation technique.

In spite of these improvements one should not lean too heavily on the qualities of the aeroplane or depend on the fat provided by the requirements. Take-off distance can be greatly influenced by the rotation speed, the

182

rotation rate and attitude and it is important to understand immediately that *varying V_R cannot possibly effect an improvement in take-off distance without reducing the overall safety of the manoeuvre.*

Rotation can be abused in eight out of the nine possible permutations which are shown in figure 7.2.

We need not go through the exact consequences of all eight incorrect techniques in detail but it is worth mentioning that early and high rotations produce large increases in drag which greatly extend the take off distance, and that late and low rotations will obviously extend the ground run. Cases 1 through 4 and cases 6 through 9 therefore all produce extended take-off distances . . . . . Q.E.D.(!).

Having established the importance of the V_R speed it is worth discussing rotation rate and lift-off attitude. There is a 'natural' rotation rate appropriate to each aircraft type; a few take-offs will soon show you just what this is. One can say that this rate then becomes the datum rate of a mid-weight I.S.A. sea-level take-off. That is, it relates to a mid-performance level. This datum rate should be modulated according to the level of performance available for each take-off. Under a high performance condition (low weight, low altitude and low temperature, etc.) the aeroplane will have a high rate of acceleration and the rotation rate will need to be that much faster. Similarly under a low performance condition (maximum weight, or high altitude, high temperature, etc.) a lower rotation rate will be required, reflecting the slower acceleration of the aeroplane.

Unlike rotation rate, which requires some degree of sophistication in order to match it to the expected level of performance available, the lift-off attitude is constant at all times, regardless of weight. This is a great help. Rotation at the right speed and rate to the right attitude will therefore get the aeroplane off the ground at the right speed and within the right distance. Easy to say? Certainly, and also not at all difficult to do.

Remember also that, on some modern aeroplanes, the all engines take-off can be more limiting than the engine out take-off in terms of obstacle clearance in the initial part of the climb out. This is because of the rapidly increasing airspeed causing the achieved flight path to fall below the engine out scheduled flight path unless care is taken to fly to the correct speeds. Furthermore, remember that, in the event of a continued take-off following engine failure at light weight, quite a high level of acceleration remains in the aeroplane. Don't let your concentration on maintaining directional control cause you to overshoot V_R by a significant amount.

The execution of a good take-off demands a smooth rotation of the aeroplane from V_R, through the lift-off speed, through the screen at V_3 (approximately $V_2 + 10$ knots) to a settled V_4 by, say, 300 feet, in the all engines case. In the engine out case the same principles apply except that V_2 is maintained from the screen onwards.

Finally, a word of warning. Don't indulge in 'snatch' rotations; apart from the risk of getting near the stall under 'g' conditions after lift-off it frightens those dead-heading pilots riding in the back.

Reverse thrust

Jet transport aircraft have high kinetic energy ($\frac{1}{2}mv^2$) during a landing roll or an aborted take-off, because they are heavy and fast. It is difficult to dissipate the energy because they have low drag with the nosewheel on the ground and retain forward thrust with the power levers at idle. While wheel brakes can normally cope, there is an obvious need for another retarding method. The solution is the drag provided by reverse thrust.

A thrust reverser is a device fitted in the exhaust system which effectively reverses the flow of the exhaust gases. In one typical system the reversal occurs in two parts; firstly the clamshells close and deflect the stream outwards and secondly the cascades, uncovered when the clamshells move, turn the flow further forwards. The flow does not reverse through 180°; the final path is about 45° from dead ahead. This, together with the losses in the reversed flow paths, results in a net efficiency of about 50%, i.e. a 10,000 lb. thrust engine at full power reverse produces about 5,000 lb. of reverse thrust. It will produce even less, if restricted to an r.p.m. less than maximum

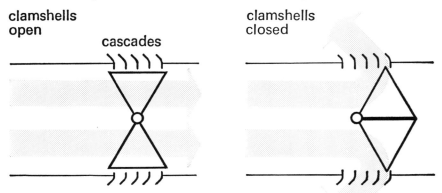

clamshells open

cascades

clamshells closed

forward thrust　　　　**reverse thrust**

Figure 7.3　A typical thrust reverser.

in reverse. Reverse thrust is normally obtained, with the main power lever at forward idle, by pulling up the reverse lever to a detent; this merely operates the reverser through full stroke but leaves the engine still at idle r.p.m. (a light illuminates immediately the reverser leaves the full ahead position and a power lever baulk is removed once the reverser has travelled full stroke and is locked in the reverse position). Power may then be applied

184

in reverse by further upwards and backwards movement of the reverse lever. Reverse is cancelled by closing the reverse lever to the idle reverse position then dropping it fully back to the forward idle position. This last movement operates the reverser back to the forward thrust position when the light goes out indicating that the forward locks have engaged.

Figure 7.3 illustrates, for a simple reverser, the gas flows in forward and reverse thrust.

The use of reverse thrust in flight, which at the present time is limited to two aircraft types, is comparatively uncomplicated. It is used as a speed brake and, within its limitations, is very effective. It produces a little buffet due to the disturbed flow.

The attraction of reverse thrust on the ground, after landing and for a rejected take-off, is that, provided it is used symmetrically, it is not compromised by a slippery runway surface. Note, however, that in cross wind conditions the aeroplane can start sliding sideways when control might become difficult. In this case reduce all engines to idle reverse and maintain control by brakes and steering.

Reverse thrust is much more effective at high aircraft speeds than at low speeds, for two reasons. Firstly, the net amount of reverse thrust increases with speed because the acceleration imposed on the (constant) mass flow is greater. This is because the aircraft forward speed is additional when in reverse thrust as opposed to subtractional when in forward thrust. Secondly, the power produced is higher at higher speeds because of the increased rate of doing work. In this context it means that the kinetic energy of the aeroplane is being destroyed at a higher rate at the higher speeds. Wing podded reversible engines have the additional advantage in reverse thrust at high speeds of suffering a general blockage of airflow under the wing causing a higher velocity over the upper surface and hence higher drag. To get best value from the reverse facility therefore it is important that it is used as soon as is prudent after touch-down.

The word prudent needs a little elaboration. Some aircraft tend to pitch nose up on selection of reverse on landing, and this effect, particularly when combined with the nose up pitch effect from the spoilers, can cause the aeroplane to leave the ground again momentarily. On these types the aircraft must be firmly on the ground, with the nosewheel down, before reverse is selected. Other types have no change in pitch, and reverse idle may be selected after the main gear is down and before the nosewheel is down. So, while it is important not to rush the selection of reverse at the expense of neglecting some other aspect of control, it is equally important not to delay the selection of reverse any longer than is necessary — get it in early where it can do most trade for you.

There is a difference between reverse pitch on a propeller and reverse thrust on a jet which has been discussed earlier in this book. It was stated that idle reverse on a propeller produces about 60% of the total reverse thrust available at full power reverse and is therefore a very useful setting when full reverse thrust is not needed. On selecting idle reverse on a jet engine, however, there is very little actual reverse thrust produced, the difference being from 1,000 lb. of forward thrust to 500 lb. of reverse thrust, which is not much of a net change. It is therefore quite useless bowling along with only reverse idle selected. Not only must you select reverse as soon as is reasonable but you must then open up to full power reverse as soon as possible.

Don't cancel reverse too early. Having decelerated from 130 knots to 90 knots there is a temptation towards the feeling that the landing is as good as over. This is far from true at 90 knots. Reverse thrust should always be held until you are satisfied that the landing roll will be contained comfortably within the distance available.

The need to cancel reverse for engine handling considerations comes under two headings. The first is where, in a four podded reversible installation, the reversed flow of the inners, being ahead of the outers, tends to upset the intake flow of the outers. This occurs at about 80 knots in a head wind, and slightly earlier in a cross wind. In this case, at 80 knots start to throttle down the inners smoothly and progressively so that they are at idle by about 60 knots. The second is where any engine in isolation tends to breathe its own reversed exhaust; this occurs at about 50 knots in a head wind and again slightly earlier in a cross wind. Just before 50 knots therefore throttle down the remaining engines. Apart from engine handling considerations it must be remembered that reverse held to a low speed on a loose surface, dust or snow, etc., can destroy all forward visibility as the cloud is blown ahead of the aeroplane.

Because thrust reversers are usually operated by compressor bleed air their rate of operation is a function of engine r.p.m.; the higher the r.p.m. the faster they operate. This is why, on a rejected take-off, where the engines are at high r.p.m., reverse comes in very quickly. On landing, where the engines are running down to idle, reverse thrust is slower to come in; the slowness being compounded by the poor basic acceleration qualities of the jet engine from low r.p.m., as discussed earlier. This is also why reverse thrust should not be cancelled quickly. If it is, the reverser will operate while engine r.p.m. is still high, and there will be a momentary push from the forward thrust. So throttle down progressively to reverse idle, then cancel reverse in slow time.

It should be emphasised that in an emergency full reverse must be held right down to a stop. It is much better to risk some engine damage than to overrun the hard surface.

In the event of any directional control difficulties due to suspected engine or reverser malfunction don't attempt to try to work out which engine has to be throttled up, or down, and whether in reverse, or forward thrust, to compensate for the swing; it is too difficult in the time available. In such cases always reduce all engines to idle immediately; it doesn't matter if some

186

are at forward idle and some are at reverse idle, because that amount of asymmetry is not significant.

For the engine-out landing case, where the aircraft has large yawing moments, only the remaining symmetrical pair should normally be reversed. However, on a dry runway the remaining odd engine may be reversed so long as the asymmetry can be held on rudder and steering only. As soon as differential braking becomes necessary for directional control the odd engine reverse should be cancelled. The amount of braking which is not being used is more valuable overall, particularly at the ground speed then obtaining, than the extra reverse thrust. On aircraft which have small asymmetric yawing moments, however, reverse may, and should, be used asymmetrically, even on other than dry runways, again so long as the small swing can be held without the need for differential braking. Asymmetric reverse should never be used on a very slippery runway surface. The Flight Manual for the type should indicate the degree of controllability you have; know what you have and be prepared to take full advantage of it.

One particular aeroplane is cleared for the use of reverse thrust before touch-down on landing. Reverse idle is selected after the threshold has been crossed and full reverse just at touch-down. There is no pitch change on this particular aeroplane. This use of reverse before touch-down tends to worry some pilots. It can only be said that every failure and reasonable mishandling case has been fully investigated and the technique found to be quite acceptable. The aeroplane is cleared for rollers using this method of reverse and reverse can be selected and cancelled very quickly indeed. The engine failed case can be held on rudder alone while still airborne.

Aquaplaning

Aquaplaning is not new, neither is it peculiar to jet transport aircraft. It can occur on those older types of aeroplane which are fast on and off the ground and equipped with low pressure tyres. It is, however, much more significant on jet transport aircraft because nearly all of them have the qualities which lead to aquaplaning; and it is a real problem.

Aquaplaning is caused by a layer of water beneath the tyre which builds up in increasing resistance to displacement and finally results in the formation of a wedge between the runway and the tyre. This resistance has a vertical component which progressively lifts the tyre and reduces the area in contact with the runway until the aircraft is completely water-borne. In this condition the tyre is no longer capable of providing directional control or effective braking. The drag forces are very low and approximate to the sort of braking coefficient which would be achieved on an icy runway.

Aquaplaning can occur when running in water and in certain depths and densities of slush. Present indications are that simple dynamic aquaplaning is unlikely to occur in water depths much below 0.2 in. although under some

conditions the minimum depth may be as low as 0.1 in.   Once aquaplaning
has commenced it can be sustained over areas where the water depth is less
than that required to initiate aquaplaning and to lower speeds than that
required for initiation.

A simple formula has been derived from data obtained during trials which
shows the relationship between the minimum speed at which aquaplaning
may commence and the aircraft's tyre pressure.   This states that the minimum
initiating aquaplaning speed in knots is approximately nine times the square
root of the tyre pressure in pounds per square inch.   Speed in this context
is of course true ground speed and not indicated airspeed, although it need
not be precisely calculated.   It is sufficient merely to allow for the wind in
order to arrive at a 'local' ground speed.   One typical jet transport of
170 lb. per sq. in. tyre pressure has a main wheels aquaplaning speed of
112 knots.   Compare this speed with a maximum take-off weight balanced
field length V_1 of 148 knots and a touch down speed at maximum landing
weight (target threshold speed -10 knots) of 136 knots: in the first case
there is a gap of 36 knots and in the second 24 knots.

The seriousness of aquaplaning is best illustrated by the following values
of braking coefficients:—

Normal dry surface	0.3
Normal wet surface	0.15
Icy surface	0.05

A condition of complete dynamic aquaplaning equates to an icy surface.

Knowledge of aquaplaning is accumulating all the time.   Although the
distinction is perhaps a trifle academic, there are now stated to be three types
of aquaplaning:—

(a) **Dynamic**   This is due to standing water on the runway when the tyre is
lifted off and completely supported by the water.

(b) **Viscous**   This occurs when the surface is damp and provides a very thin
film of fluid which cannot be penetrated by the tyre.   Viscous aquaplaning can occur at, or persist down to, much lower speeds than simple
dynamic aquaplaning.   It is particularly associated with smooth surfaces
and is quite likely to occur in the touch-down area which is often liberally
smeared with rubber deposits.

(c) **Reverted rubber**   This refers to the tyre becoming tacky and looking like
uncured rubber.   It requires a long skid, rubber reversion and a wet
surface.   The heat from the friction between the tyre and the wet runway
surface boils the water and reverts the rubber, which forms a seal, which
delays water dispersal.   The steam then prevents the tyre from contacting
the runway.

All three types of aquaplaning can occur during one landing run if the
conditions are right.

There are several factors which influence aquaplaning. Multi-rib tyre treads, with grooves of adequate dimensions to give good drainage, tend to relieve the hydrodynamic pressure and hence increase the depth at which aquaplaning will occur. Depending on the tread design critical depths can range from 0.1 to 0.4 in. Tyre wear is very obviously a most important factor; the more worn the tyre the more likely it will be to aquaplane. The arrangement of the main undercarriage assembly also has a bearing on aquaplaning characteristics. With tandem bogies the clearing action of the front wheels tends to reduce the depth encountered by the rear wheels, thus delaying the speed or alternatively increasing the depth at which these wheels will aquaplane.

Runway surface texture is important. Surfaces with a coarse matrix or grooves will take longer to build up to limiting depths particularly in windy conditions. They are better able to accept the short term build-ups of water which would occur under similar conditions on a smooth runway. Under zero wind conditions most runways have adequate crossfall to provide good drainage under quite high rates of precipitation. However, it appears that drainage can be seriously affected in winds above about 10 knots. Thus a crosswind blowing up the transverse slope of a runway could have a significant effect on water depth. This would lead to aquaplaning on that side and hence asymmetric braking action.

More recent Flight Manuals contain data on the landing distance required under very slippery runway conditions with an assumed coefficient of friction of 0.05; this can be read across to the potential aquaplaning condition. It is difficult to generalise, but those aeroplanes with a significant amount of reserve reverse thrust need about 25% extra distance while those without need up to 50% extra distance.

A 'significant amount of reserve reverse thrust' means symmetrically obtainable reverse thrust above that assumed in the scheduled performance, i.e. an emergency reverse power, or four engines equipped with reversers where, after one failure, symmetrical power can still be drawn. No twin-engined aeroplane is likely to qualify unless both engines keep operating and an emergency power is available because asymmetric reverse must not be used under slippery conditions.

So much for the facts. Now, what can we do about them? There are five distinct things you must do, in the following order:—

1. Be equipped with certain essential knowledge.

2. Make an assessment of the criticality of the landing.

3. Fly the aeroplane properly on the approach.

4. Be prepared and ready to overshoot from the threshold.

5. Handle the aeroplane properly on the ground.

Let us now consider each of these in detail.

14

General knowledge

You should know your tyre pressures and your aquaplaning speed. You should know the condition of your tyres. Make a particular note of this when you do your walk-around inspection prior to flight. You should know the significance of your gear and brake design — anti-skid coupled fore and aft on a tandem bogie will cause the leading wheel sensor to relieve braking pressure on the trailing wheel for example. Not that there is much you can actually do about all this but if the landing is likely to be critical you must know what the contribution of your aeroplane will be in order to come to a proper decision.

Assessment of the criticality of the landing

This you must achieve before you start the approach, otherwise you might be setting up an impossible task for yourself. At least one accident report has concluded that the landing distance available was not long enough under the prevailing conditions even accepting that the aeroplane was handled with a fair regard for the circumstances. To come to a sensible assessment you must listen to the landing forecast; know your landing weight and threshold speed; appreciate the wind effect, not only on your adjusted approach speed but also on the probable water effect on the runway; know the runway length, slope, approach glide path angle and extra distance required under slippery conditions (where known); use any local knowledge you might have (because for example of your constant use of the particular aerodrome). Think all these things out and come up with an assessment of the criticality of the landing. If you decide the landing is going to be too tight then either stand off until it stops raining or divert to a better aerodrome. Most runways drain adequately under normal rates of precipitation. Very heavy precipitation rarely lasts long and a stand-off of 15 to 20 minutes should be sufficient to get rid of really critical water depths. If you decide that the landing can be made without undue risk then start the approach.

Flying the approach

There is only one object in this part of the flight and that is to fly the approach in such a fashion as to arrive at the threshold at the right height, right speed, right rate of descent, right attitude, right power, etc. etc. There is no acceptable operational variation of technique which will give you a shorter landing distance than the standard technique. Any aiming short, ducking under the glide slope or speed below target speed will tend to cause more trouble than you are seeking to avoid.

At the threshold

If you have assessed the approach as 'critical' but nevertheless have elected to make it — a perfectly proper decision — this is your last chance to salvage

190

what could be a mess. Proceed with the landing only if you are absolutely satisfied with your flight conditions at the threshold. If you are not absolutely satisfied, don't hesitate; open up and go around *at once*. If you are high and/or fast you are taking a risk. If you proceed and slide off at 50 knots and smash the aeroplane — and survive — your first reaction will be 'what wouldn't I give to have that last five minutes over again' (who hasn't said this at some time in his life?). Well now, at the threshold you have that five minutes, so think about it. Remember that once you are down and start aquaplaning there is very little you can do about it on a tight runway. If you are fortunate enough to know the slippery landing distance required then there should be no undue risk even if you should aquaplane, provided that you can keep it straight. Don't chance your arm in crosswinds above 10 knots component.

Technique on the ground

Do not indulge in a prolonged flare, because it wastes distance. As soon as you reasonably can put the aeroplane firmly on the ground and start the drills without delay. Wheel braking on the ground is much more effective than floating along just above the ground. A firm touch-down is necessary to bang through the water just in case aquaplaning conditions are absolutely critical when a really smooth touch-down might just be enough to induce aquaplaning. Once down, push the control column forward to get the incidence, and therefore the lift, off the wings and the weight on to the wheels. Pull full spoiler immediately to achieve the same result. Now pull full reverse thrust *and hold it*. As soon as the aeroplane is firmly on three points start braking and increase brake pressure progressively to just below a moderate rate of anti-skid cycling as indicated by the foot-thumpers or by the pressure gauges. If braking action appears reasonable then proceed with a normal short landing procedure. If braking action appears poor, hang on to full reverse power until the engines start to object then reduce thrust progressively.

Summary

This sub-chapter on aquaplaning has been written rather forcibly — and for good reason. While some accidents are truly unavoidable and others the result of a most unusual chain of circumstances, aquaplaning accidents are nearly all avoidable. It is not the end of the world to stand off or divert occasionally. But it is asking for trouble to attempt a landing on a tight, very wet runway. · Think well *before* you expose yourself to this kind of risk.

Slush

For the purposes of this sub-chapter only, slush connotes water, slush and snow. Like aquaplaning, the problem of slush is not new or peculiar to jet transport aeroplanes; it has been an embarrassment to the older aeroplanes. But it is a more significant hazard to the jets because of their higher speeds on the runway and also because early lift-off is not possible as on most propeller-driven aircraft.

Ignoring the wave drag, which is the extra energy needed to pick up and form the slush into a wave pattern ahead of the wheels, the drag on the undercarriage when running through slush is of course proportional to density and the square of the velocity. This is our old friend $\frac{1}{2}\rho V^2$ all over again, where this time ρ = slush density. Figure 7.4 illustrates the increase in drag at high speeds for acceleration through slush of three different density values. Remember the significance of the speed squared law. If you double the speed you increase the drag four times; if you treble the speed you increase the drag nine times, and so on.

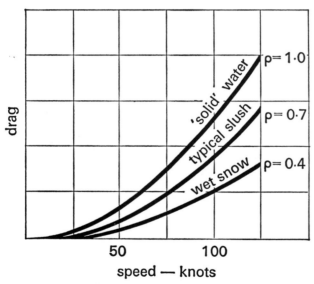

Figure 7.4   Slush drag.

Running through slush at speed produces the following hazards:—

(a) Impact damage to the aeroplane due to the slush being thrown up by the wheels. The nosewheel spray can impinge on the wing leading edge and pack slush into the main gear legs and wheel bays. The main gear spray can damage the wing undersurface, the flaps and the tail assembly.

(b) Engine malfunction due to ingestion of the spray thrown up by the wheels. Water in sufficient quantity will put the fire out in spite of ignition being selected on.

(c) Marked reduction in performance both in acceleration and braking. In acceleration this is because of the increase in drag and in braking because of the reduction in friction coefficient between the tyre and the runway.

(d) Reduction in controllability due to lowered coefficients of friction on the nosewheel in terms of steering and on the main wheels in terms of differential braking.

The problem of slush is being tackled in two ways. These are the provision of more, and more efficient, snow clearing equipment at major airports so that snow will be removed before slush can form, and the provision of more reliable means by which the effects of slush can be established. The latter is being tackled on the aerodrome side by the provision of devices which give an accurate measurement of depth over the whole runway and on the aircraft side by the determination of the amount of deterioration in field performance when running in these conditions.

Methods of measurement

While efforts are made to clear runways from which jet aircraft operate some snow will remain and eventually turn into slush. Information is then provided on the depth and density of any precipitation which remains. Two methods of depth assessment can be used:—

(i) A simple depth gauge with which readings are taken every 1,000 ft. along the runway and at 15 and 30 ft. either side of the centreline. These measurements are for virgin slush clear of any effects or rutting. Depth information in millimetres is for each third of the runway and each value is the mean of all readings taken in that section. The type of precipitation is described as one of the following:—

Dry snow (approx. density 0.2 to 0.35)

Wet snow (approx. density 0.35 to 0.5)

Slush (approx. density 0.5 to 0.8)

Standing water

(ii) A device pushed in front of a road vehicle providing integrated drag action on a free rolling wheel against time and distance. The vehicle weaves about the centreline in order to obtain a mean effect along the length of usable runway. This system provides Water Equivalent Depth (W.E.D.) in millimetres and information is passed to pilots in this form. The relationship of actual depth to W.E.D. is dependent on the density of the slush. Hence if the runway is covered by a depth of 15 mm. of 0.6 density the W.E.D. is 9 mm.

193

The determination of slush effect on aircraft performance has been done mostly under simulated conditions. From this admittedly second best method there has been built up a background of information from which it is possible to predict the sort of changes in performance which can be expected. Naturally, there are many problems which are not readily solved and a pilot may well be forgiven if he questions the accuracy of slush accountability. The answer lies in the manner in which the information is used. To obtain results which are suitable for analysis it must be assumed that nature has been considerate enough to lay an even bed of snow over the length of the runway, a situation which is unlikely to prevail even in zero wind conditions. Once this starts to turn to slush it must also be assumed that even drainage will exist to maintain constant density. In practice it is unlikely that either of these conditions will prevail and it is therefore important to allow for the worst depths and densities which exist for a particular operation.

Effect on take-off distance

When depth and density against distance information is provided in the Flight Manual this can readily be done. If W.E.D. information is provided, and if there is only a single published figure, then the worst combinations of

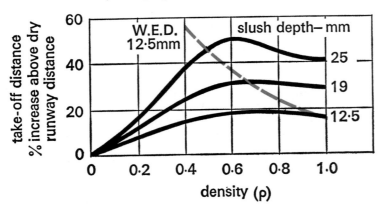

Figure 7.5   A typical W.E.D. chart.

depth and density have already been allowed for. Figure 7.5 illustrates a typical W.E.D. curve derived from varying depths, and from this a basic pitfall in W.E.D. is apparent. Different depths and densities which when multiplied together may produce an identical W.E.D., do not necessarily produce the same percentage increase in take-off distance. Hence:—

> 12.5 mm W.E.D. and 25 mm of slush produce an increase of 46%
> 12.5 mm W.E.D. and 19 mm of slush produce an increase of 31%

194

From this it is apparent that, without knowledge of depth or density, W.E.D. information cannot be applied to charts which give the full range of these parameters.

Penalties can occur on take-off if aquaplaning does not take place at the expected speed. Instead of lifting up and aquaplaning, with a reduction in drag and a lowering of the spray profile, the aeroplane will plough on and suffer increasing drag and a more damaging spray pattern. So for this reason too it is highly desirable that the correct density be established to minimise inaccuracies in distance.

For aircraft without slush data in the Flight Manual only the broadest advice can be given here, and this is best done by some examples. For two quite different early types of jet transport the following figures have been published.

	Aeroplane X	Aeroplane Y
Increment to be added to 'Take-off Field Length Required' (a) for 15 mm *actual depth* (b) for 15 mm *W.E.D.*	20% 55%	20% 30%

Remember that without density information the most adverse density must be assumed. The significant increase in field length required for aeroplane X in 15 mm W.E.D. (15 mm = 0.6 in.) corresponds to a much lower density (i.e. greater actual depth) condition than does the corresponding increment for aeroplane Y.

Finally, pilots should also be aware of the fact that published increases in distance are associated with all engines operating; no provision is made for an engine failure during the ground run. For guidance on the effect on stopping distance, reference should be made to the accelerate-stop information associated with icy runways (braking coefficient 0.05). Note that this will not allow for the deterioration in acceleration up to V_1 which must be computed from the take-off data.

If you wish to take account of a possible engine failure during take-off in slush you must consider these points:—

(a) An attempt to stop from V_1 will almost certainly result in the runway being overrun.

(b) An attempt to continue on three engines might be compromised by a significantly increased take-off distance.

195

As will be discussed later there is a recommended V_1 for wet conditions of 'dry $V_1 - 10$ knots'. This improves the stopping capability back to evens, as it were, and results only in a reduced screen height (by 20 ft. in the worst case) in the event of a continued take-off. If, in slush, you choose to work to the wet V_1 of 'dry V_1—10 knots' you improve your stopping chances but further degrade your take-off chances. The last grains of comfort that can be drawn are that the possibility of an engine failure on take-off at the worst point is remote when coupled with a distance limited slush take-off and that the slush data is, in general, conservatively drawn. Having thought out the whole of the problem perhaps the best possible decisions are:—

(a) Don't attempt a take-off in more than 12.5 mm ($\frac{1}{2}$ in.) of slush.

(b) In 12.5 mm ($\frac{1}{2}$ in.) of slush or less, select a wet V_1 equal to '$V_1 - 10$ knots' and be prepared to stop for a failure up to this speed. (After V_1 dry you should make a successful take-off following engine failure. You cannot be sure of success on a limiting field from about 'V_1 wet -5 knots' to V_1 dry.)

If in doubt at V_1, stop anyway. It is safer to slide off the end at 40 knots than fail to get off having lost an engine.

General operation in slush

The following points can be made with reference to operations in slush:—

(a) In planning the operation remember that small temperature differences can make a significant alteration to surface conditions quite rapidly. Continual rutting by the passage of other aircraft can lead to unexpected build-up in depth. Therefore, either have some distance margin in hand or have available a recent runway survey.

(b) Some of the later aircraft have been tested with chined nose wheel tyres. These deflect the nose wheel spray pattern downwards thus reducing drag due to slush impinging on the airframe and reducing the amount of slush ingested by the engines. When effects are quoted for standard and chined tyres make sure you are using the data appropriate to the tyres fitted.

(c) Wherever possible, operation in crosswinds should be avoided because of the difficulties involved in maintaining directional control. On take-off rudder control usually becomes effective around 70 to 80 knots; on landing rudders lose effectiveness at a higher speed because of the influence of reverse thrust. The difficulties of attempting to regain directional control by use of asymmetric reverse thrust have already been emphasised. At speeds below say 80 knots, therefore, directional control has to be maintained with just a touch of steering and some delicate use of differential braking. If the operation looks like getting out of hand, keep the aeroplane straight at all costs and accept that

196

running off the end of the runway, straight, at low speed, is a lesser hazard than sliding off sideways at high speed. The gear is much stronger fore and aft than sideways and the overrun area is better able to take the aeroplane than the ground alongside the runway.

(d) Use engine 'ignition override' on to lessen the possibility of ingestion causing engine malfunctioning on the ground.

(e) If distance is limiting the normal dry V_1 offers the best compromise in risk associated with a continued or aborted take-off. If there is distance to spare a progressive reduction in V_1 to V_1 wet reduces the risk associated with the aborted take-off without unduly compromising the continued take-off.

(f) Where alternative take-off flap settings are scheduled use the more extended one to keep distance on the ground to a minimum.

(g) Don't forget the importance of clearing snow, frost or ice from the aerofoil surfaces before attempting to take-off. The consequences of attempting to fly a jet aircraft in this condition are more critical than on a propeller-driven aeroplane.

(h) Occasionally, take-off power is limited to a defined maximum in terms of engine life when a higher power can be drawn without exceeding any engine or airframe limitations. Use the highest power available to keep distance on the ground to a minimum. This philosophy does not apply to EPR limited engines.

(i) On some aircraft early nose wheel raising is permitted during take-offs in slush; this technique is desirable in order to reduce ingestion as well as to reduce take-off distance and damage to the airframe. The earliest speed at which the nose wheel can be raised is a function of CG position: the further aft the CG the lower the speed. Early nose wheel raising, however, should not be indulged in unless specifically permitted in the Flight Manual.

(j) After take-off, while there is very little you can actually do about the slush which might have accumulated anywhere on the aeroplane, at least be aware of the possibility of its effect on operation of the flying controls, gear and flap retraction, either directly or after freezing.

(k) After landing get the aircraft inspected for damage from slush and check that flap, slat and control surface gaps are clear and that accumulations are removed from the undercarriage legs and wheel bays and also the engine intakes.

NOTE:

In the broad field of operation of modern jet transports there are three critical areas all of which have quite properly earned themselves expanded sections in this book. These are stalling, operation on contaminated runways and flight through severe weather. Some pilots might dismiss stalling as a risk which they are confident they can avoid. The other two risks to a certain extent are also avoidable. But the chances are that operation on a contaminated runway is bound to come your way sometime.

In dealing with this problem it is no good trying to short-circuit the size of the task; in order to understand the problem fully it is necessary first to explain the construction of the scheduled take-off and landing data contained in Flight Manuals. Only with a full understanding of this basic material will you be able to change your flying techniques under demanding circumstances in order to achieve the very best performance and highest level of safety in the operation of your aeroplane.

Without apology therefore there follows in the next three sub-chapters some basic background material. If you have had the application to read all the explanations of why things occur on jet aeroplanes so far in this book then do please continue. Don't skip these next three sub-chapters, they are important to you. With air transport operations becoming so very much pre-planned, opportunities for captains to exercise their command responsibilities are becoming fewer and fewer. Operation on contaminated runways is one of the, perhaps, few remaining areas where a captain needs the ability to exercise his command responsibility swiftly and accurately and completely unaided.

The scheduling of take-off performance

Distances

Piston-engined aircraft have been operated to three different groups of take-off rules; jet aircraft only to 1951 British Civil Airworthiness Requirements et seq. and comparable requirements.

'**Unclassified**' These rules were applied to wartime aircraft which passed into civil use and aircraft built in the immediate post war era. When these aircraft persisted in significant numbers they were operated in accordance with information published in 'Performance Schedules'.

Take-off rules were simple. For four-engined aircraft the scheduled distance to 50 ft. had to be within 85% of the runway length available, whilst

198

for twin-engined aircraft the factor was 75%. The effects of take-off altitude, runway slope, wind and temperature were allowed for.

Some measure of control on the minimum acceptable acceleration and climb away was provided by rather generous Weight — Altitude — Temperature (W.A.T.) curve limitations. These rules made no specific allowance for the possibility of an engine failure during take-off but in practice the size of the factor was sufficient to provide a fair measure of safety, together with the ability provided by the W.A.T. curve to climb away as the aircraft was cleaned up.

C.A.R. 4(b) These are the rules to which all the major U.S. piston-engined transport aircraft were certificated.

Take-off distances were scheduled as balanced field lengths, i.e. the unfactored take-off distance to 50 ft. following an engine failure at the critical speed V_1 is equal to the distance required to accelerate to the speed V_1 and thereafter to stop the aircraft on a dry runway.

As in the Unclassified group this distance is related to the runway length available, and allowance is made for the effect of take-off altitude, etc. Temperature was also allowed for in scheduling the take-off distance but only half the temperature above standard was used operationally.

Taken at face value these rules appear more comprehensive than the Unclassified rules and the critical speed is clearly identified. However, with a lightly loaded four-engined aircraft, when the acceleration after unstick is high, the distance provided by the Unclassified rules would have been slightly longer.

C.A.R. 4(b) climb performance rules did not take account of temperature in fixing Weight — Altitude limitations. Although these rules were more severe under low temperature and altitude conditions they were less stringent under high temperature and altitude conditions. Nor was temperature considered in determining the one engine inoperative flight path after take-off so that under some conditions the safety margins were small.

B.C.A.R. and S.R.422, A and B. The present Rational Code was introduced in 1951 and, although detailed improvements have been made, the underlying principles remain unchanged. These requirements have been applied to a few British piston-engined aircraft *and to all turbine driven aircraft.*

It must be mentioned at this point that in 1957 the U.S. introduced Special Regulation No. 422, which was superseded in 1958 by 422A and then 422B in 1959. These Regulations were applied in place of the performance requirements of C.A.R. 4(b) to all turbine-driven aircraft. Whilst there have always been technical differences between the U.K. and U.S. codes, the intent of both authorities has been to provide a uniformly safe level of performance.

The latest changes to B.C.A.R., which were made at the end of 1965, have

199

gone a stage further than the U.S. Regulations by allowing for the reduced braking performance on wet runways and requiring the appropriate V_1 speeds and distances to be scheduled. Take-off distances are divided into three parts and compliance with the operating regulations in each part is necessary. In every case the scheduled (factored) distance must not exceed the appropriate available distance. The most significant difference between these and the C.A.R. 4(b) regulations is that unbalanced field lengths are permitted. When a cleared area exists beyond the end of the paved runway it is possible, depending on the loadbearing capacity of the surface and its freedom from solid obstructions, to take advantage of this in computing the take-off weight. The existence of any such over-runs and clearways is declared by the aerodrome authorities concerned.

It goes without saying that the weights determined by distance considerations from any set of rules will only hold good so long as there is adequate obstacle clearance during the flight path after take-off. Comprehensive flight path performance is given by these rules and because the required minimum levels of performance are specified, obstacles will always be cleared by at least the calculated margins, *provided* the detailed techniques are closely followed in flight.

Noise abatement techniques were discussed earlier in this book. Techniques which are approved by the A.R.B. have been investigated to ensure that the scheduled take-off distances and flight paths will not be infringed.

The scheduled take-off distances are determined as follows:—

(a) *Take-off run* (i) All engines operating. This is the measured run to unstick plus one third of the airborne distance between unstick and the screen height of 35 ft., the whole distance being factored by + 15%, or (ii) With one engine failing at the critical speed V_1. As (i) but without the margin of 15%.

(b) *Take-off distance* (i) All engines operating. This is the measured distance achieved by accelerating to the rotation speed and thereafter effecting a transition to climbing flight to achieve the scheduled screen speed at a height of 35 ft. The whole distance is factored by +15%, or (ii) With one engine failing at the critical speed V_1. As (i) but without the margin of 15%.

(c) *Emergency distance* This is the distance required to accelerate on all engines to the critical speed V_1, at which point an engine failure is assumed to have occurred, and then, following reasonable time delays, bring the aircraft to a halt. British rules permit reverse thrust to be used in establishing these distances, but when so used a factor of 10% is added to the stopping distance.

At first sight fulfilment of all the above limitations may appear to be a

200

formidable task. In practice the situation is not so difficult because, usually only the limiting conditions are scheduled, i.e. for take-off run, say, only (i) or (ii) or the worst combination would be given. Furthermore, most modern Flight Manuals contain graphical presentations which give the user the limiting weights and speeds when the available distance and conditions are fed in.

Finally a word about the wet runway accountability which is provided for on the latest aircraft. The requirements dealing with this subject are predicated on the assumption that there is a short risk period of up to 4 seconds during which, should an engine failure occur on take-off from a wet runway, the aircraft will achieve a height of less than 35 ft. at the screen. The minimum height which will be reached will be 15 ft. but in most cases will be more.

The reduction in speed needed to meet these requirements is not as great as most pilots would expect. On one large four-engined jet transport a reduction of 10 knots from the dry V_1 is recommended. This will produce screen heights varying from 15 to 25 ft., but not at V_2 of course. V_2 will be achieved when the aeroplane reaches 35 ft.

Some pilots believe that the stopping distances scheduled for dry surfaces could not be achieved on a wet day even if 20 knots were knocked off the dry V_1, and there are many pilots who would not consider stopping near V_1 even on a dry surface.

Since the stopping distances from a given speed vary from a half to a third of the distance to accelerate to this speed their lack of confidence is perhaps not surprising unless they have tried it for themselves. However, on a jet aircraft the risks associated with early rotation on a continued take-off are unacceptably high and because of this pilots are urged to place their confidence in the advice contained in Flight Manuals on wet V_1 speeds.

Whether or not you like this philosophy, be encouraged by the thought that although jet operation margins are based on engine failure rates experienced with piston engines, the jet engine failure rate is only a quarter of this.

Rotation and safety speeds

Most piston-engined aircraft have safety speeds (V_2) which were determined by a margin of 15% above the power-off stalling speed. Because the unavoidable acceleration after rotation was small, the rotation speed was close to V_2 and no great effort had to be put into determining the best speeds. In a few cases minimum control speed (V_{MCA}) considerations were limiting and in these instances a margin of 10% was added to the control speed to achieve V_2.

With the advent of the jet aircraft the hidden benefit of slipstream over the wing was lost and it became necessary to increase the margin above the stall. A minimum of 20% has been used but this is often influenced by the rotation criteria which in turn affect the speed at the screen, and may increase this speed.

The rotation speed is determined by one of the following criteria:—

(a) $1.05 \times$ the free air minimum control speed V_{MCA}

(b) $1.10 \times$ the minimum power off stalling speed V_{MS}

(c) 1.1 or $1.05 \times$ the minimum unstick speed V_{MU}

(d) A speed which allows the greater of 1.1 V_{MCA} or 1.2 V_{MS_1} to be achieved at the screen height of 35 ft. with one engine inoperative.

Clearly the most important difference between these and earlier rules is the introduction of the minimum unstick speed concept.

This requires that a factor of 10% shall be applied to the minimum demonstrated unstick speed and the resultant all engines take-off distance to 35 ft. shall not be greater than the scheduled distance. When an aircraft is limited by lack of elevator power, or where it is possible to drag the tail on the ground from 0.9 of the final V_{MU} speed, the factor on minimum demonstrated unstick speed may be reduced to 5% provided the resultant distance is still not greater than that scheduled.

Once the rotation speed has been established by the above means further abuse tests must be complied with. These require the aircraft to be rotated 5 knots early, following failure of the critical engine, and the resultant distances must not exceed those scheduled.

Whilst from the foregoing it can be seen that safety margins do exist in the speeds determined for jet aircraft, it must be understood that such machines are far more sensitive to abuse than their propeller driven predecessors. Accurate flying is now the order of the day, and it is important for pilots to try to achieve the scheduled speeds where performance is critical. As an example of the importance of this, an increase of 10 knots above the correct speed at the screen on an all engines take-off on some aircraft is enough to consume the whole safety margin of 15% which has been applied to the distance. Remember too that on four-engined jet aircraft the take-off distance is frequently determined by the all engines and not the one engine inoperative case.

Reduced thrust take-offs

In recent years a reduced thrust take-off procedure has been developed in order to improve engine reliability and to conserve engine life. Clearly it can be used only when full take-off thrust is not required to meet the various performance requirements on the take-off and initial climb out. The object of this note is to explain the philosophy and point out the circumscribing conditions and safety precautions rather than instruct in its use in detail.

202

Those aeroplanes approved for this procedure have Flight Manual appendices containing all the information necessary.

A take-off can be limited by many considerations. The three which are significant in terms of reduced thrust are:—

(a) Take-off field length.

(b) Take-off WAT curve (engine out climb gradients at take-off thrust).

(c) Net take-off flight path (engine out obstacle clearance).

Where the proposed take-off weight is such that none of these considerations is limiting, then the take-off thrust may be reduced, within reason, until one of the considerations becomes limiting.

There are several possible methods of applying this philosophy, but the most usual is the 'assumed temperature' method. A temperature higher than the actual OAT is determined, at which the actual take-off weight would be the Regulated Take-off Weight, all other parameters having their actual values. The take-off thrust appropriate to this higher temperature is then used for the take-off. This method ensures that all the take-off performance requirements are met at the reduced thrust, with a small additional margin because the density effect of the actual take-off temperature is lower than that of the assumed temperature. While this means that, in the event of a continued take-off following engine failure the whole take-off would be good in terms of performance, it is nevertheless recommended that full take-off power be restored in the event of an engine failure above V_1.

The following general principles apply:—

(a) While the procedure is optional and is generally used at the captain's discretion it is not unreasonable for an operator to require it to be used when there is no resultant loss of safety.

(b) Under FARs, the thrust reduction may not exceed 10%. B.C.A.R.s demand that a minimum thrust, easily identifiable by the pilot (e.g. maximum climb), shall be imposed. The net result is about the same.

(c) The speeds V_1, V_R and V_2 used in the reduced thrust procedure must not be less than those which will comply with the required controllability margins (V_{MC} etc.) associated with the maximum thrust available for the actual ambient conditions.

(d) All performance requirements must be met within the above constraints.

(e) The take-off configuration warning must not be compromised.

(f) The overall procedure should include a method for periodically checking the availability of full take-off thrust.

(g) The reduced thrust procedure should not be used in any of the following conditions:—

    (i) free-standing water, ice, slush or snow

    (ii) a mixed engine configuration

    (iii) any non-standard take-off.

(h) The procedure should not result in a significant increase in flight deck work load nor change the take off drill significantly.

(i) With ungoverned engines the instrumentation shall be such that full take-off power may be achieved without risk of exceeding limitations (i.e. a single E.P.R. bug set to the full take-off thrust value will do provided that achieved E.P.R. is presented clearly in digital form, otherwise two bugs must be used, with the second set to the reduced thrust).

Although this may seem rather a lot of general principles, most of them refer to the overall rules and pre-planning stages. The take-off itself is quite straightforward, simply a matter of setting up the reduced thrust and flying an otherwise normal take-off. The only real difference is the recommendation to restore full normal take-off thrust on the remaining engine(s) in the event of a continued take-off after engine failure.

There are some particular variations applying to aircraft with contingency ratings; details are given in the Flight Manuals. All Flight Manual appendices on reduced thrust contain a worked example. Finally, remember that the performance consideration which is limiting at full thrust (field length, WAT curve, net flight path) is not necessarily the limiting one at reduced thrust.

The overall safety level of reduced thrust take-offs is something which bothers some pilots, who believe that the average exposure to 'near critical' take-off conditions is increased. The proof that this worry is groundless is, as one would expect of something produced by performance experts, long and detailed. However, the following is a brief outline:—

When reduced thrust is used for take-off *the risk per flight is decreased* because:—

(a) The 'assumed temperature' method of reducing thrust to suit take-off weight does so at constant thrust/weight ratio, and the actual take-off distance, take-off run and accelerate-stop distances at reduced thrust are less than at full thrust and full weight by approximately 1 % for every 3°C that the actual temperature is below the assumed temperature.

(b) The accelerate-stop distance is further improved by the increased effectiveness of full reverse thrust at the lower temperature.

(c) The continued take-off after engine failure is protected by the ability to restore full power on the operative engines.

Furthermore, although there is inevitably *a slight increase in average risk*, this increase is minimised by two factors:—

(a) A significant percentage of take-offs are at weights close enough to R.T.O.W. not to warrant the use of reduced thrust.

(b) The excess margins on lighter-weight take-offs are largely preserved by the maximum thrust reduction rule.

In any case it is anticipated that more than adequate compensation will be provided by enhanced engine reliability.

A Boeing 727 shortly after take-off with its leading edge flaps fully extended and triple slotted trailing edge flaps extended to the take-off position. Plate 14 (overleaf) shows details of a typical triple slotted trailing edge flap design, that of the Boeing 737.

These devices increase lift by increasing wing area, cambering the total section and controlling the airflow so that it does not separate until a very late stage.

Photographs: The Boeing Company

Photograph: The Boeing Company

The photograph is of a Boeing 707 seen at the commencement of the landing run. The surface extended on the wing upper surface at the trailing edge is a spoiler in the lift dump position to which it was set immediately after touch-down. Also shown are the leading edge flaps extended and the fan reverser ring in the reverse position.

Plates 16 and 17 Thrust reversers

Two views of a typical American thrust reverser design. (A typical British design is shown diagrammatically in figure 7.3 on page 184.) The side elevation illustrates how the deflector doors serve to direct the exhaust gases in a forward direction to provide thrust reversal. From the rear view it can be seen quite clearly that with the clamshells closed there is no flow to the rear.

Photographs: The Boeing Company

Plate 18 What the passenger sees

This remarkable photograph of a Boeing 727 immediately after touch-down might come as a surprise to those who spend all their time up at the front end. It also serves to underline dramatically what has been written about the jet aeroplane having (basically) low

drag and therefore needing sophisticated devices to produce drag on landing. Working from inboard to outboard, notice the following:—

1. The inboard spoiler fully extended.
2. The inboard double-slotted flaps fully extended.
3. The high speed aileron deflected slightly up.
4. The outboard spoilers fully extended.
5. The outboard double-slotted flaps fully extended.
6. The low speed aileron slightly up.

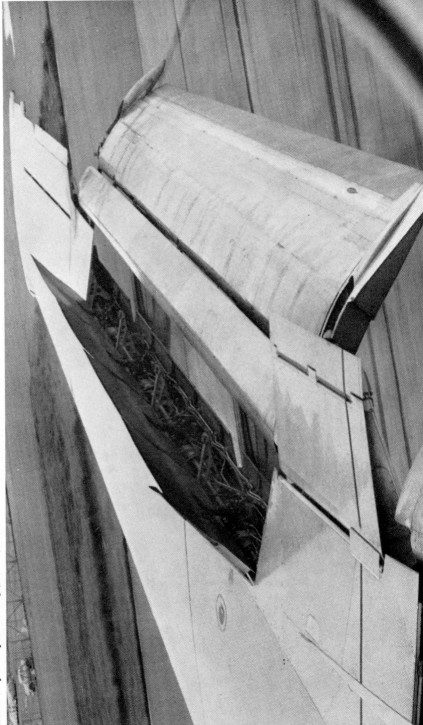

Photograph: The Boeing Company

There remains a possible argument concerning the way in which the benefit to the engine is likely to be distributed. There is undeniably a small increase in overall risk when using reduced thrust take-offs. This is justified if it can be made up elsewhere. If it were allowed to result in an improvement to reliability for the same engine life this would be totally justified. If however the benefit were all to be taken out in increased life this would be unreasonable. Where the line should be drawn is clearly a subject for debate.

The scheduling of landing performance

Distances

Most landing distances for aircraft certificated in the 'Unclassified' group and to C.A.R. 4(b) and SR 422 requirements were determined by flying the aircraft down to the 50 ft. height point in a steady condition, at a glide slope which was chosen at the applicant's discretion, and thereafter taking off the power, touching down and stopping in the shortest distance possible. Such tests are conducted on a dry runway, and with the exceptions that excessive tyre wear and burst tyres are not permitted, and that reverse thrust cannot be used, anything goes. The minimum speed for the approach down to 50 ft. is 1.3 V_{MS} and the resultant distance is multiplied by 100/60 to produce the required field length. Altitude, wind and runway slope are taken into consideration, but the temperature is taken as standard at all altitudes.

For propeller driven aircraft, similar techniques are still permitted by B.C.A.R. and these are known as 'Arbitrary Landing Distances'. There are, however, three notable exceptions:—

(i) The glide slope down to 50 ft. must not exceed 3°.

(ii) Credit may be taken for limited reverse thrust provided the asymmetric handling qualities are satisfactory.

(iii) The speeds used for establishing the arbitrary distances must be consistent with the 'Reference Speeds' which are scheduled (see Speeds later).

For propeller driven aircraft the Arbitrary Landing Distances have proved generally satisfactory and the large margin applied to the dry distances has taken care of wet runways.

With jet aircraft, however, the contribution of wheel braking compared with aerodynamic retardation has increased, so that circumstances can arise when the wet runway performance is unsatisfactory.

To meet this contingency the U.K. developed the Reference Landing Distance method, to which all jet aircraft have been certificated since the 1951 B.C.A.R. were applied, and the U.S. has recently introduced an operating rule imposing an extra 15% on the landing distance required on a wet surface.

With the U.K. technique, distances are measured on wet runway surfaces from a speed at 30 ft. which is 15 knots in excess of the speed recommended for normal operations. The aim is to determine a similar distance to that which would be achieved in service following a fast approach when landing on a wet runway and to provide a small factor to cater for further misjudgements such as excessive height at the threshold, excessive float and slow application of retarding devices.

In establishing these distances the aircraft is flown down a 3° glide slope at constant speed and power to a height of 30 ft. At this point power may be reduced, and if permitted, reverse idle may be selected, depending on the recommended technique. Touch down is delayed for about 7 secs. after passing through 30 ft. (the actual time is determined by a formula which is dependent on the maximum threshold speed) and following touch-down, actions such as braking, spoiler operation and selection of reverse thrust follow with time delays inserted to represent what would happen in well disciplined operational service.

Tests are conducted with all engines operating and with one engine inoperative. Unless directional control problems exist asymmetry has little effect on distance, but loss of a reverse thrust unit can be important. Reference Landing Distances incorporate minimum factors of 11% on the all engine distances and 8% with one engine inoperative. The scheduled distance will be the greater of these.

When use of reverse thrust is permitted asymmetric handling is assessed against requirements, and fault cases allowing forward thrust on one engine with reverse on the others are considered.

For many jet aircraft the resultant Reference Landing Distance is similar to that obtainable with the Arbitrary technique. Aircraft certificated to both techniques have shown that although the distances are often close they are never identical over the whole weight range. However, these requirements will highlight the poor directional characteristics which necessitate increases in approach speed in asymmetric conditions.

Speeds

Aircraft certificated in the 'Unclassified' group, C.A.R. 4(b) and S.R. 422, A and B have the approach speed at 50 ft., used to determine landing distance, quoted in their manuals. No guidance is given on the effect of deviating from these speeds.

Flight Manuals of all aircraft certificated to B.C.A.R. since 1951, whether using Arbitrary or Reference distances, contain recommended and maximum threshold speeds.

Reference Speeds as required by the latest B.C.A.R. provide the following protection:—

(a) The ability to undershoot the recommended threshold speed (V_{ATO}) at 30 ft. by 5 knots using an otherwise normal landing procedure. This margin is only to prove the validity of the recommended speed and is not for normal operational use.

206

(b) The ability to touch down at speeds at least 5 knots higher than those used for measured landings from the maximum threshold speed V_{Tmax}.

(c) A margin of 15 knots between the recommended threshold speed V_{AT_0} all engines, and V_{Tmax}. The achievement of a speed at the threshold of a distance limited runway in excess of the maximum threshold speed should normally cause a pilot to abandon the landing and overshoot for a second attempt within the range V_{AT_0} to V_{Tmax}.

(d) For those aircraft where asymmetric conditions necessitate an increase in speed to maintain satisfactory directional control, this high speed is used at the threshold when determining distances. On a four-engined aircraft the effect of the two critical engines being inoperative is allowed for.

From the foregoing it will be seen that whilst the pilot of a modern jet aircraft is likely to be faced with higher approach speeds, this disadvantage is to some extent offset by the greater detail which has been applied to evaluating the consequences of misjudgement and asymmetric handling problems.

As with take-off procedures it is important that recommended landing procedures are strictly observed, and if this is done the scheduled distances will prove to be adequate.

Remember too that an aircraft decelerates much more quickly on the ground than floating just above it. If distance is limiting place the aircraft firmly on the runway at the earliest opportunity and start the braking drills as rapidly as possible.

Summary of scheduled field performance

We can now summarise and compare the scheduled field performance of a typical piston-engined aeroplane and a jet aeroplane, using some simple diagrams.

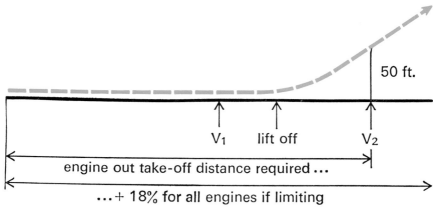

Figure 7.6   Take-off—piston.

Take-off

Figure 7.6 shows the scheduled field performance of a typical piston-engined aeroplane according to 1951 B.C.A.R. The take-off distance for 'Unclassified' aircraft was all engines only $+18\%$. C.A.R. 4(b), however, did not include the all engines case.

Figure 7.7 shows the jet situation. Up to quite recently the British factor

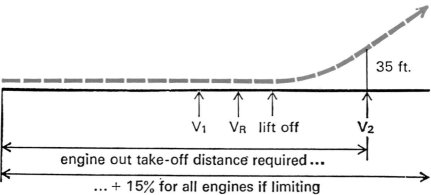

Figure 7.7 Take-off—jet.

on take-off distance was 18% and one-third of the airborne distance added to the ground run. The American factor on all engines take-off distance is 15% and one half of the airborne distance added to the ground run.

The factor in the all engines case is to allow for the general inaccuracies in flying and general random variations. There is no factor on the engine out distance in either case, apart from the proportion of airborne distance added to the ground run in the jet case because of the extremely remote possibility of the engine failure occurring at the worst point.

The jet 'appears' slightly worse off than the piston-engined aircraft because the screen height is 15 ft. lower and the all engines factor is 3% less. In the light of the better achieved jet engine failure rate these small reductions do not seem unreasonable (see also Conclusion, (c) (ii), page 211).

Only against the latest B.C.A.R. is the jet V_1 good for wet conditions although it is associated with a reduced screen height of 15 ft. Early B.C.A.R. for piston-engined aircraft gave an increased accelerate-stop distance for wet conditions with no change in V_1 or screen height.

Accelerate-stop

There is no basic difference between the piston and jet distance. There is no factor because the full distance is required only when the failure occurs at the worst point. Only against the latest B.C.A.R. is the jet V_1 good for wet conditions although it is associated with a reduced screen height of 15 ft.

Early B.C.A.R. for piston-engined aircraft gave an increased accelerate-stop distance for wet conditions with no change in V_1 or screen height.

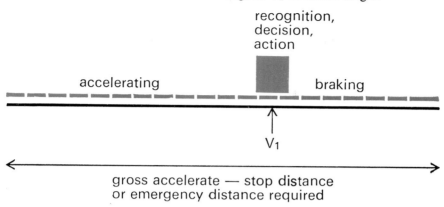

Figure 7.8   Accelerate-stop—piston and jet.

Landing

The piston-engined aircraft distance is measured with one major means of retardation inoperative, i.e. either an engine out or no reverse thrust.   The piston-engined aircraft distance $+67\%$ is supposed to look after excess speed at the threshold and also wet runways.

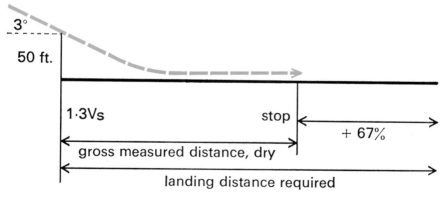

Figure 7.9   Landing—piston.

The jet distance is measured using as much asymmetric reverse as can be controlled on a wet runway.   In the jet case the longer of the engine out distance or the all engines distance is scheduled.   Jet aircraft which have been tested to both the piston-engined aircraft and jet philosophies have come out with similar distances.

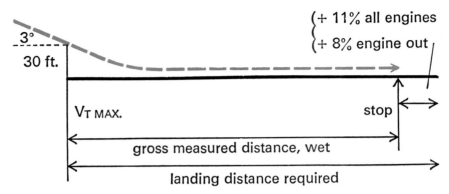

Figure 7.10   Landing—jet.

Definitions

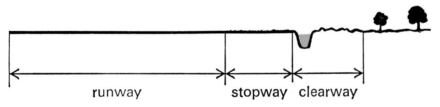

Figure 7.11   Take-off—terrain accountability.

Note the following definitions of the distances shown in figure 7.11.

Take-off run available   = the length of the runway

Take-off emergency distance available = runway + stopway

Take-off distance available   = runway + stopway + clearway

Runway is the length of the hard prepared surface.

Stopway is the length of the hard but unprepared surface capable of supporting the aeroplane without too much damage.

Clearway is the length of obstacle free distance.   The surface is not defined and could be water for example (if under the control of the aerodrome authority).

Therefore the stopway can be used for the accelerate-stop.   Both stopway and clearway can be flown over for take-off purposes.

210

Conclusion

Having compared the field requirements for both types of aeroplane the following broad statements can be made:—

(a) All jet operations on dry surfaces are generally satisfactory and equivalent to those of piston-engined aircraft.

(b) Wet surface operations are hazarded by reduced braking force, slush and aquaplaning due to the jet's higher ground speeds.

(c) The jet's scheduled performance however has hidden benefits: (i) the V_{MU} requirement imposing a V_2 higher than the minimum demanded on the basis of Vs and (ii) more rational time delays built into the accelerate/stop distances.

Take-off techniques

Before you even walk out to the aeroplane, unless nothing can possibly make the take-off limiting, you should have carefully worked it all out, made your decisions in the light of the prevailing circumstances (choice of wet V_1, etc.) and be quite confident that your planned take-off is as gold-plated as it possibly could be and would stand any criticism. Having done this, stick to your plan. If you have considered all that you should have considered then nothing should come up at short notice and cause you to act in an irrational fashion.

As you start up and taxi out go over the take-off (and the possible abort) and your departure clearance and make sure you know exactly what you are going to have to do from the moment you let go the brakes until you trim the aeroplane out in the en route climb. Make quite sure that the stabiliser is properly set according to the C.G. position.

Just before you turn on to the runway first ask yourself if everything has gone properly so far (brakes still nice and cool, no system deficiencies which need taking into account) and mentally rehearse the abort drill (depending on slipperiness and crosswinds, which reversers you are going to use, etc.). Brief the other crew-members so that everyone knows his responsibilities under all circumstances.

Line up without wasting valuable distance, set the power and off you go. Now remember that the optimum take-off is the one flown strictly to the Flight Manual Technique. There is nothing you can add which will improve the overall quality and safety of the next few minutes. Up to V_1 be ready to go straight into the abort drills without wasting time and distance, but not so fast that the quality of each of the things you have to do is spoiled.

After V_1 rotate at V_R to the known pitch attitude for lift-off, then lift off and go through the screen at V_3 (V_3, the all engines screen speed, is on average about $V_2 + 10$ knots); a further gentle rotation to the first segment noise abatement pitch attitude, wait for a good positive indication of a sustained climb away, then select gear up. Now hold that pitch attitude, monitor airspeed, altitude, rate of climb, attitude and heading, and the aeroplane will settle down into a steady climb away at V_4. Trim out longitudinal stick forces.

If you have to make a turn in this segment roll to 15° to 20° of bank, steady it there, then hold it there. Remember spiral stability — you probably have not yet achieved an accurate trim state on rudder or ailerons so watch that bank angle all the way around the turn. At the noise abatement time, reduce power, reduce attitude simultaneously and then *keep your eye on the VSI. Don't let the aeroplane go downhill.* Maintain the second noise abatement segment speed and you will continue to climb away slowly. At the next significant height or time start the acceleration and clean up drill. First reapply climb power and start the aeroplane accelerating. At the flap raising initiation speed, select flaps up and again *keep your eye on the VSI. Don't let the aeroplane go downhill.* Monitor the flaps until they are fully retracted, accelerate in a gentle climb to the en route climb speed then trim the aeroplane about all axes. You can now relax and engage the autopilot. Nothing to it; but a great sense of satisfaction in having flown an immaculate take-off.

If the take-off is at night then latch on to those instruments immediately after lift-off and *stay on them.* Fly attitude with great care and monitor the rest of your primary flight instruments frequently.

If the take-off is made into not worse than moderate turbulence fly substantially the same technique but add some airspeed in both segments of the noise abatement procedure (the amount depending on the degree of turbulence). Delay flap retraction to a higher altitude if necessary and arrange to be close to the flap limit speed just as the flaps retract fully. Then accelerate in level flight to the rough air speed and climb away.

If severe turbulence is met soon after lift-off accelerate slowly to $V_F - 20$ knots and climb away in this condition. Reduce from take-off power only when you are satisfied it is safe to do so. Maintain the flap angle and the speed and continue to climb until the level of turbulence falls to a value you deem prudent for selecting flap retraction.

So much for day, night and turbulence. Very heavy rain should call for ignition on. Icing is covered by normal operational drills, but remember the thrust loss associated with engine anti-icing and hot air airframe de-icing.

In the event of an engine failure below V_1 go quickly but smoothly into the stopping drill. All power off, start gentle braking, *keep it straight,* up spoilers, then reverse and again, *keep it straight.* Now modulate your braking to the amount of runway left. If you are tight on distance hang on to full reverse. Reduce thrust on the inners only when an engine begins to object. Bring these to idle then reduce the others when they begin to object. Slush and aquaplaning included, if you planned the take-off properly and handled the abort properly you'll stop before the end of the stopway.

In the event of an engine failure after V_1, while still on the runway, apply rudder and aileron to *keep it straight.* Now back to the ASI (because V_R still comes up quite rapidly) rotate at V_R and climb out at V_2. When a positive climb away indication is seen, select gear up. Now the only thing you have to worry about is maintaining V_2. Under performance limiting conditions, particularly on a twin, there is not much climb gradient available. So fly V_2 accurately.   Now wash out of your mind the all engines procedure and departure clearance and switch on to the engine out flight path and the clearance to the overshoot beacon.   At the appropriate height for flap retraction, retract the flaps, accelerate and climb away at the scheduled engine out en route climb speed.   Regardless of the five minute limitation on take-off power, don't reduce power until you are quite happy with your achieved performance.   Jet engines are pretty tough, and a few extra minutes at full power will not bother them a bit.

It is difficult to summarise the take-off techniques for all jet transports. They vary so much in their handling qualities and performance capabilities. There are those which are known to be a bit of a handful in the event of engine failure; there are those which are known to be critical in the flap retraction segment.   All aircraft, engine out, under WAT limiting conditions are left with a comparatively poor rate of climb which, in turbulence, will need very careful flying to achieve their predicted flight paths.   At the other end of the scale a four-engined aeroplane, with good asymmetric qualities, taking-off at medium weights, goes off like a rocket and is not a bit disturbed in the event of engine failure.   For the type you fly you should know what sort of a beast it is and in which areas you need to exercise special care.   Any certificated aeroplane will do what the flight manual says it will do.   All *you* have to do is to fly it properly.

Landing techniques

Like the take-off, the approach for a landing on a particular runway under the prevailing circumstances should not be started (unless there is obviously nothing limiting) until the whole problem has been thought right out and a proper decision taken that the landing is acceptable without undue risk.

If conditions are demanding and the distance is going to be tight then work out the speeds and drills required and brief the crew so that everyone knows exactly what is going to be done.

Now work back a bit and remember that a good landing needs a proper flight condition at the threshold, which itself, in turn, needs a well flown approach. It is unwise to fly a high speed or high descent rate initial approach, or a close-in approach needing steep turns.   Jet aeroplanes need a lot of sky for manoeuvring and a lot of time to pick up steady state conditions, so don't set up an approach philosophy which is likely to be beyond the capabilities of your aeroplane or yourself.   Stand back a bit and make the last couple of thousand feet down the glide slope under properly controlled flight path conditions.   Do not indulge in high descent rates and, in the absence of glide path guidance, go back to the simple arithmetic of distance out and height or ground speed $\times$ 5, etc. and fly an average 700 ft. a minute rate of descent.

213

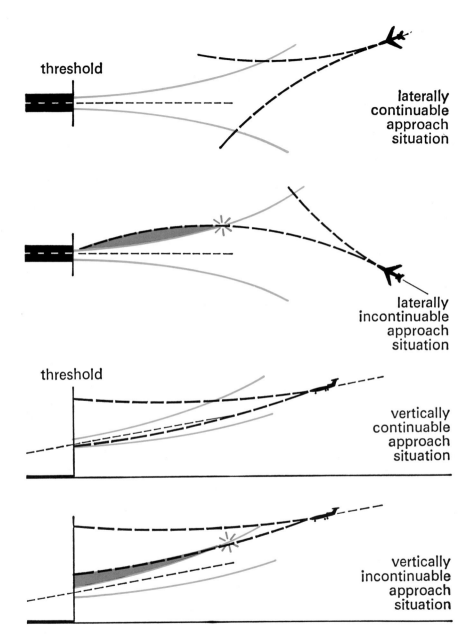

threshold

laterally
continuable
approach
situation

laterally
incontinuable
approach
situation

threshold

vertically
continuable
approach
situation

vertically
incontinuable
approach
situation

Figure 7.12 Approach manoeuvre envelopes.
214

Having achieved this then just keep coming. Keep your subconscious mind open, be sensitive to the primary parameters, and their rates of change, which control your flight path, and make the necessary gentle corrections in good time. Remember that, in terms of lateral and vertical displacement from the real or assumed localiser and glideslope, there is an expanding funnel of manoeuvre limitations pointing back up the approach path, the small end of the cone of which is located at the threshold (see figure 7.12). It is not circular actually, but rather oblong, with its major axis horizontal. (For Category II operations for example the gate at 100 ft. is assumed to be about 14 ft. deep and 90 ft. wide). As you fly down the approach you have two primary tasks. One is to keep within this narrowing funnel of displacement from which the approach can be continued (be in readiness to abort the approach if you suspect you are outside this limit at any time) and the other is to keep your speed, rate of descent and attitude within required limits.

If the approach is in IMC to very low limits *don't duck under the glide slope on contact.* There is a strong psychological urge to do this, but it must be resisted. Don't take the power off too high. Particularly when one, or two engines are inoperative, keep the power on and don't let a high sink rate develop, as it can do even at these very low altitudes. Keep the stabiliser in trim so that full elevator effectiveness is available for the flare. Shoot for a touch down at around the ILS reference touch-down point which is about 1,000 ft. in from the threshold.

If you have been maintaining a higher approach speed than standard for some good reason reduce it so as not to exceed V_{AT} + 15 knots at the threshold. On a distance limited runway a threshold speed higher than V_{AT} + 15 knots should call for an immediate overshoot. From the threshold on, simply flare (if necessary), reduce to idle thrust, *push* off drift (if necessary) then land — firmly if the runway is wet. Now, stick forward to hold the nose down, keep it laterally level on ailerons, up spoilers, reverse, and start braking according to the distance available and state of the runway. Keep it straight and get full value out of reverse thrust. Don't cancel reverse early and don't go back to forward idle thrust until you are down to taxying speed. Let the engines reduce to idle before cancelling reverse, to avoid a burst of forward thrust. In a crosswind landing remember that extending the spoilers loses some lateral control. In order not to let this compromise you, make sure that you hold on some into-wind aileron control; it is easier to stop the wing lifting than it is to put it back after it has lifted.

While a great deal is always made of not abusing the brakes unnecessarily this shouldn't cause you to be too gentle with them when you need them. If you really need to use them in order to stop, use them hard, and they won't give any trouble. For maximum braking effort, with anti-skid working normally, the foot pedals should be held just into the cycling range, as will be indicated by the foot thumpers (if fitted). When landing with anti-skid inoperative, however, take care. Use only light braking pressure at high ground speeds and slowly increase the pressure as the speed falls. Anything approaching maximum can be used only at very low speeds otherwise there is a very real risk of blowing the tyres.

Again it's no sweat on a fine day on a long dry runway. But neither is it difficult under demanding circumstances if you remember the value of thinking it out before you start an approach to a possibly difficult landing. If *you* make a bit of a mess of it, it means that (a) you were not up to scratch or (b) you asked more of the aeroplane than it could give. In either of these cases you should not have started the approach but should have held off until conditions improved or diverted to a less demanding runway.

Flying a modern jet aeroplane under most circumstances is not difficult. The only manoeuvre left worth doing, the only manoeuvre calling for any real native flying skill, is the landing. This is where you are leaving the air for a hard, unyielding piece of ground — you are leaving an area of three-dimensional freedom for one of two-dimensional freedom. You have to fly a required flight path under certain limitations of attitude, track, speed and rate of descent. However, if you could land a piston-engined aeroplane, you can land a jet aeroplane. And there is a real sense of achievement in making a good landing, especially under difficult circumstances.

Overshoot techniques

If a perfectly acceptable approach has to be turned into a go-around, simply increase thrust to maximum and rotate the aeroplane nose up to the approximate pitch attitude known to be required for the initial climb out path, gear down, full flap. Now monitor altitude and airspeed. The descent will reduce, then stop and turn into a climb with increasing airspeed. Having done this there is no need to do any more immediately; there is plenty of performance available (all engines at maximum landing weight) and a safe flight path will follow.

When you are satisfied that the aeroplane is nicely under control, accelerating and going uphill, proceed in your own time with flaps to take-off and gear up, etc. You will then be back in the take-off configuration and you simply fly the rest of the climb out as if you had just taken off.

Three specific points need to be made about a go-around:—

(a) Accurate pitch attitude flying is the key to the whole thing. So long as the approach was steady in all respects down to the overshoot point it is only necessary to apply full thrust and rotate to the appropriate pitch attitude. This attitude seems to be around 10° nose up — but you *must* get the correct angle for your particular aeroplane.

(b) The static and pressure sources for ASI, Altitude and VSI instruments on some aeroplanes are located where they suffer a temporary extra position error with changes in incidence, i.e. pitch attitude. While the aeroplane

216

is being rotated in pitch the instruments may give false information. The changes in airspeed and altitude are normally small and can be ignored. The change in VSI reading, however, can be completely misleading; it can indicate a significant descent while the aeroplane is actually climbing. Ignore the VSI under these dynamic conditions. When the aeroplane settles down in its new flight path the instruments will settle down and read properly.

(c) In the choice of sequence for flap and gear retraction the flaps should be retracted to the take-off setting before the gear is retracted, for three reasons: (i) in general the flaps produce more drag than the gear so the larger increment should be removed first; (ii) with the gear remaining locked down a very late baulk causing the aircraft to contact the runway will not result in damage so long as the initial contact is not too hard; (iii) the arrangement of some gear warning systems is such that a gear up selection at full flap will cause the warning to sound thus providing an unwanted distraction at that time.

Operation on contaminated runways

An essential piece of background information is the derivation of braking force. This is a factor in directional controllability as well as total stopping capability.

A tyre develops a braking force when it slips relative to the surface on which it is running. The braking force increases as the slip increases up to some maximum slip, beyond which the braking action will decrease again. Since this characteristic changes with speed and runway surface it will readily be seen that the tuning of any anti-skid braking system will of necessity be a compromise; in order to avoid the area where efficiency is decreasing due to increasing slip, such systems try to keep well clear of the locked wheel condition. Remember that the best rolling coefficient of friction is always higher than any sliding coefficient of friction. In addition to slip, braking force is dependent on the friction between the tyre and the runway surface. Since we are concerned with friction as it affects braking force, it is normal to refer to this as the braking force coefficient.

On a dry runway braking force coefficients are high and show only a small fall-off with speed. On a reasonably uncontaminated surface, that is, one free from traffic films of rubber and grease, there is little variation with tyre tread condition and pattern, although as might be expected, there is some reduction with increasing tyre pressure. Braking force coefficients on a dry runway are fairly consistent and predictable; a fact which is borne out by the almost total absence of overrun accidents and incidents on dry runways.

On wet surfaces, however, due to the lubrication which exists between the tyre and the runway, the braking coefficients fall off markedly with increasing speed, and also vary with tyre and tread patterns. At low speeds, the braking coefficient of a wet runway may be as high as 75% of the dry case, whereas at high speeds the value will have reduced to about 30%. Furthermore, the variability between good and bad wet surfaces can produce a variation of something like 3 to 1 in effective braking performance.

Increases from the recommended tyre pressure will bring about a further decrease in the coefficients although this may delay the onset of aquaplaning. It will be seen also that just as braking action is reduced on slippery runways, so is the directional control which can be achieved through the aircraft's wheels.

Having discussed at some length all the background to operations on and off contaminated surfaces and given detailed recommendations specifically for aquaplaning and slush, it is not necessary here to repeat all the details. But a few reminders of the guiding philosophy need to be stated. Remember that aquaplaning is a stopping problem on the landing and the accelerate–stop, and that slush is primarily a take-off problem in terms of damage, engine malfunctioning and aircraft acceleration.

As in any other critical area of operation your strategy, and tactics, should follow logical lines, in the following sequence:—

1. Make sure you have the essential background knowledge. Jet transports are no longer new and different and most of the material in this book can now properly be called 'basic airmanship (jet aircraft)'. Without an adequate knowledge of slush and aquaplaning you should not attempt to operate a jet aircraft in such conditions.

2. Make an assessment of the criticality of the operation and then stand by your decision. If, having thought the whole thing out, you decide in your responsibility as commander of the aeroplane that it would be imprudent to take-off or land — *then don't*. Delay the take-off, delay the landing or divert. Don't let the fact that your competitors might still be operating cause you to change your mind. If you should bust something, the fact that someone else got away with it a few minutes before or after will be little consolation to you, your company, the passengers or the accident investigation people.

3. Having decided to proceed, handle the aeroplane properly with due regard for the circumstances and keep your escape route open for as long as possible. Do not hesitate to use it if you do not like the way things are developing. If on take-off you find the slush deeper than forecast then *stop immediately*. If on the approach you find that you are not going to be nicely placed at the threshold then *initiate the go around at once*.

4. Once committed, press on. If you have planned properly and flown properly you should not go wrong. This simple statement is true for the accelerate/stop and the landing even if you aquaplane; it is also true for the continued take-off, all engines and engine out, if you have been prudent in terms of the slush depth and density. It is all true provided you have not committed yourself to a significant cross wind component.

218

8 Flight through severe weather

Introduction

How about this?

'. . . we encountered the most violent jolt I have ever experienced in over 20,000 hours of flying.

'I felt as though an extremely severe positive, upward acceleration had triggered off a buffeting, not a pitch, that increased in frequency and magnitude as one might expect to encounter sitting on the end of a huge tuning fork that had been struck violently.

'Not an instrument on any panel was readable to their full scale but appeared as white blurs against their dark background.

'From that point on, it could have been 10, 20, 60 or 100 seconds, we had no idea of attitude, altitude, airspeed or heading. We were now on instruments with no visual reference and continued with severe to violent buffeting, ripping, tearing, rending crashing sounds. Briefcases, manuals, ashtrays, suitcases, pencils, cigarettes, flashlights flying about like unguided missiles. It sounded and felt as if pods were leaving and the structure disintegrating.

'The objects that were thrashing about the cockpit seemed to momentarily settle on the ceiling which made it impossible to trust one's senses although I had a feeling that we were inverted as my seat belt was tight and had stretched considerably. As my briefcase was on the ceiling, I looked up and through the overhead (eyebrow) window and felt that I was looking down on the top of a cloud deck. (The First Officer) later said he had the same impression at the same instant as we acted in unison applying as much force as we could gather to roll aileron control to the left. The horizon bar at this time started to stabilise and showed us coming back through 90° vertical to a level attitude laterally. At this time, I had my first airspeed reading decaying through 250 knots. The air smoothed out and we gently levelled off at between 1,400–1,500 ft. . . . .' *(extract from an airline pilot's report)*

Well how about that?

The history of jet transport flying has been marked by well-defined classes of accidents, interest in which has reared up, run its course, then simmered down again. It started with the original take-off accidents and has run through to the structural failures in severe turbulence. One of the most significant of these classes was, and probably still is, the 'jet upset', mostly, but not always, associated with severe weather. A lot of valuable material has already been written on the subject and some of it is repeated here. More and more knowledge is being accumulated as each day goes by.

219

The arrangement of this book was chosen so that no subject was discussed in advance of a full treatment of its foundation material. Having reached this chapter we should therefore have a fair knowledge of the following subjects, all of which are important in flight through severe weather:—

Momentum, variable incidence tailplanes, low drag, speed margins, poor lift at low speeds, yaw and roll dampers, stall qualities, high Mach number, Mach trimmers, reduced manoeuvrability and damping at high altitude.

In order to arrive at the end product — recommended flight techniques for severe weather — it is necessary first to discuss a number of other related subjects. Reference to the Contents will make it clear that the sub-chapters which follow form three distinct groups, which are all part of the 'system' under discussion. Firstly, the various types of severe weather and their occurrence are considered; secondly, the aeroplane is considered in its role as a machine likely to be affected by weather, and finally, what is perhaps the most important part of the system, the man in control, is related to the other parts.

The history and choice of rough-air speeds

For flight in rough air the recommended air speed must provide protection against the two possibilities which stem from the effect of the rough air. 'Rough air,' in this context, means a gust of a defined value. When this defined gust is encountered the speed must, coincidently, be (a) high enough to avoid the aircraft being stalled and (b) low enough to avoid damage to the structure. These apparently conflicting requirements are made compatible by calculating the stall speed in the gust and then building in sufficient strength for this speed.

The key to the problem is, therefore, the value of the gust; this dictates· the strength required and therefore the weight, which is a dominant parameter in the operating economics of the final design. The gust velocity is, naturally, associated with the speed, V_B, at which the aircraft is required to be flown under these conditions and the value of the gust is 66 ft. per second in a vertical sense. This in itself, however, is not enough because there are the possibilities of hitting a gust before slow-down can be initiated and hitting a gust if upset at high speed. Because these probabilities are lower, however, progressively lower values of gust velocity are chosen at the higher speeds. These values are 50 ft. per second at the design cruise speed V_C and 25 ft. per second at the design dive speed V_D.

At the present time, when structural failures in rough air are causing some concern, it is worth tracing briefly the history of the design requirements. The values of 66, 50 and 25 ft. per second for gusts at the design speeds of V_B, V_C and V_D have existed since World War II. In the U.K. they came originally from the military requirements and were established as a

Plate 19 Severe weather

This is a good illustration of a typically ugly Cu Nimb with another lurking behind it. The nearer cloud is beginning to develop the classic anvil shape, already more developed in the farther cloud. Note the active dome surmounted by its pileus cloud, indicating considerable air motion and turbulence outside the visible cloud. Hail may be encountered under the overhanging cloud mass as well as inside the cloud. The photograph was taken from a height of 20,000 feet over Africa.

Photograph: Andrew McClymont

Plates 20 and 21 Slush

Here we see the effect of slush under actual conditions. Notice the spray pattern from the nose wheel and the build-up ahead of the main wheels. In the first case (nose wheel down) the aircraft was travelling at approximately 75 knots and in the second case (nose wheel up) at approximately 85 knots. In each case the depth of the slush was approximately 25mm (1 inch).

Plates 22 and 23   The 747 flight deck

Two views of the 747 flight deck. In the top picture the well-ordered layout and uncluttered simplicity of the systems control station can be seen. This layout has round dials for the pilots' engine instrumentation.

The lower picture shows the layout of the pilots' stations. This is the version with vertical tape engine instrumentation. Note (a) the generally clean and simple layout, (b) automatic flight control system panel on the glareshield, (c) the tailoring of the glareshield lower edge to give optimum instrument visibility and (d) the horizontal reference provided by the top of the glareshield.

Photographs: The Boeing Company

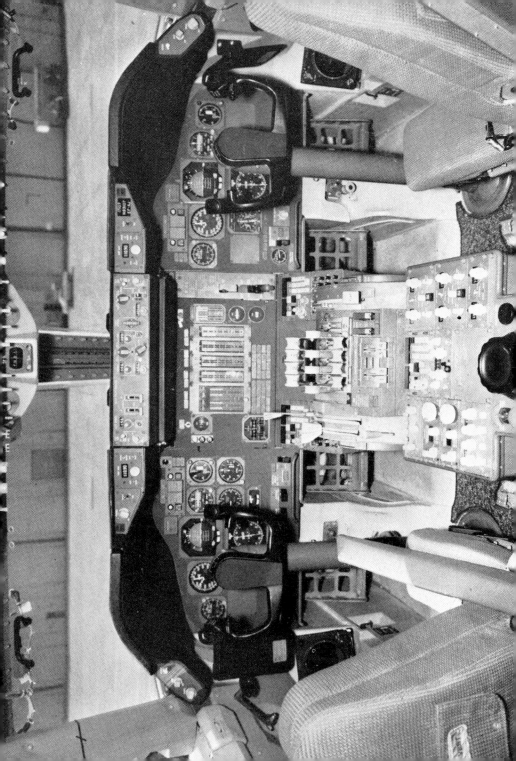

Plate 24   The man who started it all

Sir Frank Whittle, flanked by two jet engines which clearly illustrate the almost unlimited possibilities for development. It is quite obvious that the real root of all jet aircraft flying qualities is the jet engine. In fact, it would be possible to draw a stage 0 order of differences in figure 1.1 on page 2 and explain that all the differences stem from the jet engine. It is the engine which gives the aeroplane its capacity for size and weight and its ability to fly fast and high.

Photograph: General Electric

result of the earliest Vg recorder results combined with truly inspired estimation by the structural design people. It is a remarkable, and comforting, tribute to the early designers that, right up to this time, all the most modern flight recorder results and sophisticated design analyses continue to support the original boundaries of the design gust envelope and nothing has appeared to suggest the need for any change. If theory and practice have become a little divorced in recent years then the divergency is more likely to lie in the relationship of the strength of the aeroplane at various rough-air speeds than in the design gust values.

This translation of design requirements into actual aircraft strength is a most difficult job. It is generally admitted that prediction at the design stage of the likely behaviour of an aircraft in turbulence is an inexact science when judging stability, control and strength implications. It is one of the many areas of which a hackneyed but true description would be 'more of an art than a science.' The pattern of local air motion generated in turbulence is a very complex one and this places severe limitations on the manner in which turbulence can adequately be interpreted in making practical design calculations for strength.

Up to the end of the piston-engined era, design for strength was based on the comparatively uncomplicated process of relating the simple response of the aeroplane as a rigid body to discrete forms of gusts; then, by use of an alleviation factor, converting these gusts into equivalent sharp edged gusts and calculating the increase in load on the aircraft as a function of an instantaneous increase in angle of attack on the wing. This gave a satisfactory result in agreement with the interpretation of Vgh records, and continued to support the requirements.

On jet transport aircraft however, additional allowances have to be made for several reasons:—

(a) The greater dynamic response due to increased structural flexibility.

(b) The possible implications of the smaller margin between actual cruise speed and design cruise speed.

(c) The significance, in the more advanced designs, of the effects of build-up of gusts and unsteady flow generally.

(d) The frequency of storm penetrations.

(e) The implications of the limited slow-down capabilities.

In spite of these added difficulties the jet transport's operating record remains broadly acceptable. Certainly the requirements continue to be supported by positive evidence of the behaviour of the atmosphere. If any adjustment needs to be made it is more in the choice of rough-air speed than in any other field.

Before we leave the history and design philosophy of rough-air speeds a brief word about the reduced design gust value at altitude which seems to

16

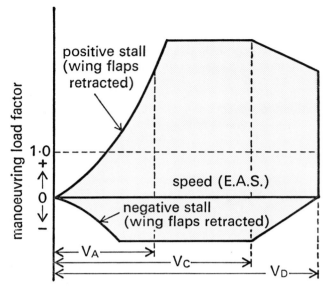

Figure 8.1   Manoeuvring envelope.

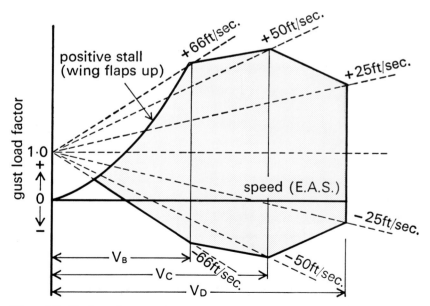

Figure 8.2   Gust envelope.

puzzle a lot of pilots. All design speeds, and design gust values, are EAS values. This is quite proper, because the aircraft is sensitive, as it were, only to EAS. However, those people concerned with the behaviour of the atmosphere generally talk in terms of true air speeds. The relationship of EAS to TAS varying with altitude is generally understood and at altitudes around 40,000 ft. for example, 66 ft. per second TAS is equivalent to a much lower value of EAS. Hence the reduction in EAS design gust velocity with altitude. The reduction is made in a simple step linearly above 20,000 ft. instead of an accurate curve from sea level. This means that the added protection at what was high altitude for a piston-engined aeroplane is retained for the jet, while the reduced EAS values are applied only where it is unavoidable.

Figures 8.1 and 8.2 illustrate the traditional manoeuvring and gust envelopes.

The choice of rough-air speed to be used operationally must be consistent with the strength philosophy outlined above. At the same time the aircraft must comply with both minimum stability and control criteria. There is also the important consideration of what maximum speed reduction can be achieved in a slow-down technique — as a typical example, over 10 nautical miles at a maximum horizontal retardation of 0.15g. We can now construct a typical chart of the speeds to which the rough air speed is related.

Figure 8.3 is drawn for a single (mid) weight.

Line AB is the 1g stall speed.

Line CDE is the stall speed in a 66 ft. per sec. gust.
(This assumes the 66 ft. per sec. gust up to maximum altitude and ignores line DF which reflects the reducing design gust velocities above 20,000 ft. Note that point E would represent an extremely high *true air speed* gust value).

Line GHI is the V_{MO}/M_{MO} line.

Line JKL is the V_{DF}/M_{DF} line.

Line MN is an example of a maximum strength speed line for a 66 ft. per sec. gust.

Line RS is the maximum altitude at which the aeroplane can sustain a $\frac{1}{2}$g increment without too much buffet.

At all speeds above the line CDF the aeroplane will sustain a 66 ft. per sec. TAS gust without stalling and at all speeds below the line MN the aeroplane is strong enough to withstand a 66 ft. per sec. gust. The rough-air speed therefore should lie somewhere between these two speeds, and the line OP seems a good place to put it.

The line MN is a curious shape because different parts of the structure become critical at different altitudes. This line is actually the lowest speed boundary of a collection of curves at the higher speed end of the chart.

In piston-engined days rough-air speeds were close to V_B. This appeared

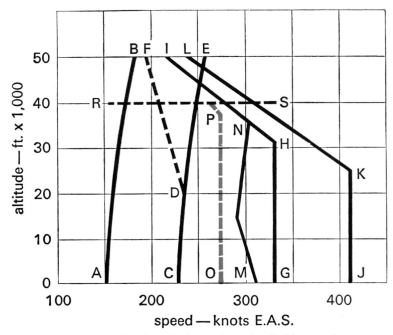

Figure 8.3 Relationship of rough air speed to other limiting speeds.

to stem from a concern not to subject the structure to too much of a hammering at high speeds in turbulence. This philosophy existed well into the early years of jet transport flying and changed only when there were increasing worries about (a) the hazard of a stall in severe turbulence (although it is difficult to find any substantiated cases of a stall, other than a pilot-induced stall, having occurred) and (b) the inducement to an unsteady flight path from the need to slow down such a long way from a high speed cruise to a low rough-air speed.

In the desire to avoid these two difficulties rough-air speeds have been increased, and it could just be that the swing to the high speed end has been taken a bit too far. Several recent aeroplanes have had rough-air speeds which leaned right up against the structural boundary. It is very difficult to prove or disprove the validity of the many arguments which are made in this area. Clearly it would be as unwise to absorb all the surplus strength which might be available as it would be to get too close to the gust stall line in order to preserve maximum strength. A sensible compromise would appear to be for the rough-air speed to be chosen halfway between V_B and the maximum strength speed for compliance with the 66 ft. per sec. gust. Because of the obvious attraction of a single speed at all altitudes up to that at which the rough-air speed becomes a rough-air Mach number, the line could be adjusted slightly so as to avoid any variations with altitude. As turbulence is generally completely random, this halfway speed would give equal protection against the 50–50 probability of being forced too fast or too slow.

It has been stated that the diagram is drawn for a mid weight. The effect of weight change in terms of the lower and upper limits to rough-air speed is, of course, significant, but self-cancelling. At low weights the stall line for a 66 ft. per sec. gust falls to lower speeds and the maximum strength speed line increases to higher speeds. There is therefore no point in attempting a sophisticated variation of V_{RA} with weight. The maximum altitude limit does, however, vary significantly with weight, and also varies for the level of manoeuvre capability chosen. A $\frac{1}{2}$g increment to buffet is not too much protection in severe turbulence. A lower altitude will therefore be required for a higher level of protection, and, for a given level of protection, a lower altitude will be required for higher weights.

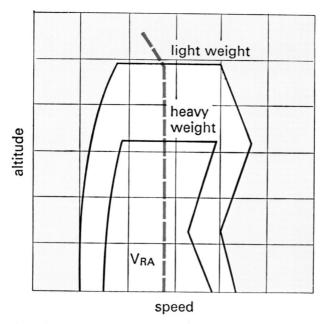

Figure 8.4   Variation of manoeuvre capability with weight.

Figure 8.4 shows, for a $\frac{1}{2}$g manoeuvre to buffet, how the envelope changes with weight. Note that the rough-air speed does not change but that the maximum altitude does.

225

The various types of severe weather

Types other than turbulence

Before we discuss turbulence, which is our primary task in this sub-chapter, let us dispose of the less critical aspects of severe weather.

Heavy Rain   In or beneath a violent thunderstorm it is possible to suffer extremely heavy rain of 50 grams per cubic metre (= 1 in. per minute) and this could cause engine flame out. This rate, however, is extremely rare and occurs only in an area where the aeroplane shouldn't be anyway.   Leaving this and other exceptionally heavy rates aside we come to normal very heavy rain of 2 grams per cubic metre (= 2 in. per hour).   This has no significant effect on the aeroplane or its engines, except that the water might impact on the pitot head and cause temporary fluctuations of airspeed, in the under-reading sense, even with the heaters on.   Free water can exist in large quantities at high altitudes down to extremely low temperatures.   This can cause ice-accretion at a rapid rate due to the naturally low temperature of the outside of the aeroplane.   Depending on the efficiency of the rain dispersal system forward visibility can be significantly reduced.

Hail   In the field of thunderstorm forecasting it is still not possible to forecast or recognise a storm which is likely to produce hail.   Remember that weather radar does not 'see' *dry* hail.   It is safest to assume that *all* thunderstorms are likely to produce hail; and the bigger and more violent the storm the greater is the possibility of hail of damaging size.   Hail is frequently thrown out of a storm in the area below the characteristic anvil. Stones up to 5 in. diameter have been found on the ground; 4 in. stones can be met at 10,000 ft. and large damaging stones can be found at much higher altitudes.   Stones of 2 in. diameter can cause severe damage to an aeroplane and there are at least four such cases in any twelve month period of world-wide operation.   There is no point in going down any further in size; when the awful battering starts there is no means of establishing the size of the hail.   All hail is potentially dangerous and any area suspected of hail must be avoided.   If hail should be struck suddenly don't attempt to turn away; encounters with hail are usually of short duration and the quickest way out is straight on.

Lightning   Lightning can occur in cloud, between clouds and between clouds and the ground.   Most strikes appear to occur within 5,000 ft. either side of the freezing level, but the risk exists outside this band, particularly at higher levels.   A lightning strike is quite frightening, first time; the flash, the noise and the burning smell are all alarming, but the risk of serious damage is actually quite small.   To date, only two accidents are attributable to lightning strikes. Strikes can of course affect compasses and therefore all remote reading indicators.   Turn up the flight deck lighting fully, and switch

226

on the high intensity storm lighting if you are so equipped. If you avoid flying beneath or between thunderstorms, which you should attempt to do anyway for other good reasons, you will lessen the chance of being struck.

Static This is noticed as noise on the radios, particularly on HF and MF, but much less on VHF. As it builds up the noise increases. It can develop into a visible discharge (St. Elmo's fire) around parts of the aircraft and particularly around the edges of windscreens. Static can build up under conditions not associated with thunderstorms. Static can completely upset the performance of MF and HF radio navigation and communication equipment to the extent that communication is impossible and the performance of NDBs (ADF), Radio Ranges and Consol is completely unreliable.

Ice Ice accretion must be expected when flying through clouds or rain at temperatures below 0°C. In thunderstorms the significant range is down to $-40°C$ where super-cooled water drops are in heaviest concentration. Below $-30°C$, however, the water normally consists of ice particles or snowflakes which are less likely to stick. With the protection provided on modern aeroplanes there should be no difficulty with ice affecting either the airframe or the engines — provided the systems are switched on in good time. The significance of ice formation lies mainly in its spoiling effect on leading edges and unbalancing effects if it should form in the areas of pressure balance panels, etc. Some of the later jet transports have dispensed with tailplane de-icing equipment; flight tests with representative ice-shapes have shown that control characteristics are not significantly altered. The most critical conditions are likely to be found when climbing through rain to above the freezing level: under these conditions it would be wise to fly manually and gently exercise all controls to avoid the possible formation of ice. If ice forming conditions have been penetrated unknowingly don't switch all engines anti-icing on at the same time, because ice dislodged from intakes can cause damage and flame out. Switch it on either singly or in pairs allowing sufficient time between each selection to establish that the engine continues to run properly.

Turbulence

To deal with our primary subject of turbulence we must consider it in its three forms:—

(a) Clear air, primarily associated with jet streams, but also with thunderstorms and mountain waves.

(b) Storm, associated with the convective activity in clouds and thunderstorms.

(c) Mountain wave, associated with orographic uplift.

Clear air turbulence This particular type of turbulence is less well understood than the other two types. Because it occurs in clear air *it cannot be*

227

seen in flight. It is primarily associated with jet streams and appears to be more marked on the cold side. It results from wind shear, that is, rapid changes in wind speed over comparatively short distances, which are more significant in the vertical than the horizontal sense. As the discontinuities are contained within a relatively shallow altitude band its upset potential is not great in terms of enforced large height variations.

Apart from 'classic' clear air turbulence associated with jet streams, any other turbulence, not accompanied by cloud, can also generically be called clear air turbulence. The most usual forms of the latter are the turbulence associated with, but significantly removed from, the cloud formation of a thunderstorm, and the high altitude, rather longer-wave turbulence, reflected from a lower altitude mountain wave. These will be discussed separately.

Flight through clear air turbulence at high true airspeed is very like a fast ride over a cobblestone road in a solid-tyre unsprung vehicle. The shocks are hard and sharp but there is little total displacement of the aeroplane involved.

Apart from a slow reduction to rough air speed there is little more that one can do or needs to do about it. Jet streams are marked on route forecasts and appear to be fairly reliable. If it is possible to alter the route clearance a change in altitude, downwards only, will probably clear it. If the jet stream is being parallel tracked the turbulence will last for a long time. In this case a lateral translation of the track might well clear it. If the jet stream is being crossed at right angles the turbulence should not last too long.

Storm turbulence   In a single cell of a thunderstorm, turbulence is due to convective activity. If a mass of air has a lapse rate greater than its surrounding air it will cool more quickly as it rises, be denser than the air alongside and therefore tend to settle and become stable. If the lapse rate is less than the surrounding lapse rate it will always be less dense than the surrounding air, will be unstable and will continue to rise at an accelerating rate. The initial discontinuity in low level temperature can be caused by surface heating or by the penetration of a cold frontal system initially lifting the warm air. As the wet adiabatic lapse rate is always less than the dry rate, severe vertical movement is more likely under these conditions and hence the mass of clouds associated with thunderstorms. The central core of a thunderstorm can contain air moving upwards at extremely high rates. The column bursts and spreads at the top and subsides over a wide area. A cell penetration therefore will be through a downdraught, a violent updraught and another down-draught. In the mixing areas of these air movements conditions can be quite chaotic and extremely violent gusts occur. Furthermore they can hit the aeroplane from any angle.

So much for the mechanics of a single cell. A thunderstorm has, of course, many cells, with each in a different stage of development. The new and developing cells can be recognised by their defined cumuliform shape and cauliflower tops. Mature and decaying cells are less well defined and frequently surrounded by fibrous clouds. There are often, however, large masses of associated clouds which deny the pilot this classic view of the storm. Within a typical thunderstorm composed of developing and decaying cells, severe updraughts and downdraughts of up to 5,000 ft. per minute velocity occur very close to each other, and in their mixing areas sharp edged gusts of up to 10,000 ft. per minute velocity have been recorded. The tops of a storm can rise at 5,000 ft. per minute and the system can spread laterally up to 6 miles in 20 minutes. Line squalls can stretch for hundreds of miles. Storms can reach 40,000 ft. in temperate climates and up to 60,000 ft. in tropical climates. While the life of a cell rarely exceeds one hour the system can remain active for several hours. The areas of the world and the times of the year in which thunderstorm activity can be expected are fairly well known, however, and the forecast system is rarely caught out.

The two main characteristics of thunderstorm turbulence are the high velocity updraughts and downdraughts and the extremely violent sharp edged gusts buried in their mixing areas. In severe cases these impose almost ultimate loadings on the aeroplane. The aircraft is thrown about violently and in some cases has been known to have been completely out of control. To this already dangerous state is added the possibility of the pilot, in attempting to maintain or regain control of his aeroplane, inducing additional loads which will then take some part of the structure beyond its ultimate strength. The same risk is involved in the recovery manoeuvre after a prolonged complete loss of control.

Severe turbulence can be experienced well above the top of a thunderstorm, so never attempt to climb in this area. While it is generally true that turbulence is less at lower levels, the possible altitude excursions which might be experienced must be weighed against the terrain clearance. While turbulence (ordinary rough day type, not thunderstorm type) and windshear on take-off and landing have been covered in other parts of this book, these two qualities, when associated with thunderstorm activity, must be treated with much more respect. It is very dangerous to attempt a take-off or a landing in the area of a thunderstorm. Cancel, delay or divert.

This discussion of storm turbulence makes pretty frightening reading. There is a tendency on the part of those of us who have never experienced it to wonder whether it is actually as bad as it is painted, but conversation with a pilot who has flown through a severe storm will remove all doubt. You must avoid severe storms if you possibly can. If you happen to penetrate one inadvertently then you must fly the aeroplane properly in order to survive.

Mountain Wave Turbulence While this longer wave turbulence can have short term gusts buried in it, its main characteristic is a complete upward or downward movement of a large mass covering a very large area. Very high (and long) mountain ranges which lie broadside to a strong wind will cause a wave effect up to very high altitudes. This effect causes a rising air motion on the windward side and a falling motion to leeward followed by a subsiding wave motion for a long distance downwind. Close downwind at low altitude there can be a rotor effect which can be extremely dangerous. The areas of the world in which mountain wave effect occurs frequently are becoming better established (the Sierra Nevadas and the Andes for example).

Apart from the 'short' long wave effect associated with large thunderstorms and the pure long wave turbulence of large mountains, long wave turbulence at high altitude can also exist. This is due to differing wind speeds and gradients, lapse rates and the general instability of large air masses. The significance of long wave turbulence, once positively identified, is that it requires a flight technique different from that used in 'short-wave' turbulence.

The contribution of the autopilot

In some ways an autopilot is cleverer than a human pilot, but in other ways it is much more ignorant. While it cannot get frightened and always performs well within its limitations it has no memory or experience and cannot act outside its design limits.

Without anticipating what will be said under the heading of recommended techniques for flight through severe weather, let us look at the task and assess the capability and limitations of the autopilot.

Essentially, flight through turbulence requires the achievement of only two sub-tasks:—

1. The maintenance of substantially straight and level flight at the rough air speed.
2. The matching of the actual flight path with the required flight path (depending on the degree and type of turbulence there can be a required flight path or there need not be a required flight path; in the latter case sub-task 1 stands alone).

Sub-task 1 on autopilot

If the autopilot were never thrown out of engagement there would be a lot of evidence to support the many claims that the autopilot would do a better job in turbulence than the human pilot. With real live practice virtually unobtainable, it is difficult to refute these claims, particularly as airline pilots' abilities vary over such a large range. In any case, one thing is certain. If pilots never attempt hand-flying in turbulence they will surely never develop any experience or ability.

In terms of being thrown out of engagement there are basically four types of autopilot design:—

230

(a) **Torque-limited** This type will never drop out. If an excessive demand is made it will do its best and then hold that control angle until the demand subsides. There is every chance that this type will make a good job of attitude flying in severe turbulence.

(b) **'Long-stop' torque cut-out** Very similar to (a) but under a most extreme demand compounded by other unusual circumstances the type could disconnect.

(c) **Torque cut-out** A high level of turbulence will call up control loads or angles which will cause this type to drop out quite frequently.

(d) **Limit switch cut-out** Similar to (c).

So far as types (a) and (b) are concerned it is suggested that they can be trusted with the task of attitude flying with some confidence. Types (c) and (d) can of course be allowed to try, but when they drop out the pilot must take over control. This question of the pilot taking over control can be argued both ways. On one hand he will be rested and refreshed and ready to do a good job. On the other hand he will have been denied the experience of the preceding few minutes and will therefore be less able to do well.

Sub-task 2 on autopilot

We should first define the required flight path. In other than severe clear air or storm turbulence, and in really long wave turbulence, it is quite proper, while struggling to maintain attitude, to overlay the control of the aeroplane with a persuasion not to depart too far from the required flight level. In really extreme turbulence this requirement must be thrown away. Attitude and speed stand alone. If the autopilot is chosen to fly attitude in severe turbulence, no other lock (height, speed, Mach, etc.) must be engaged and the auto-trim must be very carefully monitored.

If, for example, height lock is engaged, the autopilot will have a good stab at maintaining height. If the aeroplane is then forced above the selected altitude it will immediately try to regain that altitude, wind in a lot of nose down control and cause a large increase in airspeed. Similarly, if airspeed lock were selected and the aeroplane forced to a high speed momentarily a lot of nose up control would be applied and a high rate climb started. In both these examples the aeroplane would be left in a poor position to cope with the next demand (which would be in the reverse sense) and the flight path would become rapidly divergent — the very opposite of the basic need.

Auto-trim will obediently perform its task. If a long time demand for a longitudinal control application is made the auto-trim will follow up and wind in a lot of stabiliser, for example. When the demand is finally reversed the stabiliser will have a long way to run back.

The biggest danger of auto-trim and a manometric lock taking the stabiliser too far away from the correct position is that, if the autopilot should then cut-out (and this condition is conducive to a cut-out), the pilot will be left with the aeroplane grossly out of trim and perhaps rushing downhill at high Mach, all set for the difficult fight of an increasingly less effective elevator against a powerful, or perhaps a stalled drive, stabiliser.

Depending therefore on the design philosophy of the autopilot limiting or cut-out circuits, a capable autopilot may be allowed to fly the aeroplane through severe turbulence; but only in the attitude mode and with careful monitoring of auto-trim.

The flight instruments

Before we tackle the general problem of flight instruments in turbulence let us remind ourselves of the following 'particular' possibilities:—

Altimeter and VSI   Local pressure field variations can give rise to errors of up to $\pm$ 1,000 ft.   Heavy rain is a guide to this possibility and gusts and draughts can also cause instrument fluctuations.   Make allowance for this error at low level.

Airspeed indicator   This can be affected by very heavy rain, causing it to under-read.   If the power is consistent with the cruise speed and altitude don't alter it for violent or short term changes in airspeed.

Compass   This can be affected, *and remain affected for the rest of the flight,* by a lightning strike.   Report any such effect on landing.

Having disposed of these particular possibilities we can now proceed with the general problem.   In isolation, all the flight instruments, assuming the gyro driven ones have not been toppled, will continue to tell the truth in severe turbulence.   They will certainly be shaken, the needles will be hopping about markedly, and they may be very difficult to read, but they will mean what they say (with the exception perhaps of the VSI due to a position error which is the result of rapid incidence changes, as previously explained).   If the altimeter says you are going up, the aeroplane is going up (but not necessarily pointing up); if the ASI says you are going faster, the aeroplane is going faster (but not necessarily going downhill or indeed pointing downhill; if the attitude indicator says you are nose up, you will be (but not necessarily climbing).   Just think it out.   For example, in the voilent very short term gusts which can exist along with larger vertical movement of the air, the aeroplane could be fairly hard nose up, but descending rapidly, and with an airspeed which could be increasing or decreasing according to the head-on component of the immediate gust pattern. As will be suggested later in the sub-chapter on flight technique, attitude flying is the primary parameter and this information can be drawn only from the attitude indicator; no attitude inferences must be drawn from any of the pressure instruments. The pressure instruments serve only to indicate airspeed and the vertical profile of the achieved flight path.

The attitude indicator is the primary flight instrument for turbulence flying. Depending on their design and presentation qualities, and the date of their design, attitude indicators vary enormously in their efficiency. There are many deficiencies, in the pure sense, in some of the instruments currently fitted. Knowledge on this subject has increased rapidly over the last few years and opinions have firmed up even more rapidly over recent months. In some ways it is unfair to criticise instruments designed years ago, as they remain in service in a much more demanding atmosphere than was dreamt of in their design stage, but it is proper that their limitations should be known to the pilots who use them. Taking a wide range of current instruments it would appear that the following limitations should be understood:—

(a) The generally small size of the active part of the basic attitude information.

(b) The preponderance of director and other information which suppresses the attitude information and makes it difficult to get at.

(c) The poor contrast between earth and sky on some coloured backgrounds and the inadequacy of an all-black background.

(d) The inability, where pitch and roll information is split, to convey true attitude information at large pitch and roll angles in combination.

(e) The still absent full aerobatic capability of many existing presentations.

(f) The absence of sufficient freedom in pitch indication.

(g) The lack of pitch scale markings.

(h) The apparent confusion which can arise with a top mounted roll index.

Most of the above limitations are self-explanatory and the correct use of the instrument in the presence of a certain limitation is quite clear. However, limitations (d), (f), (g) and (h) need perhaps a little elaboration:—

(d) Where pitch is indicated by a vertically moving reference aeroplane, and bank by the rolling of the background horizon, the instrument is almost completely useless in terms of pitch attitude at 90° of bank. The horizon is then vertical and the reference aeroplane lies on the horizon at all pitch angles. In this case, pitch attitude must be gleaned from the position of the reference aeroplane in relation to the instrument case.

(f) Some instruments are limited to $\pm 27°$ in pitch indication. Where pitch angles exceed this, no rate of change of pitch attitude can be obtained. The recovery therefore from an extreme pitch attitude cannot be programmed according to the amount by which it is adrift from the required pitch attitude.

(g) In the absence of pitch scale markings some manoeuvres, particularly the first segment of the noise abatement departure procedure, can be demanding to fly. Airspeed, instead of pitch, tends to become the primary parameter and the flight path is poorly damped.

(h) This is controversial so we will keep it short. With a top mounted roll index there is an apparent conflict between the reference aeroplane and its horizon and the position of the 'sky pointer' in terms of identifying a roll attitude to port or starboard. A number of pilots have misinterpreted this and rolled the aeroplane the wrong way. With a bottom mounted roll index this conflict does not exist and the whole instrument is compatible in roll. If in doubt ignore the top roll index and establish roll attitude from the relationship of the reference aeroplane to the horizon. Remember that attitude information is, and always has been, *displacement* information. It is wrong to turn a part of it into *director* information. It is this conflict in philosophy which causes the trouble.

One last point on attitude instruments. Where an aeroplane is fitted with remote reading horizons the airworthiness rules require a third standby instrument, regardless of the sophistication and capability of the comparator and failure warning systems of the main horizons. The standby then serves as an umpire in the event of disagreement between the two main instruments and quickly allows the failed main horizon to be voted out. The presentation of the standby horizon is, so far as is possible, kept compatible with the main horizon but it is rarely exactly the same. It can differ significantly in pitch sensitivity and deflection of the horizon for a given pitch attitude. Make sure that you are familiar with its presentation and get to know what it looks like under typical flight conditions.

Physiological behaviour in violent turbulence

The problem of spatial disorientation is at least known and appreciated, if not fully understood, by most pilots.

Without going too deeply into the detailed physiological effects of motion and 'g' in their various forms on the ability of the pilot to control his aeroplane, it is worth noting that recent research indicates that two separate conditions are important; true spatial disorientation due to loss of space references and false tactile stimuli due to accelerations. Both may be encountered simultaneously during severe turbulence. In the presence of both of these conditions all sensory cues other than visual must be completely ignored. Almost any manoeuvre, however gentle, is always accompanied by significant accelerations along the aircraft's axis as well as by the usual 'g' through the seat of the pants. The effects increase with the duration and sharpness of the accelerations and are particularly severe during reversals of manoeuvres in pitch and roll. The human body cannot cope with these and they serve only to confuse the balancing system. Cues for control in turbulence must be visual only — either direct from the outside world or from the instruments.

Negative 'g' is a particularly disturbing experience. Some personal discipline is necessary to avoid the instinctive heave on the control column to re-establish positive 'g'. Depending on the attitude this might be quite the wrong thing to do. If you suffer negative 'g' do nothing about it until you have established its cause.

It is now also known that a pilot's visual acuity and task performance deteriorate fairly rapidly when he is subjected to body vibrations of low frequencies, for example between 3 and 4 cycles per second. The ability to read instruments as well as the ability to respond to their cues is sharply curtailed. Vision becomes tunnelled and limited to virtually one instrument. Head nodding follows at a slightly higher frequency and while this can be resisted by a conscious effort another $\frac{1}{2}$ cycle increase is sufficient to make it uncontrollable. The early large jet aeroplanes have fuselage natural frequencies which tend to be a good way below these critical values, but some of the later types presently flying approach these critical values. Even more recent aeroplanes with higher operating speeds and stiffer structures (because of their extremely long forebodies) show a trend towards these critical frequencies occurring in the flight deck area in severe turbulence. The picture on supersonic transports is not at all clear as of this time.

Use of weather radar

Airborne radar must be regarded as a most useful but crude tool. It must be used only as a means of storm avoidance and not to enable natty penetration patterns to be evolved. Those who have tried the latter have met a host of problems. Severe wind shear between cells, dry large hail, new cells growing in an otherwise dead space in about two minutes up to the levels at which the jet transport operates. (A cell has been observed by ground radar to appear and decay in fifteen minutes; it exceeded 40,000 ft. and produced

2 inch hail on the ground.)   Lastly, you may be led up a blind alley, due to one cell shielding another from your radar, or perhaps the gap closes ahead of you.

A few facts about your radar.   Remember that it relies on dispersion and reflection from water droplets to produce a picture.   The greater the discontinuity as the precipitation is penetrated by the beam, the 'harder' the picture and the better the contour facility will work.   This device is simply an electronic measurement within the set of the radar reflectivity of the storm. This has been set at a value known to mean the presence of severe turbulence within the storm; it does not mean that severe weather does not exist just outside the contour level.   Because of its design function, weather radar as we know it today will not see dry hail which has been flung out of a storm; neither can it differentiate between rain and *wet* hail.

Like any other tool, weather radar is only as good as its operator will allow. Get to know what your radar will do.   Don't be content to look at one level in the storm, but search above and below you, before making up your mind, and make sure that the radar is correctly adjusted.   Varying the control settings on the radar set can significantly vary what it will tell you; for instance you can destroy its capability of seeing a storm by misuse of the gain control. Some operators calibrate their sets and set the controls before take-off. If severe weather is forecast down the route, and if the gain control is not in the narrow band required to produce a correct picture, the set is considered unserviceable and the flight delayed until a new and correctly adjusted set has been fitted.   From then on, in flight, these controls should not be altered. The pilot can then be confident of his interpretation of what he sees.

To sum up.   Don't use radar to penetrate severe storms, but use it to circumnavigate them.   Two good rules of thumb are 'the avoidance of all echoes by 15 miles at reduced airspeed' and 'a 20-mile separation from the nearest echo when above 30,000 ft.'   Avoid echoes with scalloped edges or with pointed or hooked fingers attached.   Invoke the assistance of ground radars.   Know how to get the best out of your radar.   Remember that it sees only water concentrations.   Do not alter gain controls from their best setting in flight.

Review of piston versus jet flying qualities

The comparison between a piston-engined aeroplane and a jet-engined aeroplane is very similar to that between a cart-horse and a race-horse.

The cart-horse is slow, stable, placid and devoid of temperament; it can be ridden quite safely by a yokel.

The race-horse is fast, temperamental and a little bit unpredictable; it needs a trained jockey to control it.   That is, someone who is in sympathy with it, knows when to crack the whip (and, more important, when not to crack the whip), when to give it its head and when to start to bring its divergences under control.

Enough has been said about piston-engined and jet-engined aircraft in this book to emphasise the technical differences between these two classes of aeroplanes in terms of stability, control and performance. In particular, we have highlighted the great increased airspace needed for control of a jet transport in severe weather and the many problems involved in recovering the aircraft from a significant flight path divergence.

Control of the flight path of a modern jet aeroplane, particularly in severe weather, needs a full understanding of all the qualities of the aeroplane which bear on the subject. These have been described in some detail in the preceding chapters of this book. The importance of understanding them cannot be stressed too highly.

Closing the loop

Ergonomics, which is the relationship of a man to a machine system, involves the man as an essential part of a servo control system. Any control system, if it is to be stable, needs a closed loop relating the end product to the original demand so that the required task can be executed. If any part of the servo-loop is deficient or missing the system cannot function and satisfy the original task.

In flight through severe weather we have a typical ergonomic system. There are three parts to it; the aeroplane and its flying qualities, the weather and its effect on the aeroplane and the pilot with his knowledge and control capability. Two of these — the aeroplane and the weather — are fixed. The third must be present in adequate measure in order to produce compatibility between the other two, match them together, make them meet the requirements in order to achieve the end product, thus satisfying the original demand; thus closing the loop. In any surviveable set of circumstances therefore the pilot must be adequate in terms of knowledge and ability or else the whole system goes 'open-loop'.

The aeroplane and its flying qualities in relation to severe weather have been fully discussed. *The weather* has been discussed in sufficient detail to give a good idea of its effect on the aeroplane. The knowledge and ability of *the pilot* are the last link. The knowledge required has also been discussed. We are left, finally, with the detailed flight techniques for severe weather necessary to tie it all up.

Flight techniques in severe weather

Having carefully spelled out all the background material the final recommendations on this subject are comparatively simple and straightforward.

There are four basic rules you must observe. Do not take-off or land in areas of severe weather. Avoid predicted areas of turbulence by flight planning if possible. When airborne, avoid turbulence by visual observation, use of weather radar and by monitoring weather and communications frequencies. If committed to severe weather, fly the right techniques.

Meteorological forecast services give guidance on clear air turbulence, jet streams and thunderstorms. Your broad geographical knowledge and detailed local knowledge of the route, in combination with the forecast weather, should provide guidance on the possibility of long wave turbulence being met en route. If any of this is forecast, or likely, select an altitude at which you can enjoy *at least* $\frac{1}{2}$ g manoeuvrability.

Once airborne, use visual observation and weather radar to circumnavigate storms and keep well clear of them. If in doubt *turn back*, and live to fly another day.

If, in spite of these precautions, you suspect, or find out, that you are committed to a severe weather penetration, proceed as follows. (This technique is for all kinds of violent turbulence. The overlaying extra technique for *positively identified* long wave motion will be covered later.) Remember that storms can play innumerable tricks; if you are prepared for them you will be less disturbed. Radio devices may stop working and static noise levels can be very high. Aircraft electrical systems may be affected temporarily by very strong local electrical fields and compasses will be similarly affected. Turbulence can be severe. You may see or be struck by lightning, or the whole aircraft may be surrounded by St. Elmo's fire. You may get sparks or shocks off controls. There can be a loud battering noise if you fly into hail. You might even fly into torrential rain at sub-zero temperatures. Don't waste time investigating things. Just accept it and get on with the job.

Here is a check list of the things you should make sure of before entering severe turbulence:—

1   Passenger signs on.
2   Check your height for manoeuvrability and terrain clearance and do not attempt to climb over the storm.
3   Monitor the weather radar for best passage.
4   Check all flight instruments and supplies.
5   Check de-icing as required and ensure pitot heat on.
6   Turn off the radios spoiled by static.
7   Turn flight deck lighting full on, night and day.
8   Strap yourself in tight, and stow all loose equipment.
9   Settle the aeroplane at the rough air speed and establish a compatible power setting.

10 Note the position of the tail trim.

11 If you decide to use the autopilot, take out all the locks, but keep the yaw damper in.

12 Be prepared for all the hazards associated with severe weather.

If severe turbulence is encountered unexpectedly, attend to as many of the above items as you can. Take particular care to reduce speed to the rough airspeed only slowly and progressively, and monitor autopilot auto-trim very closely if it is engaged.

From here on this is what you must do. As the pilot in control of the aeroplane you must give your whole attention to control of the flight path and allow nothing else to distract you. You must fly attitude on the attitude indicator alone and ignore all other attitude inferences. Try to stay around the rough air speed. Don't chase airspeed or height unless they reach extreme values. Don't alter longitudinal trim and don't change the power setting. If the autopilot is engaged monitor auto-trim very closely; if it moves very far, take out the autopilot. Don't alter your heading.

Because of the violence of the storm the primary requirement is to keep the aeroplane in substantially straight and level flight. Don't keep too tight a rein on the aeroplane but make required control movements smoothly and firmly. Avoid large and harsh control movements unless absolutely necessary. Leave the power setting alone unless you identify a long term trend away from the rough-air speed. Don't use longitudinal trim; keep control of the aeroplane on the elevator alone. Ignore even large changes in height and never try to climb out of the storm. If you observe an unusually large change of trim position due to the autopilot, cut out the autopilot and put the trim back to its previous setting. Don't let large roll attitudes persist, because they lead to nose down pitch changes.

If you have positively identified the fact that you are in mountain wave turbulence (which you can do by noting long term trends in height and speed, obviously pointing to flight in updraughts or downdraughts, and an absence of the short term very violent turbulence usually associated with thunderstorms) you should overlay your technique with an additional one targeted towards keeping your height and speed excursions within reasonable bounds. In this case very high rates of climb should be countered by a reduction in thrust, and extension of the brakes if necessary, and a very high descent rate by the application of full thrust for as long a period as is necessary. Similarly, for massive speed excursions. If, in an extreme case, you are obviously chancing your arm in attempting to keep height excursions within reasonable limits then throw it away and maintain attitude and speed at all costs. If the power lever settings have been altered for some good reason then, as soon as possible, return them to the previous datum position.

A very recent extremely violent turbulence penetration—and, happily, survival—has brought to light the need for some more thinking. In this incident the turbulence was so appalling that on several occasions all three crew members were attempting to control the aeroplane, power was going from idle to full and all combinations of full primary control angles were being used.   Not having been there and suffered this ride, I am aware that it is a bit of a sauce to comment on the manner in which the report suggests the crew managed the aeroplane.   However, writing this in the peace and calm of an office as opposed to flying through severe turbulence, it would seem reasonable to make the following observations:—

(a) Only one pilot should fly the aeroplane.   It is unlikely that two pilots will work in perfect unison and the second man will only compromise the first.   This rule also extends to control of power.   If the captain decides to make a power change, but has both his hands fully occupied, he should call for whatever he needs and the second pilot should make the change strictly in line with the commands.

(b) Unless it is clearly necessary, don't change the power.   Net thrust takes a long time to run down and run up again.   This, together with the inertia of the aeroplane, makes it unlikely that even a major change in thrust will be effective in less than about ten seconds, by which time the original need for change may have been superseded by an opposing one.   The speed brakes however should be used; their effect is immediate and their rate of operation very high.

(c) Don't use the rudder.   This is virtually an unqualified recommendation because of the always poor and frequently reversed effect of rudder at high Mach number and the possibility of structural problems due to large angles in an overswing manoeuvre at high speed.

(d) Use height to control the wilder divergencies of airspeed and Mach number, but come back to level flight as soon as the divergency has been contained.

(e) Finally, be very conservative in the use of the lap-strap sign.   If there is any doubt whatever, switch it on; and require the cabin staff to strap themselves in immediately they are satisfied that the passengers and equipment are secure.

The 'jet upset'

A final word on the rather loosely labelled 'jet upset'.   This type of high speed dive manoeuvre does not always follow from an upset in high altitude turbulence.   High speed dives have also stemmed from the quiet dropping out of an autopilot which has gone unnoticed by the crew, and from the pilot flying to a failing or failed attitude indicator.

What should you do to avoid this? The answer is: keep your eye on the ball. It doesn't matter what systems trouble you might have run into, let the rest of the crew sort it out while you (the pilot in charge of the aeroplane at the time) maintain a constant watch on the actual flight path. In the event of a suspected failed attitude indicator, immediately check both against the standby, reject the failed one and fly on one of the good ones.

Recovery from upsets

Jet aircraft are more likely to become upset simply because they are jet aircraft; and when they have become upset they are more difficult to bring back under control and need a lot more space in which to do it.

A review of the Table of Differences in Chapter One shows this to be true in many of the areas connected with en route flight. Compared with a piston-engined aircraft the jet aircraft is different in the following ways, all of which are relevant to upsets:—

(a) It has higher momentum, an enormous amount of thrust and low drag, all of which give it gross overspeed potential.

(b) It can fly high and fast, thus exposing itself to the hazards of high Mach number instability, reduced manoeuvrability and restricted speed ranges.

(c) It suffers poor lift at low speeds and much greater height losses if the stall is penetrated to any depth.

(d) It needs devices like variable incidence tailplanes, Mach trimmers and yaw dampers which can malfunction or fail thus reducing the level of handling qualities even further.

All the above characteristics have been explained in detail and their influence on the stability and controllability of the aeroplane should be well understood by the reader.

An aeroplane can be upset in two basic modes—*attitude* and *speed*; it can be rolled or pitched too far and get too slow or too fast. Before we go on to discuss gross upsets let us first define and discuss moderate upsets. A moderate upset is an excursion to a defined degree beyond any normal limit and the following definitions would seem reasonable:—

(a) Too slow = not slower than the stall warning.

(b) Too fast = not faster than $V_{MO} \times 30$ knots or $M_{MO} \times 0.03$ Mach number.

(c) Excessive pitch = not beyond 30° nose up and 20° nose down.

(d) Excessive roll = not more than 60° bank.

A gross upset will then be anything beyond these limits.

Recovery from moderate upsets

This is not difficult — it is just a question of recognising the condition and flying the aeroplane smoothly out of it.   No instruments will have toppled and the aeroplane will not be going fast enough to involve any really significant reduction in controllability.

If you get down to the stall warning or stick shake, apply down elevator to reduce incidence and more thrust (if at low thrust setting) to reduce the height loss. Then fly a required flight path which is the best compatible with accelerating the aeroplane back to normal flying speed and keeping the height loss to a minimum.   If in doubt, and in a position where you can afford a height loss, trade height for speed and get back to a proper flying speed as quickly as possible.   Don't relax until the sink rate has been arrested and the aeroplane is straight and level again.

If you get too fast, fly your recovery according to the amount by which you are too fast and the rate at which you are accelerating.   Reduce thrust and operate the speed brakes if necessary.   If you are accelerating fast down hill then pull the nose up, reduce thrust to idle and operate the speed brakes. Be prepared for the buffet with speed brakes and the buffet with 'g' if at high Mach number.   Don't use the longitudinal trim unless stick forces become very high and then only in a short burst, because nearly all variable incidence tailplanes are very effective at high speed and consequently induce a large 'g' increment.

If you get too much nose up, push gently to reduce attitude.   Don't come below zero 'g' unless it is essential.   Apply up to full thrust to maintain speed over the top.

If you get too much nose down, pull up to recover to level flight.   Don't pull more than 1g increment estimated unless it is essential.   If at high speed reduce thrust to keep the speed down.   If at high Mach number don't pull much beyond the buffet threshold.

If you are at a large bank angle remember that the nose will be falling down into the turn.   Don't try to screw the aeroplane out of this position immediately by assisting ailerons with rudder because excessive sideslip will be induced and the recovery in roll might be a lot quicker than you bargained for.   It is better to fly the aeroplane out on ailerons alone in a gentle diving turn.

A number of these upsets can occur in combination.   Don't delay the recovery; but don't rush it either.   Just get at it in a smooth and co-ordinated fashion keeping a strict check on your progress in *attitude*, *speed* and *height*. Don't relax until the aeroplane is properly back under control and trimmed-out straight and level again.

Recovery from gross upsets

By definition now these are speed excursions down to the stall and up to V_{DF} or M_{DF}, pitch attitudes exceeding 30° nose up and 20° nose down and roll angles exceeding 60°.

Let us take this in two parts; one, where the primary attitude references are still working and, two, where they have toppled. Before we go into this rather hairy field we should remind ourselves of the following possibilities:—

(a) Reduced rolling ability due to aileron effect reducing with Mach number, possibly very high stick forces at high speeds and virtual loss of rolling ability due to spoiler blow back on some types.

(b) Reversed rudder effect at very high Mach numbers compounding the difficulties in roll.

(c) Reduced control in pitch due to elevator effect reducing with Mach number, very high stick forces at very high speeds, limited elevator capability due to jack-stalling at very high stick forces, the extreme sensitivity of tailplanes at high speeds and the fact that some stabiliser drives stall in the face of very high stick forces.

(d) Reduced manoeuvrability at high weights and high altitudes and the certainty of high buffet in positive 'g' manoeuvres at high Mach number.

(e) The effects of failure or loss of yaw dampers and Mach trimmers.

Before the budding jet pilot decides to stick to piston-engined aircraft he should remember that each jet transport has only a few of these possible deficiencies, and furthermore that you don't get into upsets if you fly properly!

Gross upsets, primary attitude indicators still reading This is a bit like recovery from moderate upsets, only more so. If a modern jet transport gets grossly upset, because of its high momentum and low drag, it will quickly reach an extreme attitude and speed from which recovery will need a vast amount of height and will be made more difficult by a certain reduction in controllability and manoeuvrability. Some of the milder jet upsets to date come within this category and have involved a descent at extreme attitudes and very high speeds. Although there is little evidence of pure stalling, or wild excursions steeply upwards, we should cover all of the following five cases:—

(a) *Recovery from the full stall* is similar to recovery from stall warning except that full down elevator should be applied and held until a rapidly increased airspeed is seen. At the same time apply full thrust to keep the height loss to a minimum. In the recovery from the dive take care you do not again increase incidence to another stick shake. A heavy aeroplane stalled at high altitude needs a good steep recovery attitude

243

initially in order to get the airflow cleaned up and flowing in the right direction. Too early an attempt to recover from the dive will surely bring the aeroplane close to the stall again.

(b) *An excursion to a very high speed* is usually combined with a steepish nose down attitude. In terms of speed alone the recovery action is, in quick order; reduce to idle thrust (not, however, in a steep descent on a type with reducing elevator effect) and extend full speed brake, then pull the nose up to increase the rate of speed reduction. There will be buffet from the brakes and from the 'g' if at high Mach number.

(c) *A very steep nose up attitude* is fortunately rare. Up to about 50° nose up (if you have proved positively that you are at this angle) push just into the negative 'g' area, apply full thrust and the recovery should be good, though unpleasant. Remember that if you have done this you might be very slow over the top; keep the recovery going to about 10° nose down then gently ease off the push force as the speed builds up. Because of the effect of static stability the aeroplane will be seeking a return to the original trim speed which means that at any lower speed it will want to go nose down. Having returned to level flight at a lower speed you will therefore have to hold a decreasing pull force until you regain your original speed. Having contracted, as it were, to talk this subject out we must cover the extreme nose up case with a rapidly falling airspeed. *If you have positive proof* that you are in excess of 50° nose up you might stall or run out of elevator effect during the push over; so roll the aeroplane to near 90° of bank (while you still have the speed to do so) and allow the nose to fall. Recover smoothly as the airspeed build up again.

(d) *Recovery from a very high speed dive* must be made quickly and with some determination. Pull full speed brake and then pull into the buffet a little way if at high Mach number or an estimated 1g increment if at high speed. When you arrive at the position where the speed stops increasing you've got it made. Just hang on and it will come around nicely. Ease off the pull force as the aeroplane returns to level flight. Now remember this: if you were upset from a, say, *trimmed* 260 knot cruise at, say, 35,000 ft. and you finish up at 390 knots at 22,000 ft. the longitudinal stability will have exerted itself and the aeroplane will be seeking to return to 260 knots; this means that it will want to pitch fairly hard nose up. So, if you want to maintain 22,000 ft. for a while, you are going to have to push quite hard. Don't trim this push force out — just wait for the speed to decay. If you should suffer a reduced elevator effect at very high speed or Mach number there is not a lot you can do about it except to hang on tight. As the Mach number falls with reducing altitude the elevator effectiveness will return and recovery will be made progressively. If the aeroplane should be forced to a steep dive angle so as to achieve a high speed very quickly, do not reduce the power on those low-thrust-line-engined types known to be short of elevator effectiveness in the recovery; the nose down trim change with reduced thrust cannot be afforded. It is better to leave cruise power set and wait until you have proved that you have enough up elevator effect before you start reducing power. On those types which suffer a stalled stabiliser drive in the face of high elevator loads the recovery is not necessarily difficult or disturbing if you follow the recommended drill (see page 41). Simply keep the trim button activated and ease off the elevator load. As the force falls through the critical value the stabiliser will run and recovery will be effected. Remember to ease off the pull force as the stabiliser responds.

(e) *Large bank angles*, in isolation, are recovered in the same way as moderate bank angles. Don't use the rudder — just roll it out smoothly on the ailerons. Now remember this: if you are upset at a large bank angle in a steep dive *you must recover the aeroplane laterally before you recover it longitudinally* otherwise you will simply pull into an ever-tightening spiral. So roll it substantially level first then recover in pitch. If you are at very high Mach number in a type on which you are not sure of the rudder effectiveness in the way in which it rolls the aeroplane then *leave the rudder alone* and recover on ailerons only.

Gross upsets, primary attitude indicators toppled. First let it be said that many of the later attitude indicators retain full freedom in roll. A manoeuvre including inverted flight from a roll therefore leaves the horizon still functioning. These horizons have about 85° freedom in pitch so it is most unlikely that a civil jet transport so equipped will ever suffer a toppled primary attitude indicator. Some of the very latest horizons have what is known as controlled precession in pitch around the vertically up, and vertically down, attitudes. At these points the instrument does a 180° twizzle so that it reads properly keeping the sky and the ground in the right place, and again as the other datum is traversed to bring it back to normal presentation. Different symbols identify straight down (the *nadir*) and straight up (the *zenith*) and the controlled precession is quite obvious. These instruments are effectively fully aerobatic and they will not topple. However, there are a number of jets flying with instruments that will topple, so the subject should be covered.

In order to keep this treatment within reasonable bounds a simple analysis has first to be done and certain assumptions made. If a civil transport aeroplane is upset sufficiently violently to topple the attitude indicators it is a fair bet that the pilot will be disorientated and not know what position he is in. The first thing to do therefore is *nothing*; if you do not know what position you are in you cannot know how to get out of it. So wait until the

245

aeroplane settles into a recognisable manoeuvre before you take hold of it.

The aeroplane will certainly finish up by descending; in a straight dive, erect or inverted, a spiral or a spin, erect or inverted. To date there has been no recorded instance of an aeroplane spinning out of an upset. Furthermore, judging from conversation with military personnel, it is a fair bet that the inverted spin is not in the repertoire of civil jet transport aircraft. The erect spin, however, is still a possibility. We need therefore to cover four of these cases.

(a) *The spin* is recognised by a high rate turn on the turn indicator (ignore the slip reading — it can be stuck hard either side in a modern aeroplane), a general sloppiness of the controls (if manual) a lot of banging and clattering *and a fairly low airspeed*. The recovery is effected by applying hard opposite rudder against the turn, strictly centralising the ailerons and pushing forward the control column. When the turn indicator comes off its stop centralise the rudder. You will be left in a steep dive (see later).

(b) *The spiral* is recognised by a high rate turn on the turn indicator and not much slip, a definite feel of increasing speed *and a rapidly increasing airspeed*. Recovery is effected by recovering lateral level first by applying aileron against the indicated turn until it is substantially central, then centralising the ailerons. You will be left in a steep dive (see later).

(c) *The inverted dive* will be obvious by all the loose equipment flying around the flight deck and the fact that you are hanging on your straps. The recovery in this case is simply to roll the aeroplane on the ailerons for about 8 secs. flat; this is *approximately* the time it will take the average *older* jet transport to roll through 180° (for the newer aeroplanes it could be nearer 4 secs.). Whether or not you judged it properly you will most probably find yourself near enough right way up in a spiral (see above).

(d) *The erect steep dive* will be confirmed by a rapidly increasing airspeed. Maintain lateral level on ailerons by keeping the turn indicator substantially central, then pull up elevator. Maintain up elevator until the airspeed stops increasing — this means that you are passing through the level flight attitude — then *push*, because at the much increased speed the stability will be causing a strong nose up pitch (remember?). Now wait for the altimeter to steady and fly on both altimeter and airspeed for pitch control and the turn indicator for lateral control. You are now home and dry. Just press the fast erect button on the standby horizon and relax. If you should have overcooked the dive recovery and find yourself rushing uphill, push until the speed stops decreasing; this identifies the level pitch attitude again. Now change to a pull and slowly relax as the speed increases, and maintain altitude.

Note that the above drills, particularly (d), are absolutely conditional upon the thrust not being altered from its original cruise setting. If it should be altered, then the relationship of stick force to speed will be lost and the search for level flight will have to be made through intelligent use of the VSI and altimeter. These recoveries are *not* overwritten. If you have the ability and personal discipline to fly them using the basic instruments, recovery can be guaranteed from the most extreme positions.

Instrument failures

Finally some advice on flight techniques in the event of failure of various flight instruments. The secret of most techniques of course is *the known relationship between configuration, attitude, power and speed.* Let us put aside failure of single instruments because these are usually well duplicated and backed up by the read-across from other related instruments. There are two areas which need to be discussed:—

(a) A total (temporary) failure of all pressure instruments (airspeed, altitude, VSI and Mach) should not cause you any distress. In an en route climb at night for example you should know that, if you maintain climb power, compass heading, wings level and a typical climb attitude on the horizon indicator, you are bound to continue the climb in a broadly acceptable manner. Similarly in any other configuration; the relationship of power and attitude will give you a safe airspeed and/or rate of descent or climb.

(b) A total (temporary) failure of all attitude information is just as easily coped with. Maintain lateral level by reference to the compass and turn indicator; maintain pitch attitude by reference to airspeed and height associated with a known power.

As a conclusion to this sub-chapter it is suggested that the reader will agree that it is easier to avoid falling into a hole than to dig yourself out having fallen in. All the recovery techniques elaborated here are quite flyable and work out in practice. But they need practice. Better of course to avoid the need to apply them in real life altogether.

Good as we all think we are, there comes a time when we are forced to find out just how good we really are. Under demanding conditions keep your eye closely on the aeroplane's flight path and watch any tendency for it to start sneaking away. Prepare yourself for the 1 in ? chance when things have gone wrong by keeping up your instrument flying ability. Go back and find out just how a turn and slip indicator works, practise flying without pressure instruments or without attitude guidance. For each segment of a typical flight profile get to know a standard relationship between pitch attitude, power and airspeed. It gives enormous confidence to have this knowledge and ability behind you.

9 The very big jet

Introduction

Since the second edition of this book was published the phrase 'big jet' has taken on a new meaning. Where in the past we would have been referring to 330,000 lb. of aeroplane we are now describing something which weighs 710,000 lb. At the present time however there is only one civil aircraft of this size in the Western world and it seems unlikely that there will be any other produced during the next decade. Hence in this chapter there is a departure from the previous practice of making only general comments applicable to several aircraft types. The description is of one aeroplane in particular — the Boeing 747.

The 747 is a most impressive aeroplane with a number of exceptionally fine qualities. Any problems which might have been caused by its size and inertia have been fully resolved by the size and power of its primary flight control surfaces. Additionally the lightness and fine resolution over small angles of its powered flying controls give a high degree of response and encourage very accurate control of the flight path. More than adequate redundancy exists in the designs of its primary and secondary flight control systems to cater for all likely combinations of failures and still leave a high level of controllability available. The aeroplane complies with all the flight requirements as currently interpreted, in most cases with ample margins in hand, and fixes, in a thoroughly adequate fashion, all the problems long associated with jet transport aircraft; the latter is itself an achievement.

Among its very good qualities are its high speed and high Mach number handling, stall characteristics, controllability with engine(s) out, its ability to demonstrate 0.97 true Mach number, its lack of need for Mach trimming and yaw damping and the significantly lower than usual flight deck workload. In all forms of take-offs and landings, where stability and control matter most, its precise and easy controllability sets an example to many aeroplanes one-tenth its weight and to some one-hundredth its weight.

The only important criticism the author can make is that there is initial difficulty in judging both the extra clearance needed on final approach close to the threshold and the landing flare height; this is due to the aeroplane's size and the high pilot eye level. Additional minor criticisms concern rather thin longitudinal stability at aft C.G., particularly at high cruise Mach, lack of performance at high altitude at high weights, a slightly rough ride in marked turbulence, a feeling of rather a tight fit at the pilots' stations (initially, anyway) and only just adequate ability to trim directionally with two engines out en route.

The low speed stability augmentor required for U.K. certification in the flaps up pre-stall range is a simple installation and is effective. The marked buffet identifying the flaps-up stall in the absence of a nose down pitch is thoroughly acceptable.

Well now, although there are one or two minor criticisms here and there the above is a most flattering summary of an aeroplane's flying qualities. Furthermore, little significance need be attached to these minor criticisms. It is merely the practice of a certification pilot to log these in the hope that the constructors might be inclined to effect an improvement. Surprisingly and to give them credit they frequently do and then we all get a bonus in terms of having a better aeroplane which is nicer to fly.

To readers who are not familiar with the certification of civil transport aeroplanes perhaps it should be explained that, with very few exceptions, most prototypes have a bit of a struggle to get through to certification and usually they finish up either with a handful of small areas where some generous interpretation of requirements are necessary or one large area where a major change in requirement interpretation is necessary: a significant number need both. Good examples of major changes in requirements interpretation are the need for the secondary stall recognition system (SSRS) on the Douglas DC9 and the stick pusher system on the Hawker Siddeley Trident, to show compliance with the stalling requirements.

Apart from one disagreement in principle, which will be described later, the 747 had a pretty good run through the tests for U.K. certification. Fundamentally it has no snags and its most comforting quality is that it doesn't fly as its looks or its stately departure procedure suggest it might. In spite of looking from the side a bit like an airship with wings, it is very easy to fly, very light to handle, responsive and manoeuvrable.

There are two reasons for this high standard of controllability, which is surprisingly high for such a large aircraft. The first is that its primary flying control surfaces are big enough for the job and the second is that they are fully power operated. In Chapter 3 we discussed the in-flight momentum of a large aeroplane, as illustrated in figure 3.1, and this remains true of aeroplanes with fundamentally manual control systems. A good illustration of this is to compare the manoeuvrability of, say, a Dove with that of, say, a CL44, both having purely manual controls. The Dove is small, light and responsive; the CL44 is large, heavy and not very responsive. Hence the latter requires time and space in which to change its flight path. But with very large control surfaces which are fully power operated an enormous amount of control power is given to the pilot: more than enough to overcome the effect of high momentum. The parameter that counts here then is not simply momentum, but *momentum/control power ratio*. Clearly the 747 has ratios of a conservative order about all axes.

250

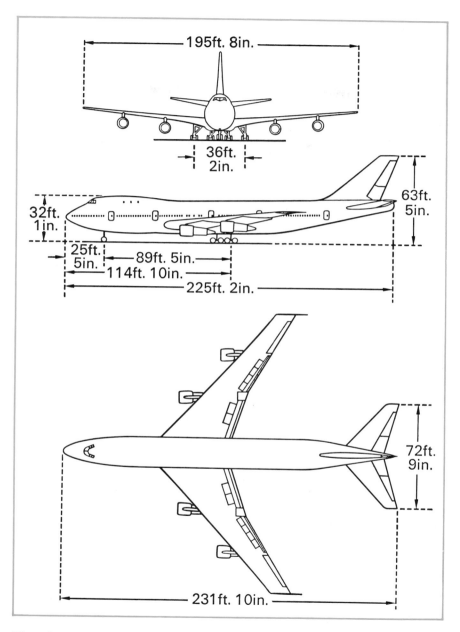

Figure 9.1   Three-view general arrangement.

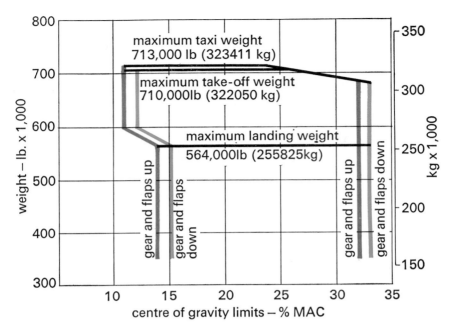

Figure 9.2   Weight/C.G. limits.

Most of the primary dimensions and values are shown in figures 9.1, 9.2 and 9.3.   The last graph relates to a model 747-136 certificated to the U.K. requirements, and the following points should be noted:—

(a) The V$_{DF}$ line should be read against the CAS scale at the top.

(b) The V$_{MO}$ restriction to 330 knots below 8,000 ft. is for windscreen bird impact protection.

(c) The four vertical lines at 15,000 ft. indicate stall speeds, thus:—
    A — flaps 30° at 400,000 lb., 181,500 kg.
    B — flaps 30° at 564,000 lb., 256,000 kg.
    C — flaps 0° at 564,000 lb., 256,000 kg.
    D — flaps 0° at 710,000 lb., 322,000 kg.

The remainder of the primary values are as follows:—
    Approximate A.P.S. weight — 360,000 lb., 164,000 kg.
    Lightest practicable landing weight — 400,000 lb., 181,500 kg.
    Weight of full fuel — 314,600 lb., 142,700 kg.
    Gear speeds — 270 knots/320 knots.
    Flap speeds, 1° through 30° — 265 knots to 180 knots.

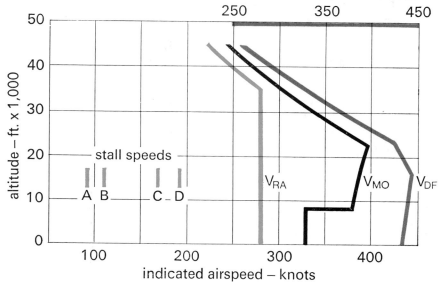

Figure 9.3   Flight envelope speeds.

Range of V_2 speeds $\begin{cases} 710{,}000 \text{ lb., } 322{,}000 \text{ kg. } - 170 \text{ knots, } 10° \text{ flap.} \\ 450{,}000 \text{ lb., } 204{,}000 \text{ kg. } - 133 \text{ knots, } 20° \text{ flap.} \end{cases}$

Range of V_{AT_0} speeds $\begin{cases} 564{,}000 \text{ lb., } 256{,}000 \text{ kg. } - 148 \text{ knots, } 25° \text{ flap.} \\ 400{,}000 \text{ lb., } 181{,}500 \text{ kg. } - 118 \text{ knots, } 30° \text{ flap.} \end{cases}$

Maximum altitude — 45,100 ft.

JT9D-3A $\begin{cases} \text{static take-off thrust } - 43{,}500 \text{ lb.} \\ \text{static maximum continuous thrust } - 36{,}400 \text{ lb.} \end{cases}$

LCN values $\begin{cases} \text{rigid pavement } - 77.5. \\ \text{flexible pavement } - 83.0. \end{cases}$

Remember that all the specific values quoted in this chapter relate to a 747 certificated to the U.K. requirements.

Having considered a brief outline of the aeroplane let us now take a closer look at the specific areas which interest us as pilots.   These are principally:—

(a) Flight deck layout.

(b) Flight control system design and associated hydraulics.

(c) Flying qualities, i.e. performance and handling characteristics.

We will take each of these in turn, then conclude with a summary including the few areas of 747 operation where some particular care is needed.

Flight deck layout

Brief description

The flight deck generally is well-designed and, in spite of some limitations, makes a good professional office. While some of the flight instruments can only be described as average the attitude indicator is a big improvement on previous instruments. This, combined with the light and precise control available, makes accurate flying easy. The systems station is well laid out and encouragingly simple, although in fact it controls many involved systems. The only one involving any apparent complexity in control is the air system. The automatic flight control side is well up to standard although not quite as refined perhaps as, for example, that of a Trident 3B. The U.K. fit is triplex autopilot with a good flight director and all the currently required facilities. Auto-throttle, duplication of all the traditional navaids and, above all, triplex INS (which to a non-expert is quite unbelievably capable)— everything the pilot needs is there and it all works. After so many years of anticipation of all these facilities it is most satisfying finally to find them all in one aeroplane.

Some points of interest

Location The flight deck is located on top of the fuselage primarily because of the need to keep the fuselage structural design common with the upwards-opening-nose-type cargo versions. While this pleases the structures people it does impose a high pilot's eye position in the three point attitude, which becomes higher still (due to fuselage length) during the take-off and landing flares. The disadvantages of this will be discussed later.

Canopy shape With the very high M_D of 0.97 true Mach number there was a need to tailor the canopy shape carefully so as to keep local Mach numbers as low as possible. This results in rather a tight fit for the pilots at upper body level and initially the pilots' stations feel cramped. Additionally the roof panel is a shade close and the glareshield rather dominant. The glareshield is shaped carefully to give adequate instrument visibility with maximum effectiveness as a glareshield and as a horizontal reference. This all sounds a bit constraining and initially one does miss the lebensraum enjoyed on other types; but one rapidly gets used to it and after a while it turns out to have a distinct advantage. In fact, my conclusion after about thirty hours flying that '. . . . the enforced proximity to structure and the feeling of sitting 'in' rather than 'on' the aeroplane both lead to a close identification with the aeroplane and raise the accuracy of flight path control' is reinforced by subsequent experience. Because of the closeness of the windscreen posts it would seem good practice to tighten, and lock tight, the shoulder harness whenever a rough ride is anticipated, either in turbulence or on rough

254

runways. The ride in marked turbulence can be uncomfortable when a lateral motion is superimposed on the vertical motion. One small penalty of the flight deck canopy position and shape is a slightly higher than usual level of aerodynamic noise at high airspeeds with a low cabin differential pressure — not however a very usual flight condition. The other source of noise is the third air conditioning pack.

Reference eye position A reference eye position indicator is fitted. While I am not a supporter of imposed seating positions, in this instance I believe that it should be used, at least initially; otherwise there is a tendency to sit low and as a result lose a significant amount of downwards vision on the approach.

Powered seats Some operators fit powered pilots' seats. While these are a big improvement over manual seats there are two points to be watched on the early versions; the starting torque is high and acceleration surprisingly fast. The drill on these seats is to pull the circuit breakers for take-off and landing. Later seats have reduced torque and speed of operation, and the pilot is able to stop seat movement with his feet.

Rudder bar adjustment The rudder pedals have quite a long travel. For pilots who are short in the leg it is essential to adjust the rudder bar and seat so that full rudder and brake can be achieved comfortably without restriction on up-elevator control.

Lateral trim There is no lateral trim control actuator position indicator. The trim scale is mounted on the boss of the control column. It is necessary for the wheel to be trimmed to zero on its scale with no hand force on it.

Fixed side windows There is no openable Direct Vision window. From an airworthiness point of view this raised the question of a side window landing in the remote event of all forward screens being obscured. A side window landing in a 747 is remarkably easy and is described later in the chapter.

Standby attitude indicator The main instrument panels are canted about 16° out of vertical. This makes them easy to read but it has an effect on the standby Horizon which is fitted without a wedged adaptor. While the standby Horizon is unaffected over the majority of its working range its controlled precession limits are out by the amount by which its pitch datum is displaced. Instead of precessing at around 85° of climb and dive it will precess at 101° nose up and 69° nose down. All this may seem a bit academic, but had the slope of the main panel been much more, bringing nose down precession close to 60°, then a wedged adaptor would certainly have been necessary. Sixty degrees nose down may seem an appalling attitude for a very big aeroplane but other aircraft have been there and on those occasions a precessing standby horizon wouldn't have helped. There is, of course, no effect of panel slope on the main horizons because their knowledge is obtained from the INS platforms which are untoppleable.

Audible warnings All the flight deck audible warnings are electronic and come out of the same box. While they are all different they nevertheless have the same generic 'electric organ' flavour. Hence familiarisation with these warnings is important. There are a lot of them — nine altogether — and this is probably about the limit that a human being can be expected to cope with. Work is going on to rationalise warning systems and reduce the number of audios and it is hoped that future aircraft will show a marked improvement in this respect.

Flight control system design and associated hydraulics

Description

This is the area in which the 747 is truly outstanding and demonstrates about an order better in terms of redundancy and failure survival than any current airworthiness level would require. There are no areas in this part of the design earning criticism or needing any special attention or warnings but a quick run down of the system will enable the design philosophy to be understood and appreciated.

Figure 9.4 is a schematic diagram of the flight control system design and associated hydraulics.

The flight control system design is fully hydraulically powered and a clever mix of the 'single surface multiple supply' and 'split surface single supply' philosophies is applied. The stabiliser and trailing edge flaps are hydraulically powered, the leading edge flaps are pneumatically powered; all the flaps have alternate electric operation. The gear is hydraulically powered with free fall back up.

There are four separate main hydraulic systems. Each system has an engine-driven pump (EDP) and an air-driven pump (ADP). The ADPs are fed by an engine bleed air gallery running across the wing. The EDP normally runs the system but the ADP joins in automatically when the demand becomes high, during gear retraction for example. In the event of an engine shut-down the hydraulic system remains active and fully capable on the ADP. This is bonus number one; loss of an engine does not result in loss of its associated hydraulic system.

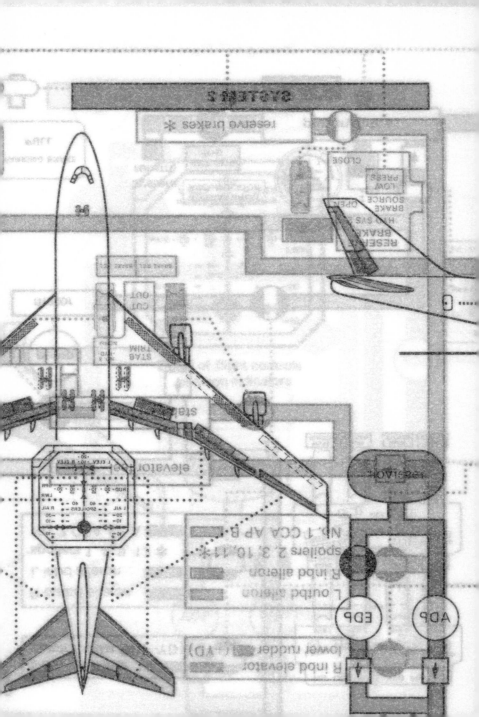

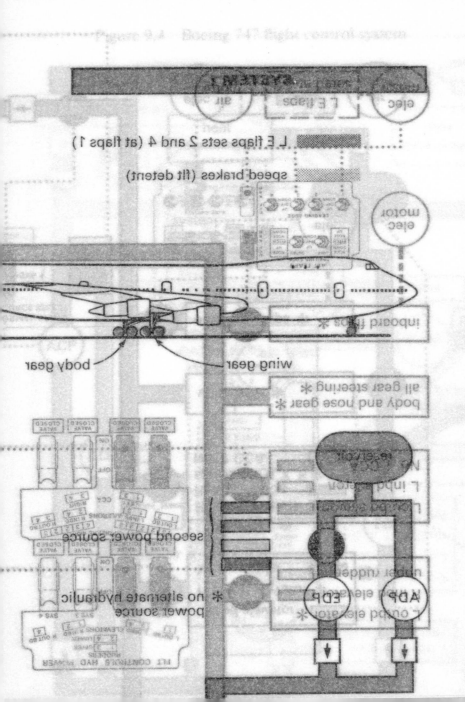

Figure 9.6   Boeing 747 flight control system

The flight control surfaces are split and supplied by the hydraulic systems in such a way as to minimise the effect of single and double systems failures. The distribution is as follows:—

Service	Item Controlled	System
Pitch control	Four elevators— left outboard left inboard right inboard right outboard Stabiliser— one piece	 1 3 and 4 1 and 2 4 2, 3 and 1
Roll control	Four ailerons— left outboard left inboard right inboard right outboard Ten spoilers	 1 and 2 1 and 3 2 and 4 3 and 4 2, 3 and 4
Yaw control	Two rudders— lower upper	 2 and 4 1 and 3
Gear	Body and nose Wing All steering	1 4 1
Flaps	Trailing edge— inboards outboards Leading edge— four sets	 1 4 pneumatic

A good deal of far-sighted philosophy has gone into the relationship of hydraulic systems with flight control surfaces. The distribution of the hydraulic systems is such that single failures and double failures leave the aeroplane substantially symmetrical. Systems 2 and 3 are primarily the flight control systems. A situation with two engines inoperative on one side, and with both ADPs also failed, still leaves full rudder available.

257

Single surfaces with a double hydraulic supply will still operate effectively in the event of a single hydraulic failure.   The following are the design rates for those primary surfaces with two hydraulic supplies:—

Surface	Two hyd. systems rate (°/sec.)	One hyd. system rate (°/sec.)
Inboard elevators	37 down 37 up	30 down 26 up
Rudders	50	40
Inboard ailerons	40 down 45 up	27 down 35 up
Outboard ailerons	45 down 55 up	22 down 45 up

The one-system-out rates are thoroughly adequate.

The only circuits with no alternate hydraulic power source are as follows, but in the event of failure most are supported in other ways as indicated:—

(a) Outboard elevator — three surfaces remaining.

(b) Gear steering — differential thrust and braking.

(c) Gear retraction — nil (body gear *or* wing gear stays down).

(d) Trailing edge flaps — alternate electrics.

(e) Four spoiler sections — eight sections remain.

Out of all this enormous redundancy the only significant single failures which exist are Systems 1 and 4, resulting in half the gear failing to retract. While this would be an embarrassment operationally it is not of any safety or airworthiness significance.

The spoiler panel scheduling is fairly complex.   Its detail is a good example of how carefully the tailoring has been done to give optimum performance in the speed brake mode and roll control mode without unnecessary buffet.   The panels are grouped as follows:—

1 2 3 4	5 6	7 8	9 10 11 12
left outboard	left inboard	right inboard	right outboard

They are used thus:—

(a) *In-flight speed brakes* selection uses panels 3 4 5 6 and 7 8 9 10
where 3 4 9 10 go to 45° ⎫
and 5 6 7 8 go to 20° ⎬ with lever in flight detent

(b) *Ground spoilers* selection, with lever going beyond the flight detent, picks up all the remaining panels.

(c) *Roll control* selection uses panels 1 through 5 and 8 through 12, where 1 through 4 and 9 through 12 go to 45° and 5 and 8 go to 20°.

(d) *Partial speed brake* selection results in the roll control spoilers acting differentially.

What about control in the event of all engines flame-out? This would mean no bleed air and no ADPs. Survival depends on the EDPs. They produce enough hydraulic power provided they are kept windmilling fast enough. This will be achieved if 1.3Vs with a minimum of 160 knots is maintained. To keep the demand low the controls should not be waggled unnecessarily and other hydraulic services — flaps for example — should not be used.

There is considerably more to the design than this brief description suggests. In order to maintain a high standard of ease, precision and lightness of controls there are systems like central control actuators (CCA) to reduce lateral control circuit loads, mechanical coupling of inboard-with-opposite-outboard elevators to reduce longitudinal control circuit loads and so on. There is too much to cover in detail here. But the great care which has gone into the philosophy of the design is shown by these brief examples.

Failure analysis

This is the most rewarding part of this sub-chapter; however one tackles the subject, the design of the 747 is difficult to fault. Taken in isolation, single and double engine failures have no effect on controllability and to see any effect at all one has to assume either a hydraulic system failure or a control surface failure (other than the stabiliser which is accepted as not capable of failure). A single hydraulic system failure however is really of no significance — there remain plenty of surfaces to do the job — and a single surface failure is just as innocuous for the same reason.

To show any real degradation of controllability one has to go to double failures; either double hydraulic systems failures, double surface failures (with fair allowance for their probability) or a mixture of one hydraulic and one surface failure. Even then, any combination of double failures still leaves the aeroplane comfortably flyable. (Compare this with the landing technique necessary on a DC8 or 707 in the event of a double hydraulic system failure.)

A full analysis shows that the worst double failures are as follows:—

(a) For pitch control — failure of systems 1 and 2 (or 3 and 4) resulting in the loss of one outboard and the opposite inboard elevators.

(b) For lateral control — failure of systems 2 and 3, resulting in the loss of all outboard roll spoilers and reduced rate on all ailerons.

However, the resulting degree of controllability remains very high and the aeroplane can still be flown to its destination and landed without difficulty. (As a generalisation it is true that any aeroplane can be flown quite adequately on only one half full control power about all axes.)

The U.K. airworthiness requirements do not go beyond any likely combination of double failures. This includes engines, hydraulics, primary and secondary flying controls. The 747 design is more than a match for every one of them. When all this capability is considered in combination with the fact that the aeroplane flies very nicely anyway, it will be understood that we are dealing with a very impressive aeroplane indeed.

Flying qualities

Performance

The 747 is certificated as a Performance Group A four engined aeroplane. It meets all the U.K. requirements and will do everything claimed for it and scheduled in the Flight Manual.

It is U.K. practice during certification to conduct an engine out take-off at maximum gross weight under WAT limiting conditions if possible and fly the complete net flight path departure up to the point of entry to the engine out en-route climb. This the 747 does admirably and with about the right amount of gross performance in hand. It was most impressive at a weight of 716,000 lb., 324,800 kg. Regular gross performance climbs are also conducted on every new delivery in the engine out take-off and two engines out en-route configurations. The results to date are running in excess of the scheduled gross data. So the aeroplane's airworthiness performance is of course good.

But if by 'performance' one means does it get up and go — well, it's no 720B! Maximum continuous thrust is needed at very high weights to show a gross gradient of 4% in the second segment of a noise abatement departure procedure. Like all fan-engined aeroplanes, it is also short of thrust at altitude. It is performance limited in terms of cruising levels and 45,000 feet, at any operationally useable weight, is out of reach with the present engines. We all look forward at least to the –7 engine.

But then, this is little different from the fan-engined versions of the bigger DC8s and 707s. So long as operational use of the 747 is planned within its abilities it is perfectly satisfactory and the lack of thrust at high altitude is really only a nuisance to test pilots who have to run for example a high Mach programme at high altitude in order to clear the extreme boundaries of the flight envelope.

Handling characteristics

This is the second major area in which the 747 is outstanding. This is due primarily to its light and precise controllability but its other fundamentals, like stability and stalling, are very good too. It is convenient to run through the handling qualities in the order of the airworthiness sections of stability, controllability, ability to trim, stalling and take-offs and landings.

Stability Apart from two particular areas in the longitudinal sense which are debatable the overall stability of the aeroplane is good. There is no significant dutch roll anywhere and while yaw dampers are fitted they are not mandatory for despatch. The lateral and directional stability is good throughout. Negative dihedral effect at high Mach number is small, particularly for 37.5° of sweep. With the speed brakes in, roll response to rudder is still positive; with the brakes out it is zero; all at 0.97 true Mach number. This is of little real significance because the roll rates on lateral control alone are remarkably high. Spiral stability is good at low speeds at low altitudes, where it matters most; a bit weaker but still positive in the cruise. Speed stability on the approach is positive and this contributes to already good approach handling characteristics. Static longitudinal stability at aft C.G. is characterised by very light stick forces over small angles of elevator. Manoeuvre stability over large angles of elevator is good at around 75 lb. stick force per 1g increment. One small point on the quality of the ride: up to the point of moderate turbulence it is good, but above this it can be quite rough. This flight deck shaking seems to go with the lack of stiffness associated with very big aeroplanes.

The two debatable areas are:—

(a) *Stability at high Mach number* at aft C.G. is approximately neutral and no Mach trim system is fitted. The aeroplane is quite willing to fly between say about 0.84 and 0.90 true Mach number without any real stick force gradient against speed. The stability however is not negative. Strictly speaking this is not quite up to requirement level for a 1970 aeroplane although types like the VC10 and the Trident, certificated some years ago, fly perfectly well at about the same level of stability. The choice was to accept the aeroplane as it was or impose a Mach trim system; this being a case where the aeroplane complied with the intent of the requirement but failed to show literal compliance. In view of other compensating features the requirement for the Mach trimmer was not imposed.   There is high speed warning and tremendously impressive qualities above 0.92 TMN.   At around 0.94 TMN the aeroplane has an inherent nose up pitch of just about the right amount to provide a good recovery from an overspeed condition and at 0.97 there is all the stability and controllability necessary for total control of the aeroplane.   Large amounts of 'g' can be pulled without difficulty and the roll rates are perfectly adequate.   The speed brakes are of course always effective. Without qualification this is the best high Mach number aeroplane I have ever flown and there was no doubt in my mind that the Mach trim system was not needed.   Having however made this sophisticated interpretation of the requirements there is an obligation on the ARB to adjust the written requirement to accommodate it and this will be done in due course.

(b) *Longitudinal stability before the flaps up stall,* again at aft C.G. only, is a bit thin; this is the point of disagreement in principle referred to earlier. With a trim speed of 1.3Vs, after a small elevator force to start the speed reduction, the stick force falls to zero while the aeroplane quietly progresses all the way to the stall on its own.   With the speed brakes extended the self stalling tendency stick free is more marked.   It is common know-ledge that the U.K. attitude to stalling is quite firm and this degree of instability, although slight, was declared unacceptable.   The fix was the nudger.   This is a gentle stick force augmentor of about 16 lb. in the nose down sense which operates when the stick shaker starts to operate and remains effective until the stick shake cancels.   In a fairly rough and ready manner it restores the pre-stall longitudinal stability and satisfies the requirements at little cost and with no snags.   It is similar to the nudger fitted to 707-320B/C aircraft certificated in the U.K. which, while not taking out all the pre-stall pitch up at full flap at aft C.G., at least restores a positive stick force gradient down to a point very close to the stall.

These explanations of the U.K. authority's support for the absence of a Mach trim system and the presence of a stick nudger having been made they should not be written off as merely 'certification history': the backgrounds in both cases are, of course, of continuing interest to pilots who fly the aeroplane.

Controllability   Once more, an area in which the 747 excels.   Faced with the problems of high inertia, particularly in roll and pitch, the designers provided large primary surfaces such as fin and stabiliser and then backed them up with large and powerful controls in yaw, roll and pitch.   Having provided the fundamentals they then made the controls light and precise, with a fast response rate, capable of resolution over very small angles and powerful enough to cope with abuse cases.   Combined with good stability, this results in an aeroplane which is easy to fly, light to handle, responsive and capable of being flown to a very high level of accuracy without effort.

262

Directional control is good. In normal operation a turn co-ordinator system applies rudder proportional to roll rate in a 'turn co-ordinating' sense, i.e. in the conventional fashion to assist the turn, thereby suppressing the adverse aileron yaw effect and smoothing the roll control response generally. This system is operative at flaps 1° and more when the yaw dampers are on high gain also. With the flaps up at the higher airspeeds this system is inoperative and the dampers revert to low gain.

For a type with wing-mounted engines directional control is particularly good in the engine(s) out cases. With zero trim the maximum foot force at full rudder is only about 70 lb. The engine(s) out critical speeds are all low and easily demonstrated with this very comfortable rudder force. This will be welcome news for those pilots coming to the 747 from the 707, where engine out work in the circuit involves very heavy rudder forces which are tiring after a minute or two. A comparison of approximate values (all for ISA, SL with 7 knots cross wind allowance in the V_{MCG} figures) is as follows:—

Condition	707-336C	747-136
1 engine out V_{MCG}	117 knots	118 knots
2 engines out V_{MCG}	Not established	143 knots
1 engine out V_{MCA}	117 knots boost on	102 knots
	156 knots boost off	—
2 engines out V_{MCA}	149 knots boost on	137 knots

These speeds do not tell the whole story: the 707 foot forces are high and tiring, while the 747 foot forces are low and comfortable.

There is one directional control feature on the 747 worth special mention. This is the rudder ratio changer system which reduces maximum rudder angle obtainable as a function of increasing airspeed. Other aeroplanes have similar protection as step changes, with flap retraction for example, but this one is smooth and progressive. In figure 9.5 the red curves show how full pedal rudder angle varies from its full value 24° (constant up to 132 knots) to 1.5° at 340 knots and also the range of full rudder trim available, the latter being equal to about two-thirds of the full rudder angle available at any given airspeed. The rudder bar travel however is not restricted. While this could be said to support the philosophy of constant response the system would have been more compatible with expected human behaviour had the rudder bar travel been related to achieved rudder angle. It is rather an odd feeling to be flying along at V_{MO} with one or two engines out, the others at a high power, with a lot of rudder bar travel applied.

Similarly, the indicated rudder trim range is not restricted: full trim is always 10 units. In spite of this reduction of rudder angle with speed there is never a lack of rudder for control. There is always enough for any normal

263

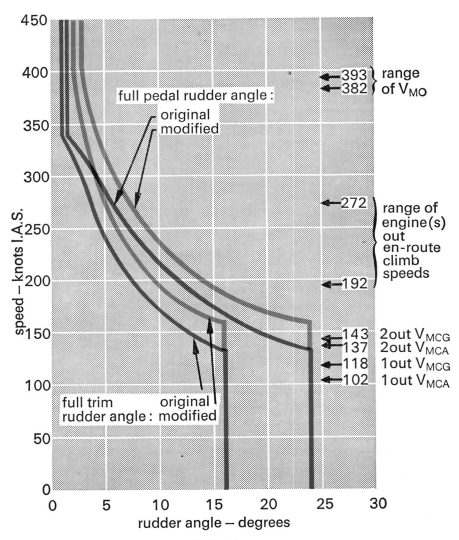

Figure 9.5   Rudder ratio changer speed schedule.

flight condition at any speed. Returning now to figure 9.5 let us consider the
blue curves. These represent an improvement to the rudder ratio changer
speed schedule which gives more rudder, and trim, throughout the speed
range. The modification is primarily intended for the later –7 engines, **when**

264

it will be necessary, but is also a desirable improvement for the –3A engined aircraft. The extra rudder travel will ease the tightness in what is presently the only limiting area (the two engines out V_{MCG} for a three engine ferry condition) and remove the tightness of ability to trim, two engines out en route, which will be discussed later in the chapter.

The constructors use the term 'tameness' in describing the 747's good directional qualities and support this claim by showing how easily the aeroplane will cope with an engine failure after take-off on roll control alone, without using rudder. It is true, the aeroplane will do it, and it is a remarkably good feature — one of the design parameters apparently. But this should not be used by training organisations as one way of coping with such a situation. It is wrong in principle to allow a swept wing aeroplane to suffer significant angles of sideslip. So, always use the rudder in the conventional sense to keep sideslip to small values.

Lateral control The mix of two sets of ailerons and several spoiler panels provides all the roll power necessary throughout the flight envelope and in the single and double failure cases. Maximum wheel force at full throw is only 13 lb. This perhaps above all others is the reason for the ease of controllability on this enormous aeroplane. To obtain this light force, power boost to the control runs was necessary to suppress the effect of control circuit friction. These are the items labelled CCA in figure 9.4. The pilot merely signals these and they do all the work to the aileron and spoiler power units. The roll rates are good throughout, particularly in the engine(s) out configurations and all the way out to V_{DF} and M_{DF} of 445 knots EAS and 0.97 TMN. It is at M_{DF}, around 0.95 to 0.93 TMN that some current aeroplanes are rather poor in terms of roll rate, needing enormously high forces to produce very low rates. The 747 is not critical to the second decimal point in terms of Mach number. The author has flown it to 0.98, the company to 0.99, and it is understood that it still handles remarkably well.

To illustrate the roll rate ability consider the following results for the approach configurations. All cases are the time taken fully to reverse a 30° bank turn (i.e. to roll through 60° including the time for acceleration into the roll) using full lateral control alone, no rudder.

	Roll time
(a) *All engines*	
All hydraulic systems operative	4.8 seconds
Gear down full flap	
$V_{AT_0} = 134$ knots	
(b) *Two engines inoperative*	
All hydraulic systems operative	4.3 seconds
Gear down 25° flap	
$V_{AT_2} = 143$ knots	

(c) *All engines*

Nos. 2 and 3 hydraulic systems inoperative   8.3 seconds

Gear down full flap

V_{AT_0} +20 knots = 154 knots

The last case is particularly impressive for a double hydraulic system failure condition.   On some aeroplanes which revert to manual in this condition one is lucky if one has much roll control at all.   All the above times are well inside the requirements: in case (a) for example the requirement time is 7 seconds maximum.   Cases (b) and (c), being remote double failure cases, do not have specific values tied to them, but if they did they would lie somewhere in the range 11 to 14 seconds.

Longitudinal control is as good as directional and lateral control.   For normal flying the elevator is light, effective and with a very low break-out force, all of which not only allow but actively encourage extremely precise control of the aeroplane in pitch.   This is helped by the first class presentation of pitch attitude on the artificial horizons.   The feel system is an elaboration of the sophisticated ones we rather expect these days (as on the 737).   It takes in knowledge of airspeed and stabiliser angle to trim and produces a characteristic which tends to suppress, for example, C.G. effect.   The result is a pretty constant, or at least not widely divergent, stick force per 'g' flavour to the aeroplane.

The normal trim changes on the aeroplane, gear, flaps, speed brakes, power, etc., are all low and comfortably held with one hand.   The abuse cases are equally comforting.   The mistrimmed take-offs for example, going right to the 'wrong' end of the green band for each extreme C.G. position, result in maximum stick forces of only 40 lb. pull and 20 lb. push.   Such is the value of powered elevators with a good feel system.

A badly mistrimmed stabiliser is easily handled.   Because of the characteristics of the feel system the elevator handles aircraft nose up mistrim at lower stick forces than aircraft nose down mistrim.   In the nose up sense a large stabiliser mistrim can be held for a maximum stick force of only about 40 lb. push.   In the nose down sense the stick force can peak as high as about 95 lb. pull.   There is also a stabiliser trim brake system, which has an electrical interconnect and is completely silent in operation.   There is none of the clanking that occurs on the 707 with the control column actuated stabiliser trim brake system.   When the 747 stabiliser trim brake operates, because it is silent, one can momentarily confuse it with a stalled drive condition.   One reason for the rather high pull force before the brake operates in the aircraft mistrimmed nose down sense is that the system was planned to be compatible with a Mach trim system; the latter was however deleted from the design before certification.   Recovery from high Mach upsets with the stabiliser mistrimmed to the forward electrical limit can be made with

266

reasonable stick forces and the ability to pull plenty of 'g' increment for a good recovery with a very low buffet level.

One word about recovery from a high Mach run with the aeroplane initially in trim. The nose up pitch around 0.94 TMN is very good; it is equivalent to about 20 lb. pull force on the control column. The speed brakes on their own also produce just about the 'right' amount of nose up pitch for a good recovery. If therefore the brakes are pulled in the presence of the nose up pitch above 0.94 Mach the aeroplane will provide all the recovery necessary. There will certainly be no need for any up elevator; in fact there might be a need for a little down elevator to restrain the recovery to about the $\frac{1}{2}$ g increment level.

The stabiliser is easy to operate, with a nice choice of rates (varying as a function of airspeed) and with complete ability to meet any flight demand. The stabiliser trim rate schedule is 0.5°/sec. up to 185 knots, then decreasing linearly to 0.3°/sec. at 255 knots and above. The stabiliser drive system is very capable. It will not stall against any stick force likely to be applied. The probability of a high stick force itself is low because of the high level of control available on elevator alone with moderate stick forces. It should be noted that the stabiliser trim brake is active only when the pickle switches are being used: control of the stabiliser by means of the double levers on the throttle pedestal by-passes the trim brake system.

Ability to trim With only one exception this again is good throughout. Longitudinally, the stabiliser has the range to trim out all flight conditions throughout the flight envelope at all combinations of weight and C.G. This is creditable for an American aeroplane certificated against U.K. requirements: FARs and BCARs being different in this respect there is usually some difficulty involved. Two small points worth noting on stabiliser trim: (a) occasionally, when the trim switch is given only a short blip, the stabiliser wheel does not move; this does not mean that the stabiliser itself has not moved, so don't confirm trim action by movement of the wheel but rather by the variation in stick force; (b) as the aeroplane ages the noise made by the trim wheel tends to diminish; this noise is useful as a confirmatory signal and the maintenance people should be required to keep the noise at its proper level.

Laterally, again the trim system is fully capable. In common with most jet aeroplanes however it is very rarely needed, even in the engine out cases. It should be noted that there is no direct trim actuator position indicator and that the wheel has to be trimmed to zero on its scale with no hand force on it.

Directionally, for all normal and abnormal flight conditions the rudder trim system is adequate, but only just adequate for the more limiting cases. Due to the shape of the original rudder ratio changer curve (see figure 9.5) there is presently only just enough trim to cope with the more demanding conditions of two engines out en-route climb for example; and a slightly irritating feature is that, unlike most other aeroplanes, the position does not improve as the airspeed is increased. Rudder angle available by trim falls steadily with increasing airspeed and the aeroplane is just as tight at V_{MO} as it is at the climb speed. However, it does cope. With two engines out en route advantage has to be taken of 2° to 3° of bank angle by using aileron trim. The tightest case, although its probability of occurrence is clearly extremely remote, is the failure of two engines on the same side as the fifth pod when installed for ferrying. In this event the required bank angle gets up to around 4°. With the improved rudder ratio changer speed schedule proposed for the −7 engined aircraft these criticisms of tightness of ability to trim directionally should be removed completely.

Stalling Basically, compliance with the stall requirements simply demands only adequate warning, clear identification and acceptable qualities at the stall. While the 747 has all these in good measure, one particular feature, in one particular configuration, proved to be very much an 'equivalent level of safety' exercise. This was the flaps up stall characteristic, which is unique and will be explained shortly.

It is easiest to describe stall qualities according to flap angles, which are as follows:—

Flaps up = Trailing edge flaps up with leading edge flaps up
Flaps 1° = Trailing edge flaps at 1° with half leading edge flaps down
Flaps 5° = Trailing edge flaps at 5° with all leading edge flaps down
Flaps 10° = Trailing edge flaps at 10° with all leading edge flaps down
Flaps 20° = Trailing edge flaps at 20° with all leading edge flaps down
Flaps 25° = Trailing edge flaps at 25° with all leading edge flaps down
Flaps 30° = Trailing edge flaps at 30° with all leading edge flaps down

The gear incidentally has no effect on stall qualities.

We will first consider the flaps down stall behaviour, which is exceptionally good.

With the flaps in the range 5° to 30° the aeroplane has immaculate stall qualities. Longitudinal stability and lateral control are good. Warning is by natural buffet with a good margin and by the conventional stick shaker system. At the stall there is a clean, straight nose drop. Recovery is straightforward and the aeroplane remains laterally level throughout.

With flaps up however the aeroplane's behaviour is quite different. Natural buffet starts very early and builds to a high value with decreasing airspeed. Stability is maintained by the stick nudger at and after stick shake. There is no nose drop and no change in pitch attitude. The aeroplane does not pitch nose up or nose down as incidence increases with reducing airspeed. The buffeting simply increases until at Max. C_L the violent vertical bounce experienced on the flight deck reaches a very high level, sometimes with a lateral component. This identifies 'the stall' and at this point the pilot must initiate recovery by applying down elevator. The recovery is straight-forward although the buffeting takes a little time to clean up. Throughout this pounding the aeroplane remains absolutely level laterally. This lack of a nose down pitch is unusual but the stall identification is so unmistakable, the qualities so good and the recovery so straightforward that there was no hesitation on our part in accepting the flaps up stall qualities. Hence the 'equivalent level of safety'. Like high Mach number stability, this variation of requirement interpretation will also necessitate some adjustment of the written requirement.

The flaps 1° stall characteristics are a mix of the flaps up and flaps 5°-and-beyond qualities. Flaps 1° is where only those leading edge sections inboard of each engine pylon are extended. The natural buffet which is generated by that part of the wing leading edge where the leading edge flaps are retracted is again early and builds to a very high value. Just as the buffet becomes quite violent (and instinctively one is expecting the lateral or increased vertical motion at any moment) the aeroplane stalls with a straight nose drop.

The criticisms of rather early buffet flaps up (generally similar to VC10 Type 1101) and early buffet and stick shake at flaps 1°, around 1.3Vs, are avoided by the imposed operating procedures which keep the aeroplane well away from these incidences. As a guide the following stall speeds are quoted from the Flight Manual:—

Weight	En-route configuration	Landing configuration
Maximum take-off 710,000 lb., 322,000 kg.	193 knots	—
Maximum landing 564,000 lb., 256,000 kg.	168 knots	110 knots
Very light 400,000 lb., 181,500 kg.	138 knots	92 knots

Take-off and landing

Normal all engines and one engine out cases

Normal all engines and one engine out take-offs and landings are easy to fly accurately. Controllability is good and control forces light. The view is good.

All engines take-offs are straightforward. The stick force to rotate is light: hence *an ugly snatch could cause a tail strike;* be particularly careful if you are flying with the attitude warning system as an allowable deficiency. Rotation is through quite a large angle to about 9° for lift off. The pilot should remember that he will be a long way off before the main gears leave the ground. Climb out is comfortable at V_2+10 knots. It is important to follow the flap retraction sequence accurately because of the large changes in stall speed, the early shake and buffet at flaps 1° and early buffet flaps up. The Boeing recommendation is $V_2 \ldots +20, +40, +60$ and $+80$ knots for selection of flaps 10°, 5°, 1° and up respectively, although some operators have alternative techniques.

An engine out take-off is equally straightforward. Controllability is very good right down to V_{MCG}, rudder forces are light at full throw and there is no problem in flying a V_2 climb out.

General handling in the circuit is easy and precise. However, due to the chosen angle of the wing rigging in relation to the fuselage, one feature which is surprising initially is the nose high attitude for level flight on the downwind leg with the gear down and some flap on. The aeroplane is around 6° nose up and one must get used to this amount of 'blue' on the horizon. This is one area where the rather dominant glareshield takes a bit of getting used to: there is an instinctive urge to push the control column forward so as to get the glareshield out of the way.

In an all engines approach the required approach path can be held exactly and, in calm conditions, to a knot of airspeed. Due to the size of the aeroplane and its high pilot eye level there are initially two potential difficulties: the first is that it is easy to get too low close in and the second is that judgement of flare height and of height above the runway generally is not easy. The first point is very important, the second much less important.

Let us consider the problem in four parts:—

(a) threshold clearance
(b) visual aiming points
(c) ILS approach
(d) the flare and landing.

(a) **Threshold clearance** Figure 9.6 illustrates the reduced threshold clearance on a 747 compared with a 707. In the 747 there is a lot of aeroplane beneath you and a long way behind you: you must allow for this and give plenty of clearance over the last part of the approach and threshold. The diagram however needs some explanation. It is intended only to show the difference in threshold wheel clearance between a 707 and a 747 for one given set of parameters. The basis of the drawing is that the visual aiming point is 1,000 ft. from the threshold, the approach slope is 2.5° and the aeroplane is not flared for the landing. This is perhaps rather academic, but the fundamental difference is important. Whereas the 707 wheel clearance is about 25 ft. the 747 wheel clearance is only $2\frac{1}{2}$ ft. *That's right, 2.5 feet!* At the threshold the eye height is 44 ft. and the touchdown point only 60 ft. from the threshold. In practice the screen height assumed for performance purposes (in the U.K.) is 30 ft. and aeroplanes are of course flared for landing to a flight path asymtotic to the runway which would increase the clearance slightly.

The choice of an aiming point 1,000 ft. from the threshold is not all that academic: it is attractive by tradition and habit and, although 25 ft. is 5 ft. short of 30 ft., an approach flown like this could be considered a well disciplined approach to a shortish runway in a middling size aeroplane. But, clearly, it won't do for the 747. By the simple process of drawing similar triangles it can be deduced that an aiming point of 2,000 ft. from the threshold will give an eye height of 88 ft., a wheel clearance of 46 ft. and a touch down point of just over 1,000 ft. from the threshold. This is much more like it. However, we cannot abandon the performance implication of the screen height of 30 ft., so as a result the aiming point becomes around 1,625 ft. from the threshold. All we have to do now is locate that point.

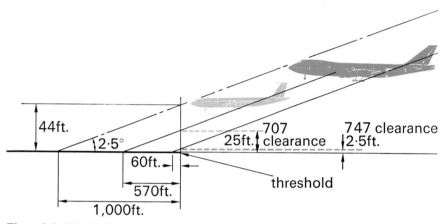

Figure 9.6   Threshold clearances.

(b) **Visual aiming points**   Figure 9.7 illustrates for both day and night the runway markings and lighting for what is known in the U.K. as a precision instrument approach runway.   The VASIs are shown in both cases and the 3rd (distant) light unit proposed for big and long-bodied aeroplanes is included.   The day illustration shows touchdown zone markings at 500 ft. intervals from the centre of the threshold longitudinal bars with an elaborate one at 1,000 ft. from the threshold.   The night illustration shows white barrettes at 200 ft. intervals from the green threshold expanded bar.   The VASIs are shown with the first unit at 500 ft. then the next two at 700 ft. intervals.   We now have all we need to pick a point around 1,600 ft. from the threshold, like this:—
    Without VASIs by day — use point 'D' just beyond the 3rd touchdown zone mark (1,600 ft.)

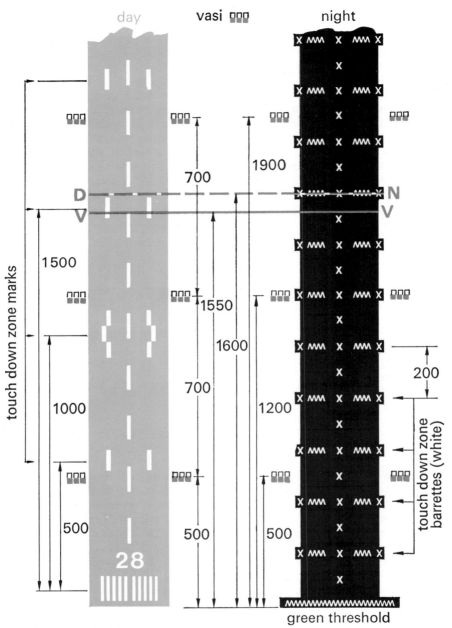

all distances in feet
Figure 9.7 Visual aiming points.
272

Without VASIs by night — use point 'N', the eighth row of white barrettes (1,600 ft.)

On VASIs day and night — use point 'V', the further two light units (1,550 ft.)

In fact, in the case of the 'night — no VASIs' aiming point it is just a little academic to say 'shoot for the eighth row of white barrettes': this is not so easy to do in real life against a veritable fairground of illumination. An alternative is to use the radio height 100/50/30 feet calls and ensure that at 50 ft., called or uncalled, the threshold is just disappearing from view under the nose — otherwise you are too low. On a properly flown 2.5° approach slope these aiming points should give adequate minimum threshold clearances. It should not be forgotten however that threshold clearance is a function of approach slope. If a 2° path is flown clearances will be less; if a 3° path, they will be more. If you are denied VASIs you must discipline yourself to an intended say 2.5° approach slope. Use the 'times 3' formula for height against distance out and stick to approximately 700 ft./min. rate of descent, adjusted for longitudinal wind component. If you are denied all runway markings you must still calculate a 1,600 ft. aiming point, even if it is only by some simple proportioning of known runway distance available, for example. If in doubt, stay high. The aeroplane stops well on the ground if it has to.

(c) **ILS approach** The ILS glideslope beam is so arranged that, regardless of angle, it crosses the threshold of the runway at a height of 50 ft. nominal. Fundamentally, the difference between a visual approach and an ILS approach is that the tracking point changes from the pilot's eye position to the glideslope aerial position. On the 747 the aerial is on the nose gear doors which are considerably lower than the pilot's eye, hence in theory the aeroplane will be higher at the threshold by this difference in height which is of the order of 22 ft. Therefore if an ILS glideslope were to be flown accurately right down to the ground the aeroplane would cross the threshold with the pilot's eye at 72 ft., the glideslope aerial at 50 ft. and with a wheel clearance of 36 ft. all of which is acceptable in terms of wheel clearance and performance distances. These numbers are theoretical minima because, on a flight director approach, the glideslope is abandoned, certainly by 100 ft. minimum, and the pilot then enters the pre-flare thinking phase. He starts the flare, it is suggested, at a wheel radio height of 50 ft., so that the actual threshold wheel clearances are greater. To complete the picture, on an autoland the glideslope is abandoned by the automatics in the region of 50 ft., the computed flare programme is flown and again threshold wheel clearances are satisfactory. What is comforting to know is that an accurate ILS approach, whether manual, flight director or automatic, will result in adequate wheel clearances at the threshold.

(d) The flare and landing Having disposed of the approach clearance problems we now have the final task of landing the aeroplane. It has been stated that knowledge of exact height is not necessary and this is true; in the early part of the flare, within say 5 feet is good enough. But radio height is an enormous help during one's early landings. A good average landing can be flown as simply as this: at 50 ft. radio height and at V_{AT} make one small flare movement on the elevator; at 30 ft. slowly close the throttles and merely *resist* any nose down pitch change with the elevator, thereafter maintaining a substantially constant attitude; by about 10 ft. the power should all be off, ground effect is quite marked and reduces the rate of descent; a few seconds later there is a comforting rumble as the main gears run on to the ground. That is really all there is to it. Because one is so far away from the ground and the gear it is unreasonable to pretend that the aeroplane can be landed with any real precision, measured in small values of feet of height or distance, knots of airspeed or seconds of time. One simply sets up a projected flight path and waits for the aeroplane to achieve it. The constructors claim that if there is no flare (and a late flare is always one's first error) the gear will take a straight fly-on to the runway without any problems. They are right — I proved this on my first landing. Once the aeroplane is down the rest is conventional. The spoilers having extended automatically, you simply lower the nose, pull reverse and stand by for some gentle braking. There is however one trap at the end. Due to the high pilot eye-level again, one is not very conscious of ground speed and it is very easy to taxy too fast or attempt a fast turn off much too fast. Keep your eye on the INS ground speed: get down to about 25 knots for a convenient fast turn off and down to about 12 knots for sharp turns on taxy ways. The aeroplane has a wide track and you are not likely to tip it up but there is no point in putting an unnecessary burden on the main legs. Ground manoeuvrability is generally very good, again particularly so for such a big aeroplane. This is due in large measure to the body gear steering system. Note that when the body gears unlock and start to assist turns they track the *opposite* way to applied nose wheel steering angle. This point needs to be remembered when taxying on very slippery surfaces. If too much nose wheel steering is applied, causing the nose wheel to skid, the aeroplane will then track bodily sideways in the 'wrong' direction, away from the required turn. So, taxy very slowly and do not let the nosewheel skid.

In the early days of operation of the 747 a lot of emphasis was put on its ability to land in a significant cross wind with a fair amount of drift on without distress. It is quite unnecessary however to make use of this ability. The aeroplane handles well in the flare and as one waits for it to sink majestically on to the ground some of the drift can be taken off by a gentle push on the rudder. So why not do it?

Next, reverse thrust.   It is common knowledge that there is a little way to go yet on this part of the aeroplane.   The drills change with the modification state of the engines but the net result is that reverse thrust is not quite as effective yet as it is on many other aeroplanes.   If too high a power is held to too low an airspeed the engines get upset and are likely to overtemperature.   They can do this quite silently and your line of defence is someone's eagle eyes on the EGT gauges.   When they start rising they can't be stopped just by bringing the engines to idle — it is necessary to cut the fuel.   The present drill without the reverse actuated bleed system (RABS) is: no more than 75% N_1 down to 90 knots, then modulate to idle by 50 knots; don't exceed 50% N_1 below 60 knots. With RABS the drill is full reverse down to 90 knots then a reduction to idle; don't exceed 50% N_1 below 50 knots.

An engine out landing is as straightforward as the engine out take-off, with good, light, precise controllability.   There are no problems whatever.

One point worth noting here on the subject of flap operating times. Most selections are achieved quite quickly but the movement from 1° to 5° (and back) is an exception — it takes from 32 to 34 seconds.   Hence care should be taken to stay within the required speed range until the required flap position is fully established.

Abnormal and double failure cases

Abnormal and double failure cases cover a variety of conditions. They are all, without question, very easy to fly and the drama that some pilots associate with, for example, two engines out work has all gone.   Let us just go through a selection of them.

(a) **Unintentionally low threshold speed**   This does not present any problems, down to at least V_{AT} –5 knots.   There is plenty of elevator for the flare and plenty of lift left in the wing.

(b) **Unavoidable high touchdown speed**   There is no problem up to at least V_{AT}+15 knots.   The aeroplane doesn't bounce and stays down with no difficulties.

(c) **Two engines out landings and go-arounds**   These need to be handled together because they are absolutely related.   (In this chapter only the essentials of two engines out work in terms of the 747 are considered. A discussion of asymmetric flight training, including a defence of the author's philosophy regarding the continuation of this training, can be found in Chapter 10.)

The 747 is particularly good with two engines out and it is disappointing to see the now usual U.S. conservative approach being read across once more and reflecting unfairly on the aeroplane. A two-out approach and landing, and a go-around within certain weight limits according to flap setting, are both perfectly straightforward and easily flown with complete control at all times. The aeroplane is a lot more capable than the company and Flight Manual write-ups suggest. The minimum recommended asymmetric control speed for go-around EPR on the remaining engines, which is $V_{MCL}+5$ knots, is comfortingly low at 142 knots for ISA SL conditions. This speed does not become dominant until the weight comes below 460,000 lb., 209,000 kg., for a 10° flap approach and 500,000 lb., 227,000 kg., for a 20° flap approach. There is also a close relationship with the target threshold speed for the landing at 25° flap. There are therefore no problems concerning a high speed on the approach, nor is there a need to lose a lot of speed by the threshold. The performance of the aeroplane gear down on two engines at go-around EPR is perfectly reasonable as the following figures show:—

Flap position	Maximum weight for:	
	Level flight	200 ft./min. gross rate of climb
10°	520,000 lb., 236,000 kg.	480,000 lb., 218,000 kg.
20°	500,000 lb., 227,000 kg.	460,000 lb., 209,000 kg.

These weights are conservative by about 20,000 lb., say 9,000 kg. By proper control of weight, two engines out circuits can be flown during training day or night, with the ability to make a go-around comfortably from 300 ft. Even if the aeroplane is placed deliberately in a performance limiting condition, unable to achieve level flight at go-around EPR, the change to a higher performance configuration should be achieved in a height loss not exceeding say 200 ft. This assumes go-around EPR on the operating engines, flap retraction 20° to 10° in 5 seconds, gear retraction in 24 seconds and 7 knots acceleration from an initial 500 ft./min. rate of descent condition. For training therefore there is no problem: the aeroplane is easily flown on the approach and just as easily landed or taken around. For the landing the threshold speed should be quite close to the target value for 25° flaps. The stopping ability on the ground is good; two in reverse on one side on a dry runway are quite controllable. Distance therefore is not a problem either. For the go-around controllability is very good with light rudder forces at full travel. It is simply a matter of applying the EPR and cleaning up the aeroplane progressively. Operationally, with the ability to dump fuel to a reasonably light landing weight exactly the same level of protection and performance can be enjoyed.

The 747, given knowledge of its performance ability on two engines, is capable and easy to fly in this asymmetric condition. Reference to figure 10.1, in which all the parameters discussed in this sub-chapter are plotted, should make their relationships quite clear and indicate the weights at which the aeroplane has level flight performance ability on two engines for ISA SL conditions.

(d) **Part flap failure landings** There are many permutations of failures of these. For any single failure, for example outboard trailing edge flaps only, one simply flies a Vref +20 knots approach and makes an otherwise normal approach and landing. The double failure cases, which are remote anyway, are no more demanding but in such cases the increment of +20 knots is added twice and the approach flown at Vref +40 knots. The one chosen for the U.K. certification test was Group 2 leading edge flaps retracted and all inboard trailing edge flaps retracted. The approach and landing were straightforward. The float was rather long and the speed thought to have a lot of conservatism in it. In this particular case it was necessary to have the stick shaker inoperative because its datum was at the flaps up datum with the inboard trailing edge flaps retracted; otherwise it would have shaken all the way in.

(e) **Hydraulic system failure landings** A single hydraulic system failure landing is no different from an all hydraulic systems operating landing. To see any difference one must, as with the high lift devices, go to the double failure cases. The case chosen by the author was the worst case for pitch control, which is Systems 1 and 2 inoperative leaving only the left inboard and right outboard elevators working; i.e. only half elevator power available. With Vref +20 knots the approach was good. There was no cheating on the use of power because it was all off at 30 feet, and the landing was good with plenty of elevator power available. This test was of course flown on full forward C.G.

(f) **Side window landing** Without a Direct Vision panel there was the need to demonstrate a landing with the forward screen blanked off and using the side window only. To the author's surprise this was easy and considerably more comfortable than using an open window. It is necessary to get well over to the left, jam one's face up against the windscreen post and leave the control of power and airspeed to either the co-pilot or autothrottle. The runway can be kept in view the whole time with the left eye while the right eye monitors pitch and bank attitude. A conscious effort has to be made not to apply right rudder when using it as a prop to keep over to the left. Very close in the runway centre-

277

line has to be abandoned as a sighting point and the left-hand edge used instead. Apart from a slight tendency to overflare with a bit of a float there is no difficulty in making this landing. The co-pilot calls radio height as usual. All of this might sound a bit academic but a severe hail encounter could make it necessary if, for example, an automatic landing could not be made on that flight. The worst hail damage to date has left the main screens usable but badly pitted. The next one could however granulate the whole area.

In the event of the main screens becoming totally opaque it is likely that the very thin, hard, outer layer of glass will splinter progressively and break away from the screen, improving vision enormously. If by the time of the approach, not enough has gone to provide sufficient vision, the wipers should be given one cycle and this may remove a lot more. Don't overdo it however; the exposed layer is comparatively soft and somewhat sticky and extended use of the wipers might make matters worse.

Well now — so much for take-offs and landings. There isn't one of them that need raise a bead of perspiration.

Miscellaneous flight items

There are a number of flight items which do not fall easily into either performance or handling categories but nevertheless are worthy of mention.

Buffet boundaries

The 747 wing is obviously a good one in terms of its lift generating ability and its control of flow at high Mach numbers. The buffet onset boundaries are conservatively drawn and it is possible to pull beyond them before buffet becomes noticeable to the flight crew. The manoeuvre 'g's to reach the maximum demonstrated buffet boundaries are almost always at and frequently above the minimum values demanded by the airworthiness requirements for manoeuvre capability. At high speed and high Mach numbers more than adequate increments of 'g' are available. For example consider the following figures:—

(a) 630,000 lb., 285,900 kg. 28,000 ft. 0.90 TMN 1.25g *increment* with no significant buffet.

(b) 626,000 lb., 284,000 kg. 24,000 ft. 0.97 TMN 0.6g increment with *no* buffet.

Both of these results are considerably in excess of the airworthiness minima. The limitation most easily reached is at V_{RA} at high weights at high altitudes; the exposure to this is unlikely and in any case would be very limited in time.

Half main gear retracted landings

In the event that one body gear leg cannot be extended the aeroplane is cleared to be landed on the remaining three legs. If however a wing gear leg cannot be extended then the other wing gear leg must be retracted and the aeroplane landed on the body gear (and nose) alone. This is because a landing with only one wing gear extended would cause the wing-body gear levelling system to tip the aeroplane away from the extended wing gear. In all such cases the weight should be reduced to a minimum and care taken to make a smooth touchdown. If the landing should be on the body gear only, where the track is narrow indeed, care must be taken to maintain lateral level and the aeroplane should be taxied off the runway at a very slow pace.

Special systems

The 747 has three systems which rate brief explanations. These are:—

(a) **Attitude warning** which is provided on take-off through a system coupled to the stick shaker. It is set to operate at 11° body angle at a very low rate of change of pitch, where the tail scrape angle is 13°. At high rates of rotation it is phase advanced to come in much earlier at around 6° body angle at a pitch rate of 7°/sec. It works well — and yet *the tail has been struck several times*. Once more, be aware of this problem if you accept an aeroplane with the attitude warning system unserviceable.

(b) **Throttle bar protection** which is provided because the JT9D is sensitive to rapid reversals of the thrust lever at high altitude. While it will accept a straight acceleration or deceleration it doesn't like a change of mind half way through. The engine tends to surge and overtemperature. To prevent this there is a throttle bar which is slid into place to limit the idle setting at altitude. The particular altitude limitation varies with modification standard and is between 29,000 ft. and 35,000 ft. depending on bleeds. While it is a pity that this bar has to be there at all, in normal operation it is no embarrassment except that an initial descent from a very high altitude is quite slow. In the event of a real need to descend quickly the throttle bar should be removed and the throttles fully closed. The wing gear may also be lowered for additional drag but the speed limit remains as for the main gear.

(c) **Flap load relief** which is provided by a system sensitive to airspeed. This is a structure weight saving device which limits the maximum speed at which full (30°) flap can be achieved and hence the stresses involved. Figure 9.8 illustrates its operation. It operates only between 25° and 30° flap.

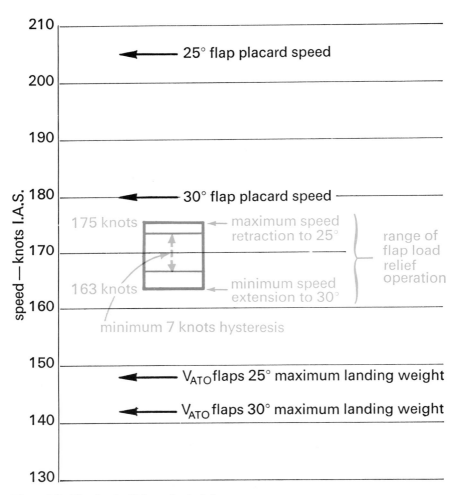

Figure 9.8　Flap load relief speed schedule.

While it is possible to select 30° flap at any speed say below 205 knots, the flaps will not run beyond 25° until the airspeed falls below 170 knots nominal. Equally, if 30° flap is on and the airspeed exceeds 170 knots nominal the flaps retract automatically, with no movement of the selector lever, to 25° and stay there until the airspeed again falls when they return to 30°. There is a minimum hysteresis band of 7 knots on any particular installation to prevent unwanted flap movement over small changes in airspeed. With the system on bottom tolerance the pilot can achieve full flap at V_{AT} 25° flap +15 knots at maximum landing weight so the system is never limiting although, fundamentally, it is not as accommodating as a traditional system. Whenever the flap load relief system operates an amber warning light is illuminated.

Flight deck workload

There is no part of the operation on this aeroplane where the workload is any higher than on previous types and in many areas it is significantly lower. The overall effect therefore is an appreciable reduction in workload. Whether one thinks of workload as physical effort, mental effort or the rate of doing things this broad statement is true. Of the six definitive areas of workload (Command, Lookout, Flight Path Control, Engineering, Navigation, Communication) there are of course no changes in Command, Lookout or Communication. However, of the other three Navigation is helped enormously by the INS, Engineering by the simplicity of control and operation of the systems panel and Flight Path Control in manual flight by the ease of handling and precision of the aeroplane and in automatic flight by the very high capability and wide range of facilities of the automatics. The INS and the Autopilot share the credit for the big lowering of flight deck workload, producing altogether a most relaxed atmosphere for the crew.

Special operating clearances

In the U.K. the 747 is cleared for the majority of Flight Manual Supplementary Operations.

Engine out ferrying Engine out ferrying is fully approved. For an aeroplane with four engines in wing pods, meeting the U.K. requirements in this respect is a pretty significant achievement. Controllability is required in the event of a further engine failing on take-off and this demands a two engines out V_{MCG}. The aeroplane copes comfortably and the take-off is as satisfactory as all the other engine out procedures. Full thrust can be achieved on the 'third engine' by 110 knots for an outboard inoperative case and by 90 knots for an inboard inoperative case. The V_2 speeds are higher to cater for the further engine failure and, in this event, the flap retraction schedule is altered to V_2, V_2 + 20 knots, and 1.25 V_{MS_1} for selecting flaps 5°, 1° and up respectively. For this ferry clearance the maximum permitted weight is reduced to around 562,000 lb., 255,000 kg., (just below maximum landing weight) and V_{MO} reduced to 320 knots and 0.85 Mach. The inoperative engine must be plugged and made secure for take-off. Note that if the No. 3 thrust lever is not in the take-off position the take-off configuration warning system will be inoperative. Also that if the gear warning horn cancel is operated before advancing the thrust levers for take-off the horn will not sound on gear retraction.   In the event that another engine should fail en route the handling qualities remain good and the landing is quite straightforward.

Fifth pod ferry   Fifth pod ferry is also fully approved.   The spare engine is installed between No. 2 and the fuselage.   The fan blades and spinner are removed but the fan stators remain and an ice deflector shield is fitted.   It looks a big lump and one imagines that it would have a significant effect on flying qualities: proportionately however it is about the same as any other fifth pod installation.   If you weren't told it was on the aeroplane you certainly wouldn't know by any change in flying qualities in normal operation, except that perhaps just a touch of lateral trim is necessary in the cruise when flying manually. V_{MC} speeds and stall characteristics are similarly unaffected. When the pod is installed an ASI overlay is fitted as a reminder of the reduced operating speeds. V_{MO} is reduced to 330 knots/0.85Mach and V_{RA} to 280 knots/0.80Mach.   This is to retain an adequate margin below the reduced M_{DF} value which is 0.92 Mach.   These reductions are usual on fifth pod installations due to the effect of the pod at very high Mach numbers. (The VC10 is exceptional in having no speed reductions with a fifth pod fitted.) The fifth pod installation on the 747 slightly highlights the tightness of directional ability to trim in the engine out and two engines out en-route configurations due to the scheduling of the original rudder ratio changer as already discussed. In the worst case with a fifth pod, that of Nos. 1 and 2 engines out, full rudder trim is necessary together with some lateral trim to produce up to 4° of bank before the aeroplane will fly controls free on a constant heading.   In this event try to keep the bank angle as low as possible otherwise the spoilers will be just cracked.   When the modified rudder ratio changer system is fitted this tightness of ability to trim should disappear.   For fifth pod ferry the maximum take-off and landing weights are reduced by about 22,000 lb., 10,000 kg., below their normal values.

Gear down operation   Gear down operation is approved.   There are no problems here other than the reduction in operating speeds due to the gear. V_{MO} becomes 270 knots and V_{RA} reduces to 240 knots.   Because the effective performance ceiling at a sensible take-off weight is around 18,000 ft. there is no need for an M_{MO} limit.   A maximum altitude of 30,000 ft. is imposed. While there is no weight limit imposed the ISA SL WAT curve imposes an effective maximum of around 584,500 lb., 265,000 kg.

Automatic flight

The Autopilot and Flight Director Systems impress with their range of abilities, ease of control (when thoroughly mastered) and accuracy of performance and display. The inertial navigation system is pure magic. When the author asked a certain airline pilot flying with him how far they were from the airport he took a delight in replying .... 'You are seventy-eight miles *from the hangar!*' The U.K. fit is three autopilots, three INS and a flight director system that is compatible with the autopilots and capable of displaying most of the same knowledge. The flight director chosen for U.K. operation is of the two needle type which fundamentally permits a very high accuracy and offers great flexibility in selection. Equally important, it offers facilities for rejection which one cannot enjoy with a one piece director. (Unfortunately the U.K. fit is configured in such a fashion that the unwanted axis, i.e. pitch, cannot be readily rejected: an azimuth steering needle alone can be most useful on so many occasions when one does not want the burden of keeping the pitch needle tied to an intelligent source.) All this is supported by good primary flight instruments, the horizon in particular encouraging very accurate control of attitude and hence of the flight path. The auto-pilot manual controller is mounted on the throttle box but all the other switching, including that for the flight director, is grouped in a panel on the centre glareshield. In the pitch mode the following are available: altitude hold and pre-select altitude, vertical speed, airspeed hold, glideslope and autoland; in the roll mode, heading select and tracking on VOR, ILS and INS. There is a turbulence mode on both axes where the gain is reduced and automatic pitch trim disconnected. Auto-throttles complete the picture. All this equipment works and is a major contribution to the reduction in flight deck workload. Good as it is, it is necessary to make the points, in fairness to other design teams, that the 747 automatics lack some finesse and that the two-axis auto-pilot as presently installed precludes the possibility of kick off drift and roll out control. In spite of these criticisms the 747 automatic flight system remains a good piece of engineering design to which probably less than justice has been done here. But a full treatment of its philosophy and particular application in the 747 would need a chapter of its own.

Main engine relighting

The initial flight start envelope was optimistic. While a light up could be achieved at the low speed boundaries, N_1 failed to increase; there clearly was not enough ram energy to spin up the fan. In this condition the engine would slowly overtemperature. The boundaries were revised after the clearance of the –3A yoked engines and the flight start envelope is now as shown in figure 9.9.

Emergency descent procedure

The constructor's recommendation is to reduce speed, if above 270 knots, to the gear operating limit, then extend the gear and descend at the speeds of 0.82 Mach and then 320 knots. The disadvantage of the procedure is that, while it achieves a high descent rate eventually, it imposes a comparatively long period of exposure at high altitude with the possibility of a rapidly rising cabin altitude (depending on the particular failure, of course). The author is convinced that if something serious occurs at very high altitude then the important thing is to get rid of the high altitude as quickly and as

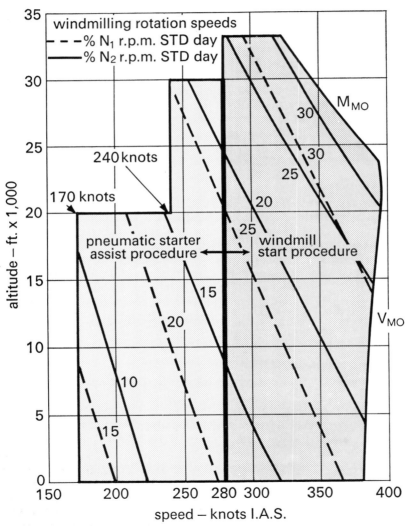

Figure 9.9 Flight start envelope for JT9D-3a.

early as possible. This is best done by an immediate power off, brakes out condition and a descent at M$_{MO}$ then V$_{MO}$ at lower altitudes. Figure 9.10 illustrates the alternative emergency descent profiles and shows the difference in exposure to possibly very high cabin altitudes. Note that the immediate descent technique without the gear brings the aeroplane 8,000 ft. lower after one minute than the 'wait-for-the-gear' technique.

A cruising level of 30,000 ft. is about the most critical height in terms of which technique to employ. At very high altitudes it is likely that the cruise speed will be close to 270 knots/0.82 Mach in which case the gear can be used

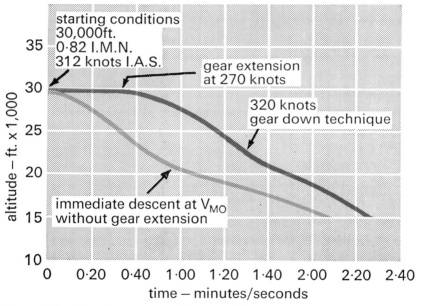

Figure 9.10   Alternative emergency descent profiles.

immediately. But at around 30,000 ft. there could be a long wait for a reduction to 270 knots even with speed brakes. A simple way to avoid height as a discriminant in the drills is to use speed only. If the speed at the time of need for a rapid descent is say 280 knots or below, reduce to 270 knots, drop the gear and descend using a maximum airspeed of 320 knots. If the cruise speed exceeds 280 knots don't use the gear but shoot for a target airspeed of M$_{MO}$ or V$_{MO}$. To those who, rightly, raise the point of possible structural damage the answer is that this becomes an ad hoc command decision at that time.

This is what command is all about: the captain has to take in as much knowledge as possible as quickly as possible, make an intelligent decision, then act on it. If significant structural damage is believed to be a risk then a compromise has to be struck between the highest likely safe speed compatible with the best achievable rate of cabin altitude control. This last point of course applies equally to all other high altitude jet transport aircraft.

Flight deck roof escape hatch

This is primarily for use on the ground. If ever the need should arise to open it in flight for, say, severe smoke evacuation, 200 knots is the speed limit and at that speed it needs a 200 lb. crew member pulling on it. Maximum speed with it open is 250 knots because of excessive roar.

Crew training

Because the 747 is such a well-engineered aeroplane, with a lot of systems redundancy up to the double failure level and with extremely good flying qualities, the pilot type rating final test form should be a very simple one, with a number of the traditional jet aircraft checks deleted. The aeroplane has no dutch roll, no high Mach number instability, good stall qualities and no particular reasons to be taken above V_{MO} or M_{MO}. All systems failures, including the likely double failures, leave a very high level of flying qualities and there seems little need to plough through a variety of failure landing cases.

Weight has a big effect on recommendations in terms of asymmetric training. Fundamentally the aircraft handles very well on two engines and this training (with the inoperative engines at *idle* of course) should be encouraged. On the other hand at very high weights with one engine shut right down (fuel off) the real failure of a further engine would leave the aircraft badly placed unless there were sufficient height for a relight. These conflicts are best handled by discriminating in terms of weight, height and shut down states. The following set of rules should always be observed:—

1 The fuel should never be taken off an engine merely to simulate a failure in terms of flying qualities. The thrust at idle is not very great and is a close enough approximation.

2 The fuel should only be taken off one engine at a time for completeness in demonstrating shut down and relight drills.

3 A weight of 500,000 lb., 227,000 kg., is a good round number in terms of performance. Below this weight the aircraft will, in standard conditions, maintain level flight in the circuit with gear down and 20° flap at

the appropriate approach speed. For drills purposes therefore this weight should be observed with a height restriction of say 1,000 ft. above terrain.

4 A height of 4,000 ft. is currently proposed in the U.K. for complete shut down for drills purposes where adequate performance in the event of a further failure relies on the relighting of the inoperative engine. For shut down drills therefore at weights exceeding 500,000 lb., 227,000 kg., the height of 4,000 ft. above terrain should be observed.

Having listed the weight and height restrictions it is worth repeating that the 747 flies very well on two engines — on the approach, go-around and landing — and that this training should be done. The idling engines are there to enable a training captain to salvage a mess if it should be necessary. All that is needed is a little anticipation in terms of engine acceleration times. Two engines out training produces confidence in the aeroplane and also gives confidence and ability to the pilot and the 747 is just the aeroplane to do it on.

There are two final points worth mentioning on crew training. One is a very practical point, the other rather academic. Firstly, the only really unusual feature of 747 flying is the pilot's eye height on approach and landing. Care must be taken to allow plenty of clearance on the approach to the threshold and practice is needed for pilots to become familiar with the initial flare height and judgement of height above the ground generally. Sufficient landings should be allowed (finally including some approaches with no approach guidance at all, no VASIs and no radio height) so that the pilot is confident of making a good landing under all conditions. Secondly, it has been stated that there is no particular reason for going out beyond M_{MO}. This is because the only point of interest here is the nose up pitch at around 0.94 TMN. As this is a good feature it would be sufficient merely to acquaint the pilots with this piece of information. (This is quite different from a *bad* handling feature beyond M_{MO} where training in coping with it could perhaps be said to be necessary.) However, if anyone should want to see this feature, in order perhaps to decide on a training procedure, then he should be aware of the Machmeter errors beyond about 0.92 TMN. With the variations of position and instrument error, while the nose up pitch at 0.94 TMN is nominally 0.922 indicated, it can vary between 0.913 to 0.931 indicated.

Routine testing

The aeroplane is comparatively simple so far as routine testing is concerned. There are no special handling checks. The usual performance climbs should be made with the inoperative engine(s) at idle (not fuel off) and the gross performance data is compatible with this condition. The fuel should be

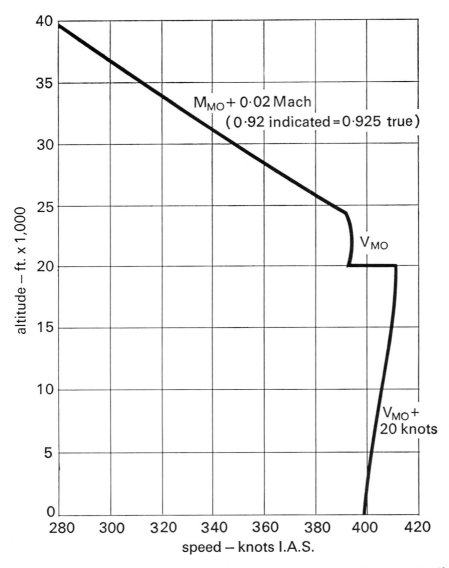

Figure 9.11 Routine testing VMO. (This chart may also be used for Crew Training if desired, although there is little point—see text.)

taken off one engine only at a time for relighting tests.   The only high speed work is to test the overspeed warnings.   Figure 9.11 illustrates the routine testing V_{MO}, which allows $M_{MO} +0.02$ Mach and $V_{MO} +20$ knots below 20,000 ft. for this purpose.   The only system of any complexity is the air system.   There are no particular autopilot or flight system checks.

The engines—JT9D

By this time no doubt some of the more critical readers will be wondering just when something will be said about the engines; without some comment this could not be said to be a wholly rounded picture of the 747.   However, the author is not an engine expert and there is little he can add to what is common knowledge of the subject.   We know — indeed the whole world was told — of some of the problems associated with the JT9D in its early months of operation: but these have been or are being fixed and the record of the engine now is certainly quite acceptable.   Producing an engine of this size is a major task and some early problems can be forgiven.   As far as the author is concerned that funny 'wanging' noise of the JT9D at high power is a great comfort.

Summary

The purpose of this chapter has been to describe the flying qualities of a very big jet aeroplane, to point out the areas of difficulty and to provide guidance in those areas.   The aeroplane described had to be the 747 because it is the only very big jet aeroplane presently certificated.   Big and heavy it certainly is.   The first model is cleared at 713,000 lb., 323,500 kg., maximum weight; there is another model (the 747B) at 738,000 lb., 334,200 kg. and another (the 747C) at 778,000 lb., 352,200 kg.   As a matter of interest the 747B has been taken off at an all-time record weight of 820,500 lb., 374,000 kg.

There are also two *fairly* big civil aeroplanes flying — the Douglas DC10 and Lockheed L1011.   The author has not flown these aeroplanes yet but is familiar with their flight control system designs and predicted flying qualities. In many cases a number of airworthiness requirements as minimum design aims have long since been left behind.   With the ability to tailor flight characteristics within close limits and the superb control which full hydraulic power offers, it is now sharpened competition which is the spur to competing design organisations.   This serves us, as pilots, well.   It will be most surprising if the DC10 and L1011 do anything but fly exceptionally well.   So we have a good present and a good future to look forward to in terms of these very big aeroplanes.

Certainly as far as the 747 is concerned it is true to say that nearly all our traditional complaints have been taken from us and there is now no excuse for not flying this aeroplane *properly*.

This book is characterised by a 'what to do about it' bit after each 'what it is' description. To finish off this part on the 747 I can only suggest in relation to 'what to do about it' the following four things:

1 Get posted to the 747 as soon as you can—and enjoy it
2 Don't taxy too fast
3 Don't smack the back end on take off
4 Do allow plenty of clearance on approach and landing.

I can't advise you how to fix the first point, but on the others:

2 Keep your eye on INS ground speed and *slow down*
3 Use a bit of finesse
4 Remember the visual aiming points and *don't get low*.

10 Asymmetric flight

Engine out ferrying

Engine out ferrying is the process of flying a multi-engined aeroplane from one place to another with one of its engines inoperative. It is a convenience to an operator in that it avoids the necessity of holding a costly spare engine at all stations on the operator's route network. It is sometimes called three-engine ferry, which of course is not inaccurate for a four-engined aeroplane. Three-engined aircraft can also be ferried with one engine out so long as they meet the rules; some have demonstrated this. However, while some twins have been taken off on one engine as a demonstration it is really only a circus trick. The safety level on an engine out ferry is, of course, lower than on an all-engines operation, hence passengers may not be carried. Depending on the performance and handling qualities of the type and its certification standard, the actual risk can vary from very little more than that associated with a normal take-off to considerably more than with a normal take-off.

The rules

A simple recital of rules can be boring but for a proper understanding of this operation it is necessary to examine the following précis and attempt to appreciate the purpose of the rules.

There are two sets of certification rules that concern us, FAR and B.C.A.R. The significant difference between them lies in the degree of accountability for failure of a further engine during the take-off. Broadly speaking, under FARs the take-off is an all operating engines operating manoeuvre with no performance or handling accountability for failure of a further engine until the aeroplane is in the en-route configuration, i.e. with gear up and flaps up. Under B.C.A.R.s the take-off procedure gives full protection against failure of a further engine from a controllability point of view and limits the period of exposure to an inadequate performance level to a few seconds around the lift-off point.

The fundamentals of the FARs are that:—
(a) The take-off technique must be fully spelled out.
(b) V_R and V_2 must not be less than their normal all engines values and must be good for control with one engine inoperative.
(c) The distance required is the engine out distance to 35 ft. $\times 1.15$.
(d) Performance with two engines out is not required until the aeroplane is en route, when it is 1.2% gross climb gradient.

(e) Equally, controllability with two engines out is not required until the aeroplane is en route and then it must be capable of being trimmed out at the climb speed.

(f) The ferry weight is limited to the minimum necessary for the flight irrespective of the weight permitted by performance capabilities.

(g) Only dry runways are permitted unless operation on wet runways is tested and approved.

Whereas the fundamentals of the B.C.A.R.s are that:—

(a) Three items are established and published:—
  (i) The two engines out V_{MCG}, good for 7 knots crosswind.
  (ii) The two engines out V_{MCA}.
  (iii) The take-off technique.

(b) Controllability is provided for both a continued take-off and an accelerate-stop in the event of an engine failure; for example V_R and V_2 are not less than 1.03 and 1.07 respectively of the two engines out V_{MCA}, and V_R may not be below V_{MCG}.

(c) The distance required is the engine out distance to 35 ft. $\times 1.18$.

(d) A continued take-off performance ability exists from the 'gear locked up' point, i.e.:—
  (i) The WAT curve gives a positive gradient from the second segment on.
  (ii) The Net Flight Path permits adequate obstacle clearance if it is constructed and matched to the obstacle.

(e) The runway performance is good for a wet surface unless it is specifically limited to dry.

(f) There is no guarantee of a stop within the distance from V_{MCG} but a maximum stop speed for the distance is scheduled.

(g) The stop may be either with brakes alone or with any controllable combination of reverse thrust, which must be good in the wet if the data is wet.

So say the rules. These however are minima. If some conservatism is used in weights, involving several short legs instead of a few long ones, the safety level can be raised considerably against both sets of requirements. This conservatism however must not be taken to extremes otherwise the risk will increase again with the additional number of take-offs. The minimum overall risk is achieved by a sensible compromise between weights and number of legs. But if full advantage is taken of the rules under limiting conditions then the following differences become obvious. The FAR technique is strictly an all operating engines operating take-off and a failure around lift off could leave the aeroplane with inadequate continued take-off performance, inadequate stopping performance and no guarantee of controllability. In contrast the B.C.A.R. technique provides full controllability in the event of failure of a further engine and limits the risk of inadequate performance to a period covering the maximum stop speed to the speed at the 'gear locked up' point. A failure in this period would result in an overrun during a stop and a very low screen height during a go.

It would be unfair to allow the reader to assume that this distinct difference in safety level between FARs and B.C.A.R.s lies to the sole credit of the ARB—it doesn't. There was a lot of help and pressure from the British Air Line Pilots Association. Coming from the pilots who were likely to be doing this work the help was welcome and the pressure entirely reasonable.

Circumscribing considerations

Having examined the ground rules let us now consider the operation. There are at least five major points to be considered before we discuss the actual take-off technique:—

(a) The effect on services and systems of an engine failure. It is necessary to consider the consequences in terms of electrics, hydraulics, etc. of the most significant engine failure. A good example of such a consequence is that which could occur with the VC10, where a particular engine failure in combination with a particular engine inoperative could result in half the gear failing to retract. This is avoided by a commoning of the two otherwise independent hydraulic systems just for the engine out ferry take-off. In an instance where, for example, the gear could not be retracted following the engine failure, then the ferry climb performance would be scheduled gear down. Whatever special drills apply to a particular type should be contained in the Appendix to the Flight Manual.

(b) It is always necessary for take-off weight to be restricted, for obvious reasons. The restriction is not great on a high performance four-engined aeroplane but is very much more on a low performance four-engined aeroplane, and can be quite crippling on a three-engined aeroplane. If there is any doubt the solution is to take off light and fly shorter legs, within reason.

(c) Nearly always, reduced flap settings are chosen for take-off. This is to increase the climb gradients available in the event of a failure after take-off and also to keep the aeroplane comfortably ground-borne up to the higher speeds necessary for directional control in the event of a failure during the take-off run.

(d) On some types, if there is a need for a high speed to meet the two engines out V_{MCG} requirement, this can get very close to the tyre ground speed limitation.

(e) If the take-off is going to be limiting it is necessary to decide on a V_1 speed. (V_1 as used in this context is a convenient shorthand expression for a decision speed in relation to engine out ferry: it does not imply the performance protection in its usual context in relation to normal all engines operation.) Minimum V_1 clearly cannot be less than V_{MCG} and maximum V_1 effectively equals V_R (exceptionally, $V_{lift-off}$). As

293

the speed range V_{MCG} to V_R is normally very small it is best to settle for $V_1 = V_R$ for the majority of cases. However, there are two extremes of conditions to be considered which would merit departures from this general rule. The first is where the limiting field length is dominant to the extent that the weight is well below any climb-out or obstacle clearance limitations. In this case one should choose to continue the take-off from as low a speed as possible, i.e. $V_1 = V_{MCG}$. The second is where climb or obstacle clearance limitations are dominant to the extent that the field length is clearly not limiting. In this latter case one should choose as high a V_1 as possible. In practice it would be unreasonable to expect a pilot to stop from a speed probably exceeding V_R and certainly exceeding $V_{lift-off}$. Hence one of these speeds becomes the effective top limit of the available range of V_1 speeds. In all but exceptional cases maximum V_1 is V_R. Equally, don't take too much advantage of an exceptionally low V_{MCG} otherwise the lift off could be beyond the end of the runway. The scheduled stop speed data will indicate whether a decision to stop from the chosen V_1 would result in a significant overrun. Incidentally, it must not be assumed that the best choice of V_1 will always avoid problems; the choice of a particular V_1 is always a compromise between two evils—the probability of damage being incurred in an overrun and the significantly reduced obstacle clearance in the event of a continued take-off.

Take-off technique

In principle the take-off is quite simple. The aeroplane is clearly going to want to swing, due to the asymmetric thrust, and this swing must be countered by the two means of directional control available, i.e. nose wheel steering in the early part of the run and rudder in the latter part of the run. The method of using available thrust is quite logical; the symmetrical pair of engines is set at full power before brake release and the third engine is brought up to full power progressively and balanced initially by steering and subsequently by rudder.

Basically that is all there is to it, but a little sophistication can make it a much smoother operation. Let us consider a take-off with No. 4 inoperative. It should be performed like this:—

1 Set in about half left rudder trim (where the Flight Manual gives a specific value, use it). This is a good compromise between the 99.9% certainty of needing the rudder and the 0.1% chance of a second failure turning the take-off into a symmetric one.
2 Get the co-pilot to hold the control column well forward to get a good bite on the nose wheel in the early part of the run.
3 Establish full power on numbers 2 and 3 engines and about one third power on number 1 before brake release. This amount of asymmetry can be held on steering from start of roll.

4 Apply full left rudder. Although this isn't strictly necessary until the rudder becomes effective, if it is not done there is a strong tendency to control the whole take-off on steering, resulting in a surprising swing at V_R.

5 Let go the brakes and keep straight on steering using quite a coarse angle while the ground speed is very low.

6 When the aeroplane is rolling at about 20 knots start bringing up number 1 engine. Balance the increasing thrust against steering angle. This is comparatively easy after a little practice. If you overdo the thrust increment just throttle back a little, wait for a few more knots then re-apply the thrust.

7 As the speed increases use smaller steering angles and feel for the transfer of control to the rudder. Now match increasing thrust against rudder control and abandon steering when you have full control on rudder alone. Finally achieve full thrust on the third engine against full rudder and you have it made.

8 Proceed to V_R, rotate and climb out at the ferry V_2, which, under B.C.A.R., will look after failure of a further engine.

Where an aeroplane is fitted with coupled steering (limited nose wheel steering through the rudder bar) this device will clearly interpose itself between the two phases of control, i.e. control by nose wheel tiller steering and control by full rudder. The net effect will be that the tiller can be abandoned quite early in the run and control maintained on the rudder bar. Be aware, however, that if the steering is still making a contribution up to V_R, an increase of rudder angle will be necessary as the nose wheel leaves the ground.

Because the take-off is essentially a 'static' manoeuvre directionally, i.e. there is no sudden swing to kill as in the unexpected engine failure case, full thrust can be achieved on the third engine on full rudder alone at a speed considerably less than the one engine out dynamic V_{MCG}. This speed difference can be around 15 knots. With an inboard engine inoperative the take-off is easier because the asymmetric yawing moments are less. In this case full thrust on the third engine can be achieved at about 10 to 15 knots less than the outboard inoperative case.

If, in spite of doing your best, you begin to lose the place early in the run, don't hesitate—chop and stop. Go back and start again with a little more finesse. Even on a superb engine out aeroplane such as the VC10 don't treat the take-off casually—keep it firmly under control until you are well airborne. Finally, don't forget to retract the gear when you see a positive rate of climb after lift-off. This reminder isn't so ridiculous as it sounds. With the concentration necessary for this type of take-off gear retraction can be overlooked.

With the B.C.A.R. procedure, in the event of failure of a further engine at or above your chosen V_1, continue and accept the lower screen height. Get the gear up smartly and fly out at V_2. If the failure occurs below V_1, stop and accept the overrun. If failure of a further engine occurs on a FAR type take-off the choice is very limited. If close to the two engines out V$_{MCA}$ speed, continue, and establish control by using a mix of a bank angle slightly in excess of 5° together with a temporary change of departure heading, if the terrain allows it. If it doesn't, put all your faith in extra bank angle. But if you are not close to the two engines out V$_{MCA}$ don't risk total loss of directional control; close all throttles instantly and re-land regardless of distance remaining.

So much for the take-off. The rest of the flight is straightforward. All aircraft handle well enough with only one engine out and most engine out landings are close enough to the all engines procedure to make no significant difference. An engine failure in the cruise however calls for a two engines out landing. No problem—read all about it in the next section!

Asymmetric flight training—with particular reference to two engines out on four-engined aircraft

Soon after the introduction of big jet aircraft into service in significant numbers, around 1958, concern arose about the accident rate associated with asymmetric flight training. The rate was high and generated much discussion regarding the propriety and the value of the training. Indeed, opposition to this training grew and has become very deep-seated. Opinions, whether properly founded or not, are held very strongly, facts have become distorted and the whole problem has become confused by emotion. Some parts of the arguments against engine(s)-out training are certainly valid in isolation but the overall flavour is not well proven. In fact, it is in direct contradiction with the philosophy of civil aircraft certification.

So much has been written and published on this subject that it is difficult to present some simple facts without having them compromised immediately by some well-remembered opposing argument. However, if we hope to get at the truth after years of good and bad, well—and ill—founded debate we must try to put aside the last ten years of argument, get down to the elementary bones of the problem and build up the whole case again from square one. Having done this it should then be possible to draw out a simple accurate conclusion at the end.

The case for asymmetric flight training

Consider an aeroplane in flight. Its overall level of safety is made up of three distinct parts:—
(a) The qualities of the aeroplane as a vehicle.
(b) The ability of the commander as a pilot.
(c) The effect of the weather.
In order that the total sum shall be satisfactory each of these three contributions must be satisfactory individually. We are primarily concerned

with the inter-relationship of the first two contributions. Hence we shall get rid of the effect of the weather by saying that for weather conditions up to a given severity the aeroplane and the pilot must be capable; and that for weather conditions beyond the capability of the aeroplane and the pilot (e.g. extreme crosswind landings and flight through thunderstorms) operation is either forbidden or strongly discouraged.

We are now left with the aeroplane and the pilot. Each must be individually capable, otherwise their sum will be deficient. It would be just as unreasonable to provide an aeroplane which is very capable in failure cases and man it with an incapable pilot as it would be to provide a capable pilot with an inadequate aeroplane. In both cases, in the event of a high demand state of affairs arising, the inadequate half would fail and the aeroplane would be lost. It is clear therefore that there must be compatibility between the demand made by the aeroplane and the response offered by the pilot, and just as true that there must be compatibility between the level of ability offered by the pilot and the demand made by the aeroplane. This corollary has occasionally been exercised; there are to the author's knowledge at least two occasions where aeroplanes had to be modified significantly to reduce their level of demand for 'skill, alertness and strength' on the part of the assumed average pilot.

We now turn to the design requirements for civil four-engined jet transports. The certification authorities have long been convinced that the design of such aircraft should be such that all likely single failures will be contained at very little hazard and that all reasonable combinations of double failures will be survivable without too much hazard. It is inescapable therefore that, for any aeroplane properly certificated in accordance with the design and flight requirements, the pilot must be able to match the demand made by the aeroplane.

It is generally agreed that single failures do occur, not frequently perhaps, but certainly often enough for the aeroplane to be designed to cope with them without difficulty. Hence the generally good qualities of aircraft with one engine out and the training of pilots to the required level of ability. The double failures are admittedly rarer but still sufficiently frequent for them to be accountable, both in design and therefore piloting ability. Two good examples of significant double failures are those which can occur in the hydraulic systems supporting powered flying controls and of course the engines. In one thirty-month period of operations in the two U.K. state corporations there were three two-engines-out landings, equal to a rate of 1 in 250,000 flights or twice the assumed rate for such occurrences.

One of the arguments used by the opponents of two engines out flight training is that the real life occasions are too few to need consideration in terms of demonstrated pilot ability. If we make a logical extrapolation of this argument, then it could be said that the need for an aeroplane to survive a double engine failure on one side could be removed from the design and flight requirements! It goes without saying that any such suggestion would meet total opposition. But the compatibility between design/flight requirements and piloting ability must be maintained otherwise the loop becomes open-ended. The aeroplane/pilot combination should be capable of returning from a flight with two engines on one side inoperative and making an approach, a go-around within certain constraints and a landing; certainly without any danger and, just as important, without any shadow of doubt concerning the success of the three manoeuvres. All contemporary four-engined jets are capable in this respect: it is illogical for pilots to refuse to demonstrate their share of the contract. To close the loop of course it becomes necessary to require that pilots train for the manoeuvre and demonstrate their competence. It isn't good enough to write up a drill, make a gesture of practice in a simulator (probably lacking fidelity) and hope that the pilot will make a good enough shot at it on the day that it occurs. This approach begs the question and throws some doubt on the likelihood of success. It causes pilots to be suspicious of the aeroplane's qualities and to doubt their own level of competence. The only reliable way is to ensure that pilots train for these manoeuvres and thus become confident that the real life application lies well within the capabilities of both the aeroplane and themselves.

Asymmetric flight, two engines out

It is generally accepted that flying with two engines out en route is no problem; the difficulties, if any, are in the approach to land and its permutations. To illustrate the author's contention that, with a proper knowledge of the subject, even these 'problem' areas are perfectly straightforward, we shall now consider two aeroplanes, the Boeing 747 and the Boeing 707–320C, in detail. The 747 has been chosen because its particular qualities are such that it favours neither side in this debate. In addition this material will support what has been written about the aeroplane in a previous chapter. In contrast, the Boeing 707–320C is an aeroplane which is acknowledged to be demanding with two engines out and therefore cannot be considered a biased choice.

In a two engines out approach there are three fundamentals to be considered. They are:—

(a) The performance level of the aeroplane at full power on two engines for a range of configurations.
(b) The minimum directional and lateral control speed on two engines at full power (V_{MCL2}).
(c) The effect of (a) and (b) on the approach path, and also on the airspeed at the threshold.

The Boeing 747 Figure 10.1 shows the appropriate values for the 747. There are two flap settings on the aeroplane which are clearly usable for a

298

two engines out approach; 10° and 20°. The lines marked V$_{AT}$ 10° and V$_{AT}$ 20° flap are the 1.3Vs approach speeds for these configurations all engines. So long as V$_{MC}$ is not limiting these speeds give the usual protection above stall speed and can be used with confidence. They are plotted from maximum landing weight down to a very light landing weight.

The line marked V$_{MCL_2}$+5 knots is the lowest recommended speed for operational use in terms of lateral and directional control against the

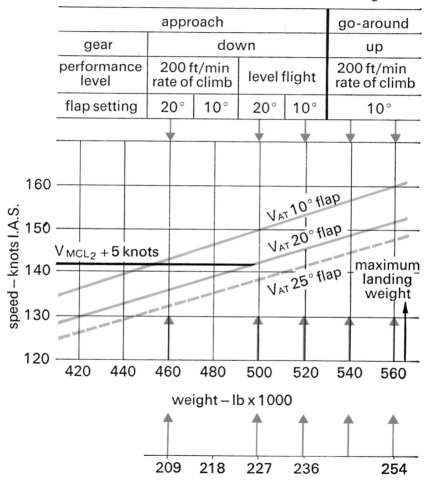

Figure 10.1   Boeing 747–136 two engines out (windmilling—fuel off) approach, landing and go-around data, ISA (valid up to 27°C) sea level, one A.C. pack on.

asymmetric yawing moment of two engines on one side at full power with the other two engines inoperative. This line is exactly what it says it is; the actual V_{MCL2} corrected to the highest possible power at sea-level is 137 knots. So, from controllability considerations this speed too can be flown with confidence. This speed of course does not vary with weight or flap angle.

The table in Figure 10.1 indicates the performance level available at full power on two engines for various combinations of gear, flap and weight. All climb rates quoted are 'gross' but conservative.

Finally, the target threshold speed for a landing with 25° flap is plotted against weight.

These are all the basic figures necessary for a two engines out approach, a possible go-around and a landing at all permitted landing weights at sea level and at temperatures up to 27°C.

In using this chart there is only one decision which has to be made if the weight at the time exceeds 460,000 lb., 209,000 kg. and that is the performance level which is desired on the glideslope. (At and below 460,000 lb., 209,000 kg. the application of go-around EPR will give a 200 ft./min. climb rate without change of configuration and this should be enough for any pilot to fly a satisfactory ILS approach.) If the approach conditions are good a decision to accept level flight capability would be quite proper. In this case the approach can be started at 10° flap, gear down, up to a weight of 520,000 lb., 236,000 kg. So, depending on the approach conditions, either select the performance level you need for your estimated landing weight or dump fuel to a weight at which you can enjoy the performance level you want. Having done this now use the higher speed of V_{AT} for the flap angle chosen or the $V_{MCL2}+5$ knots value. At weights above 500,000 lb., 227,000 kg. at 20° flap use the V_{AT} 20° flap line against weight; below this weight stick to the $V_{MCL2}+5$ knots value. This means that you will always have a safe margin above the stall speed and the minimum control speed; you can go up to go-around EPR on the operating engines and draw at least your expected level of performance without the need to change speed.

From here on the three manoeuvres of approach, go-around and landing are all easily flown with accuracy and confidence in the aeroplane's abilities.

On the approach the aeroplane is easy to fly. It is nicely stable and very steady. All control forces are light, including the rudder at full stroke which is only 70 lb. There is no difference in handling between flaps 10° or flaps 20°. The localiser and glide path, and of course a fully visual approach, can all be flown comfortably and with high accuracy.

For an intended landing the final approach and touchdown are perfectly predictable. If a positive climb performance level weight/flap combination has been selected there is of course no commit point in terms of performance; a go-around can be made at any time the speed is at or above 142 knots. If the aeroplane is above the weight for a positive climb gradient there is of

300

course a commit point—but there is no drama about it. This point can be quite close in—say 200 ft. height—when all that is necessary is the selection of 20° flap from 10° flap followed by the selection 25° flap at say 50 ft. This will have taken some of the speed off and, with the co-pilot winding the rudder trim to zero at the beginning of flare a normal landing can be made from this point on. The threshold speed should be very close to the target speed for 25° flap so there should be no worry over distance. Asymmetric reverse thrust is quite comfortably held; use both engines on a dry runway, the inner only on a wet runway. If the approach is flown at 20° flap, select 25° again around 50 ft. There is no objection to the selection of 30° flap for the touchdown; its use, in fact, should be encouraged.

A go-around is just as predictable. So long as 142 knots is maintained full power on two engines can be applied and the aeroplane controlled on the rudder very comfortably. Coincident with the power application the aeroplane should be rotated nose up to an angle of about 10°. This rotation destroys the descent rate very quickly and the thrust maintains the speed. The performance level will settle at the chosen value without change of configuration. However, the performance level can be improved rapidly and considerably. Gear retraction (16 to 24 seconds depending on how many EDPs are operating) will improve the climb rate significantly. Flap retraction 20° to 10° (5 seconds) will also improve the performance. The speed increment of 7 knots necessary before retracting flaps to 10° will normally be achieved automatically as the gear drag disappears. Note from the chart that at maximum landing weight the 747 has a 200 ft./min. rate of climb capability gear up flaps 10°.

Those are the basic facts of two engines out work on the 747. However, in case readers should think that the simplicity of flying the 747 on two engines has been overstated the following additional information is offered.

Figure 10.1 as drawn is conservative in its performance by approximately 20,000 lb., 9,000 kg. weight. This means that an average 747 will actually fly level, gear down with 10° flap, two engines out and two at full power at a weight of 540,000 lb., 245,000 kg. This is only 20,000 lb., 9,000 kg. short of the maximum landing weight.

In any case it is rather academic to consider an in-service two engines out landing at a very high weight. Even with a high payload it should still be possible to dump fuel to a landing weight of around 480,000 lb., 218,000 kg. and still have plenty of fuel left. At this weight the 747 has a performance potential on the approach of 100 feet per minute rate of climb gear down 20° flap.

The performance of the aeroplane at lighter weights is impressive and much better than most pilots are given to understand. This is an area where the author disagrees with Boeing and the U.S. philosophy in general. In the U.S., the emphasis is placed on a gear up initial approach, with a commit philosophy with gear extension (possibly at 1,500 feet!) and a very small flap angle for the approach, 10°. This degree of conservatism is excessive and undermines the pilot's confidence in the aeroplane, which will in fact do what is claimed for it in figure 10.1. At and below 500,000 lb., 227,000 kg., for example, an approach can be perfectly well flown gear down at 20° flap with a commit point as low as 200 feet if necessary.

The relationship between speed and flap angle is convenient so that speed reductions are not at all difficult to achieve. In a 10° flap final approach for example the selection of 20° at the right point will incur sufficient extra drag to just about get rid of the 7 knots required. Similarly, the selection of 25° flap close to the threshold will get rid of the next required decrement of 4 knots; all without the need to do much fiddling with the thrust levers.

At very light landing weights, around 440,000 lb., 200,000 kg., there will be the need to lose 13 knots between the point of decision to land and the threshold because the speed down to this point will have been maintained at 142 knots. There is no need to get rid of all this speed because the landing distance (to the U.K. rules at least) allows for a threshold speed of V_{Tmax}, which is 15 knots above the normal threshold speed anyway.

The height loss during the go-around manoeuvre is remarkably small, as was demonstrated in a recent test flown by the author. The aeroplane was set up on an approach, two engines out, gear down, 20° flap at a weight of 550,000 lb., 250,000 kg. approximately, very close to maximum landing weight. The weight and flap setting were chosen deliberately to place the aeroplane in a limiting performance condition, i.e. where go-around EPR on the remaining engines would not reduce the descent gradient to zero. The object was to make a go-around at exactly 1,000 ft. QNH and measure the height loss. It was a miserable day, gusty and IMC throughout the exercise, so nothing was in favour of the manoeuvre. The approach down to 1,000 ft. was good on a 3° glideslope without the need for a very high power on the operating engines. The speed of course was 150 knots. At 1,000 ft. EPR was advanced to go-around and the aeroplane rotated to the go-around attitude. The rate of descent ceased very quickly and the additional thrust sustained the speed. The gear was selected up and as the gear drag disappeared the airspeed increased by the required 7 knots. When the gear was locked up the flaps were retracted to 10°. *The height loss was exactly eighty feet*—an astonishing result! With the aeroplane now settled at go-around EPR on two engines, gear up, 10° flap, the next three minutes indicated an average rate of climb of 250 ft. per min. All in all a most impressive performance on the part of the aeroplane.

The discussion so far has related fundamentally to the in-service double engine failure cases. In terms of training procedures however there are three points which need to be made. Firstly, there can be positive control of weight. If two engines out work is restricted to weights below 500,000 lb., 227,000 kg., the performance level on the approach (100 ft. per min. rate of climb, gear down at 10° flap) should be quite adequate. Secondly, figure 10.1 is drawn for fuel off the windmilling engines; in training, with idle thrust, the performance will be better. Finally, if a pilot under training *should* make a hash of it (although I find this hard to imagine) the idling engines are there for the training captain to salvage the manoeuvre.

Before drawing a line under '747 with two engines out' it is necessary to give a little space to two areas where the circumstances of a possible two engines out landing would be less favourable and not capable of being adjusted so readily. They both concern performance on the approach and they are of course (a) the case of freighters with higher than usual landing weights and (b) operations into hot and high airfields.

In the first case the penalty of a high landing weight, say around 540,000 lb., 245,000 kg. is the inability to guarantee level flight on the approach, gear down, even at 10° flap. But the amount by which the aeroplane will be short will be very little—anything from virtually nothing to 100 ft. per min. rate of descent—and this should not cause any difficulty. The commit point can be as low as 300 ft. if necessary and from that point on the approach should be flown at flaps 10° and 156 knots to 150 feet, then flaps 20° and 150 knots to 50 feet and finally flaps 25° with a normal flare and touchdown.

In the second case the performance picture will change quite considerably but it is not the intention in this dissertation to go beyond the ISA sea level work. It must be the operators' responsibility to ensure that the necessary information is established and made available to their crews. The result will be of course to slide the top part of figure 10.1 some way to the left, the amount depending on the thrust decrements due to altitude and temperature.

It will be clear from the foregoing that there is no inherent difficulty in flying the 747 on two engines. But of course the 747 is an average two engines out aeroplane; it is easy to fly, all the speeds seem to fit and the approach performance on two engines is adequate. So what about all the other four-engined jet transports? Well, the scatter is enormous. It ranges from the VC10 at one end to the 707–320C at the other. The VC10 has a very low V_{MCL2} speed and a very high performance level on the two-engined approach. The –320C however has a high V_{MCL2} speed and an only just adequate performance level on the two-engined approach. It would be useful if someone would undertake to provide data similar to that given in figure 10.1 for the 747 for all other four-engined jet transports currently flying. The precise procedures could then be properly established. However, that is beyond the scope of this book and we will therefore limit further discussion to the –320C. This aeroplane is not actually as demanding as it is generally thought to be.

The Boeing 707–320C Figure 10.2 gives Flight Manual data together with some ARB performance data (all at ISA sea level) for a Boeing 707–336C (a –320C series) with JT3D–3B engines of 18,000 lb. thrust. Note the following features:—

(a) $V_{MCL2}+5$ knots at 152 knots.

(b) The Flight Manual recommended two engines out approach speed for
14° flap, gear down, equal to target threshold speed (full flap)+30 knots.
This is based on the traditional Boeing Vref+30 knots for a flap angle three
stages up from full flap (add 10 knots for every stage less than full flap).

	approach	go-around	approach
gear	down	up	down
flap setting	14°	14°	14°
performance level	200ft/min rate of climb	300ft/min rate of climb	level flight

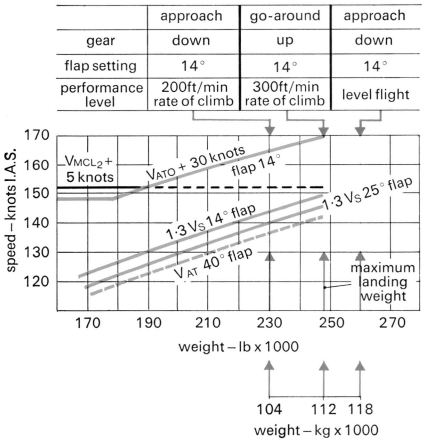

Figure 10.2   Boeing 707–336C two engines out (windmilling—fuel off) approach, landing
and go-around data, ISA (valid up to 29°C), sea level, no bleeds, one T.C. on.

(c) The $1.3V_{MS_1}$ speeds for 14° flap and 25° flap (these are the *all engines*
final steady approach speeds for a landing with these flap angles).

(d) The target threshold speed for a landing using 40° flap (all engines).

(e) The significant weight of 230,000 lb., 104,000 kg. which would give a
go-around climb rate of 200 ft. per min. at 14° flap with the gear
remaining down.

304

(f) The significant weight of 260,000 lb., 118,000 kg. for level flight capability at full power on two engines on the approach, gear down, 14° flap.

Before we discuss the significant differences between figures 10.1 and 10.2 there are two points concerning –320C performance which should be discussed. Firstly, the difference in 1.3 times stall speed for 25° flap compared with that for 14° flap is very small and, as both speeds are so far below the recommended two engines out initial approach speed anyway, the performance penalty of using 25° flap (at any weight) rules this setting out completely if you wish to retain the ability to make a go-around. Secondly, the 200 ft. per min. rate of climb weight of 230,000 lb., 104,000 kg. is fairly close to maximum landing weight and the level flight weight of 260,000 lb., 118,000 kg. is above maximum landing weight. The –320C series therefore, in spite of its very high maximum landing weight, isn't really all that much of a performance limited aeroplane on a two engines out approach.

We come now to the major differences between the 747 and the –320C. The first is that on the 747 the V_{MC} parameter fits nicely into the middle of the landing weight range and is therefore dominant only over the lower half. On the –320C however the V_{MC} parameter is so high that it is dominant over the whole of the landing weight range; 152 knots drawn across to maximum landing weight still exceeds $1.3V_s$ 14° flap by 3 knots. This is the heart of the matter on the –320C. It is the penalty of unbalancing the development of the type by not matching improvements in lowered stall speeds by improvements in lowered directional control speeds. One could argue of course that half a loaf is better than no bread. But, where an aeroplane has to live with 'landing distance required' rules which read across two engines out and one engine out V_{MC} speeds to the all engines threshold speeds (i.e. B.C.A.R.) some of the potential improvement in distances is forfeited.

The second difference between the two aeroplanes is in the quality of the V_{MCL} speeds. In terms of raw numbers of course they are the same, with the exception of the reduced maximum rudder pedal force which goes with the later requirements. V_{MCL2} as interpreted in the U.K. over a long period of time is the minimum speed at which an aeroplane can be flown straight in a given configuration with two engines inoperative on one side and the other two engines at maximum go-around EPR without requiring (a) more than 5° favourable bank angle, (b) a rudder pedal force exceeding 180 lb. (old rules, changed to 150 lb. under the new rules) and (c) a lateral control force and angle which would prevent sufficient control for reasonable manoeuvring and for containing reasonable short term changes of power. Both aeroplanes met, and still meet, the appropriate requirements. The 747 demonstrates compliance with ease. All control forces are light, the maximum rudder force is only 70 lb., and the aeroplane can be flown comfortably and with precision. It can be flown at V_{MCL2} (137 knots) for long periods quite comfortably. The –320C, however, is more demanding.

305

With its fundamentally manual controls it is not so precise over small angles. Longitudinal and lateral control are not difficult but directional control is, relatively so, because of the size of the rudder control forces. It is some time since these forces were measured accurately on a flight test programme. Boeing states that the company records show that the force can be as low as 90 to 100 lb. with the aeroplane flown immaculately. Undoubtedly this is true but the need to make sure that full rudder is held is of course very great and there is a tendency to overdo the foot force. As a result, the last part of the foot force is simply squashing the mechanical stops, but it is difficult to avoid doing this. There is some other evidence to show that the 'real-life' foot force is around 140 lb. in this condition. The forces are certainly high and about two to three minutes is as long as a pilot could be expected to hold this force level and fly with accuracy. It is wrong to get this out of perspective however: flight at V_{MCL2} is never required operationally and flight at $V_{MCL2}+5$ knots is only required for the first part of a go-around. Incidentally, the maximum rudder force required does not fall very much with increasing airspeed. Subjectively it is just as tiring to fly at a steady 170 knots as it is at 152 knots.

While the V_{MC} part of the picture is not very good we must remember that it is only one, unlikely, part of a two engines out landing. Using figure 10.2 as a basis, we will assume a landing weight of 220,000 lb., 100,000 kg. (one should normally be able to dump fuel to about this figure). The approach should be flown gear down, 14° flap, at around 160 knots. Control of the aeroplane is actually quite good. At this flap setting a 3° glideslope can be flown comfortably at a power which doesn't require full rudder, so the foot forces are reasonable.

The ability to make a go-around can be exercised down to 300 ft. If the go-around is required go up to the required EPR and push and hold full rudder while rotating the aeroplane to the climb out attitude. Select the gear up and shoot for 170 knots. The aeroplane will settle down to a climb rate of around 300 to 400 ft. per min. The need now is to get rid of some of the foot force which means getting away from go-around EPR. When a safe height has been reached increase speed and throttle back to maximum continuous thrust. At this point the rudder trim will have taken out a lot of the very high foot force. The only real demand in this manoeuvre is the ability to push full rudder and hold it for possibly up to two minutes.

For the landing, let us go back to 300 ft. on the approach. With the aeroplane nicely placed the new target is to get from 160 knots at 14° flap to say 140 knots at 40° flap. This, to some extent, is a manoeuvre in which the speed adjusts automatically with flap extension. At 300 ft. select 25° flap, at 100 ft. select 40° flap. Watch the rate of speed decay and control it by changes of power. Finally, with the aeroplane crossing the threshold and flaring in the normal fashion there is no reason for not selecting 50° flap.

Other types It is too great a task to cover the two engines out behaviour of all the other four-engined jet transports in depth but the following general remarks may be helpful as a guide. The VC10 is exceptionally good with a low VMC and high performance. Two engines out work on this type is most predictable and not in any way demanding. The DC8 variants are generally a little better than the 707s, vintage for vintage. The smaller Boeings, the −138B and −720B for example, are also better than the −320C series. This is due primarily to their much lighter maximum landing weights and vastly increased performance on the approach. VMCL for these aircraft however is just as limiting.

Remember that with any type it is always possible to improve your position by unbalancing the power of the two operating engines on the approach. Set a high power on the inboard engine and use the outboard over small ranges to control your flight path. Also, in a one-engine-out, rudder-boost-off condition, which is the other significant failure case, life can be made generally much easier. Rather than come in on three engines and suffer the problems of a badly degraded rudder, make the approach with symmetric power by setting the 'odd' engine to idle.

In this sub-chapter we have dealt with some of the details of two engines out work on a range of aircraft from average to somewhat demanding. Even in the worst case the demand is only for a high push force on the rudder bar. This is within the capability of all pilots. There is in fact nothing which lies outside their abilities.

The case against asymmetric flight training

Those people who oppose asymmetric flight training do so on the basis of three main points:—
(a) It is dangerous, as shown by the accident record.
(b) It is unnecessary, as shown by statistics.
(c) It can be done equally well in the simulator.
It is not intended to précis the supporting material for these points, which has been frequently publicised together with long lists of training accidents. Rather the intention is to show the weaknesses of the three arguments, taking each in turn.

The risks involved There are two lists of accidents which are frequently quoted. These are the U.K. Flight Safety Committee list of Training Accidents involving Destruction of, or Substantial Damage to, the Aircraft (1954 to 1968) and U.S. Air Carrier Training Accidents, Jet Transport Aircraft, 1958 to 1968. Whichever record one reads certainly makes poor reading. Most of the accidents listed shouldn't have happened; only a few were truly unavoidable accidents.

Various conclusions may be drawn from these lists. Traditionally, they are produced as evidence of the danger involved, but it can equally be argued (on the basis of the very same details) that some training organisations were deficient in their evaluation of the task and/or allowed themselves to be unreasonably constrained by factors fundamentally in opposition to the principles of good training, like shortage of time and money.   The demand of the task exceeded the ability of those training organisations.   Some of the pilots accepted as training captains were in the first place not suitable for the job and in the second place not properly trained.   Their level of instructional ability was not high enough.   The discipline which was imposed was at much too low a level.   There was a lack of knowledge and an occasional failure to curb recklessness.   Proper motivation was clearly lacking in many instances and the incentives and rewards were inadequate.

These are pretty powerful conclusions, but the majority are privately admitted by some major airlines to be true.   However, these difficulties are inevitable and must be faced when attempting to set up a competent training organisation.

In the second edition of this book it was said that 'Far too many aeroplanes have been lost in training due to ignorance, overconfidence and recklessness'. To this could be added lack of ability on the part of training captains. The people who are responsible for engine out training are also responsible for *all* flight training so it is relevant to consider the total record before isolating the asymmetric record.   Within the total record a number of aeroplanes have been lost absolutely unnecessarily—how else would one describe a deliberate roll or attempts at all engines flame out landings? These were civil transport aeroplanes, not designed for aerobatics or beyond the double failure level case, and required to be flown by sensible responsible adults not a bunch of clowns.   Anyway enough of recklessness and lack of discipline.

Let us turn now to asymmetric training and consider the levels of knowledge and ability indicated by the accident record.   A number of aeroplanes have been lost through being placed, deliberately, outside their capabilities.   A good example is the switching off of rudder boost at low airspeed with two engines on one side already at idle.   As a triple failure this is outside the design limitations of the aeroplane and is not even considered during certi- fication.   Small wonder the aeroplane was lost.   By far the majority of losses however were due to lack of flying ability, not so much on the part of the pupil but on the part of the instructor in allowing the aeroplane to reach a position where control was hazarded and finally lost.   It is not within the scope of this book to produce a complete breakdown of accident causes but in the first list of accidents referred to, out of the twenty-seven accidents listed eighteen were the result of ignorance, recklessness and lack of ability or discipline and thus were avoidable, while the remaining nine accidents were unavoidable; in the second list out of a total of twenty-one, thirteen were avoidable and eight were unavoidable (three were gear failures not related to training and one a mid air collision).

308

This leaves us with a training accident record three times higher than it should have been. Had it remained at the one-third level there would have been normal acceptance of unavoidable accidents and no evidence to support the discontinuation of two engines out work because of its danger. If the aeroplane is flown properly (which isn't difficult), within its limitations (which isn't difficult) and with due regard for circumscribing conditions like weather (which isn't difficult) there is no danger in two engines out asymmetric flight training, merely a slight increase in risk. The risk in such training is higher than that in normal operation; this has to be accepted. There is also a higher than usual risk in engine out ferrying, for example, but it is accepted. In the same way there is a risk in one engine out training on twin-engined jet transports (very similar to two engines out on a four-engined aeroplane, and in one obvious respect, much worse) yet the world of twin jet pilots is and always has been totally silent about it. The risk in training is only slightly higher than in normal operation, and the difference is, in general, tolerable.

The need for training This part of the argument against asymmetric flight training is based on the fact that while there are some two engines out training accidents there are no two engines out operational accidents. This bald statement is of course true but the inference (i.e. that if two engines out training is stopped, ipso facto, all two engines out accidents will be stopped) is false. It is much more likely that if two out training were stopped the operational two out accident rate would appear. It is in fact reasonable to assume that the reason there are *no* two engines out accidents in line service is because pilots are trained in two engines out work to a satisfactory level.

Certainly two engines out landings occur sufficiently frequently to be accountable. In one two-and-a-half-year period in the operations of the two U.K. state corporations there were three such landings in service; all well executed because the pilots had trained for the manoeuvre. This is an achieved rate of 1 in 250,000 flights which is twice as frequent as the assumed rate for two-out landings (at the 'Remote' level this is 1 in 1,000,000 hours—say 1 in 500,000 flights for a mix of short and long haul revenue sectors). Apart from this example, some very recent work by the ARB on the probability of two engines out landings concludes with the following interesting remarks:—

(a) The overall figure is around 1 in 1,000,000 landings.
(b) For smaller samples the rate may vary by a factor of five, i.e. up to 1 in 200,000 landings.
(c) For individual types or operators, over a 'bad patch' period the rate may rise alarmingly, i.e. up to 1 in 5,000 landings.

In any case a statistical record is only valid in retrospect for a given type with a given engine, and then with certain reservations. A period of poor engine reliability can occur; this has been demonstrated recently on a certain four-engined jet transport. Additionally, when a new aeroplane type starts service with new engines *it has to prove itself;* it has no right to ride on the record of previous types of aircraft or engines. It could have a crop of engine problems leading to, statistically speaking, frequent two engines out landings in service. Trying to lean on statistics entirely is rather like trying to show for example satisfactory stall qualities by accident record rather than by compliance with the requirements; by the time one has enough data to prove the point the aeroplane type is due for retirement.

To sum up, the need for two engines out survival exists. This is recognised by designers and certification authorities and for the same reasons it should be accepted by pilots and training and licensing authorities.

The limitations of the simulator In this case the contention is that the simulator is as good as the aeroplane, or at least sufficiently good for the shortfall to be insignificant. But there are three reasons why this is not true. Firstly, of present day simulators there are more which fail to simulate adequately *one* engine out characteristics than there are those which succeed; and this only in terms of control motion, control characteristics and instrument behaviour. With *two* engines out very few simulators come anywhere near the qualities of the aeroplane; in some cases simply because they just don't perform very well in this condition and others because either the original specification did not call up this case or the operators have allowed the facility to lapse. Secondly, without an acceptable visual attachment the parts of the manoeuvre which matter cannot be simulated. These include not only the lift-off engine out but also the last stages of the approach and landing with one and two engines out. (For the same reason, lack of reality, a go-around at 10,500 ft. cannot equate with a go-around at 500 ft.) Finally, for a number of pilots the psychological difference between the simulator and the aeroplane is unbridgeable. You can't do any damage and can't get hurt in a simulator and this knowledge can have an appreciable effect on a pilot's performance. In the aeroplane things are quite different; it has to be flown reasonably well and the consequences of a large deviation from the flight path could be significant.

This is not to say there is no value in simulation of asymmetric flight training. Some of it is good and capable, and certainly saves time and money. In due course when everyone is equipped with six-axis simulators with high quality visuals we will be a lot closer to an acceptable level of fidelity. Even then a final simulator check can never satisfactorily take the place of the aeroplane, for the psychological reasons quoted. It is particularly disturbing to read of those training organisations who are attempting to do virtually all training and testing on the simulator. It is also difficult to accept that pilots themselves will be satisfied with so little flight experience.

310

Summary

Certification test pilots have the responsibility of ensuring that no aeroplane put up for certification makes an undue demand for flying skill on the part of the average line pilot. As a general rule the world's airline pilots place their confidence in the decisions made by the certification authorities' test pilots. It is therefore unreasonable for them to quarrel with one item out of the many which exist in the whole field of safety.

In the last few years the author has flown many two engines out approaches, go-arounds and landings on a wide variety of aeroplanes. With the exception of having to hold high foot forces on the 707 (which requires strength, not skill) there were no problems. Any line pilot with a regular 800 hours a year on one type should be able to fly his aeroplane more fluently than a certification test pilot who is denied a long experience of any one particular type. Two engines out work is predictable and repeatable and if a pilot cannot cope with it he shouldn't really be flying multi-engined aeroplanes at all.

Appendix

Some work done recently in the U.K. on asymmetric flight training has caused the ARB to produce some information which should be of value in the training field. Two extracts from this work are reproduced here. The first is some height guidance for the complete shutting down of an engine during training according to aircraft performance classification and ability. The second consists of limited two engines out approach performance data for the VC10 and the B707.

While asymmetric flight training can be, and should be, perfectly well done with the simulated inoperative engine at idle, fuel on (the residual thrust being comparatively insignificant), it is recognised that the complete shut down of a power unit is necessary for drills purposes. To guard against a further real failure with one engine already shut right down it is however prudent to provide height protection to allow for this possibility. The heights quoted in the following table allow for the shutting down of a second engine while the first engine is being restarted.

The restriction of 4,000 ft. AGL on four-engined jet transports for the complete shut down of one engine for drills purposes was found to be an embarrassment to training captains who, naturally, wanted to be able to do this work in the circuit. A first attempt to meet their needs by quoting the only (at that time) proven data of two engines out en route climb performance was equally unacceptable, because nobody wanted to fly a circuit flaps up at the two engines out en route climb speed. Finally there was no alternative but to accept a typical engine out initial approach configuration and speed, and to calculate conservatively and then flight check the weight at which the aeroplane would have a positive climb performance in the event of one of the remaining engines failing. Figures 10.3 and 10.4, which

Aircraft classification	Recommended minimum height for full engine shut down—fuel off
Group A, four engines (full performance accountability for a single failure; en route capability for a double failure, e.g. B747, VC10).	4,000 ft. AGL
Group A, three engines (as for Group A fours, e.g. B727, HS Trident).	5,000 ft. AGL
Group A, two engines (full performance accountability for a single failure, e.g. DC9, BAC 1–11).	8,000 ft. AGL

NOTES: (i)   The classifications of the aircraft are in accordance with the provisions of the U.K. Air Navigation (General) Regulations 1970, Regulations 6 to 10 inclusive. For the benefit of those readers not familiar with these rules one U.S. and one U.K. type are quoted in addition to the brief explanations of the classifications.

(ii)   The heights quoted in the table are conservative by a factor of about times two, i.e. if a real engine failure occurs with one already shut right down it should be possible to restart the inoperative engine and shut down the failed one in about half the height allowed.

(iii)   The height for Group A fours may be reduced to 1,500 ft. AGL provided that the weight is such as to permit a gross rate of climb of at least 200 ft. per min. in the two engines out initial approach configuration.

show the results available to date for the VC10 and the B707 respectively, are encouraging.

The VC10 is a most capable aeroplane with two engines out. Its V_{MCL_2} speed is very low and it has plenty of performance. Figure 10.3 shows the approximate rate of climb available at 2,000 ft. in ISA for VC10 and Super VC10 aircraft with two engines inoperative, two engines at take-off power, approach flap 35°, gear down, and speed 1.3V_{MS} for 35° flap. Clearly the aeroplane is capable of two engines out go around performance of 200 ft. per min. rate of climb at all weights effectively up to maximum landing weight. Circuit work therefore in this configuration with one engine shut right down is an acceptable practice.

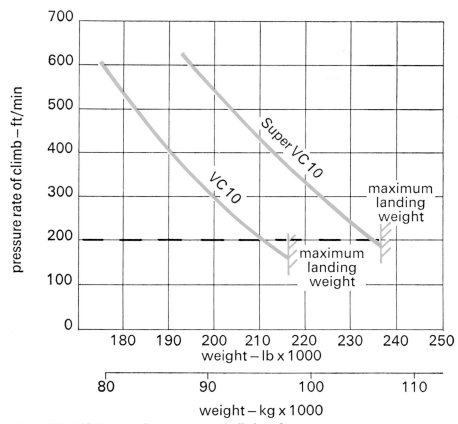

Figure 10.3   VC10 two engines out approach climb performance.

The VC10 and Super VC10 performance is based on calculation from Flight Manual data. The Flight Manuals for both aircraft recommend that the speed should not be reduced below 130 knots IAS with two engines inoperative if take-off power is likely to be required. At weights below 209,500 lb., 95,000 kg., where a constant speed of 130 knots would apply, the performance shown will vary slightly as the speed increases above the 1.3V$_{MS}$ assumed in the calculated data.

The B707 too provides an adequate level of performance provided that the flap angle is restricted and the airspeed kept at or above 170 knots. Figure 10.4 shows the approximate rate of climb available at 2,000 ft. ISA for Boeing 707–321, –436 and –336C aircraft with two engines inoperative, two engines at take-off power, flap as noted and gear down at 170 knots IAS. It is clear that, with the two considerations observed, the –436 and –321 versions both have substantially 200 ft. per min. rate of climb in the

313

two engines out go around and may be used in the circuit with one engine fuel off up to maximum landing weight.

The 707–321 and –336C performance is based on limited flight test data. The 707–436 performance is based on calculation from Flight Manual data, at a speed close to V_2. The aircraft can probably achieve a better performance level than that shown by calculation.

Although not shown the performances of the –138B and 720B versions are known to be very high; thus these types may also enjoy the same level of clearance. The limiting aeroplane is the –336C (a basic –320C) but only because of its much higher maximum landing weight which drags the performance down. Notice however that it will still *just* go uphill at its maximum landing weight. If the weight is restricted to 220,000 lb., 100,000 kg., then the –336C can be used for engine out training like the others.

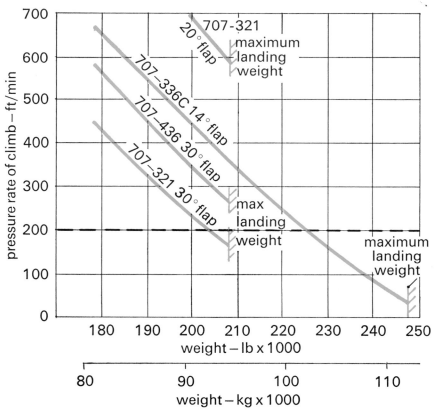

Figure 10.4   Boeing 707 two engines out approach climb performance.

11 Conclusion

To airline pilots

The most important thing, now that you have come to the end of this dissertation on the flying qualities of jet transport aeroplanes, is to *keep the whole thing in perspective and balance.* In writing about the more demanding areas of flying qualities I have taken great care not to overstate the case, and equal care not to understate it. My object has been to warn pilots who might be over-confident of the possible difficulties and at the same time to encourage those pilots lacking in confidence not to overrate the difficulties. This is where the reader must now step in and help me out. In assessing the level of difficulty which exists in certain areas it is important to realise that while the difficulty is as great as is stated it is *no more* than that. The use of the word 'difficult' is itself a difficulty — jet aircraft, compared with piston-engined aircraft, are merely *different.*

With a proper understanding of their qualities, and a reasonable measure of native flying ability, handling them is no problem for the average pilot. They have their limitations of course, and are less forgiving of errors in certain areas, but by and large they are a delight to fly. A real sense of achievement can be gained from the smooth, controlled execution of one of the slightly more demanding manoeuvres under difficult operating conditions. It is a great pity that so much was made of the alleged difficulties in flying the original jet transports, because it was entirely unwarranted. The job of flying jet transports needs to be approached, however, with a proper mixture of determination, prudence and confidence. This is most important. If you decide that you are going to fly the aeroplane, and not let the aeroplane fly you, then you are off to a good start.

The second most important point is that you should never commit yourself to a position from whence extraction could be beyond the capability of you or your aeroplane. Time and again I have emphasised that if you do not like the look of something, you should think it out before proceeding any further. Do not just barge on hoping that everything will work out all right in the end. Once in so many times it does not and we have another accident on our records. Keep your escape route open at all times and never hesitate to use it.

Next, know your aeroplane — and I do not mean only your system drills. References have been made in this book to all sorts of qualities that the aeroplane may possess and, to be a complete commander of the aeroplane, you should know the values of them all for the type you are licensed

315

to fly. Let us name a few: powered flying controls capability after significant failures; V$_{DF}$ and M$_{DF}$ values; the capture capability of individual yaw dampers; stalling qualities; high speed roll rates and high Mach manoeuvre limitations; brake cooling periods where temperature gauges are not fitted; asymmetric reverse thrust capability; aquaplaning speeds; very low altitude baulked landing qualities; the design limitations on your autopilot; the limitations of your attitude indicator — and umpteen more. All this information exists, and can certainly be obtained from the constructor and the airworthiness authority. Go and dig it out or have it dug out for you. Under normal operating conditions of course you can live without a lot of the more exotic information; but when things go badly wrong then having this background information might make all the difference.

Finally, do not become lazy in your professional lives. The autopilot is a great comfort, so are the flight director and the approach coupler. But do not get into the position where you need these devices to complete the flight. Keep in practice in raw I.L.S., particularly in crosswinds. Keep in practice in hand-flying the aeroplane at altitude and in making purely visual approaches.

Airline flying really is money for old rope most of the time; but when things get hairy *then* you earn your pay. The old saying that 'Flying is years and years of utter boredom punctuated by moments of sheer terror' is always true. As we get older we all become slightly more lazy, slightly more tired — and this is a bit of a trap. The demand of jet transport flying can best be met by enthusiasm. Personal enthusiasm for the job is beyond value because it is a built-in productive force, and those who have it do not have to be pushed into practice and the search for knowledge. Enthusiasm thus generates its own protection. This is the frame of mind which needs to be developed for the best execution of the airline pilot's task.

To training captains

Never having had any training responsibilities I feel a little hesitant about handing out advice to pilots who have done this work very well for a long period of time. However, there are some points I wish to put across.

The first one I think is that airline pilots are no different from any other sort of people and they carry with them into maturity some of the fears of their childhood. The greatest fear of course is the fear of the unknown. Once the unknown has been exposed and identified it loses its terrors. There is no greater mistake therefore in the field of instruction than to prevent a pilot under training from doing something for himself. Allowing a pilot to carry out a manoeuvre himself and thus prove to himself that he can cope will give him enormous self-confidence. If you deny him this he will never really know whether he is up to scratch or not. I appreciate that airline pilots vary a great deal in their flying abilities, and that certain prudent measures have to be taken in some cases, but the principle should be applied wherever possible.

On the subject of 'prudent measures' during training we would do well to look at the accident record. Far too many aeroplanes have been lost in training due to ignorance, overconfidence and recklessness. This has allowed those who are instinctively opposed to training to develop the line that more aeroplanes are lost in training for emergencies than are lost through the emergencies themselves — and it is hard to deny this. It isn't however the right line. Pilots must be properly practised in manoeuvres which they might be called upon to cope with at a recognised frequency. If proper measures are taken, no risk is involved and the safety record can be held at the right level.

It is worth listing some elementary points:—

1 Write an accurate, complete training schedule — and stick to it. Training captains should not favour their personal procedures.

2 Know the aeroplane's flying qualities at the boundaries of the flight envelopes (V_{DF}, M_{DF} and high Mach number position errors, for example).

3 Have a complete, fully qualified flight crew on board for all training flights. Trainees are 'additional' and should not replace licensed crew members. Should they fail to cope with the demands of their station the training captain will become overloaded.

4 Make an analysis of the training captain's actual workload during the more critical exercises and if you find it too high for one man *do something about it*. During simulated low weather approaches and auto-land training, for example, one can find a right-hand-seat training captain responsible for command, circuit procedures, nav. and com., lookout, injecting faults and being ready to take over control. This is too much for one man. Offload some of the tasks and spread them around the flight deck, even if it means putting another senior pilot on board.

5 Insist on a special check for 'command from the right hand seat'. Not only are there a lot of controls on that side with which some captains are not familiar but also the view and feel of flying from there are entirely different.

6 Never go beyond the approved crew training limits given in the Flight and Training Manuals. While some types are still safe some distance beyond these limits, others are not.

7 Never give a trainee a manoeuvre which is beyond the aeroplane's capability.

8 Be aware of the flight condition in which you take over control from a

pupil. In a runaway stabiliser check, for example, if he is a lot stronger than you are, you might have quite a surprise.

9   Be careful in areas known to be critical such as high Mach runs with the Mach trim off and dutch roll.   Aeroplanes have got away from training captains in these situations on a number of occasions.

10   Intersperse continuous circuit training with extended circuits with the gear down to cool-off the brakes and tyres.

11   *Never* shut an engine right down when simulating engine failure at low altitude; put it to idle but leave the fuel on.   The engine will then be always 'there' when you want it (but remember the acceleration time required).

12   During relight practice at altitude never shut down a second engine.

13   Examine the practice of roller landings (touch and go) in terms of its overall safety.   Because of occasional difficulties with the selection and cancellation of reverse thrust, some ground runs are very much extended. In the event that the difficulty cannot be resolved both the stop distance and the take-off distance can be severely compromised.   Have in mind a point on the runway by which, if all engines at full power is not achieved, a stop becomes mandatory.

14   Learn from the mistakes of others and keep your training procedures right up to date.   This includes checks on the training captains' training techniques and practices.

15   Finally, be aware of the inevitable dilution of fundamental aircraft type knowledge as generations of training captains succeed each other. Usually, the first group of training captains on a new type get their information direct from the manufacturer's pilots.   As this knowledge is passed on to succeeding groups however some parts of it get lost and the emphasis in certain areas weakens.   At regular intervals you must refresh the current group of training captains using all the accuracy and punch of the original introduction.   Don't let familiarity soften the edges of the bits which matter.   This precaution certainly needs to be taken when a smaller operator eventually operates a type which in its early years was used almost exclusively by the major carriers, particularly when the airline selling the aeroplanes also does the flight training. If the original manufacturer can't supply a pilot for this purpose the certification authority can usually produce a pilot on whose memory is engraved the certification history of the type in question.

All this is elementary stuff, you might say.   But look at the list again.   There are more big airlines not doing some of these things than I care to think about.

The next point is this.   Some of us regret the passing of small flying units (such as a war-time squadron) where the chief was personally acquainted with all the pilots and they were all known to be of high quality. A verbal briefing was all that was necessary to ensure an acceptable safety record.

But things have changed. A modern airline can employ many hundreds of pilots and (with respect) neither of the two qualifications of the old philosophy apply. However, the same end product is necessary. The only way of achieving this is to write good, simple and unambiguous procedures in the Operations Manual, keep them right up to date and then ensure their correct application at all times by high standards of personal and crew discipline.

I have suggested that many pilots are short of some essential knowledge concerning the more advanced areas of their aeroplane and its operation. The training staff of course are the people best able to obtain this information and pass it on to the pilots. Remember this particularly when you do your own training on a new type at the manufacturer's facility. There are many engineers, designers and test pilots there who know all about the aeroplane — its design philosophy, flight test history and flying qualities. Get hold of all of this before you take the aeroplane away, and then pass it on to the line pilots during your own training programmes.

Finally, a word about basic flying training, instrument flying and recovery from unusual attitudes on limited panel. A number of airlines are now buying small executive jet type aircraft as trainers for their major transport fleets. In these, some attempt is made to make the instrument panel layout resemble the transport aircraft. This is probably the most significant step forward in training programmes for years. It provides a small, comparatively cheap aeroplane on which pilots can practise and exercise their flying skills.

Even this does not go quite far enough. The real need is for a fully aerobatic training aeroplane to be provided so that airline pilots can practise real flying manoeuvres and recovery from unusual attitudes on primary instruments. The defence offered to an attack like this is always that the outlay is never worth the insurance against such a remote risk. I do not agree. There are too many senior transport pilots flying who have just about forgotten how to *fly* an aeroplane. The only way to put matters right is to give all airline pilots a couple of hours on an appropriate aeroplane, say, once every six months, so that they can practise limited instrument flying and refresh themselves with the confidence which comes from having proved to themselves that they can still *fly* (as opposed to operate) an aeroplane. In comparative terms the cost involved is not large. A lot of people pay lip service to the cause of aviation safety, but actually do little about it; this is one area where some positive advancement can be made. A proportion of all transport accidents can be attributed to errors of judgement and lack of flying ability. If the proportion can be reduced significantly by this means it is bound to be worthwhile.

Index

The list of Contents serves as the main guide to the location of the various subjects covered in the text. There are, however, a number of places where subjects are mentioned out of their main sub-chapter in relation to other qualities and many references to items not distinguished by a sub-chapter title. It is to these items that this index gives guidance.

Index to illustrations

This index is arranged alphabetically with the most likely word as the primary reference and the preamble in brackets.